Welcome to the new

Teen Guide

Teen Guide is a classic. Since 1961, thousands of students have enjoyed and benefited from four different editions. During this time, *Teen Guide* has constantly grown in scope and appeal. Today it is the favorite resource for teachers of introductory home economics courses and a popular source of useful information for teenagers. Here's why we think the fifth edition is the best yet:

- The **topics covered** are of lively interest and practical value, as a glance at the Table of Contents will prove. You'll find new material on growing up (p. 55), the future (p. 252), school and community (p. 221), international and regional foods (p. 480), safety (p. 185), management of time and money (pp. 214 and 226), and careers (p. 145).

- **Chapters** are short and built around a single concept to help in lesson development. And they contain such instructional helps as "A Quick Review" and "Words to Know." The scope and sequence chart on pp. 6-9 presents the big picture and helps you plan.

- **Readability** is enhanced by a compelling writing style, clever ideas, meaningful subject matter, and a reading level appropriate for average students as measured by the Dale-Chall formula. New terms are defined as they are used.

- The **photographs and illustrations** are great. Thumb through the book and see for yourself.

- **Sketches and drawings** clearly illustrate how-to-do-it (pp. 290 and 315) and dramatize important concepts (pp. 38 and 254).

- The **third columns** running throughout the book contain supplementary material (p. 140), activities (p. 359), and resources (p. 148) related to each chapter. They are color-coded for quick access to each unit.

- There are marvelous **charts and boxes** to pore over. Look at pages 143 and 304.

- The complete *Teacher's Resource Guide*, new with this edition, provides objectives, motivating lesson openers, discussion questions, test questions, bulletin board ideas, and reproducible activity sheets.

from *The Home Ec Professionals*

Webster/McGraw-Hill

Teen Guide

FIFTH EDITION

Other Home Economics Titles:

Child Growth and Development   Hurlock

Concepts in Clothing   Graef, Strom

Focus on Foods   Peck, Moragne, Sickler, Washington

Guide to Modern Meals   Ohl, Duyff, Hasler

How You Plan and Prepare Meals   Carson, Ramee, Cobe

Parenting and Teaching Young Children   Hildebrand

Personal Perspectives   Paolucci, Faiola, Thompson

Survival: A Guide to Living on Your Own   Kelly, Chamberlain

The Home: Its Furnishings and Equipment   Morton, Guthrie, Inman, Geuther

The McGraw-Hill Guide to Clothing   Faiola, Pullen

Your Marriage and Family Living   Landis

Professional Resource:

Creative Home Economics Instruction   Chamberlain, Kelly

Webster/McGraw-Hill   *The Home Ec Professionals*

CONTRIBUTORS

Marion Bartholomew
Dorothy A. Brown
Joanne DeCristofaro
Roberta Duyff
Marian Faux
Gale Flynn
Janice M. Hamilton
Debbie Henderson
Elaine Muller
Ceanne Pelletier
Cynthia Richardson
Debra Sawyer
Janis Wilson

Teen Guide

FIFTH EDITION

Valerie Chamberlain

Peyton Bailey Budinger
Jan Perry Jones

Webster Division/McGraw-Hill Book Company
New York St. Louis San Francisco Auckland Bogotá Düsseldorf Johannesburg
London Madrid Mexico Montreal New Delhi Panama Paris São Paulo Singapore
Sydney Tokyo Toronto

Project Director: Martha O'Neill
Editors: Pattyann DesMarais (Unit 6)
  Carol Newman (Units 1 and 4)
  Martha O'Neill (Units 2, 3, and 5)
Coordinating Editor: Charles Wall
Senior Designer: Tracy Glasner
Photo Supervisor: Rosemary O'Connell
Production Supervisor: Angela Kardovich

Photo Research: C. Buff Rosenthal
Layout: William Dippel

Illustration: Evelyne Johnson Associates: Carolyn Bracken, Frank Daniel, Sharon diBlasi, Tom LaPadula, Tien, and Tom Utley; Marcia Goldenberg
Charts and Other Illustrations: Blaise Zito Associates

This book was set in 12 point Garamond by Lehigh/ROCAPPI.
The color separation was done by Lehigh/Electronic Color, Inc.

Library of Congress Cataloging in Publication Data

Chamberlain, Valerie M.
  Teen guide.

  Fourth ed. by J. H. Brinkley, published under title:
  Teen guide to homemaking.
  Includes index.
  SUMMARY: A textbook dealing with relationships, family, home, decision-making and consumerism, clothing, and food.
    1. Home economics—Juvenile literature. [1. Home economics] I. Jones, Jan Perry, 1942–   joint author. II. Budinger, Peyton Bailey, 1939–   joint author. III. Brinkley, Jeanne Hayden. Teen guide to homemaking. IV. Title.
TX167.C4   1982   640   80-39901
ISBN 0-07-007843-2
ISBN 0-07-007844-0 (teacher's resource guide)

1 2 3 4 5 6 7 8 9 10   VHVH   90 89 88 87 86 85 84 83 82 81

TEEN GUIDE EDITORIAL BOARD

ABOUT THE AUTHORS

Valerie M. Chamberlain is both an author and a teacher. In addition to *Teen Guide,* her writing credits include McGraw-Hill's *Survival: A Guide to Living on Your Own* and *Creative Home Economics Instruction.* Dr. Chamberlain holds the rank of professor in the Home Economics Department at Texas Tech University. Her work involves teaching, research, and in-service presentation. She is a graduate of the University of Vermont, with graduate degrees from Florida State University. Dr. Chamberlain lives in Lubbock, Texas.

Peyton Bailey Budinger is best known to young people for her column "Talking it Over," which appears monthly in the magazine *Co-Ed.* Her work also involves writing books and magazine articles on contemporary topics. Ms. Budinger is a graduate of Skidmore College and lives in Kennett Square, Pennsylvania.

Jan Perry Jones writes on a variety of home economics topics. She is the author of a clothing and textiles textbook. Her experience also includes high school teaching and consumer information projects in business. Ms. Jones is a graduate of Ball State University and lives in Midland, Michigan.

SCOPE AND SEQUENCE

	UNIT 1	UNIT 2	UNIT 3
Aesthetics, Art, and Design Principles		14•children's art	18•aesthetic needs met in the home 19•designing and decorating rooms 21•inexpensive room decorations
Careers	9•helping people careers/looking good careers/personnel manager/executive director of a boys' club	16•baby-sitting 17•careers related to families and children/starting a summer business/recreation superintendent/day-care center director	24•home design and construction careers/interior design careers/home maintenance careers/careers in real estate/construction manager/interior designer/real estate broker
Consumer Information		10•cost of raising a child 12•community services for older family members 16•inexpensive things to make for children	19•looking for bargains for the home
The Future	6•looking at your future	12•the family of the future 14•can we predict height?	
Health and Safety	5•handling conflict and stress 6•teenage tension	13•physical exercise for the family 15•kids in cars 16•accidents and emergencies guide	18•home safety 22•controlling household pests 23•falls, fires, and poisonings/illness/first aid kit/family fire drill
History and Culture	8•famous rumors	10•colonial families/the average family in 1900, 1930, 1956 15•the history of toys	

SCOPE AND SEQUENCE

	UNIT 1	UNIT 2	UNIT 3
Home Management		13●family council	20●storing your possessions 22●organized home care
Housing and Home Furnishings	2●adolescents and the neatness of their rooms 3●television as an escape	11●new conveniences	19●loft beds 20●creating new storage space 21●care of your room 22●home repair tools
Human Development	1●individual differences/human needs 2●adolescent changes 3●self-image 5●aging	11●life cycle 12●older family members/parents/children 14●child development 15●care of children	21●a place to be alone
Interpersonal Relationships	2●handling anger 3●handling hurt feelings 4●the way you look, act 5●getting to know other people/stereotypes/roles 7●making friends/cliques/problems with friends 8●boy/girl relationships/dating	10●family 11●roles in a family/tips for moving 13●cooperation/communication/telephone time	18●being good neighbors 21●sharing space at home
Laboratory and Home Skills			
Managing Resources			18●saving heating and cooling energy 21●smart energy use in your room
Nutrition		14●overweight infants 15●nutritional needs of children	

UNIT 4	UNIT 5	UNIT 6
25 • short- and long-range goals 26 • problem solving 27 • managing resources 28 • managing time 32 • credit	42 • selecting a project	55 • meal planning 61 • working in the foods lab
34 • computers of the future/housing of the future	44 • sewing machine • sewing equipment	57 • table setting 62 • kitchen equipment 63 • measuring equipment 64 • kitchen appliance safety
26 • decision making/risk taking		
28 • valuing other people's time		55 • family meals 56 • serving family meals 57 • table manners 60 • restaurant manners
	42 • taking measurements 45 • pattern layout/cutting/marking 46 • construction steps/pressing/knits 48 • recycling clothes	58 • outdoor food preparation 63 • understanding recipes 65 • cooking meat group foods 66 • cooking with milk, cheese 67 • preparing fruits, vegetables 68 • preparing breads and cereals 69 • cakes, cookies, pies
25 • abilities 27 • the individual/the family 28 • time 30 • money 33 • sources of energy/energy crises/saving energy	41 • textiles 47 • smart energy use for clothing care 48 • recycling clothing	61 • saving energy in the kitchen
		51 • nutrients 52 • daily food guide/dietary guidelines 53 • calories 54 • food fads 59 • nutritional labeling 65 • nutrients in the meat group 66 • nutrients in milk and cheese 67 • nutrients in fruits, vegetables 68 • nutrients in breads, cereals

Unit 1
RELATIONSHIPS

Unit 2
FAMILY

Unit 3
HOME

Unit 4
RESOURCES

Unit 5
CLOTHING

Unit 6
FOODS

RESOURCES

Unit 1
RELATIONSHIPS

CHAPTER 1
One of a Kind, One of Many

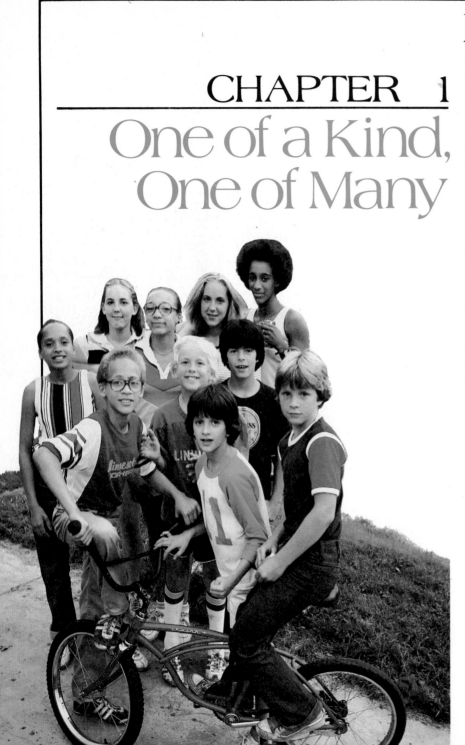

By 1980 the world's population had grown to 4½ billion people. By the year 2000 there will be about 7 billion people in the world. Yet even among all these billions of people, there is something special about each person. There is only one you. You are one of many in your school. You are one of perhaps twenty or thirty in your classroom. You are one of several people in your family. And you are one of more than 200 million people in the United States. Among all these people, you are an individual, one of a kind.

INDIVIDUAL DIFFERENCES

The sum of all the things you are makes you an individual. Such things as your sense of humor, your shyness or lack of it, your ability to learn, the color of your eyes and hair, and your height are your *characteristics*. Many of your characteristics came from your parents. They were passed along to you at birth. These are called *inherited* characteristics. You are also developing other characteristics as you grow up. These are called *acquired* characteristics. You can acquire new characteristics as long as you live.

People have much in common, but it is their differences that make them individuals. Even identical twins do not have all the same acquired characteristics. One twin may like to talk; the other talks less.

Physical Makeup. Every person inherits physical characteristics from parents, grandparents, and even more distant ancestors. These inherited characteristics are called a person's *heredity*. Carried in the sex cells, inherited characteristics are the basis for each person's general physical make-up. They also keep on affecting physical development all through life.

From babyhood on, however, a person's development is also influenced by his or her surroundings. These surroundings, which include the food a person is given, the people a person meets, and events that happen, are called the *environment*.

Environment and heredity together produce a person's individual characteristics. For example, heredity determines that your body can grow only so tall. But you need proper food, rest, and exercise in order to reach that height.

Mental Makeup. Your mental ability helps to determine the kind of person you are. This ability is centered in your brain, a mass of nerve cells located in your head. The way it works is not yet fully understood. But it is known that your brain is what makes it possible for you to understand and learn. This ability to understand and learn is called *intelligence*.

No two people are alike in intelligence. Your own intelligence depends partly on heredity and partly on how

You inherit many characteristics from your parents. You and your environment shape these characteristics into your personality.

you have developed since birth. Scientists believe that no one ever uses her or his brain to its full capacity. There is always room for mental growth.

How much brain power you develop is up to you. And it is also up to you to decide which parts of your intelligence you wish to develop.

> We all live with the objective of being happy; our lives are all different and yet the same.
> —Anne Frank,
> *Diary of a Young Girl*

19

Scientists are trying to understand how heredity and environment work together to make people who they are. One way that scientists do this is by studying twins who have grown up apart.

Recently scientists have been studying twin brothers from Ohio who were separated at birth and brought back together after thirty-nine years. What they have discovered about these twins has amazed them.

Both twins are named James. Both are 185 centimeters (6 feet 1 inch) tall and weigh 81 kilograms (180 pounds). Each grew up with an adopted brother called Larry, and each had a dog named Toy. Each married and divorced a woman named Linda and remarried a Betty. Both work as part-time sheriffs. Each does carpentry and mechanical drawing in his spare time. The twins also fold their arms and cross their legs in the same way, have the same sleep habits, and get the same kinds of headaches. For years, both also vacationed at the same beach at Florida.

What do you think about these twin brothers? How much do you think is the result of heredity? Environment? Pure chance?

There are many different kinds of mental abilities. One person may be very good at math. Another may have an especially good memory. Some people are highly skilled at expressing their thoughts in writing. People differ as to which learning areas they are good at and which they are not. That is why each person's mental ability is special.

Emotional Makeup. Notice the many types of people among your friends and schoolmates. Some are happy-go-lucky. Others always seem worried. Some are kind and generous. Others are critical and hard to please. These people are all different in their emotional makeup. How did they get this way?

People are born with different personalities. But everyone has the same basic needs for physical, mental, and emotional attention. How these needs are met affects your emotional makeup. Some people are fortunate that their needs are well met. Others are less fortunate. When a person's inherited characteristics mix well with that person's environment, the result is a stable emotional makeup.

Your attitudes are part of your emotional makeup. An *attitude* is a learned way of looking at things, people, and events. Attitudes are learned from your family and friends. You reveal your attitudes in your likes and dislikes.

Most of your actions are based on your attitudes. Positive attitudes that show you think well of yourself will be a great help when you are trying to make decisions. But negative attitudes, which are usually based on fear or insecurity, will make it difficult for you to make decisions and to work with other people.

Most feelings can be regarded as some form or combination of the three basic emotions: love, anger, and fear. Each basic emotion has its place in human life. Love can make you easy to please and understanding. Anger can make you go out and strive to overcome obstacles. Fear can help you avoid anger. No one needs to be ashamed of feelings. But we are each responsible to ourselves and to others for how we express them. One of the goals of the teen years is to increase the ability to deal with emotions in socially acceptable ways.

BASIC HUMAN NEEDS

Even though you are a special, one-of-a-kind human being, you share certain basic needs with all other people. These needs are physical, emotional, mental, and social.

Physical Needs. To stay alive, you need a steady supply of air and water. You also need food, shelter, rest, sleep, and space in which to move. The better these needs are met, the more easily the real you—the person within your body—can develop.

In the past, people assumed that natural resources such as air, water, fuels, and land were available in unlimited amounts. Today we know we must take care of natural resources. We must plan, work, and cooperate with each other to get from our environment the things we need.

Emotional, Mental, and Social Needs. Do you know the saying, "Man cannot live by bread alone"? This means that if people are to find life rewarding, their whole beings must be nourished, not just their stomachs.

Babies who are cared for physically but are given no love or emotional care are slow to develop. They have little desire to learn. The will to live seems to be related to how well emotional needs are met. Mental and social growth are also dependent on good emotional care.

Love. Much has been said about the need for love. Yet love means different things to different people at different times in their lives. When we receive love, we grow in our ability to love. To helpless babies, love means prompt attention to their needs. Even small babies know when they are wanted. Through love, they develop a sense of trust. Love helps prepare them for social growth and learning. Without it, they cannot form a firm framework into which the pieces of their personalities can fit.

Changing Environment

The environment in which people try to meet their needs is always changing. For example:

• What do scientists know today that they did not know five years ago?

• What new developments have been made in health and medicine in the last five years?

• How has family life and household management changed?

• What products are available for sale today that could not be bought five years ago?

• What changes in the environment have taken place that affect people's physical needs for air, water, food, and shelter?

You have the same basic needs that all other people have.

Making Introductions

Introducing members of your family to other people can be confusing if you don't have much practice. Here are some tips:

Say the person's name and then, "I'd like you to meet . . ." or "this is . . ." For example, "Miss Holt, this is my mother, Mrs. Ducey." Or, in less formal introductions, use the first names of the two people, as in "Tom Ward, this is Joel Palmer."

The general rule is to first say the name of the person who is older or holds a position of respect. You are introducing the other person *to* this first person.

(continued)

Young children need love too. So do teenagers. And how about parents and grandparents? Do people ever outgrow their need for love?

Acceptance. To know someone accepts you as you are is necessary for your emotional health. Some people are hard to love. They may be unusual, and their ideas may seem strange. Even so, they need friends and associates who accept them as people. We all need to feel we are included as members of the human race.

Appreciation. We each need to feel that we have achieved something on our own. We need to feel that what we have done is appreciated. Unless we feel that our efforts bring some rewards, we soon give up trying. Rewards can come as thanks, money, praise, good grades, or prizes. Rewards strengthen people's personalities and their will to try.

Security. To make the most of ourselves, we must feel safe and secure. We need to feel that the things and people important to us will be there when we need them. If they are not, we feel afraid. Fear that causes us to stop trying will make it hard for us to grow into well-adjusted people.

Variety. Human beings are naturally curious. We are quickly bored. We need to experience variety, or change. This need can be met through creative work or through the imaginative use of leisure time. It can

also be met through choice of food, clothing, and housing.

Meaningful communication. As people mature, they ask themselves questions about life and its meaning. They need to feel there is more to life than mere existence. Most people want to share their thoughts on this subject and learn what others think. This sharing and learning is a part of growing toward maturity.

Independence. To become truly grown up, a person must gain independence. Achieving independence is a process of separating what is you from what is your family. This happens little by little. From time to time during your childhood, you were allowed to do certain things on your own, to go places without your family, to make some of your own decisions. As you enter your teens, you will do more things on your own.

Independent people have learned to provide for themselves the things others once provided for them. To achieve independence, you must first recognize your basic needs and then find ways to meet them. Basic necessities such as food, clothing, and shelter are not free. In the past someone has had to work to provide you with these necessities. As you take over work that was earlier done by others, you move toward independence.

Do you want total independence? Since we depend on our environment for survival, we can never be com-

Some of our important needs are met through other people.

• You introduce: a younger person to an older person: "Mr. Cooper, I'd like you to meet Bruce Asycue."

• a boy to a man or a girl to a woman: "Mr. Porter, this is Augie Schlaffer."

• a friend to your parents: "Mother and Dad, this is Tony Mack."

• one person to a group: "Gang, I'd like you to meet my friend, Wayne Weisz."

• anyone in your family to a member of the clergy: "Father O'Brien, this is my sister Joyce."

• a guest to your hosts: "Mr. and Mrs. Newman, this is Laurie Ichino."

▶ **Words to Know**

acquired characteristics: Characteristics that develop as a person grows up.

attitude: A learned way of looking at things and people.

environment: A person's physical, social, and economic surroundings.

heredity: Characteristics that are inherited from parents and other ancestors.

inherited characteristics: Characteristics passed to a child from parents or other ancestors.

intelligence: The ability to learn and understand.

pletely independent of each other. Nor is total independence desirable. Think about the emotional, mental, and social needs in this chapter. Could you meet these needs if you were totally independent of others?

a quick review

1. What is the difference between heredity and environment?
2. What is an attitude?
3. The three basic emotions are love, anger, and fear. For each one, imagine a situation in which that emotion is handled in a socially acceptable way.
4. How do people's basic needs differ at different times in their lives?

CHAPTER 2
Changes

You are changing. You have been changing since you were born, of course. But now it's different. Things are happening fast. At times it may seem too fast. Between the ages of twelve and twenty, you will actually change from a child to a full-fledged adult. That's a lot of work for a mind and body to do in a fairly short time.

Of course, this does not mean that when you are twenty you will be "grown up," or that you will have finished changing. The process is never over, for anyone. Maturity isn't something that magically comes when you walk through a door marked "twenty-one," or "thirty-five," or "forty." Everyone is constantly in a process of change. And everyone, at any time in life, has moments when she or he feels scared, lost, or ten years old.

HOW YOUR LOOKS WILL CHANGE

Children tend to accept their bodies naturally. Many teenagers, however, feel uncomfortable about their bodies. You may worry about being too fat or too scrawny. You may notice other things, too—like your kneecaps. Why haven't you noticed them before? Your kneecaps stick out funny. Does everyone laugh about them behind your back? You are probably more self-conscious now than you have ever been in the past.

Adolescence is the period when a child matures into an adult. During adolescence, your body grows and changes in many different ways. The changes do not happen in one graceful stretch. They take place in spurts. The process of maturing usually begins about two years earlier for girls than for boys. On the average, a girl's adolescent growth begins between ten and thirteen, a boy's between twelve and fifteen. Between the ages of eleven and seventeen, the average girl will grow 17 centimeters (7 inches) and gain 20 kilograms (44 pounds). The average boy will grow 22 centi-meters (13 inches) and gain 31 kilograms (68 pounds). All of this is caused by your glands. *Glands* are small organs that send chemicals, called *hormones*, directly into your blood. The pituitary gland, which is located at the base of your brain, controls growth. The hormones sent out by the pituitary gland cause you to grow taller. They also cause other physical changes that make you look more and more like an adult. You develop more muscles, more curves. Your hair gets darker. Your nose and chin become more defined, and your eyebrows thicken. Your voice becomes lower as your larynx, or voice box, get larger. As glands in your

	Age 11	Age 12	Age 13	Age 14	Age 15	Age 16	Age 17
GIRLS cm	144.8	151.6	157.5	160.5	161.8	162.6	163.0
inches	57.0	59.7	62.0	63.2	63.7	64.0	64.2
BOYS cm	143.3	149.9	154.9	163.0	169.0	173.5	176.3
inches	56.4	59.0	61.0	64.2	66.5	68.3	69.4

Boys usually end up taller than girls, but not always. People grow at their own rate to a height that is determined by heredity and environment. On the average, girls are taller than boys at the age of eleven. The opposite is usually true by adulthood.

Fears and Phobias

An emotion is a strong feeling or reaction. When your emotions are stirred up, your mind sends messages to your glands and organs. For example, when you are afraid, a message is sent to your adrenal gland. This gland then releases a chemical called adrenalin into your bloodstream. Adrenalin causes more sugar to enter your bloodstream and your heartbeat to quicken. Your body now has more energy to defend itself.

For a few people, fear gets out of control and does not go away. An ongoing fear of this kind is called a *phobia*. Some known phobias include:

acrophobia (fear of heights)
claustrophobia (fear of enclosed spaces)
thanatophobia (fear of death)
agoraphobia (fear of open spaces)
logizomechanophobia (fear of computers and other machines)
hydrophobia (fear of water)
zoophobia (fear of animals)
ailurophobia (fear of cats)
pyrophobia (fear of fire)

Amazing Fact: Another phobia to know about is arachibutyrophobia. It is the fear of getting peanut butter stuck to the roof of your mouth!

"It seemed as though everyone in my class began maturing before I did. I was the shortest girl in the class, and I looked like a baby next to the other girls. I pretended to be as interested in boys as everyone else, but I wasn't really. I really felt much happier at home playing with my dog. Everyone was really nice to me, but until I was fifteen and my body began to catch up, I felt like the class mascot."

"My brother was good at everything. He was smart, a class leader, and an athlete. All the teachers expected that I'd be that way too. It really hurt when I saw how disappointed they were when I wasn't like him. No one could figure me out. I liked my ham radio. I liked to grow vegetables and to look at the sky at night with my telescope. Now that I'm older, I feel better about myself; in fact, I'm proud of the way I am. But for a while I felt miserable, lonely, and unlikable."

"When I was thirteen, I went through a time when I was BORED. With everything. I blamed it on other people, on the school subjects. Everything seemed so trivial. 'What's the point?' was how I felt. The turning point came when I wrote a story about how it felt to be a thirteen-year-old who couldn't feel and couldn't get interested in the world. It won a prize at school, and after that I really felt like trying again. But I never figured out why this happened."

skin develop, you notice that your skin becomes more oily and that you perspire more than you used to.

Many young people feel all alone as they go through these changes. This is especially true for a girl who is taller than anyone in her class or a boy whose voice is the last to change. Everyone's growth pattern is different. Each person develops according to her or his own biological clock, and there is nothing you can do to speed things up or slow them down.

Many teenagers are critical of themselves as they change. You may make the mistake of comparing yourself to an ideal (a gorgeous movie star, your college-age brother or sister, the perfect model that you see in a magazine). You may spend time in front of the mirror, secretly observing, criticizing, practicing. A girl may experiment with smoky eye shadow, suck in her stomach, turn sideways, and wonder, "Am I pretty?" A boy may flex his muscles, test his voice, and check his beard (will it ever grow?). You may think about going out on dates and wonder if anyone of the other sex will ever want to date you. For a while, the idea may seem impossible.

As you change from a girl to a woman or a boy to a man, you'll have mixed feelings about your changing body. These will include pride and excitement as well as insecurity and doubt. Obviously the you who goes into adolescence will look very different from the you who comes out as a young adult. At times it will seem that just about nothing has stayed the same. No wonder you sometimes look in the mirror and ask, "Who am I?" It will help if you can share some of your feelings with friends, a parent, or a trusted teacher. It will also help to see the way others react to the new you. When a clerk in a store calls you "sir" or "ma'am," you may feel a burst of new confidence. It's exciting

Fifteen is really
medieval and pioneer
and nothing is clear
and nothing is sure,
and nothing is safe
and nothing is come
and nothing is gone
but it all might be.
—*Gertrude Stein*

During adolescence, physical differences are obvious. People mature at their own speed—physically, emotionally, and socially.

It's Tough to Be 13

"When I started junior high school, my parents, their friends, and many of the neighbors told me how much fun I was going to have. Well, I don't think junior high is fun. I have so many teachers I can't even remember their names. My classes all have different people in them. Jami, my best friend, is only in my math class. The only time we get to talk is at lunch, and then we have only 22 minutes! When I look around at the other kids, they all seem so happy. What's wrong with me?"

Growing Neater

At the Gesell Institute for Child Development, researchers studied teenagers' rooms. According to their conclusions, when you were between the ages of ten and twelve, your room was probably a disaster. At thirteen, it is probably still messy, and now you are spending more time there. At fourteen, you may become a little bit neater, and by fifteen your room will probably show marked improvement. By sixteen, there is a good chance that it will finally be neat.

THINGS HAVE CHANGED

So many things are changing in your life now that it's not easy to keep track of them all. Many of the changes that are taking place for you have both negative and positive sides.

You have become more sensitive.

Good news: You are quick to recognize it when someone needs something.

Bad news: You often worry about what others think of you.

Your parents have begun to see you as an adult.
Good news: You have more privileges.

Bad news: Some of the responsibilities that come with new privileges may not always please you.

to see that you are no longer considered a child. "Hey," you may be able to say to yourself, "I guess I'm getting there, aren't I?"

HOW YOUR FEELINGS WILL CHANGE

No matter how much you learn in advance about hormones, body changes, or growth spurts, you won't know what it's like to be a teen until you are there. And some of your moods and feelings will take you by surprise. You begin to be bothered by little things you never noticed before. For example, you might be annoyed by the way your sister chews, or your best friend's habit of tapping his finger against his front tooth. You lose your temper more easily these days. Too easily, you think. But no one understands, and at times you feel strange. Maybe you have a secret place where you like to hide (behind a tree in the park, or up by the attic window). There you can see and hear other people, but no one can see you.

Your moods go back and forth. One day you feel full of laughter, happy, and self-confident. The next day you feel downright weird. You want to hit someone or cry, and you don't know why. One day the idea of

A growing spurt has added 15 centimeters (6 inches) to your height.

Good news: You look and feel great.
Bad news: Your best friend is still 4'6"

You have become more confident.

Good news: You've been elected class vice president.

MARIA WINS!

Bad news: People begin to demand more of your time.

MARIA, PLEASE, RUN THE PAPER DRIVE FOR US, NO ONE CAN DO IT AS WELL AS YOU.

becoming an adult seems exciting. You can't wait to take off, get a job, and find an apartment of your own. (That is probably the day you clean your room, finish your homework early, and do the dishes without being asked.) The next day the idea of becoming an adult seems unreal. What is real is the pressure you're under right now. "It's too much," you think. "It's impossible! How can I work with all this noise going on? Who understands algebra anyway!" You crash into your room, slam the door, or tell your troubles to the cat while it bathes itself. Today if your mother wanted to pull you down into

her lap and cuddle you, you wouldn't mind at all.

Your interests are changing, too. Yesterday you were skateboarding or playing kickball with the kids in your neighborhood. Now doing that seems childish. You'd rather be alone with a book. You used to think your sister was crazy because of the way she went on about some rock star. Now you're the one who spends hours listening to one album over and over. The other sex doesn't seem so awful anymore. You find yourself thinking about one girl—or guy—a lot. The idea of going to dances and parties seems scary, but exciting.

Catching Your ZZZs

If you are cranky and you do not know why, perhaps you are not getting enough sleep.

You spend one-third of your life sleeping. "Normal" amounts of sleep range from 6 to 8 hours per night, but the right amount depends on your body's needs.

When you first fall asleep, it is a light sleep. Your blood pressure and heart rate drop. Then you fall into a deeper sleep. Your eyeballs move from side to side. This is called REM—for rapid eye movement—sleep. REM sleep occurs every 90 minutes. It is during REM sleep that you do most of your dreaming and "work out" some of the problems of the day. After REM sleep, you become totally relaxed. Your blood pressure and temperature go down. Finally you go into your deepest sleep, and then the cycle begins again.

Some people have trouble sleeping. This is called insomnia. If you have trouble getting to sleep, follow a routine at bedtime. Read for 10 minutes. Listen to music in the dark. Drink a glass of milk; the calcium in it will calm you. And be sure to get lots of exercise during the day.

Letting Off Steam

Anger is a normal emotion. Letting out bottled-up anger can be a healthy way to clear the air. When you are angry and you don't express it, the tension builds. By putting off dealing with the anger, the explosion may be even bigger when it comes. Anger held inside too long can turn into *depression,* or feeling down. Unexpressed anger can also turn into headaches, backaches, and stomach troubles.

However, "blowing off steam" can hurt others or get you in trouble. Usually, an angry explosion makes it harder to solve the problem that caused your anger.

Here are some helpful ways to let out your angry feelings:

1. Tell a third, uninvolved person how you feel.
2. Pound a pillow.
3. Go outside by yourself.

(continued)

You may feel different about your schoolwork, too. History used to be your favorite subject. Now you have to force yourself to finish your homework assignments. And you often catch yourself staring out the window. Sometimes you feel lazy. You want to run and hide from the pressure that tells you to get good grades, be popular, and help with the yard and the laundry. When your parents ask you what's wrong, you say, "Nothing." But they look as if they don't believe you, and sometimes they shrug and say, "Oh well, it must be adolescence." That makes you angry. The feelings you have are *real.* Adolescence can't be blamed for everything, can it?

Some of these emotions are simply due to body chemistry. But your body is not the only thing that is changing. Your mind is growing, too. You are becoming more aware, more intro-spective, more able to think about what it is that you are feeling. You begin to notice more, and your feelings get hurt more easily. Teasing that used to make you laugh might now make you feel hurt or angry. You are a more complex person than you were when you were younger, and there is no going back, even though sometimes you wish you could.

WHO WILL YOU BE TOMORROW?

"What do you want to be when you grow up?" People have been asking you that since you were old enough to talk. Every year you probably gave a different answer: movie star, fire fighter, teacher, famous novelist. Some of your friends have already decided what they want to be. "I'm definitely going to be a doctor," they say, or "I'm going into my family's carpet business." When they seem so sure about the future, your own uncertainty may worry you. It shouldn't. You don't have to plan out your entire future now. But it is a good idea to think about the things you like to do in terms of what jobs exist. Obviously, a job that involves your special interests will be the one that makes you happiest. Ask yourself, "Do I enjoy working with people, ideas, or things?" Are you proudest of the work you have done in math, in English, or in woodworking

The one thing you know for sure about the future is this: the person you become tomorrow . . .

. . . is now being put together by the person you are today.

shop? If you think you would like working with people, getting experience as a camp counselor or teacher's assistant would give you a feel for it. If you love wrestling with ideas, working on your school newspaper would be a natural outlet for you. Keep on questioning and exploring. Take a part-time job in a shop, do yard work after school, or draw cartoons in your spare time. Any time you participate, you can expand your sense of your own abilities. It is not necessary to come up with answers. The idea is to experiment and learn about yourself. It would be as much a mistake to decide now what you want to be and then close your mind to other ideas as it would be not to think about the future at all.

a quick review

1. List four physical changes that take place during adolescence.
2. What is the name of the gland that controls physical growth?
3. How much weight are you likely to gain between the ages of twelve and twenty?
4. If you find yourself angry or sad for no particular reason, should you worry about yourself? Why or why not?
5. Why is it important to think about what you'll be doing ten years from now?

4. Write down exactly how you feel.
5. Exercise: jog, swim, rollerskate.
6. Turn your anger into art. Slap some clay around, bang on your drums, scribble a story.
7. Have a good cry. Often beneath anger there is hurt.

At some point, you might want to tell the person who made you so mad why you felt angry. State the reasons calmly. Use "I" statements, not "you" statements ("*I* felt bad when you . . . ," not "*You* are a . . .").

When you are feeling better, ask yourself why you got angry. This may help you to understand yourself and the person who made you so mad.

▶ **Words to Know**
adolescence: The time of life when a child matures into an adult.
glands: Small organs that send hormones into the blood.
hormones: Chemicals that direct growth and body changes.
introspective: Tending to dwell on one's own thoughts and feelings.

CHAPTER 3
How You See Yourself

Y ou have probably heard people talk about their "self-image." Your *self-image* is your opinion of yourself. It would be great if people liked themselves all the time. If only people could always say, "Sure, I have faults, but I'm learning. And, all in all, I'm a good and valuable person." It would be wonderful if no one ever felt shy or embarrassed, if people never put themselves down or held themselves back because they were afraid of looking foolish. However, all people worry about their faults. Everyone has a word to put in the sentence "I'm just not ——— enough."

HOW YOUR SELF-IMAGE IS FORMED

Your self-image began to form when you were very small. Your mother smiled at you and said, "What a beautiful baby!" You felt good. You pulled a dog's tail, someone said, "Stop it, you naughty child," and you felt bad. Other children teased you about the way you threw a ball. "I'll never be good at sports," you decided. From the beginning, parents, brothers, sisters, friends, relatives, and teachers have reacted to you. You observed those reactions, interpreted them, and created a picture of yourself—a self-image.

There is a private side to your self-image, too. This is a side that no one

32

else knows. The private side is the you who sits and listens to music and sometimes cries over the words. It is the you who daydreams, the you who goes out in the yard and talks to birds and bugs. It is the you who keeps a diary. This is a side you may not be comfortable showing to other people, a side you know is special but think no one else would understand.

For years you were not aware of having a self-image, either a private one or a public one. Now you are keenly aware of your feelings about yourself—both good and bad. Your image of yourself *fluctuates,* or changes often. One day the good things seem more real than the bad. Other days you feel all thumbs, worthless, not able to remember one good thing about yourself. You are much more critical of yourself than anyone else is, but you do not realize it. The criticism you feel from yourself and others is painful.

WHO IS THE REAL YOU?

Your self-image, that collection of decisions you have been making about yourself since you were born, is full of *misperceptions,* or incorrect views. Some of the evaluations you

You have been building a self-image since you were a baby. That self-image is your understanding of all the "messages" that people sent you.

Television: The Great Escape

Some people abuse or misuse television. They tune in their sets and tune out the rest of the world. One author even calls television a "plug-in drug."

Here are some facts that may help you to stop and think if you are using television as your great escape:

• The only thing people in the United States do more than watch television is sleep.

• Ninety-seven percent of all U.S. homes have one television set. Forty-one percent have two or more.

• The average television set is used for 6 hours and 15 minutes each day.

• The average preschooler watches more than 54 hours a week. At this rate, by the age of sixty-five, that person will have watched the equivalent of nine straight years of television!

• The average seventeen-year-old has spent 20,000 hours in front of the television set.

If you think you are using television to escape from your problems, try one of these "television tips":

1. Limit yourself to one program or one hour of television each day.

(continued)

34

made of yourself are right. But others are very wrong. Yes, you are good at helping other kids with their problems. But no, you are not the worst dancer in the class. It is not true that you will never learn to tell a joke right.

Unfortunately, some of the wrong ideas you have about yourself will stick with you, even after you have become an adult. (This is why, for example, people who were told they were too fat when they were children sometimes spend the rest of their lives feeling chubby, even when they are not fat.) The only person who can remove these wrong ideas from your self-image is you. It may take work to sort out what is true from what is not true and what is good about you from what needs improvement.

You are a mixture of pluses and minuses. The real you is the awkward one who missed the ball and lost the game for the team. The real you is also the one who aced the English test. The real you is the one with a hot, unreasonable temper that can explode without warning. The real you is also the one who took time out from a favorite television program to help put a bandage on your younger brother's cut. If your self-image is not strong enough, you may *overemphasize,* or give too much importance to, the negative things about yourself. You may then miss the point about the real you.

DO YOU HAVE A GOOD SELF-IMAGE?

If you do not think well of yourself, you may not be giving yourself enough credit. (Did you answer yes to many of the questions in "Do You Give Yourself Enough Credit?" on page 35?) In that case, you need to work harder to appreciate who you are.

What are twelve good things about you? Get a pencil and paper and write them down. Add three reasons why other people like you. Note two nice things you did for other people last week. Also, notice how you treat yourself. Do you set unreasonable deadlines for yourself and then start to blame yourself when things do not get done on time? When you look in the mirror, do you notice that your ears stick out and your nose is crooked, while overlooking the fact that you have soft, shiny hair and dazzling brown eyes? Be kinder to yourself. Do things that will help you feel good about yourself, like helping other people or forcing yourself to be the first one to raise a hand in class when you know the right answer. The more you participate, the more you realize how valuable you are.

A good self-image makes a difference in the person you will become. People who think well of themselves develop confidence. Confidence helps people to try new or difficult things. Sometimes they succeed, and some-

Do You Give Yourself Enough Credit?

Perhaps you take your good qualities for granted and spend too much time worrying about your faults. If that is true, then you are not giving yourself enough credit. The way to build a good self-image is to recognize the things you have done well. Ask yourself these questions:

- Are you always putting yourself down?
- When you do something well, do you minimize it by saying, "Yes, but ———" and come up with reasons why it was not such a great accomplishment?
- When other people pay you a compliment, do you wonder what is wrong with their judgment?
- After you have had a friendly conversation with someone you do not know well, do you often walk away wondering if you sounded foolish?
- If you do something nice for someone and they do not notice it, do you decide it was a dumb thing to have done?

times they do not. The important point is that they have given themselves a *chance* to succeed. They had the confidence to try.

Confidence also helps in dealing with other people. If you are confident and self-assured, you come across to people in a positive way. Then they are more likely to accept you. A positive self-concept and confidence can help you become successful.

SOMETIMES YOU WANT TO ESCAPE

You may think you have no escapes from life's problems, but almost everyone has them. There are many ways you can retreat from the world and from yourself without consciously realizing that you are doing it. Sometimes things become too difficult. Sometimes you feel unsure of yourself, and you do not like yourself—or anyone else—at all. You want to get away from the demands and the criticism. At times, that is okay. You sometimes need a quiet time alone. It helps to sit and think, to read, or to listen to music—alone. But sometimes escape can be harmful, a way of putting off dealing with problems that will not go away by themselves.

Drugs and alcohol are obvious es-

2. Give up television during the week.

3. Choose what you will watch when the television schedules are published. Write down your choices. Stick to them.

4. Start a "television tune-out." Give up watching television for two weeks. See how it feels. You may discover new ways to relax. You may even discover new things about yourself.

All Scrambled Up: Dyslexia and Self-Esteem

Millions of young people in the United States have learning problems. One such learning disorder is *dyslexia,* which means having tremendous difficulty with words.

People who are dyslexic may have trouble with reading, spelling, handwriting, or even speaking. They may confuse the letters *b, d,* and *p* and read the word *bid* as *dip.*

In the past, a child with dyslexia was sometimes thought to be retarded or slow. Researchers now know that the dyslexic child is usually of average or above average intelligence. The sad part is that because of trouble with schoolwork, sports, or other activities, the child often develops low self-esteem—a bad self-image.

However, despite frustration and even failure, many people learn to handle dyslexia and go on to lead lives of high achievement. In fact, some of the great figures of history have been dyslexic.

• Although he had ten tutors, Hans Christian Andersen, who wrote "The Ugly Duckling" and other famous tales, could not learn to read. Instead, he dictated all of his stories.

• King Karl XI of Sweden

(continued)

"Somewhere I got the idea that it's 'bad' to like yourself. So when I do something I'm proud of and I start to feel good, I begin to criticize myself for liking myself too much. I know it's dumb, but I always do it."

"When I walk into a room full of people, I get so self-conscious I want to shrink out of sight. It's as though everyone can look right through me and see all my faults. My mother says people are too busy worrying about themselves to be judging me. That's probably right, but I still can't get rid of the feeling."

"I have a hard time raising my hand in class, even when I'm sure of the answer. I always think someone else can give a better answer, or that what I have to say isn't that important."

capes. There are others, too. For example, there is watching television "just to see what is on." Or spending hours and hours alone getting lost in books, magazines, or daydreams. Another way to escape is to become so busy that you have no time to think. You fill your life with so many parties, projects, and school activities that you never have a chance to think about yourself—or your problems.

Teenagers are not the only ones who use escapes and hide out. People do it at any age, at times when life feels too uncomfortable. The trouble is that when you come out of hiding (and everyone has to sooner or later), the problems are still there, unsolved.

Escaping puts a screen between you and your inner thoughts. It reduces self-awareness. *Self-awareness* is knowing about yourself: your likes and dislikes, the way you react, your attitudes about things and people, your strengths and weaknesses. Although self-awareness is painful at times, it is a very important part of being human. Knowing, accepting, and loving yourself is a vital part of growing up strong and happy.

THE IMPORTANCE OF MAKING MISTAKES

Mistakes cannot always be avoided. Not only that, they are essential. If you never made a mistake, you would never learn anything new. Few people realize that. People try hard to avoid making mistakes, but no one succeeds. Even the most assured and accomplished people have moments when they say, "Why did I do that? How could I have been so stupid?"

For anyone at any age, life consists of problems and solutions. It is a process of making mistakes and learning, making mistakes and learning. And when you make a mistake, it is best to take notice of it, understand how it happened, and then let it go. If you constantly blame yourself for the mistakes you make, if you constantly worry that you'll make a mistake "just like last time," you probably

Accepting yourself—with all your good points and faults—is part of growing up strong and happy.

was a wise and beloved king. However, he was sometimes caught reading important government papers upside down.
• Woodrow Wilson, the twenty-eighth President of the United States, did not learn to read until the age of eleven. When he was a child, his teachers thought him to be an extremely slow learner.
• Albert Einstein, the famous physicist, did not learn to read until he was nine. His teachers thought he was retarded. Yet he became the best-known genius of the modern world.
• Other famous dyslexics include Auguste Rodin, sculptor; Amy Lowell, poet; Lawrence Lowell, president of Harvard University; George Patton, general; and Nelson Rockefeller, Vice President of the United States.

Facts: It is estimated that 2 to 12 million young people in the United States have learning disorders. Boys are seven to ten times as likely to be dyslexic as girls, but no one is sure why.

37

HOW DO YOU HANDLE HURT FEELINGS?

Sometimes your feelings get hurt. That is unavoidable. When it happens, do you confront the other people involved to find out what happened or to let them know how you feel? Do you withdraw, feeling neglected and alone? It

Everyone Makes Mistakes

How do you usually feel when you make a mistake? Do you feel differently if the mistake is made in front of the class? How do you usually react to your mistakes?

will. It does not help to drag yesterday's mistake into tomorrow's experience like so much baggage.

If you do badly on a test, it does no good to write it off by saying, "I guess I'm just dumb." It does help to notice why you did badly: "I was careless and read the instructions wrong," or "I watched television last night when I should have studied."

It feels good to learn from a mistake. That is a sure sign that you are growing. It is good to accept the fact that making mistakes is an important part of the learning process, to keep looking back and noticing how far you have come. You are improving all the time. Noticing your improvements should help your self-image a great deal.

takes courage to confront other people. But your feelings matter. Being able to share those feelings with people you care about helps you become a stronger, happier person. Imagine yourself in each of these situations. Visualize the way you would react in each one.

YOUR BEST FRIEND PAIRS UP WITH ANOTHER PERSON AND LEAVES YOU OUT WITH NO EXPLANATION.

YOUR TEACHER BLAMES YOU FOR SOMETHING YOU DID NOT DO, AND THERE IS NO WAY FOR YOU TO PROVE THAT YOUR TEACHER IS WRONG.

a quick review

1. Who are some of the people who play an important part in the way a person's self-image is formed?
2. Is the image you have of yourself completely accurate? Why or why not?
3. What are some signs that your self-image is not strong?
4. What are some good ways to improve your opinion of yourself?
5. What are some ways people use to escape from their problems?

► **Words to Know**
fluctuate: Change often.
misperception: An incorrect view; a misunderstanding.
overemphasize: Give too much importance to something.
self-awareness: Being aware of your feelings.
self-image: Your opinion of yourself.

39

CHAPTER 4
How Others See You

Most people care about the impression they make on others. You probably do, too. You want people to like you. And sometimes you are not sure what they think of you.

The way others see you depends on many things. Your *appearance* (the way you wear clothes, how your hair is styled, the way you carry yourself) is only part of it. What you say, the tone of your voice, and the expression on your face are important too. Whether or not you are really interested in others also plays a big part in the impression you make.

THE WAY YOU LOOK

Your appearance gives others their first impression of you. It can also affect your own feelings about being with other people. You tend to be more confident when you know you look nice.

Perhaps the most important part of "looking good" is that it lets you forget about yourself and concentrate on the people you are with. For example, you can really shine at the class play tryouts when you're not wishing you had remembered to get a haircut. Or you can really listen to what a new friend is saying when you're not worried about a rip in your shirt. The time to think about how you look is not when you're *in* a situation but before you get there.

Your grooming is a big part of how you look. *Grooming* means the way you care for yourself. Going to school with clean hair and fingernails, a freshly scrubbed face, and a shirt with all the buttons in place gives the impression that you feel good about yourself and are ready to get down to work.

On weekends at home, you may want to be more relaxed in a pair of old blue jeans and one of your dad's shirts. But what if you went to school with your hair dirty and shaggy, your toes poking out of old, scuffed sneakers, and your shirttail flapping? People would get the feeling that you were unhappy or that you did not care much about yourself. Teachers would probably expect your work to be as sloppy as the way you look.

On the other hand, if you worry about the tiniest speck of dirt, if you never have a hair out of place or a wrinkle in your clothes, you give the impression that you are nervous and insecure. "Good grooming" does not mean fussing over yourself; it means taking good care of yourself, staying clean and "pulled together." The special feature on page 42 gives you all the basics of good grooming.

Your posture creates an impression. Good posture means being relaxed without being sloppy. It means carrying yourself straight but not rigid. You do not have to be as stiff as a broom to have good posture. But if you hunch over, you look droopy, and you probably feel droopy, too.

People who hunch over or slouch are often trying to hide themselves

What impression do you get from this student's posture?

The special feature on page 42 gives you all the basics of good grooming.

Word Messages

The average five-year-old has a vocabulary of 1500 words. The average ten-year-old knows 7000 words. By the age of eighteen, the average person has a vocabulary of 20,000 or more words. The average college graduate knows 60,000 words.

Clearly, there are plenty of words to choose from. Yet many people "pepper" what they say with *fillers*—words or sounds that fill up space but do not add meaning.

Do you use the expressions "uh," "uhm," "well," "like," "and," or "you know" between sentences? These are *fillers*—words that add nothing to your conversation. In fact, they make you sound less self-assured.

Activity: Name some of the filler expressions that people use. Then carry on a five-minute conversation in class. Whenever anyone uses a filler, that person is to stand up quickly, then sit down. If you become a jack-in-the-box, you will know it is time to work on getting rid of the filler habit.

41

LOOKING GOOD FROM HEAD TO TOE

YOUR HAIR

Keep it clean and shiny. How often should you wash it? Oily hair needs shampooing every other day—or more often. Dry hair must be washed at least twice a week. Choose a shampoo that's designed for your hair type (dry or oily). Some shampoos are fine to use every day.

YOUR SKIN

Scrub yourself all over in a bath or shower every single day. A washcloth gets you super clean. After your bath, use an underarm antiperspirant to cut down perspiration and keep you fresh-smelling all day long.

YOUR NAILS

Trim them often. You need nail clippers to snip them and an emery board to smooth them. Push back cuticles with a wooden orange stick (never cut cuticles). Don't let dirt build up under your nails (a nailbrush keeps them clean). Trim your toenails as well as your fingernails. Cut toenails straight across. If your nails aren't healthy, you may not be getting enough protein. Eggs, milk, meat, and fish can provide protein for you.

YOUR FACE

Wash it morning and night. Clean oily skin more often. Use a special soap and dab with *astringent* lotion—a lotion that cuts down oiliness. Keeping your skin free of oil prevents the acne that's caused by oil-clogged pores. Acne creams are some help. For severe acne, see a *dermatologist,* a doctor who treats skin problems. If you have dry skin, pamper it with a moisturizer after you wash.

YOUR TEETH

Without brushing, flossing, and a dentist's care, your teeth and gums can be ruined by plaque. *Plaque* is bacteria that builds up on your teeth and can cause cavities. Four out of five teenagers have some damage due to plaque. Tooth decay is the most common disease in the Western world. Brush at least twice a day, after every meal if you can. Use dental floss to scrape off plaque. It's important to see a dentist twice a year.

because they feel too tall, too fat, or too skinny. Whatever problem you think you have, bad posture will make the problem look worse.

How can you find out what your posture is like? Ask people. Your parents, your doctor, or your friends will tell you. Notice yourself reflected in the window of a store as you walk along the sidewalk. Are you stooped over? Do you stare at the pavement? Take a deep breath. Throw your shoulders back. Straighten up. Notice how much better you feel.

Plan to catch yourself whenever you begin to slump. Ask your friends and family to remind you. If you are worried that your posture is really bad, ask your physical education teacher for help. The right kind of exercise is one of the best ways to correct posture.

THE WAY YOU ACT

The way people see you depends on much more than your looks. There are many other things that people notice about you. One of these things is *body language*. This is the way you express yourself without words. Whether you are aware of it or not, you use body language. The way you sit, stand, tilt your head, or move your hands tells people what you are thinking even when you do not want them to know. Consider a few examples.

When your arms are crossed, it looks as if you do not believe what someone is saying to you. A person speaking to you may get the message that you do not like the idea that she or he is presenting. When you sit with your arms back behind your head, you looked relaxed and happy. Sometimes your words and your body say two different things. You may say, "No, I'm not angry anymore."

Good grooming tells others that you feel good about yourself. Others then tend to react to you in a positive way.

Body and Face Messages

Communicating without words is called nonverbal communication. The new science of *kinesics* deals with body language, the messages that your body sends out when you move.

Did you know that the pupils of your eyes widen when you see something pleasant? Are you aware that when you are puzzled you are likely to scratch your nose? Do you realize that the muscles in your face can make 250,000 expressions?

You also communicate by how far you stand from someone. If you are a close friend, you might stand 15 to 20 centimeters (6 to 8 inches) apart. This personal space is called your zone, or bubble, by body-language experts. Sometimes you send out messages for people to come into your bubble. Sometimes your body language says "stay away".

But there you are with your arms crossed, lips twitching, and foot tapping. Your body language says you are indeed angry.

Body language can irritate people. For example, if you put your feet on a table or throw your leg over the arm of a chair, your mother may get upset. She feels that your body language is saying that you are lazy and do not care. Or you may shuffle along behind your father, head down, hands stuffed in your pockets. Your father may snap, "Will you please cooperate?" Your body language has told him that you really do not want to help him with the shopping.

People notice your tone of voice. Your tone of voice tells people a lot about your attitude and the mood you're in. Consider the following exchanges:

"Do you want an ice cream cone?"

"Yes!" (You're enthusiastic.)

"Will you wash the pots and pans tonight?"

"Yes" (with a sigh). (You're unhappy.)

"I entered a contest. Do you think I'll win a million dollars?"

"Yes." (You are teasing.)

"Does my harmonica make it hard for you to concentrate?"

"Yes." (You are annoyed.)

Often when you know you've said the "right" thing, when you really got your message across, it was because someone heard your tone as well as your words. Suppose you said, "Thanks for calling, but we don't need any light bulbs right now." Your tone of voice would tell the other person exactly what you mean. People often read your tone instead of your words.

People also notice your manners. Good manners are more than knowing which fork to use and when to say, "Thank you very much, I had a nice time." Manners also mean paying attention to how other people are feeling. Having good manners does not mean being stiff and stuffy. You can have good manners and still have fun. You just need to know how to act in different situations. When you have guests, you do not tease your sister about getting the biggest slice of cake. The roughhousing you do in the school gym can get you thrown out of a restaurant or a movie theater. Your friends may think it funny to have their shoelaces tied together when they take a nap, but your favorite uncle may not find that kind of joke funny at all. There is nothing wrong with your uncle. His humor is just different from that of your friends. Good manners mean understanding this and joking with your uncle in a way that will make him laugh and put him at ease.

However, sometimes you do not know how to put people at ease. You can get into situations where you just do not know how to act. So you tease

NOBODY UNDERSTANDS ME

It happens a lot. People get the wrong idea about you. You do something, say something, or even look a certain way and they imagine you're feeling or thinking something you're not. When someone gets the wrong impression, think back to what you said or did and see if you can figure out why you were misunderstood.

Sun Smarts

Tanning is caused by the sun's ultraviolet rays. These rays are very strong, and over time they can cause wrinkles and even skin cancer.

It is important to wear a sunscreen lotion outdoors in sunny weather. There are two kinds of sunscreens. One type blocks the sun directly. The other kind absorbs the ultraviolet rays and slows down burning and tanning.

Since 1978 an SPF (sun-protection factor) number has had to be listed on all sunscreen products. The SPF number tells you how much protection the product gives you. The numbers range from 5 to 15. The higher the number, the greater the protection.

▶ Words to Know

body language: Unspoken messages sent by your body.

energetic: Having energy; feeling strong.

grooming: Cleaning, caring for, and making attractive.

personality: A person's style of relating to others.

posture: A position of the body or a way of carrying the body.

What is happening in this picture?

people and blunder, or you get shy and make people nervous. Or you start giggling, and people get annoyed. Sometimes you will make mistakes, and there will be times when you will seem rude. But if you are really trying, people will forgive the mistakes you make. If you are really sincere, it usually shows.

Making a good impression seems like hard work at times. Your friends look beneath the surface to the real you. You may wonder why other people cannot do that. Why do you have to pay so much attention to the way you look and act? Why is it so difficult for people to see who you are inside? Think about it a minute. The ways other people judge you are probably the same ways you judge them. The key idea to remember is that you want to feel comfortable with other people and have them feel comfortable with you.

a quick review

1. What are four things that affect the impression you make on others?
2. What do certain kinds of clothes tell other people about your mood?
3. What is body language? How does it tell others what you may be thinking?
4. Say "Would you please give me that pencil?" using two different tones of voice. How does your tone affect the meaning?
5. What does it mean to have "good manners"?

W hat is a stereotype? Originally, a stereotype was a metal printing plate. All printed copies made from the plate were exactly alike.

The word is now used to describe a certain way of seeing other people. Sometimes we think that all members of a certain group are alike. We expect them to behave in the same way.

But people are not like copies made from a printing plate. Members of a group may be alike in some ways. But they are very different in others. Each person is an original.

When you form an opinion about someone, your opinion is affected by more than what you see at that moment. Ideas you have had earlier in your life play a part in the impressions you form of others now. You have been influenced by what your family and friends have said about other people. You have also been influenced by television, movies, books, and magazines. Many of the impressions you have of others are below the level of your awareness, and you don't even know you have them.

Are your impressions of other people accurate? Sometimes they are, and sometimes they are not. You may be right that your sister is nervous around boys. But you may be wrong to think that the girl who turned away when you smiled at her in the street does not like the way you look. Maybe she is just shy.

CHAPTER 5
Outsides and Insides

First Impressions

For each of the situations below, write your *first impression* of the person described:

• a classmate who volunteers to answer every question

• a classmate who never volunteers to speak in class

• a classmate you've known for years who didn't speak to you in the halls this morning

• a dentist with dirty hands

• a salesclerk in a clothing department who is dressed sloppily

• a salesclerk in a department store who is dressed neatly

• your friend's older sister who didn't speak to you as
(continued)

READING PEOPLE

You can get to know some people pretty well. Living with your family, you have probably learned how to interpret their moods. You can usually tell when they are happy or worried or feeling playful. When your father clears his throat a certain way, you know it means he is upset. When your brother's footsteps tap across the house, you can tell he's excited about a new idea. When he walks slowly, you know he's either worried or thinking hard.

But sometimes it is not easy to read people correctly, and you can be wrong, even about people you live with every day. You think your aunt is glaring at you because you gobbled down a piece of cake before dinner. She may not know (or even care) that you ate the cake. She may be deep in thought about a problem that has nothing to do with you. You may be angry at your sister for pouting because you won't take her to the mov-

ies. It may be that your sister isn't even thinking about the movies, but is feeling bad about something that someone said to her at school.

At home, you may feel safe to say, "Hey, are you mad at me?" This is a good way to start clearing the air. In the outside world, it may be harder to know what the problem is. There you are more likely to have the wrong idea about someone.

You've probably heard that it's not a good idea to judge people by appearances, but sometimes appearances are all you have to go on. And it is easy to be misled. Look at Linda, for example. Probably every school has a girl or a boy like Linda. She's smart. She's good-looking. Her personality is outgoing, and it's not fake—she is *really* nice. Everyone wants to be her best friend, but it's hard to know whom she likes best because she is so nice to everyone. Linda gets straight A's and is liked by the teachers, too. She is more than likely to become president of her class or win a lead in the school play. There is nothing wrong with Linda. And that's the problem. Whenever people compare themselves to Linda, they come out looking like losers. Next to Linda anyone would feel ugly, stupid, and unlikable. You are sure that if you had her self-assurance, her brains, her looks, her personality, and her clothes, your troubles would be over.

The fact is, Linda gets panicky be-

Sometimes even friends don't understand each other.

Women cannot work in rugged jobs.

Men do not enjoy working in the home.

BREAKING DOWN STEREOTYPES

Handicapped people miss out on so much in life.

Children cannot do anything about the adult world around them.

Beyond Rocking Chairs

Ageism is the stereotyping of people because they are old.

Fairy tales are filled with stereotyped pictures of older people: evil witches, old hags, mean kings. And too often, television shows older people as stubborn, slow, or silly.

There have been many recent efforts to strike down these stereotypes. People who formerly would not have been allowed to work once they turned sixty-five can now work until they reach seventy. And a group called the Gray Panthers has been formed to work for the rights of older citizens.

stereotype: Most senior citizens are dependent on others and live in old people's homes.
fact: Only 5 percent of all senior citizens are under special care. The majority of older men and women live in family units. And 16 percent of the men and 33 percent of the women live alone.
stereotype: Getting older is not a major problem for this country because there are not many senior citizens.
fact: More than one fifth of all men and two fifths of all women now reach the age of eighty. In 1970, one in ten people in the United States was sixty-five years

(continued)

In their traditional role, older people enjoy giving love and support to other people in their families.

you, her mother role is the most important one, and when another of her roles conflicts with that one, you may get upset. When your band recital comes just when she is having a crisis in her office, you may not understand it if she misses your performance. What could be more important than hearing you play the tuba? But if she leaves her work in the middle of an office emergency to go to a band concert, her co-workers and boss may not understand.

You fill different roles, too. You are a daughter or a son. You are also a student. You may be a brother or a sister, and you are certainly a friend. At times you may play other roles: baby-sitter, member of a basketball team, singer in the church choir. Sometimes your roles can conflict with each other. For example, suppose you have to work at your after-school job for Mrs. Poiner, do an hour of homework, *and* go with your family to Grandfather's birthday party. Juggling your roles as employee, student, and family member helps you understand the problems other people have with the roles they play.

The roles people play are important. And the way you see people is influenced by the roles in which you know them. Sometimes, in fact, all you see is the role, and you forget that there is an individual in the role. Your school principal may simply be an authority figure to you—a serious woman in a gray suit. A police officer may appear to be just a badge and a uniform. It would seem strange to you to see that same police officer out of uniform, sitting under a tree with a lemonade and a movie magazine. You might giggle to find yourself standing in line for the movies behind the school principal and her date for the evening. You expect certain role behavior from your friends and family, too. It's all right for your teacher to give you instructions, but if your sister does it, you call her bossy. It's fine for your brother to whine to you about being afraid to go to the dentist, but what would you think if your mother showed the same kind of childish fear? You'd probably feel pretty uncomfortable.

Roles help the world work in an orderly, predictable way. They tell you what kind of behavior to expect from certain people in certain situations. And that, in turn, helps you know how you should behave. But you can also find yourself seeing people as nothing more than their roles. And then it is important to remember that people are individuals, too. Your experience of each person you know will be richer if you can separate the individual from the stereotype or role that applies (mother, teacher, salesperson, uncle, garage mechanic). Each person you know is a separate, unique individual with special feelings.

Recently, many older people have added to the traditional role. They may continue in their jobs, return to school, or travel.

old or older. By the year 2000 that share will rise to one in eight.

stereotype: Old people sit around and do not accomplish much.

fact: Over forty million hours of work and service are given by senior citizens each year.

stereotype: Most old people are lonely.

fact: Some are. But surveys show that old people are less likely to feel lonely than teenagers.

stereotype: Old people look forward to retirement.

fact: Four out of every ten retired people said they did not want to retire but were forced to because of age.

stereotype: Old people stop learning.

fact: Many senior citizens are now going back to school. Under the new Elderhostel program, college courses are offered throughout the country to men and women over sixty.

stereotype: Old people do not take part in politics.

fact: Senior citizens have the best voter registration and voting records of all age groups in the United States.

fact: According to a recently completed ten-year study on the role of old people in television shows, only one in fifty characters is over sixty-five. In real life, one in ten people is sixty-five or older.

53

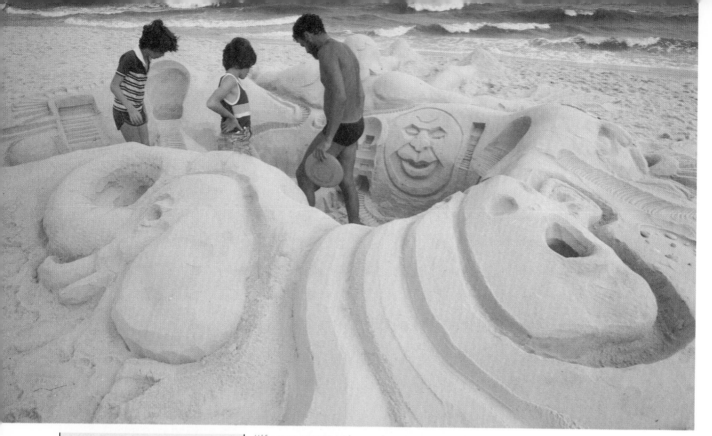

"If you approach each new person you meet in a spirit of adventure, you will find yourself endlessly fascinated by the new channels of thought and experience and personality that you encounter." —*Eleanor Roosevelt*

a quick review

1. What, besides firsthand experience, influences your opinions of other people?
2. Why is it a bad idea to judge people by appearances?
3. Is it a good idea to compare yourself to others? Why or why not?
4. Name at least four ways of stereotyping people.
5. How do roles help people understand one another? What is a drawback to seeing a person in a role?

When do you become an adult—a grown-up? At eighteen? Twenty-one? Thirty? Adulthood may seem a long way away to you, but the fact is that you are in the process of becoming an adult right now. The changes are so gradual that you may not notice them, but you can be sure that they're happening.

When you were a child, a parent or older relative probably bought your clothes and helped you clean up your room. Now you are likely to have a clothes allowance, to care for your bedroom, and to share other cleaning chores. As a child, you may have cried or worried when someone at school "said something mean." Now you are more likely to confront people when there is a problem and discuss what's wrong. You may once have had trouble getting your homework finished on time. By now, you may have learned to pace yourself. You know how much time you need. Do you remember begging your parents to stop for ice cream or to buy you one more rubber monster for your toy collection? Now you can pass up a chocolate sundae in order to lose weight, or take an after-school job when you want money for a new clock radio. Of course, you don't always budget your time and your money perfectly. Your room doesn't always pass inspection. And you are

CHAPTER 6
Becoming an Adult

The Range of Change

Sometimes when a sudden change happens in your life, it feels like you are the only person who has ever had to go through the experience. You're not. Below are some statistics to prove it.

Moving:

Have you moved lately? The average family in the United States moves once every five years.

Working:

Has your mom gone back to work? In 1978 half of all women worked outside the home. Ninety percent of all women will work outside the home at some time in their lives.

Has your mom or dad recently lost a job? In the early part of the 1980s almost six million people were unemployed.

Family:

Have your parents recently separated or divorced? Twenty to thirty percent of all marriages end in divorce, half of these involving children under eighteen years old. One out of every six children in the United States lives in a single-parent family. Half of all children up to the age of fourteen will live in a one-parent home at some time during their growing years.

often less than even-tempered when something upsetting happens. But you're learning.

As you get older, you have more privileges and more responsibilities. You may baby-sit for younger brothers and sisters, help cook dinner, and do odd jobs to contribute to the family income. You may get to stay up to watch a late movie on television, have a pet of your own, sit in on adult conversations, take subways and buses alone, or go on camping trips with your friends. You will probably get a driver's license. Eventually, you will have a job and an apartment of your own. You'll become a voter and perhaps a husband or wife, maybe even a parent. But doing things adults do does not necessarily mean you will be wiser, braver, or more self-assured. It takes time to acquire knowledge and build self-confidence. Adults need to test themselves in the world, just as you do as a teen. Being an adult, like being a young person, is a continual process of growth.

ADJUSTING

You have been making adjustments ever since you first dropped a rattle and had to crawl across the floor to pick it up. You have to make an adjustment every time something happens that you had not planned on.

As you grow older, the way you make adjustments changes. You take more responsibility for yourself. Your reactions are more adult. You no longer cry or look for someone else to solve a problem. When you miss a train, fail a test, or forget a homework assignment, you figure out what needs to be done, and you do it.

You make adjustments every day of your life. Some are minor. When you are out of corn flakes, you eat oatmeal. When it rains, you have your yard sale indoors. When your sister spills ink on the carefully lettered cover of your report, you redo the cover. Other adjustments are more major. When a grandparent or other loved one dies, it may take a long time to get used to the changes that take place in your life. When your parents get jobs out of state and you move, you have to make new friends in a new place. When you break your leg and have to wear a cast for 2 months, you have to learn many new ways of doing everyday activities.

You probably think that adjusting is something you have to do only in time of difficulty. It may surprise you to discover that it takes just as much effort to adjust to happy events in your life. Have you ever thought, "If only I were elected class president (or got straight A's, or had a car), I'd be completely happy"? But if you do get elected class president, you will have to adjust to the extra demands on your time. If you get straight A's, you may have to adjust to pressure to "keep it up." If you get a car, you will

MYTHS TO QUIT BELIEVING

ONCE A FAILURE, ALWAYS A FAILURE.

WHEN I GROW UP, I WON'T HAVE PROBLEMS ANYMORE.

WHEN I'M ADULT, I WON'T HAVE AS MUCH FUN AS I DO NOW.

IF I DON'T GO TO COLLEGE, I'LL NEVER GET A DECENT JOB.

GETTING OLD WILL BE AWFUL.

SOME THINGS WERE JUST MEANT TO BE.

Growing up means being able to do things that have to be done. The childlike feeling of "somebody-else-will-take-care-of-this" begins to change.

Teenage Tension

When you are nervous or upset, do you bite your nails or pull at your hair?

Working with a group of adolescents several years ago, researchers in Connecticut explored the most common ways that teenagers deal with tension.

(continued)

58

have to find the time and money to take care of it. Getting what you want does not mean the end of problems. If you think it does, you may worry that something is "wrong" when problems continue to crop up.

It is also true that a great deal of easy success can be as misleading as a great deal of failure. If things go especially smoothly for you as a teen, you can get the impression that life will be a breeze for you. If you don't have to work for the things that matter to you, you probably won't develop the psychological muscle you need to perform in the adult world. Failure itself may not build character, but learning to deal with failure does. It may help to remember this fact when things go wrong.

HANDLING CONFLICT

You have to handle conflict every day. Some conflict you take care of fairly easily—whose invitation should you accept, Terry's or Carla's? Which after-school sport should you take, baseball or track? But some conflicts are much more difficult to deal with.

Imagine that it's 9:30 P.M. and you are studying for a biology exam. You are already worried about how late it is. The telephone rings. It's Betsy. She's crying hard because she has had a fight with her parents. She needs help and sympathy. You are the only one she feels she can talk to. You feel panicky about your test. You know that if you talk too long to Betsy, you will do badly on the test. But if you hurry her off the telephone, she'll feel deserted and even more upset than she is now. Whose needs are more important, yours or Betsy's?

Imagine that you are out shopping. In the dressing room of a store, you find a good ball-point pen. It looks expensive. You're sure whoever lost it will never come back. And you could use a nice pen like this one. Is it fair to keep it? Should you turn it in to the salesclerk?

Imagine that you are out with friends having pizza. Someone suggests that you go out to the parking lot and have a few beers. You are all underage, and your parents would disapprove. But everyone seems to be going along with it. These friends are important to you. Besides, there will be nothing for you to do if everyone else is out in the parking lot. Should you go and have a beer, or say you have to go home?

Each of the situations above presents a conflict. In each instance, your feelings are telling you one thing and your mind is telling you another. Your mind says you should get off the telephone and study for your biology test. Your feelings tell you to help Betsy. Your mind says that the ball-point pen does not belong to you and that you have no right to take it. Your feelings say "finders keepers." Your mind says that buying beer is against the law at your age and that your parents would be upset and disappointed. Your feelings say that you want your friends to like you.

When there is a conflict between your mind and your feelings, it is important to weigh both sides carefully. Sometimes you can reach a *compromise*. A compromise is a solution that tries to satisfy conflicting needs. Other times, you just don't know

Trust is earned. Parents who feel they can count on their teenager also feel comfortable with the teenager's need for increased independence.

Stress: Getting to the Heart of the Matter

Until 1960, the people of Roseto, Pennsylvania, had a lower death rate from heart disease than the rest of the country—50 percent lower. The low heart-disease rate was due to very low stress levels in the small town. Families there were very close. There was good communication.

(continued)

what to do. You may have a very strong feeling about what is right, and yet making the decision to stand up for it takes courage. You will have to face such conflicts all your life. You will become stronger and more respected by other people if you can stand up for what you believe even when no one else agrees with you. Remember that each time you resolve a conflict, you grow.

DEALING WITH STRESS

When you are in conflict, you are under stress. Stress is also caused by things like worry, fear, excitement, and hurrying. You are under stress when you're late for school, waiting for test results, getting ready for a party, or making a choice between going to the beach with your family or on a picnic with friends. Stress is the result of caring intensely about

CALM DOWN

It is important that you be able to recover from the effects of stress—to calm down. It helps if you can find time to relax every day. What are some ways to relax? Take twenty minutes a day to:

Take a walk. Sit on a hill. Watch the clouds.

Listen to calming music.

Soak in a tub.

Sit in a quiet place. Close your eyes. Say a nonsense word to yourself over and over. Don't let yourself be distracted.

the way things turn out. Caring about the ways things turn out causes tension to build. If being late for a party did not matter to you, you would not be upset about having a flat tire on the way. You want to make the team. You want to do well on a test. You want someone to like you. The idea of not making the team, the grade, or the friendship causes you to worry and become tense.

Other people's expectations of you may cause stress. Your best friend wants you to like her parents. Your parents want you to do well in school so that you can go to college. Your teacher wants you to make the all-county debating team so that you can win for your school. Their expectations may cause you to feel nervous and tense—under stress. And stress can wear you out emotionally and physically.

Whether stress is caused by something pleasant or unpleasant, your physical reaction to it is the same. You may perspire, your heart may pound, your muscles may tense, your stomach may churn, and you may cry or laugh nervously. You can deal with stress better if you call time out, force yourself to relax, and calm down. Finding ways to relax in the course of your everyday life helps you build a calm place inside yourself, so that when a stress situation occurs, you'll be better able to handle it. (See the box on the facing page.)

Physical exercise is an excellent way to relieve feelings of stress.

You can learn to live with stress, but you cannot get rid of it entirely. Stress is a fact of life. It is important to remember that everyone undergoes stress. In fact, without the things that cause stress, life would be boring.

LOOKING AT YOUR FUTURE

How do you see your future? Do you think your teen years will be the best time of your life, or do you believe that everything will be easier when you are an adult? Do you think that as an adult you will be very different from the way you are now? Do you believe that your life is fated to turn out a certain way and that you cannot do much to change it?

Throughout your life you will experience ups and downs, successes and failures, good days and bad days. Life involves problems and solutions,

Houses were similar and near to one another. All family roles were respected, and people knew they could count on one another.

But then things changed. People moved. Some families broke up. Industry moved into the area. Cars and houses got fancier. With these changes came more stress, less communication, and more heart disease. In fact, figures show that between 1961 and 1975, the heart-disease rate in Roseto more than doubled, finally rising to the national average.

Growing up is easier when you like yourself for what you are and what you are becoming.

kinds of things you will enjoy as an adult. And some of the things that give you trouble now (speaking in front of a group, writing reports, or getting places on time) are things you can work on and change as you grow and gain more confidence.

Nothing was "meant to be." *You* are the designer of your life. Few things will just drop into your lap. If you want something, you can plan and work for it. If, for example, you want to be an actor or an actress, you would be foolish to sit in a Hollywood coffee shop waiting to be noticed by a movie producer. It would be better, instead, to prepare for an acting career by volunteering for school plays, taking acting classes at the local Y, and joining theater groups. Nothing is easy. But nothing is impossible, either. When you recognize that you are the one in charge of your life, you will be way ahead of where you would be if you think of your life as something that just happens to you.

and there is no way to change that. Problems are part of life. Solving them is part of growing.

Becoming an adult does not mean you will change from one kind of person to another. You are now basically the person you will always be. The kinds of things that give you joy today (running through the grass with your dog, getting the giggles with a friend, or playing a vigorous game of tennis, for example) will be the same

a quick review

1. Name two situations you might have to adjust to as a student and as a family member.
2. How can having great success as a teen make adult life more difficult?
3. What does it mean to have a conflict between your mind and your feelings?
4. What are three physical reactions people have under stress?
5. Who is the person who most affects the way your adult life turns out?

A friend is someone you can share things with. A movie is funnier when your friend is giggling next to you. Your fear of moving up a grade is more tolerable because your friend is nervous about it, too. Your excitement about horses increases when your friend loves horses. Doing things with a friend feels good.

THE IDEAL FRIEND

The ideal friend accepts you just the way you are, sticks up for you when you are not around, keeps your secrets, and worries about you when you are sick. If you miss a day at school, the ideal friend calls ("Hey, how do you feel?") and fills you in on what you missed. The ideal friend is loyal. You can admit that you are secretly in love with one of your teachers and not get laughed at—or told on, either. The ideal friend will not stand you up for the movies because someone else comes along with a more interesting invitation.

If you are lucky, you have a friend who fits (or nearly fits) the ideal, a person to share things with, to count on. You will have many other kinds of friends, too. In the group of people you know, you may have one friend you like to do homework with, another you like to play tennis with, one who is fun to tease, or one you see only when your families bowl together.

CHAPTER 7
Friends

(continued on page 66)

64

Many of your friends do not fit the description of the ideal friend, and that is okay. Jack is a friend who is fun to be with. You like clowning around together and having dinner with his joke-cracking family. But Jack is not as moody as you are. Sometimes, when you feel sad "for no reason," he gets impatient—he doesn't understand. Also, Jack can't keep a secret. More than once something you told him in confidence just leaked out to other guys you know. Does this mean Jack is a disloyal friend, and that you should not see him anymore? That is not necessarily what it means. But it does mean that Jack is not the guy to call when you are depressed, or when you have a piece of news you would rather not share with the world. Sometimes, in order to enjoy the good in a friendship, you have to put up with what is not so good. And you are less likely to have your feelings hurt if you do not expect more from a friend than that person is capable of giving.

Of course, a person who lies about you to other people, uses you, or steals from you is not a friend and is definitely someone to avoid. Part of the process of growing up is learning to tell when people are your friends and when they are not.

MAKING FRIENDS

It is easiest to make friends when you do things with people. You are likely to become friends with the person who is assigned to your tent on a camping trip, who shares your seat on a long bus ride to the museum, or who sits next to you day after day in school chorus. Making friends that way often comes so naturally that you do not think much about it.

But how do you get to know someone who looks interesting but has no classes or activities with you? You have to make an effort. Invite that person to join you when there's something going on. Having something to do gets your minds off yourselves, and you will not feel so self-conscious about getting to know each other.

It takes courage to initiate a friendship, whether you are inviting someone to your home, inviting someone to go to a basketball game with you, or asking someone to save you a seat in assembly. You may worry, "What if I invite Jake over and he doesn't want to come?" "What if Ginny wouldn't be caught dead at a basketball game with me?" "What if Mike is planning to sit with someone else at assembly? Am I butting in?" But often, the people you are interested in knowing are also interested in you. They have not made the first move because they are probably just as shy as you are. Being afraid of rejection can cause you to hold back, and that is a common mistake.

It can take time to make friends, and courage and *persistence* as well.

WILL YOU BE MY FRIEND?

Making new friends is difficult for everyone. Many people worry that others won't accept them, or fear that they're forcing themselves on other people when they try to make friends. If you feel insecure about yourself, you can come to many wrong conclusions when you try to make friends. How many of the following mistakes have you made?

Friendly Facts
(*continued from page 64*)

Friendly Facts
try this: Write a letter to the friend explaining how you feel about the conflict. (Do not send the letter. This is just an exercise.) Now pretend you are your friend. Write a letter back to yourself describing your friend's point of view. Write as many letters back and forth as it takes for you to understand both sides of the situation. Later, you might even want to share the series of letters with your friend.

Bits on Buddies: Quotes About Friendship
"Do not remove a fly from your friend's forehead with a hatchet."
—*Chinese proverb*

"Anybody can sympathize with the sufferings of a friend, but it requires a very fine nature to sympathize with a friend's success."
—*Oscar Wilde*

"One's friends are that part of the human race with which one can be human."
—*George Santayana*

"The feeling of friendship is like that of being comfortably filled with roast beef."
—*Samuel Butler*

"Friendship is like earthenware; once broken it can be mended."
—*Josh Billings*

Friends don't always like the same things or act in the same way. In a good friendship there is room for these differences.

Friendships you reach out for do not always "take." Sometimes you think you have much in common with someone. However, after spending an afternoon with that person, it is clear that you do not. But that is all right. Look for another friend and try again. People are like ice cream flavors: there are many varieties of them, and you will not like them all.

CLIQUES

A *clique* is a small, exclusive group of people within a larger group. In your school and in your grade, people will often form cliques. The desire to form cliques seems to be a part of human nature. If you are not accepted in the group you want, or if you find yourselves in one clique and wish you were in another, you may feel terrible.

Sometimes some groups are considered "in" and other groups are considered "out." People may not come out and talk about it, but everyone knows what is going on. Feeling shut out or being classified as a member of an "out" group hurts, even when the other people in your group are really the ones you like the best. How can you deal with the hurt you feel? For one thing, realize that you are not alone. There are many others suffering from the side effects of clique-making. And some of the other left-out people may be potential friends, with more in common with you and more to offer you than any of the members of the so-called in group.

Even if you are a member of the in group, you may still be unhappy. You may feel you do not belong there. You may worry that you are not as clever, good-looking, or interesting as others think, and you may fear that it is only a matter of time before you are found out, laughed at, and kicked out. No one on earth is free from the fear of rejection.

Are you in or out? You may not be sure. The whole thing can make you feel pretty uncomfortable—and confused. It is especially difficult when you have just entered a new school and want to fit in. You notice Jim, the star athlete, and Beth, the student council president. Jim and Beth always seem to know the right thing to say. They are so self-confident. People seem to like them instantly. They look to you like natural leaders. Having Jim or Beth for a friend would make you feel important. You would definitely be in if they were your friends. So you make it a goal to become Jim or Beth's friend. You hang around with them, laugh at their jokes, and hope they laugh at yours. You try hard. However, you never really know how you're doing. Also, you never feel completely comfortable. You feel you can never let your guard down and be yourself. You always feel as if there were something wrong, as if your hair were sticking out in a funny way or you had food on your shirt front.

Many people find themselves in a situation like this more than once in their lives. They are trying to be a friend of someone they think they should be friends with, but with

In every school there are "in" groups. What are the advantages and disadvantages of belonging to an "in" group? How important is it?

The Eyes Have It

If someone stares nonstop at you, you feel uncomfortable. But if someone never looks at you, it makes you feel ignored, even angry. Therefore, it is important that your eyes communicate interest and attention without turning each conversation into a staring contest.

Activity: Divide into pairs. Carry on a conversation with your partner. One partner should give normal eye contact. The other partner should give 100 percent eye contact for a few minutes, then no eye contact. (For this last exercise, you might even want to wear sunglasses or a blindfold.) Now switch roles. Discuss how the two extreme styles of eye contact made each of you feel.

What Draws People Together?

"We need to see ourselves, and one way we see ourselves is through someone like us. It's like looking in a mirror. We think, 'You're neat; I'm like you. Therefore I'm neat, too.'"

—*Myrtle T. Collins*

GOOD FRIENDS/BAD HABITS

Sometimes you want so much to have friends that you can do some pretty foolish things. Here are some bad habits to avoid.

whom they have little in common. They force it. And they feel miserably uncomfortable as a result. A friend made in this way is not a friend but a trophy, a stamp of acceptability. And that kind of friendship is not worth it. It is much more satisfying when you seek people out because you have things in common. You will be far better friends if you share, say, a slapstick sense of humor, a love of rock music, or even a feeling of loneliness. Being able to be yourself with someone who likes you just as you are—that is the best kind of friendship.

PROBLEMS WITH FRIENDSHIPS

Some problems you might have with a friend are as follow:

• *New friends replace an old friendship.* You used to walk home from school with your friend, to share everything. Now your friend is with someone else all the time and is always "too busy" for you. Maybe an interest in a person of the opposite sex is causing the split. Maybe your friend is always walking around school holding hands with that person and looking dewy-eyed.

• *You and your friend become competitive with each other.* You are struggling to do well. Your friend always does better. This time your friend came out with straight A's and then asked you (with a bit of a sneer, you think),

"How did *you* do?" You wanted to shrink out of sight.

• *One of you reveals a secret.* You cannot believe your ears. The deep, dark secret you shared with your best friend was repeated back to you by someone you hardly know. Your friend told! Why has your friend turned against you?

These things hurt. They make you feel angry and betrayed. In each situation your friendship would feel threatened. When you are upset with someone, it is a good idea to go off by yourself and sort out your feelings. Go for a walk, talk to yourself, look at what you feel. You may want to cry, or you may feel like punching your friend. Take some time. Allow your anger to explode where no one is around to hear you. Then calm down. Think through what you want to say to your friend. Do you want to ask for an explanation? Do you want your friend to do something? Do you want your friend to know how much you hurt? Your friend may not talk about the problem. Your friend may hope that the whole thing will blow over. In that case, you will have to deal with the problem alone.

It helps to stand back and take a fresh look at your friendship. Just because you have been very close to someone does not mean you are linked together or that you own one

Hear! Hear!
Being a good friend means being a good listener. When you are upset, you want an understanding listener, not an automatic advice machine. It is the same with your friends.

Listening Tips:
1. Listen with more than just your ears. Your body language should also communicate real interest.
2. Once in a while, give verbal cues that show you are following closely what your friend is saying. "I hear you saying that . . ." or "I understand what you mean when you say . . ." or "I have often felt the same way" are helpful phrases to use.
3. Do not interrupt.
4. Do not shift the attention from your friend's problem to one of your own.
5. Do not spend so much time planning your next response that you do not hear what is being said.
6. Try not to let your emotions get in the way of hearing.
7. Do not rush the conversation.
8. Do not try to solve the problem. You cannot. Your friend has to find his or her own solution.

Good friendships make each person better.

▶ **Words to Know**

exclusive: Shutting out all others.

infinite: Limitless.

initiate: Be the one who starts something.

persistence: Refusal to stop or give up.

vulnerable: Can be wounded or hurt.

that you need to change the kind of friendship you have. Instead of walking home from school together every day, it may be better to play tennis or do homework together once in a while. Instead of being number one in your friend's life, you may have to take second place to a steady boyfriend or girlfriend. Things will be different but still all right.

It also helps to put yourself in your friend's shoes. What would you do if you found that you had more in common or more fun with a new friend? What if you got the part in the play that your friend had really wanted? What if you told your friend's secret to someone when you did not mean to? It is painful to be the one to cause hurt feelings, too.

Caring about people—having friends—means you sometimes get hurt. Friends may disappoint you, just as you might disappoint them. But a conflict does not have to mean the end of a friendship. Often, working through conflicts together can make a friendship even stronger.

another. There should be room in your friendship for other friends, higher achievements, slips of the tongue. Sometimes conflict is a sign

a quick review

1. When you make new friends, why does it help to have an activity planned?
2. If you do not make new friends right away in a new school, is there something wrong?
3. What is a clique?
4. How do people make friends into trophies? What problems can result?
5. What should you do if a friend upsets you?

In grade school, boys and girls seem to separate into two groups: girls in the front of the bus and boys in the back. Parties are often "girls only" or "boys only." The other sex doesn't seem very important.

IN GROUPS

Gradually, girls and boys in the same class become interested in each other. A group of boys, out for pizza, might trade slices of their sausage-and-mushroom pizza for slices of a pepperoni-and-onion pizza that the girls at the next table have. The two groups might talk and joke about teachers, other kids they know, or the car with the flat tire outside the restaurant.

Before long, boys and girls stop to talk in the halls, outside school, and near the snack bar. They begin to reach out to each other, nervously at first. A boy steals a girl's shoe, and she chases him. A girl slips an unsigned note into a boy's locker. A group of girls call a boy and hang up in gales of laughter. Later on, things begin to relax somewhat. It turns out that school dances aren't so terrible after all. Dancing with each other is *fun*. After all those years of ignoring each other, everyone is a little surprised and pleased. Boys and girls can be friends.

Boys and girls may begin to do more things together. They may not actually date, but they spend time to-

CHAPTER 8
Boy/Girl Relationships

The Grapevine: Rumors and Gossip

People usually use the words *rumor* and *gossip* to mean the same thing, but there is a difference between the two.

A *rumor* is a report that is difficult to prove. It usually arises out of a confusing situation. And it often has a kernel of truth.

Social scientist R. H. Knapp has studied rumors, and he has divided them into three types:

1. *The Wedge:* This type of rumor divides people into groups and plays on suspicions. ("John said Mary said that you're a creep.")
2. *The Bogey:* This kind of rumor works on group fear. ("I heard Mrs. Johnson is going to flunk anyone who hasn't memorized the whole book.")
3. *The Pipe Dream:* This rumor builds up false hopes. ("The coach is really nice. I heard that anyone on her team will play in the all-star game.")

Gossip is more directly about people and the details of their private lives. Spoken gossip that is damaging and untrue is called *slander.* Written gossip that is harmful and false is called *libel.* You can be sued for both.

Everyone is sometimes interested in gossip. Some

(continued)

gether in a casual way. A group of boys and girls may get together and go bowling or to the roller rink. Or a few girls may run into a few boys after school and stop at a coffee shop together for a hamburger.

It's a relief to discover that boys and girls aren't all that different. Both worry about their looks, their popularity, their grades, and their futures. Both feel self-conscious about problems with their skin. Both want to get places in the band or on the team. Both want summer jobs and new winter jackets. Both have worries about brothers, sisters, parents, and friends. Both wonder whether someone of the other sex will ever really like them. Seeing the similarities makes the differences seem less awkward.

The idea of actually dating may seem unlikely, unreal, and fascinating. Older teenagers walk down the street, holding hands and talking. What do they talk to each other about? Are they in love? What does being in love feel like? Many younger teens feel curious, even envious. But they may not feel ready to date yet.

ON DATES

Some teenagers have their first date planned out in their heads months, or even years, before it actually happens. Michael expected his first date to be with someone special, someone he had wanted to go out with for a long time. He expected to look and feel great. He could picture going to a funny movie and laughing together over all the same lines. After the movies he imagined them stopping for ice cream, seeing friends in the distance and waving. How proud he would feel to be out on a date!

Most first dates probably don't turn out that well. More than likely a first date is awkward, maybe miserably awkward. For example, the person Michael really wants to be with may already like someone else. His first date may be with a second choice. He has a cold. His hair isn't right, and his clothes feel itchy. Michael's father drives them to a party, and the silence in the car is deafening. The first few jokes he tells fall flat, and then no one can think of anything else to say. His palms sweat. His throat goes dry. At the party, Michael and his date avoid each other. And after the party, he can't wait to have the whole thing over with and to go home. The next morning he feels terrible enough. Then he overhears one of his parents on the phone telling a friend how "cute" it is that Michael went out on a date. Dating isn't worth it, he decides. Who needs all the pain and embarrassment?

Dating can seem discouraging at first. It takes time to learn what to expect and how to relax when you're out with someone new. It takes time to learn that when you're on a date with someone you don't know well,

IT'S A DATE!

- Do show up on time. If you're going to be late, call.

- Do let your parents know whom you're with, where you're going, when you'll be home.

- Don't expect every date you have to be a smash hit.

- Don't give up on yourself. Yes, it hurts when the person you like doesn't like you. But keep trying. You'll find people who do appreciate you.

- Do have the courage to go out with a person you like even though no one else does.

- Don't break dates unless you absolutely must. "Something better came along" is no excuse.

- Don't take bad treatment from other teens. If someone is inconsiderate, cross him or her off your list.

- Do expect problems (you and your best friend may like the same person; someone you can't stand keeps cutting in on you at a dance; it rains on your picnic).

- Do let your date know it if you had a good time. Saying something like "You're really fun to be with—thanks" is all it takes.

psychologists think this is a healthy way of dealing with stress. But having a tremendous interest in gossip is often a sign of a deeper problem—jealousy, nervousness, poor communication, boredom, or low self-esteem.

Some Famous Rumors:
1. There is a rumor of a secret tunnel under the English Channel. This rumor returns during bad times, particularly during wars or periods of financial problems.
2. In 1938 the actor Orson Welles presented H. G. Wells' *War of the Worlds* on the radio. This is a tale of the invasion of Earth by Martians. A rumor quickly spread that Earth was being attacked by strange creatures. Panic set in.
3. In 1962, in a Southern textile factory, word spread about dangerous insects in the area. Soon over sixty people went for treatment for their "bug bites," all of them imaginary.
4. In 1967, a Michigan newspaper claimed that Paul McCartney, a member of the Beatles singing group, was dead. The rumor caught fire, and fans spent many hours searching for death clues in the group's lyrics and on their album covers.

Boys and girls get to know each other first in casual groups.

funny stories. All you need to do is be yourself, to share your points of view, experiences, and feelings. You don't need to entertain the other person with nonstop chatter. You do need to ask questions, listen, and make comments on what the other person has to share. You'll get the hang of it eventually, and then even long silences won't upset you.

Dating may sometimes surprise you. A person you have always wanted to date may turn out to be disappointing. Someone you have never paid much attention to may turn out to be lots of fun. Sometimes when you least expect it, you have a magical time and end up jogging and singing duets together.

LEARNING TO LOVE

You've experienced love feelings ever since you were a baby. As you get older, loving becomes more and more complex. Your ability to give, to share, and to understand the feelings of others grows. Your understanding of your own personality and feelings comes into sharper focus.

The first romantic feelings for the other sex are often felt from a distance. Sharon had watched Rick in history class from the first day of school. Sharon didn't see Rick outside of class often, since the high school was large and they lived on opposite sides of town. In order to get glimpses of Rick, Sharon would go

Early Romantic Lyrics
Plato, a philosopher in ancient Greece, believed that people had been split in half and they spent the rest of their lives searching for their other half—their perfect mate.

doing things together is better than sitting and talking.

It's easier to be yourself when you're bowling, ice-skating, watching a football game, or riding a roller coaster. You'll worry less about what the other person thinks of you. You'll take some pressure off yourself when you realize that it's not necessary to be dazzling or to wow a date with

down certain halls in school where she knew he would pass. She spent a lot of time thinking about him. Even though she had never spoken to him, she had a definite idea of what he was like. Sharon thought Rick was easy-going, smart, and kind. She had imagined what it would be like to walk with him after class, to stop by his locker, or to spend a Saturday with him. Sharon felt she was in love. But Rick didn't notice her. And she never got the courage to speak to him.

After a while Sharon's feelings about Rick became confusing for her. She felt rejected. She was hurt, and she felt like a failure whenever she thought about him. Her feelings made her feel frustrated and angry. She eventually wished she never had to see Rick again, and she had never even met him!

It's common for teenagers to feel "in love" with a person they have never met or spoken to. Some people dream about rock stars, movie stars, or a boy or girl in high school whose name they don't even know. Some people tell their feelings to a friend. Others may keep their feelings to themselves.

Loving someone who is out of reach is safe. It's not pretending—the loving feelings are very strong (and sometimes painful)—but the distance keeps it comfortable as well as exciting. These kinds of loving feelings can be practice for the feelings that will occur later on in a deep, caring relationship.

Some people don't fall in love until their twenties or even later. Other people believe they are in love much earlier. What does it feel like to fall in love? You may get to know some-one, and everything "clicks." You

The idea of "being in love" is often in the back of teenagers' minds. This can either be a cause of awkwardness or push a couple into an emotional relationship.

IT'S LOVE—OR IS IT?

You will hear a lot of confusing messages that can lead you to the wrong conclusions about what love is and isn't. It helps if you can see the truth behind some of the most commonly held beliefs.

MYTH	TRUTH
You can learn a lot about love from songs you hear on the radio.	If you believe everything you hear in love songs, you can get a pretty distorted view of love.
The road to true love doesn't run smooth. Pain is a sign that it's the real thing.	People in love always face problems. But a lot of pain means something's wrong.
Feelings don't lie. If you think you're in love, you are.	You can want so much to be in love that you convince yourself you are.
There's one right person for everyone. Once you find that person, the rest is easy.	There's no such thing as Mr. or Ms. Right. It takes a lot of hard work for any relationship to last.
If you fall out of love, you weren't in love in the first place.	People change. Growing apart doesn't mean you didn't once love each other.
If you haven't fallen in love by the time you're 16, something's wrong.	Many people don't fall in love until their twenties or thirties—sometimes later.
Grown-ups have forgotten what it's like to be in love.	People fall in love at any time in their lives—even in old age.

talk and talk. You can't believe how much you have in common. Before long, you go everywhere together, and when you're not together you are on the telephone or thinking about each other. Other people tell you you're too young to really be in love, and that makes you angry. You think, "How can they know how I feel?" You are sure they don't understand how special your feelings are.

Those kinds of feelings are special—and very real. The words of caution you hear come from people who are afraid for you. They are afraid you will get in over your head or that you will become too focused on one person. Sometimes people are afraid you will develop unrealistic expectations, and that you'll be hurt.

What should you do if you fall in love when you're a teen? You should enjoy the feelings and force yourself to come to terms with some realities that you may not like to face. Be aware that as much as you care for this person right now, you are both going to change. You are both going to grow, and you will very likely grow in different directions. This means that you won't have as much in common as you do now. It's a reality that's not easy to accept.

By the time you become an adult, you almost surely will have experienced the pain of breaking up with someone you have cared about. That's almost guaranteed. It may make you feel better if you realize that even though you may not love the same person forever, the good feelings you share become a part of who you are. In that sense, a person stays with you all your life. And each person you care about increases your ability to care about others. The more you love, the more you know about loving. Even a painful experience helps you grow and adds to the quality of relationships you will have in the future.

a quick review

1. Why do you think people fall in love with rock stars or people they have never met?
2. What kinds of feelings do boys and girls have in common?
3. What are the best kinds of activities to plan for a first date with someone you don't know too well?
4. Is having fun on a date just luck?
5. Is it likely that you will have as much in common with someone 10 years from now as you do today? Why or why not?

Studying Teen Social Life

• Do you ever feel as if the whole world is out having fun while you sit at home? A University of Chicago psychologist studied the moods of people of different ages. Each person in the study was given a beeper that went off several times a day. When the beeper sounded, the subject noted her or his mood at the time. The study found that teenagers felt loneliness much more often than adults, and that these feelings were strongest on Friday and Saturday nights.

• Do you assume that if you were just a little more good-looking, your social life would be better? A study showed that very attractive teenagers are not involved in boy-girl socializing more often than other teenagers. Also, particularly good-looking teens are sometimes very lonely because others assume they are always busy.

▶ **Words to Know**

fascinating: Capturing interest; attractive.
focus: Make the central point of attention.
realities: True states of affairs; actual facts.
similarities: Points of likeness.

CHAPTER 9
Careers in Helping People

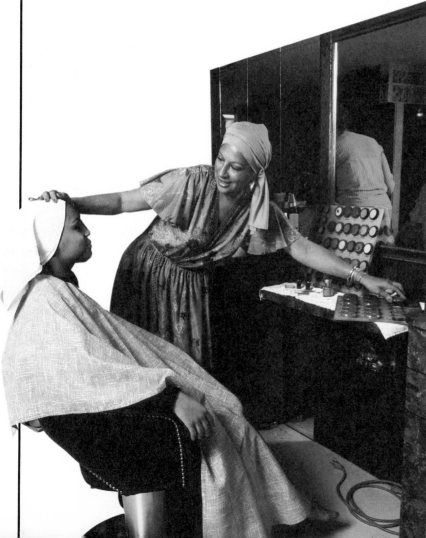

You live in a world of computers that handle your bank account, credit cards that transact your purchases, and a Social Security number that will soon record your earnings and income tax. Of course, it is really people who operate the computers, record your credit card purchases, and add up your earnings. But you never see most of these people. This means that the people you do see—your family, your friends, the neighbors around you—are more important in making your life a meaningful, personal experience.

The relationships with these people around you can become the basis for many exciting and rewarding careers. And one of these careers may be for you.

CAREER QUIZ: DO YOU ESPECIALLY ENJOY HELPING PEOPLE?

1. Do you like working with all types of people?
2. Are you a good listener?
3. Do you like to help people solve their problems?
4. Do you find it hard to sit still for long periods of time?
5. Do you especially like working in your community?

If you answered "yes" to even one of these questions, a career dealing with people and their relationships with one another may be for you!

"Helping People" Careers: Entry Level

• *Social Service Aide.* Social service aides help needy people find a professional social worker. They help new applicants fill out forms, they update clients' records, and they encourage people to seek help. This may be part-time or full-time work.

• *Homemaker Aide/Family Assistant.* This "family helper" assists in homes where the family needs help because of illness, old age, or an emergency situation. Grocery shopping, cooking, cleaning, and caring for children are some of the tasks performed. This may be part-time or full-time work.

"Helping People" Careers: Paraprofessional Training

• *Casework Aide.* Casework aides work directly with people needing social welfare help. They help the client get food stamps, medical care, unemployment benefits, and job training. They also help clients find adequate housing. This may be part-time or full-time work.

• *Personnel Agency Counselor.* This kind of counselor works for a personnel agency. People seeking jobs are matched up with companies having similar job openings. Personnel-agency counselors interview the job applicants. This is full-time work.

Homemaker aides assist in homes where families are facing emergency situations.

Thinking About a Career

Thinking about a career is both exciting and frightening. There are more career choices open to you than any person or reference book can name. By the time you are ready to hold a job, there will be still more choices.

Sometimes it's hard to know what you want and what you are best suited to do. And it's frightening to have to make a choice from unlimited possibilities.

At the end of each unit in *Teen Guide,* you will find a career chapter. Within each chapter are real career stories as well as listings of just a fraction of the career possibilities in that work area. Each chapter will list entry-level jobs, paraprofessional jobs, and professional jobs.

Entry-level jobs are the lowest level in a career area. They may be had with, and sometimes without, a high school diploma. On-the-job training or further education can lead to a higher-level job in the same area. *Paraprofessional* jobs require a high school diploma plus some training. Paraprofessionals are trained aides who assist a professional person. *Professional* jobs require a college education with some specific courses or training in the given field.

Psychologists help people learn or behave more effectively. Some psychologists specialize in helping children and teenagers.

Exploring Career Choices

Stop and think about the many interesting careers people around you have. Then read, read, read to choose a career best for

(continued)

counseling activities. This is part-time to full-time work.

• *Police Officer.* Police officers enforce local laws and assist people in distress. They help to ensure the secure atmosphere and smooth operations of a community. In large police departments, there is a range of jobs that assist patrol officers in their duties: police administrative assistant, dispatcher, community affairs officer, and polygraph (lie detector) specialist.

"Helping People" Careers: College Education with a Professional Degree

• *Homemaker Services Administrator.* This kind of administrator runs family-care programs in the community. These administrators make sure that programs for temporary emergency help are well run and are in line with the community's budget and policies. They organize and carry out training for homemaker aides. This is full-time work.

• *Social Worker.* Social workers interview individuals and families to find out what their problems are. They help people get the right resources, services, and education or job training. This may be part-time or full-time work.

• *"Help-Line" Columnist.* These columnists write newspaper or magazine columns answering people's questions about such things as dating problems,

• *Counseling Paraprofessional.* Counseling paraprofessionals work with a trained counselor, such as an employment counselor. They administer tests, score tests, and supervise some

family concerns, and social etiquette. This may be part-time or full-time work.

• *Counselor.* Counselors help people understand themselves. *School counselors* help students select courses that match their interests, abilities, and career goals. *Employment counselors* help a client plan a career path and decide on the "right" job. They work with universities, businesses, or employment agencies. *Rehabilitation counselors* counsel handicapped persons and help them adjust to changes in their personal or career lives. They help the handicapped discover how to adjust to their handicaps and still live rewarding lives. This is full-time work.

• *Psychologist.* Psychologists study how people behave and counsel or advise individuals or groups. *Clinical psychologists* examine and treat people with emotional and behavioral problems. They work toward preventing mental health problems. *Consumer psychologists* study how consumers choose products. They often work with a business firm to help that company with its advertising and marketing policies and problems. *Industrial psychologists* work in industry to select, train, and develop personnel. This is full-time work.

• *Clergy.* The clergy act as ministers of church congregations. They also counsel church members and di-

Law enforcement jobs are as much involved with helping others as with enforcing laws.

you. Here are some career resources:

Books to Read
Occupation Outlook Handbook
   U.S. Department of Labor
   Washington, D.C. 20402

This book describes many jobs and gives suggestions of where to write for more information on specific jobs. It is a library reference book.

Encyclopedia of Careers and Vocational Guidance
   J. G. Fergusen Publishing Company
   Chicago, IL

This book gives in-depth listings and short descriptions of many jobs that exist today. Check for it in your library.

Places to Go
guidance office in your high school
career planning and placement office in a college
Job Service Offices in your state. (Affiliated with the U.S. Employment Service)
Youth Office of Information Employment & Training Administration
   U.S. Department of Labor, Room 10225
   601 D Street, N.W.
   Washington, D.C. 20213

A Real Person in a Real Job

Don Williams has always been concerned about people. Today he is a manager of personnel for a large corporation. Here is how he describes his career:

"Ever since I can remember, I have always been more concerned about other people than myself. That is why I found personnel management a natural major for me in college. I also worked part-time as an interviewer in a personnel agency. I loved matching up the person with that perfect job!

"Today, I am personnel manager for a billion-dollar corporation. My days are filled with designing personnel policies, such as major health insurance programs, for our employees. I also spend countless hours meeting with department managers to discuss their job openings, interviewing present employees for these jobs, and counseling our employees.

"As you can see, I am constantly working with all kinds of people—and that is what makes my career as personnel manager just perfect for me!"

Counseling others is a skill used in many fields. Counselors need to be good listeners and observers.

rect church-related programs. Some specialize in youth ministry. This is full-time work.

• *Management-Development Specialist.* These specialists plan in-house training to teach company employees such things as how to manage their time, conduct a meeting, or supervise people. This is full-time work.

CAREER QUIZ: IS THE WAY PEOPLE LOOK IMPORTANT TO YOU?

1. Do you spend a large amount of time on personal grooming?
2. Is what you wear very important to you?
3. Do you often notice how other people look?
4. Do you read many fashion and beauty magazines?
5. Do you spend a lot of money on clothes and cosmetics?

Looking good is important to almost everyone. And this means almost everyone is willing to pay for advice and help. Giving this advice and help could be a career for you!

"Looking Good" Careers: Entry Level

• *Salesclerk in a Clothing Specialty Shop.* These salesclerks help a customer find the right size, choose the perfect garment(s), and coordinate the right accessories. They also make the sale. This may be part-time or full-time work.

• *Health-Club Worker.* Health-club workers help maintain health-club facilities. They sanitize the pool, repair exercise equipment, and keep registration records. They are usually allowed the use of the facilities during their free time. This may be part-time or full-time work.

"Looking Good" Careers: High School Diploma and Paraprofessional Training

• *Beautician.* Beauticians shampoo, cut, and style hair. They tell their customers how to care for hair. Beauticians work in a large salon or in their own shop. A special state license is required. This may be part-time or full-time work.

• *Model.* Models demonstrate products by modeling clothes in a style show or advertisement, by showing products in television commercials or print advertisements, or by demonstrating products in retail stores. Models must have above-average looks, poise, and modeling know-how. This may be part-time or full-time work.

• *Weight-Control Program Leader.* These leaders supervise exercise and weight-loss programs at weight-control salons or exercise camps. They conduct weight-reduction exercises,

help clients design their own reduction programs, and oversee client progress. There is usually some on-the-job training. This may be part-time or full-time work.

Salesclerks offer assistance and advice. This job can lead to the position of buyer or to other retail careers.

A Real Person in a Real Job

Tony Castillo has always been liked immediately by everyone he meets—young and old. Today he is the executive director of one of the largest Boys' Clubs in the country. Here is how he describes his career:

"As far back as I can remember, I have always enjoyed all types of people. They seem to like me, too—especially young children. So when the local Boys' Club in Los Angeles offered me my first job as supervisor of youth activities, I jumped at the chance. And I loved everything I did—from designing new activity programs like the Intraclub Sports Olympics to actually taking trips with the boys to a summer camp in the nearby California mountains.

"As I gained in experience, I gained in responsibilities, too. Today I am executive director of one of the largest Boys' Clubs in the country. Every day I see all kinds of people. Instead of working only with young people, I spend countless hours meeting with top executives of major corporations to raise money for things like the new swimming pool we installed last year.

(continued)

• *Department Store Makeup Demonstrator.* Makeup demonstrators illustrate appropriate makeup selections and show how to apply makeup in live demonstrations. They work for cosmetic companies or department stores. There is on-the-job training. This is usually full-time work.

• *Barber.* Barbers cut and style men's hair and often give shaves. They may have their own shop or work in a small barber shop. This may be part-time or full-time work.

"Looking Good" Careers: College Education with a Professional Degree

• *Fashion Coordinator.* Fashion coordinators manage the fashion image program of a retail or department store by planning style shows, selecting fashions for floor displays, and choosing accessories. They must have knowledge of fashion, color, and design. This is full-time work.

• *Product Manager, Cosmetic Manufacturer.* Product managers coordinate the development of new cosmetic lines. They analyze market research and sales to find out what products will sell. They help create new products and oversee the production. Finally, they must help develop the advertising and promotion that will sell the new cosmetics.

• *Spokesperson for Cosmetic/Clothing Manufacturer.* These spokespersons promote the use of products by appearing on radio programs and television shows. They also make appearances at consumer events like state fairs. They offer consumers informa-

Exercise and body-building are rapidly growing career fields.

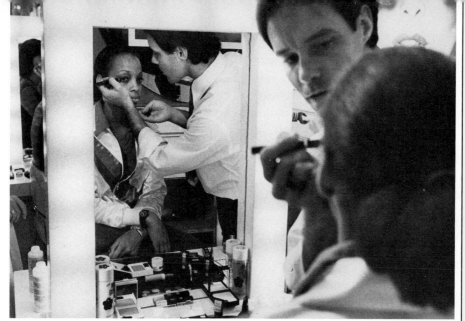

Some helping careers can be glamorous and exciting.

"My 'people-skills' are constantly being used. We are always interviewing for a new supervisor for some program. And that requires evaluating people quickly and accurately. Occasionally, one of our projects is funded by a celebrity, so that means working with the press and famous people at the same time to make the event successful."

▶ **Words to Know**

entry level: The lowest-level job in a career area. It may be had with, and sometimes without, a high school diploma. On-the-job training or further education can lead to a higher-level job in the same area.

paraprofessional: A trained aide who assists a professional person.

tion on buying and using the products. Being a spokesperson usually involves traveling a lot. This may be part-time or full-time work.

Careers involving the people around you can be extremely exciting and rewarding. The job may even pay well. If you're often described as a "people person" by your friends, you may enjoy this kind of career. Look around. You may be pleasantly surprised!

a quick review

1. Name some part-time careers that involve helping people in your own community.
2. Describe some careers that involve studying people—how they live, how they work, and how they relate to each other.
3. You are always willing to listen to your friends' problems. Name some careers you might enjoy.
4. Name some jobs not requiring a college degree that allow you to help others "look their best."
5. You plan to obtain a college degree and love the world of fashion. Discuss some careers you could follow.

Unit 2
FAMILY

CHAPTER 10
What Is a Family?

People have always lived in families. The word *family* has many meanings. If you asked fifty people to describe a family they know, you would probably get many different answers. Some of the answers might be the following:

• mother, father, sister, and stepbrother in an apartment
• father and son in a mobile home
• father, mother, and four daughters living on an army base
• mother, father, and twin daughters living in the suburbs
• husband and wife working in a city
• father, mother, two sons, and several foster children living in a small town
• mother, grandfather, aunt, and one child living over their store

It is hard to say what a typical or average family is. However, all families have certain things in common. This chapter is about families.

WHAT IS A FAMILY?

Your family may look, sound, or act different from other families you know. However, most families have one thing in common. Their members are related to each other by blood ties or by marriage. Being related by blood ties is called *kinship*. Relatives are sometimes called *kin*. There was a time when family members all lived

Being part of a group, taking your turn, and playing by the rules are a few of the things you learn about first from your family. What are some other things people learn about in families?

together in one place. This is not always true today. When parents separate or divorce, family members may not live together. Family members may be in different parts of the country or in different parts of the same town. However, they still make up a family.

When you were born, you needed your family for everything. The family was your source of food, clothing, and shelter. When you were an infant, your first relationships were with your family. Even before you could talk or walk, you were learning about love and laughter from your family. As a young child, you got your ideas about what was right and wrong from your family. Now, as a

teenager, you are beginning to move out into the world. All the feelings, ideas, and skills that your family gave you are helping you grow up. Your family is helping you to know and understand yourself. That helps you to understand other people as they come into your life.

HOW FAMILIES DIFFER

Each family is special. It differs from other families in many ways. Some of these differences are easily seen. Some are not.

As you read at the beginning of this chapter, families come in all combinations. They differ in the number of people in them and how these people are related to one another. One

Television Families

Some of our ideas about families come from the families we see on TV. How real are television families? Keep a list of all the television programs about families that you see in one week. Answer the following questions for each:

• Describe the television family by size, kinds of family members, customs, and life-style.
• Is the television family like real families you know?
• Did the television family seem real to you? Why or why not?
• If you were writing a half-hour television program about a family you know, how would your story compare to the ones you saw on television?
• Describe families you have seen in television commercials or in newspaper or magazine advertisements. Tell what you remember about them.

The Cost of Raising a Child

Inflation, the constant rise in prices that has been a problem in recent years, has also increased the cost of raising a child. A child born in 1958 cost about $30,000 to raise from birth through high school in a city area. A child born in 1976 will cost the parents about $85,000 by the time that child finishes high school in 1994.

89

Were Colonial Families Really So Big?

We are often told that colonial Americans lived in very large extended families. This picture is at least partly true. Households *were* generally larger than those in Europe. Many had from five to ten children. Fifteen or more in a family was not unusual. Benjamin Franklin, for example, came from a family of seventeen. However, the stories about large extended families do not give a true picture of all families in those days. The first U.S. census, taken in 1790, showed the average size of a household to be 5.8 persons.

How Do People Trace Their Roots?

Have you ever seen newspaper photographs in which four or five generations of a family appear together? If your great-grandparents are living, you may know at least four generations of your own family.

Some people have been able to trace their family members as far back as ten generations. In ten generations, each of us has 1022 ancestors in the direct line. This total does not include brothers, sisters, aunts, uncles, or cousins. It only includes the parents of each generation. The official name for tracing

(continued)

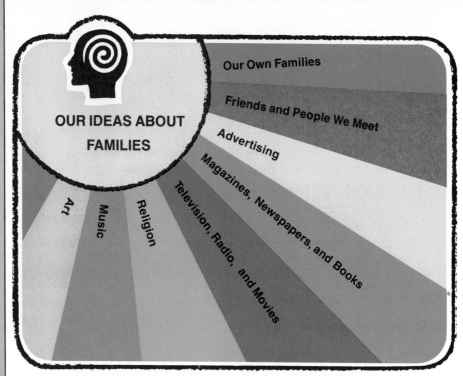

common family form is called the *nuclear family.* It includes a mother and father and their children living with them in the same home. *Single-parent families,* however, have one parent living with the children. Families may include a stepparent or some stepchildren. This is sometimes called a *blended family.* Some families have adopted children.

If grandparents or aunts and uncles live in the home, the family is an *extended family.* An extended family can include three or more generations living in the same home. A married couple without children is another type of family structure. Some families have seven or more members; others are much smaller.

The things a family can call upon to keep going also differ from one family to another. These *resources* include material goods like income, land, a house, and personal possessions. Resources also include the talents and skills of each family member. For example, one person may be good at keeping the family budget. Another person may be an excellent gardener or mechanic. A grandparent may be a talented painter, or a teenager may play the guitar for family fun. All are valuable to the family in making life more enjoyable.

Families also vary in their customs and traditions. These may have come from another time and place and been handed down by parents and grandparents. Or they may be new. Family traditions tend to change only gradually through the years. Special ways of celebrating family events may be among a family's traditions. Other traditions may have to do with a family's religious activities.

A family's *life-style* involves where and how they choose to live and work together. Parents may decide the family will live on a farm, in a small town, or in the center of a big city. They may divide the housework equally among every member or give special jobs to some members. In some homes, each person chooses from a list of jobs prepared by the entire family. Every person's job, no matter how large or small, is needed to keep the home running smoothly.

Another way families differ may be the way they express feelings toward one another. One family may be very open, even noisy, in showing feelings. Another family may be more quiet, keeping many thoughts to themselves. You may know a family whose members are sometimes emotionally *expressive* (willing to show their feelings to others) and at other times very private. Some families seem very close to one another, staying at home and keeping to themselves most of the time. In other families, each member may have several outside friends and interests in addition to life at home. Even within the same family, one member may show feelings more openly than another.

How families spend their time is another way they differ. A day in any family's life will include a certain amount of work time and playtime. However, a family's special interests usually shape their activities overall. For example, an outdoor-minded family may enjoy fishing, camping, or playing ball together. A musical fam-

ancestors is *genealogy*— the study of family. Genealogy is more than lists of births and deaths of relatives on a family tree. It is the discovery and gathering of the details of their lives. It can become an exciting hobby that will lead you to places you never dreamed of visiting. You may find yourself writing to relatives that you never heard of. This hobby can give you a better idea of who you are and where you came from.

Doing the dishes, washing the car, and helping prepare dinner may all be good times for a talk with someone in your family. This grandmother and grandson have a lot to share, despite the difference in their ages.

THE AVERAGE AMERICAN FAMILY YESTERDAY AND TODAY

What was life like for families in the United States when you were a young child, when your parents were 12 to 14 years old, or when your grandparents and great-grandparents were your age?

Year	Average Family Size	Life Expectancy at Birth	Average Income (in today's dollars)	Prices They Paid for Food					
				Bread (loaf)	Round steak (lb)	Bacon (lb)	Eggs (doz)	Milk (½ gal)	Potatoes (10 lbs)
1970 (When you were a young child)	3.58	70.5 years	$8,838	.24	1.30	.95	.61	.66	.90
1956 (When your parents were teenagers)	3.60	69.7 years	$6,007	.18	.88	.57	.60	.48	.68
1930 (When your grandparents were teenagers)	4.03	59.7 years	$1,000-$2,000	.09	.43	.43	.45	.28	.36
1890-1900 (When your great-grandparents were teenagers)	4.76	47.3 years	Figure not available	.03	.12	.13	.21	.14	.16

Source: *Historical Statistics of the United States from Colonial Times to 1970*

▶ Words to Know

blended family: Includes a stepparent or stepchildren.

extended family: Includes grandparents, parents, children, and sometimes other relatives living in the same home.

(continued)

92

ily may spend more time going to concerts and playing music. Families who like to stay home often have favorite games to play, hobbies to pursue, television programs to watch, or things to talk about together. Teenagers may find their time split in many directions. After-school activities, team sports, club meetings, play rehearsals, jobs, and just being with friends can take up much of their free time. Their families may spend time watching the teenagers competing in a sport or acting in a play.

You are a blend of your family's own special strengths, talents, and

A visit to the local art museum is a time for this family to learn and enjoy each other at the same time. Many museums have special family membership rates and after-school programs for children and teens. What other activities like this could a family do together?

feelings. You may add some new personality traits and ideas you learn on your own along the way. Yet you will always reflect that one-of-a-kind group of people that you call your family.

a quick review

1. What are some different types of families today?
2. What basic things do most families have in common?
3. What are the basic needs a family provides for its members?
4. What is meant by a family life-style?

kinship: Being related to others by blood ties.
nuclear family: Includes a husband, a wife, and their children.
single-parent family: Includes only children and one parent.

CHAPTER 11

How Families Change

Can you guess what your family will be doing ten years from now? Where will you be living? Will you have new brothers and sisters? What will your parents do after you graduate from school and leave home? This chapter will help you understand the changes families may face at different times in their lives.

HOW FAMILIES CHANGE

Once a family is formed, changes may occur in its way of life. These changes can be caused by expected events, like graduations. Or they can be caused by unexpected events, such as the sudden loss of a job.

A life cycle, or regular pattern of change, is natural for a growing family. Most changes happen gradually, allowing a family time to prepare and adjust. The chart on page 96 will help you recognize the *family life cycle*— what happens to most families during each stage of life. Most families go through most of these stages. However, no two families go through a stage in the same way. Some may skip a stage. For example, a married couple may choose to have no children. Another family may repeat a stage. When a new baby is born into a family whose other children are already teenagers, the family backtracks to an earlier stage. Some families may overlap stages. For example, when one parent dies after the children have

94

grown up, the other parent may remarry and become a stepparent to young children in a second family.

If you marry, you will share in at least two stages in the life cycles of two families. You will be part of the family you grew up in and part of the family formed by your marriage. In each stage, your family will deal with changes, face problems and opportunities, and set new goals.

CHANGING ROLES IN A FAMILY

In many ways it is harder now than it used to be to describe the roles of a mother, a father, and their children in a family. Until the late 1800s, more families lived on farms than in cities. They had to produce nearly all their own food, clothing, and shelter. Each family member, often including grandparents, had important assigned duties and responsibilities. Children were valuable because they were extra hands to help with the farm and family work. Fathers taught sons farming and building skills. Mothers taught daughters important homemaking skills such as weaving and food preservation. Everyone's role helped the family survive.

The industries that developed gradually after the late 1700s brought changes to families. Machines were invented that did the work people once had to do by hand. Families began to get most of their food, cloth-

ing, and other supplies from the outside world. They also began to count on outside sources for much of their education and entertainment. More and more people found jobs outside the home to support the family. All these factors have made the family into a *consumer group,* people buying what they need from the community. Today, children in a family are seen more as individuals than as extra workers.

Today's family is still like a team. Each member has a special role to play on that team. And within every family these roles may differ and change as the family members grow older.

As public opinion changes year after year, the roles people play in a family change. Today, more men and women prefer to share the task of earning a living for their families. They may also decide to share home-

The Way It Was.

Home life changes with new inventions and changes in life-style and social customs. Choose one part of home and family life from the list below and research how it was 50, 100, 150, or 200 years ago in this country:

- providing food
- kinds of housing
- types of recreation
- education
- cooking
- providing clothing
- rules of behavior
- family customs
- where people shop
- jobs
- household equipment
- child care
- family rules
- transportation

As a group, discuss the advantages and disadvantages of each time period.

One way that families change over the years is that children grow up. As you get older, you take on more responsibility within your family. Caring for younger brothers or sisters might be one such responsibility. Helping with chores might be another.

FAMILY LIFE CYCLE

Young Married Stage	Founding Family Stage	Growing Family Stage	Teenage Stage	Launching Stage	Empty Nest Stage
• Couple sets up a home. • Both husband and wife may be working outside the home. • Both husband and wife may have interests outside the home. • Both husband and wife may continue education or training related to their jobs.	• The couple's first child is born. • The couple invests in equipment for the baby. • Care of the baby keeps both parents busy. • One parent may give up an outside job for a while to care for the baby.	• The baby begins to grow up, changing from toddler to school-age child. • Other children may be born into the family. • The family life-style continues to be busy for both parents. • Investments are made in clothing, school needs, medical care, and play equipment.	• Children develop interests outside the home. • Children may take over some of the family jobs at home. • Children may take part-time jobs outside the home.	• Older children leave home to marry, attend school, or begin full-time jobs. • A parent who stayed home to care for growing children may return to work outside the home.	• All the children have left home. • Parents may begin to plan for retirement. • Parents may develop new interests to fill time once devoted to children. • Parents may become grandparents.

Possible variation or change that may occur during these stages:

Young Married Stage	Founding Family Stage	Growing Family Stage	Teenage Stage	Launching Stage	Empty Nest Stage
• Couple may decide not to have children—skipping middle three stages.		• Parents may divorce and remarry to begin another family—returning to second stage. (This change can also happen during the next two stages of the cycle.)	• Parents may have a new baby—beginning an overlapping of stages.		

Moving can be both exciting and sad for everyone in a family. It is a time of change when family members often look to each other for support.

making and child care to keep their homes running smoothly for everyone.

The roles people may play within a family also change as the family moves through the various stages of its life cycle. For example, during the Growing Family Stage, one parent may be the main homemaker and child-care giver. However, as the children pass through the Teenage Stage and into the Launching Stage, that parent may decide to work outside the home.

OUTSIDE INFLUENCES CAN CHANGE A FAMILY

Many outside influences affect today's families. These often cause changes that families of the past did not face. Changes may come at any stage of the family life cycle.

Changes in the *economy,* or a country's system of making, buying, and selling goods and services, affect everyone. The life of a family may be changed greatly by an economic event like a factory strike, the loss of a job, or an unexpected change in the

How One Family Changed Their Too-Much-TV Habit

By the end of summer vacation, the Shirmangs knew they were watching too much television. The television set was on from morning until night. They were watching just about anything.

They decided that this habit was getting boring and wasting a lot of time. So they decided to do something about it.

First they got a roll of tickets at an office-supply store. Then each family member received ten tickets. Each ticket was worth one hour of television.

Everyone moaned and groaned for a while. But with only ten tickets to last all week, they chose their shows carefully.

By the end of the first week, some of the children had five or six tickets left over. By the end of the second week, they had even more tickets left. There was more bike riding, talking, guitar playing, and book reading going on, too.

The Shirmangs had not given up television completely. However, they were now watching only the shows they thought really counted. They were not looking at the television just because it was on. At the end of the third week, Mom and Dad gave the ticket roll away to the neighbors.

97

Tips for Moving

There are many things that complicate your life as a teenager when your family moves. Schools are not the same in every town or state. New friends are sometimes hard to find at first. Even the school cafeteria can be confusing. Here are some ideas to help make moving easier:

• Have your former school send a complete set of your records to your new school before you arrive.

• Visit the guidance counselor in your new school. In addition to scheduling your classes, a counselor can tell you about school clubs, athletic teams, and other activities you may want to join.

• Find other new students in the school. Plan an after-school or lunchtime get-together to share feelings, ideas, and ways to get acquainted.

• Find another student, perhaps in your homeroom, with a schedule similar to yours. Ask for some help in finding your way around your new school.

• Look in the telephone book for local branches of *national organizations* (organizations with branches throughout the country). Contact those you belonged to in your old hometown. These might include the Boy Scouts or Girl Scouts, the YMCA or

(continued)

amount of money the family has to spend. Inflation can also change the way a family lives. *Inflation* is a widespread and continuing rise in prices. With inflation, people can buy less with their dollars than before.

Current events influence the style of family life. A dispute with another country may make a much-needed product like oil more difficult to get from that country. This may mean that a family must cut back on driving. Or it may mean the loss of someone's job if that job is in an industry dependent on oil, such as the automobile industry. Another example is when a young adult in the family joins the armed services in a time of international crisis.

MOBILITY AND THE FAMILY

In the past, many people were born, grew up, married, and started families of their own all in the same town. Today that pattern is changing. *Mobility,* or moving from one place to another, is more common. Each year in the United States, one family out of every five moves. Whether a move is across town or across the country, it means getting used to new surroundings, a new school, new people, and perhaps a new way of life. Relatives and friends are left behind when a family moves. If a family's life will be improved by moving, these difficult changes may be worthwhile.

Family members may have mixed feelings about moving. They may be

When parents divorce or one parent dies, the change can be frightening. A child needs the time and opportunity to ask about what has happened.

Graduation is an example of change that is both expected and happy. When one family member reaches an important goal like this, it is a time for everyone to celebrate.

happy to make a fresh start. Yet at the same time, they may feel lonely and cut off from the world. Getting used to a new home, new people, new customs, and new ideas takes time. If the move is to a foreign country, a new language must be learned. Even simple things like shopping for food can be hard. When a family shares these experiences, it may bring the family members closer together. They count on one another for help and companionship. They may get to know one another better than they ever did before.

HOW FAMILIES COPE WITH CHANGE

Change can be both frightening and exciting. Family members can help one another during times of change. Talking about your first day in a new school while your parents tell about a first day on a new job may help ease everyone's fear and loneliness. Together, you may find that

YWCA, 4-H Clubs, voluntary action groups, and church or other organizations.

•Find school organizations such as FHA/HERO that interest you.

•For help in catching up with schoolwork, find a tutor through your school counseling office. Ask for the name of a good student who might help you study and help you find your way around.

•Be sure all your teachers know you are new to the school. If they are covering topics you have not studied before, tell them so. Ask for help. Teachers will appreciate your honesty.

•Explore your new town with your family. Plan a day together. See the sights, and also conduct a group search for the best pizza or chili dog in the whole town!

•Ask your parents to be patient with you while you adjust to everything. Although you do not want them to relax their standards for family behavior, you do want them to understand you during this hard time. And that goes two ways. You will want to go easy on them while they get used to everything new, too. In time, everyone will be back into the swing of things.

99

New Conveniences

Since you were born, many new convenience products and services have become available. How have any of the following affected you and your family?

- vans and recreational vehicles
- pocket-size calculators
- blow dryers for hair
- microwave ovens
- instant color cameras
- digital clocks
- slow-cooking pots and food processors
- sugar-free soft drinks
- cassette tape recorders and players
- drive-up windows at banks
- fast-food restaurants

Can you name others?

▶ **Words to Know**

economy: A country's system of making, buying, and selling products and services.

family consumer group: The family as a group of people buying and using products and services provided by the community.

family life cycle: The regular pattern of changes that happen in stages to a family.

inflation: A widespread and continuing rise in prices.

mobility: Moving from one place to another.

things become easier as you share each day.

Some family changes involve money. This may mean having less money to spend, or it may mean having more income than before. In either case, the change will be easier if the situation is explained and shared in a family talk. When everyone understands, everyone can help.

When something happens to one family member, all the others are affected. For example, if one member is sick, the others may help care for the patient or keep the house quiet. When parents decide to separate or divorce, each family member should try to understand the feelings of the others. During these times, children as well as parents can feel lonely. Everyone has a greater need for love and understanding to get through such a period of change.

When a new baby comes into a family, many changes must be made by everyone, especially in the first few months. Older children often help their parents by sharing the household work. Later they may share a bedroom with the newest family member. If you are an older child in a family with a new baby, you may feel left out at times. You may wish you were the baby receiving all the attention. This is a normal feeling. It will pass as you get used to having a new brother or sister. If you have such feelings, it may help to tell your parents about them.

Not all the changes that face a family are difficult or sad. Sometimes happy changes come into a family's life. A son or daughter wins a scholarship. A parent gets a raise or job promotion. Someone recovers from a very serious illness. These changes also take time to adjust to. Coping with any change, however great or small, happy or sad, takes time and understanding. Asking for help or simply talking about your feelings with your parents, a friend, or a counselor may be helpful. Understanding the positive features of a change may help you and your family to find hope and plan for the future.

a quick review

1. What are the six stages of the family life cycle?
2. How are the roles of family members changing in today's world?
3. What are some outside influences that may change a family's life-style?
4. When a family moves to another place, what are some of the feelings its members may have?
5. What are some ways that families cope with change?

Close your eyes and try to picture your family. Imagine the way they looked when you were born. Think about the photos taken of your family from that time until now. These may be photos taken on vacations, holidays, and important occasions—photos of you and your family growing and changing. The photos probably show people of all ages—youngsters, adults, and older people. Besides their differences in age, the family members in these photos are also different in personality, abilities, likes, and dislikes. This chapter will look at these differences and how they affect the way people live together as a family.

CHILDREN IN A FAMILY

Each child in a family is different from all the others. Children have their own personalities and patterns of development. Parents are often surprised to see unique personality traits appear when a child is only a few days old.

Later, a child's personality is affected by the makeup of the family. How old a child is and the *age span,* or number of years between that child and her or his siblings, can affect how that child gets along. *Sibling* is another word for a brother or sister in one family. Sometimes siblings who are close in age are playmates while they are young. But later, as they be-

CHAPTER 12
People in a Family

Community Services for Older Family Members

In most towns, special help is available for people in their sixties or older. When an older person needs help or is looking for interesting activities or ways to be involved in the community, the following offices or groups can be contacted:

• the social services department of a local hospital—for information about Medicare or other health support programs

• a state, county, or city department of senior citizen affairs (sometimes called a council on aging)—for general advice, outlets for energy, ideas for creative activities, and companionship

• the local health department—for advice on health matters

• the local city department of social services—for advice and help in financial matters and other personal problems and needs

• United Way agencies—for a variety of helpful services and outlets for volunteer energy

• the regional or local Social Security office—for help with Social Security benefits

"Adopt" a Grandparent

Some communities have a Foster Grandparent Program for getting grandparent-age people
(continued)

102

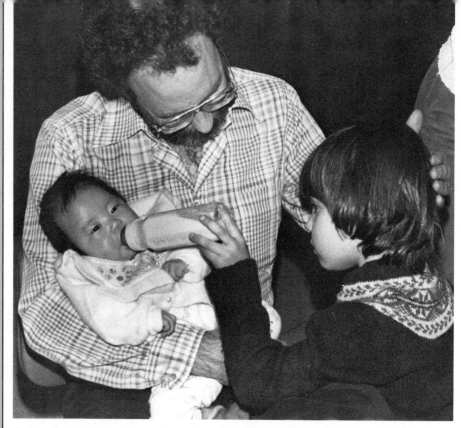

A new baby—whether adopted or born into a family—is a special part of any family occasion. What are some ways that a new family member changes the lives of the other people in a family?

gin to grow up, they become competitors with each other. Siblings who are three or more years apart in age may not be interested in the same things at the same time. However, parents of children who are three or more years apart may have more time to spend with each child during that child's infant years.

The number of brothers and sisters in a family and the order in which each was born is also important. *Birth order* is the relationship of siblings to each other—who is the oldest, next oldest, and so on.

For example, if you were the first-born child in your family, you were an only child for a while. You enjoyed the undivided attention of your parents until another child was born. As a result, you had an especially good start in life. As the oldest child in the family, you were generally the first child to try something—from a tricycle to an automobile. This gave you a feeling of independence. Also, firstborn children often have more responsibilities and sometimes more privileges. Helping your parents care for the younger children in your family can give you self-confidence. It can be a good feeling to have your little brother or sister look up to you proudly. Even when your parents ask you to act more grown-up than you feel, having responsibility can give you leadership skills and a good feeling about yourself.

Younger children in a family have a different point of view. Their older brothers and sisters help them learn things and even protect them. But sometimes younger children feel they are being treated like babies. Or they may find the achievements of their older brothers and sisters difficult to measure up to in the eyes of their family and teachers. When they see older children given more freedom, they may feel jealous. However, being the youngest child can also bring good feelings of being loved, accepted, and safe. These feelings can give younger children the confidence

---

"Chip Off the Old Block"

Have you ever heard these sayings: "chip off the old block," "like father, like son," or "her mother's daughter"? They mean that the child is just like one of his or her parents. Many children indeed do look or act like their parents. However, these old sayings are misleading.

When you were born, certain physical traits were passed from your parents to you. The color of your eyes, hair, and skin, as well as the shape of your face, were part of this *heredity*. You may also have inherited a tendency toward certain behaviors or abilities seen in your parents. A *tendency* is a natural likelihood that you will act in or be a certain way. For example, you may have inherited a tendency to be musical, graceful, athletic, quiet, or lively.

Your environment also has an important effect on you. Your *environment* is all the places, people, feelings, things, and events around you. If you grow up in a home or community where art and music are important, your environment may encourage you to become an artistic person. If your family plays many sports, you might be influenced to become an athlete. If the people around you show their feelings openly, chances are good that you will be an emotionally expressive person.

However, some very quiet people have grown up in active, noisy homes. And not every football player had active parents. Somewhere within their environment, people sometimes find something to lead them in a special direction all their own. Each person is, therefore, a complicated blend of heredity and environment. And while you may seem like a "chip off the old block" in the beginning, you will become someone special as you grow.

---

together with children and teenagers. The young people who take part in such a program may live far away from their own grandparents, or their grandparents may no longer be living. The adopted "grandparents" visit with their "grandchildren" regularly, sharing love and friendship. These visits satisfy important emotional needs of everyone involved.

The Foster Grandparent Program can be found in all parts of the United States. It was created by Congress in 1968. This program finds men and women in their sixties and older who are interested in "adopting" children in hospitals, day-care centers, other institutions, and, in some cases, private homes. There are 158 projects in all fifty states, Puerto Rico, and the U.S. Virgin Islands. Perhaps your town has such a program. Check your telephone directory or write to ACTION, 1800 Connecticut Avenue N.W., Washington, D.C. 20007.

Happy Grandparent's Day!

Congress has declared the second Sunday in September a national holiday to honor all grandparents. This holiday is called Grandparent's Day.

"My sister was an only child."

Meet Kim (age 16):

"Whenever I hear a comic on television tell a joke about his brother being an only child, I have a special reason for smiling inside. My sister Nancy was already in high school when I was born. For sixteen years, she had been an only child. Then, when she was about to graduate from high school, I came along.

"For Mom and Dad, I'm sure it was like starting over again. For my sister, having a new baby sister in the house probably seemed unreal at times. She helped take care of me sometimes. But she had school and friends to keep her busy. Then she went away to college and we never had much of a chance to get to know one another.

"Nancy is thirty-two and married now. I am sixteen. And although she lives forty miles away, we visit often. We do things together and talk a lot. We are finally feeling like sisters after all these years. I still feel a bit like an only child, and I'm sure Nancy does too. But it really feels great to have a sister to share things with after all these years."

to handle more responsibilities as they grow up.

Middle children in a family feel uneasy at times. They may wish to be free of the "shadow" of their older siblings. Or they may miss the attention being given to a younger child in the family. However, if you are a middle child, you probably enjoy advantages also. Your parents knew more about taking care of children when you were born than they did when their first child was born. You are also not as likely to be treated like a baby for as long as firstborn children are. Finally, since you are neither the youngest nor the oldest, people are more likely to recognize you just for your own personal qualities.

Some families have only one child. Being an only child in a family has advantages and disadvantages too. Only children often enjoy a large amount of attention from their parents. They may often be included in adult activities. However, they may feel a great deal of pressure to please their parents. Some only children come to feel that they are totally responsible for their parents' happiness. Although only children do not have to deal with any brother/sister problems, they must learn to get along with other young people. They do this by developing friendships with cousins, neighbors, and classmates.

When children are born eight or more years apart, each child may

The oldest, youngest, middle, and only children each have special experiences growing up.

seem like an only child. A fourteen-year-old and a three-year-old have very different activities and interests. They will not be companions or competitors like siblings closer in age. Even so, these children develop a sense of sharing and family unity. In time, as they both grow older, their age difference will become less important to them.

Twins usually have a very special relationship with one another. They also hold a special place in their family. While they are young, they may dress alike and spend much of their time playing together. They may also receive a great deal of attention from curious or admiring people. Other children in the family may feel left out when this happens. As twins grow older, they develop different needs and interests. In order for them to develop in a healthy way, it is important to treat them as individuals with different personalities.

Families have different ideas about the ways children should act. Although these ideas are not as set as they were in past generations, some families still may expect different behavior or achievements from sons than they do from daughters. Young boys may be encouraged to be more active and independent than their sisters. They may be discouraged from crying or showing fear. In contrast, young girls may be encouraged to show feelings such as affection and even fear. These ideas have all been passed down from earlier times. Children were then expected to behave only according to traditional male and female roles.

Today people can choose to follow traditional roles or to adapt these roles to fit their needs. Yet traditions fade slowly. You might recognize both traditional and new roles within your own family. Your own attitude is important. Treat your brothers and sisters like individuals. Encourage them to pursue their interests so that they will develop all their abilities and talents as fully as possible.

Special talents and abilities vary among children in a family. Some may have unusual talents as artists, musicians, athletes, writers, or dancers. While every person has things

Each family member has special abilities and goals. A person who wants to play a musical instrument must have the self-discipline to spend many hours practicing.

The disabled child on the right is an active, contributing member of his family and school group. Most such children are no longer educated apart from nonhandicapped children.

she or he does well, specially talented people seem to stand out. If you have a brother or sister who is very good at something, you may have mixed feelings. You may be proud, or you may feel envious. Your talented sister or brother may have mixed feelings, too. Being in the spotlight is exciting. However, the pressure to be at your best all the time can become hard to bear. And a talented person has weaknesses, too. When family members accept each other's talents as well as their weaker points, everyone feels closer.

A disabled or handicapped child has special needs. There are many different kinds of handicaps. Thus there are many kinds of needs to be met. But all disabled people have one need

in common. That is to be recognized for things they *can* do instead of those they cannot.

Like other children, each disabled child has strengths and weaknesses. Even though a child has a disability in one area, he or she will still be able to experience life in many ways. For example, mentally retarded children gain pleasure and learn from their senses. Some are good at active games and sports. Others are skillful at working with their hands.

A disabled child may need more of the family's time, energy, and money than a nondisabled sibling. Sometimes it is hard for the other children in the family to accept this fact. Also, many parents and siblings are very sensitive about a disabled family member. They may feel that people outside the family do not understand the disabled person's special needs. Nevertheless, many families find that the experience can build a closer and stronger family unit.

Your family group may include adopted children, foster children, or stepbrothers or stepsisters. When a child from outside the family joins the family unit, all the family members need time to get to know and trust one another. It could take months for the children who were already in the family to get used to sharing the parents' attention and space at home. Talking over all your feelings openly and calmly will help.

Most of the time, brothers and sisters who were not all born to the same parents become as close as any brothers and sisters.

PARENTS AS PEOPLE

How do you think of your parents? You may answer this question with a description of what they do. Parents are people who cook, pay for things, fix things, clean, and tell you what to do. Parents do all these things. Yet they are far more than just payers and fixers. They are people, too, very much like you.

As people, parents have strengths and weaknesses, talents and interests. Every parent has a personality. One may be quiet and serious. Another may be outgoing and lighthearted. These personality differences can affect the style of your family life in many ways. How parents express their feelings and communicate with each other and with their children will also vary from family to family. Every family includes people with different opinions and ideas. And to live together successfully, a family must make room for individual differences.

Parenthood is a big responsibility. From the day children are born until they leave home to live on their own, their parents work hard. Their task is to guide and care for their children. Being a parent can be a 24-hour-a-day job, especially when children are very young. Finding time to be alone or to enjoy personal interests and friends is not always easy. And everyone in a family, from the youngest member to the oldest, needs that kind of personal time. You want your parents to understand that you need to do things on your own sometimes. Are you ready to return that understanding?

Sometimes it can be disappointing to learn that your parents are not perfect. When you were a young child, they seemed so wise and strong. When parents make mistakes or can't do something you expect, you may feel angry or critical of them. At such times, it helps to remember that they are people just like you. Forgiveness, understanding, and love should go both ways, from parent to child and from child to parent.

OLDER FAMILY MEMBERS

Today most people can expect to live into their seventies. New knowl-

Tomorrow:

• More fathers will choose to stay home full- or part-time. A few companies are already offering *flexible working hours* to their employees. This means that the employees still work their required hours, but they can arrange their work time so that they can be at home during family times.

• Single-parent families will become more common. The U.S. Bureau of the Census predicts that 45 percent of children born in the United States in 1977 are likely to live in a single-parent family before they reach the age of 18.

• More people will live alone. According to the Census Bureau, one-fifth of the households in the United States already consist of a person living alone.

Parents need time away from their children—to be together and to be with their friends.

"Gramps"

Meet Grandpa Ben (age 70) and his grandson Aaron (age 11).

Aaron:

"We all call him Gramps, and he's a pretty popular guy around here. When Grandpa Larson first came to live with us, he stayed by himself a lot and seemed a little sad to me. He wasn't much fun to have around the house. When Mom suggested I ask him to help me with my science and history homework, I wasn't sure what to do. He didn't say much, so I left my report on his chair.

"The next day he was full of talk about railroads and canals and what they were like when he was a boy. We talked so much that day, and we've been having homework talks after school ever since. In fact, some of my friends bring their reports over to talk with Gramps.

"Last week he walked with all of us to the park and named every wildflower and tree leaf we collected for science class. He doesn't seem so sad anymore. And I think he even walks faster sometimes."

Ben:

"Aaron's right! I've been around this old world a long time. So many of my friends are gone . . . and I

(continued)

Older family members are often very involved in the community as well as with their own family.

edge in the fields of medicine, nutrition, and physical fitness is helping people live longer, healthier lives.

Grandparents in their fifties or sixties are often still working at jobs outside the home. They are usually involved with their friends and other people in the community as well as with their family. Most often, they are able to live on their own. Their children and grandchildren are a valued part of their independent lives.

Grandparents long past retirement age—in their seventies, eighties, and nineties—may prefer to live independent lives as well. Often they can and do. Sometimes they need special support from their family. This is particularly true if a grandparent is having health problems.

All of us are changing physically each day of our lives. It is important to remember that people of any age are as fit as they feel. Many people who lead active lives are healthy and strong even in their seventies and later. For others, however, physical change is dramatic during old age. Hearing and vision may weaken. Energy levels may decrease. Minor aches and pains may grow troublesome. Older people sometimes have special eating or sleeping needs. These changes and needs vary greatly from person to person, just as they do at any other age.

You may have grandparents or older relatives living with your family. Their presence can be a pleasure or a problem, depending on how they are accepted into family life. Many activities can be shared in three-generation families. This is true whether the older members live with their younger relatives or have homes of their own. People of any age can enjoy taking part in games, gardening, craft projects, hobbies, cooking, music, and many other activities. Including grandparents in activities makes them feel a part of family life. You can make a difference by trying to understand the needs and ways of older people.

Grandparents and other older relatives living further away from you need to feel in touch with you. When you cannot visit them regularly, sending them a news-filled letter and recent family photos will help keep family ties strong.

Whether older family members are healthy and active or in need of special care, their many years of care and work as parents have earned them a lifelong right to the family's affection and respect.

Although the people in every family are different in the ways you have just read about, there are also many ways in which they are alike. One of the most important of these is that family members share the basic emotional needs that all people share.

Acceptance, achievement, and affection are three of the most important emotional needs. People need to be able to accept themselves and to feel accepted by others. They need to feel a sense of achievement. This comes from knowing there is something they like to do and can do well. People also need to care about others and have others care about them. The family can play an important part in meeting these needs.

a quick review

1. What effects might birth order have on the relationships among brothers and sisters and parents?
2. What might family life be like for twins? What might it be like for an only child?
3. How are some traditional family attitudes changing toward boy children and girl children?
4. How would you explain the saying "Parents are people"?
5. What are some special feelings or needs of older members in a family?

miss my wife Emma. I was sure I'd just be in the way when I moved in with my son and his family. But when Aaron and his buddies started asking me things about their lessons and about how things were in my boyhood days, I felt alive again.

"I'm so proud of the nice grades they got on their nature collections. I haven't been in that park since Aaron's daddy was a boy, but I go there every day now. Who knows when somebody might need to know the name of a particular wildflower? And I know 'em all!"

▶ **Words to Know**

age span: The number of years between the births of two people.

birth order: A child's placement in a family according to the order in which all the children were born.

environment: All the places, people, feelings, objects, and events that surround someone or something.

heredity: All the physical traits, qualities, and tendencies that a child receives from her or his parents at birth.

sibling: A brother or sister.

tendency: A natural likelihood to act in or be a certain way.

CHAPTER 13
You and Your Family

Some families always seem to get along. They enjoy being together. Everyone cares and everyone shares. This does not mean that they have no problems. They have their good days and bad days, just like any family. What is their secret for getting along so well as a family? Seven key qualities for family living are listed in the box on the following page. As you read them, think about what each one means.

COOPERATION

Cooperation occurs when you and everyone else in the family share both the work and the fun. Family cooperation is a two-way arrangement. You give a little, and you take a little. You feel good when you know you can count on your dad to help you with your term paper or your sister to wake you up in time for school each morning. Your parents count on you to put all your dirty clothes into the laundry basket before Monday morning. Then one parent will have the time to help you with your math homework after school. When the whole family takes part in something, cooperation is a must. For example, when power bills are too high, everyone must cut down on using electricity. Or when gasoline prices go up, you join carpools or ride bicycles more often in order to conserve fuel. Sometimes cooperation means giving

Quality	How it helps families get along
cooperation	promotes sharing in order to get things done
communication	builds understanding and feelings of being safe
trust	builds everyone's self-confidence and sense of security
responsibility	helps people to become more dependable and to keep their promises
consideration/ respect	builds feelings of self-worth and thoughtfulness toward others
loyalty	gives everyone a feeling of belonging and trust
caring	shows people that they are loved

up something you really want when someone else's needs are more urgent. Then others will be willing to give up things for you as well. When you cooperate with the people in your family, they will be more likely to cooperate with you. This kind of sharing brings about a feeling of unity.

COMMUNICATION

Communication is two simple actions—talking and listening. Families grow stronger when they communicate all the time. Accepting and understanding another person's feelings is one way of keeping communications open. You are more likely to express yourself. You also listen in return. Communication becomes a two-way arrangement, just like cooperation.

Sometimes people in your family may have ideas that are different from yours. You can accept these ideas without agreeing with them. When such ideas—or actions—cause conflict in a family, talking about these differences may help to ease the difficulty. All kinds of feelings—love, anger, fear, jealousy, pride—happen naturally when people live together in the same house day in and day out. It is a healthy habit to discuss these feelings instead of keeping them hidden.

Some communication is *nonverbal*. This means that ideas are communicated without words. Sometimes when you cannot say something out loud, a special look, a hug, a tear, a smile, a groan, or a helpful favor will reveal your feelings.

Some families set aside a special time for talking. Others talk casually, whenever problems or special situations come up. However a family goes about communicating, every member needs to take part.

The Return of the Extended Family

Before the twentieth century, extended families were common. Three, even four generations sometimes lived under one roof. Often the immediate family was extended to include uncles, aunts, cousins, nieces, and nephews. Expenses, chores, and child care were shared.

Until World War II, young couples frequently moved in with their parents. The elderly often moved in with their children. In the 1950s, however, the emphasis shifted to the nuclear family, to being independent, and to owning a one-family home. Extended families became less common.

Today the extended family appears to be coming back. With rents and housing costs rising, young adults are choosing to move back in with their parents. With both husband and wife working outside the home in many families, some young couples are relying on grandparents for live-in child care. And older parents, particularly widowed ones, are moving in with their middle-aged children. In fact, one third of older men and women who are no longer married live with their children or grandchildren.

You may have something on your mind that you do not want to tell everyone in your family just yet. If that is the case, try telling your feelings to just one person at first. Grandparents often make very good listeners for your private ideas or feelings. If you have younger brothers or sisters, they might appreciate your listening to their problems on a one-to-one basis, too.

TRUST

Most families with teenagers are apt to have stress at times. You and your parents may clash once in a while. This stress can be reduced if you take time to build trust in one another. If each family member is in such a hurry to run off to activities that everyone is too busy to eat, talk, or make telephone calls, all the members soon become strangers in the same house. No matter what causes this situation, a family must find some time for talking if trust is to grow. If you tell one another about the little everyday things, the more serious matters will be easier to share. Nothing will seem too bad to talk about.

When your parents want to know where you are or whom you are with, they are not intruding. They are truly concerned. And it is their responsibility to know. To you they may seem overly protective. However, your parents may be questioning you because you have kept them in the dark about things. No one, whatever age, feels comfortable when he or she does not know what is going on.

The ability to make people trust you can become your most valued quality. As you become an adult, people will feel they can depend on you as a friend and rely on you as a trusted worker.

RESPONSIBILITY

When you were a child, things were decided for you. When your parents were children, it was the same for them. Years pass between the day your parents help you to take your first step and the time you are able to stand on your own two feet. Each

Part of the reason this father and son get along so well is that they spend time both talking *and* listening to each other. Good communication is a two-way process.

passing year, you make a few more choices and decisions for yourself. You learn, with guidelines from your family, to solve your own problems. Your family still gives you advice and sets many rules. Independence is not simply rejecting family rules and advice but rather the ability to make your own choices based on what you know is right or wrong. Independence means making a choice of action and then taking full responsibility for the results. All the things you have learned, even the mistakes you have made, help you to become a responsible person. In your family each person, from the youngest child to the oldest adult, can accept some responsibility. It may be caring for a puppy or managing the family finances. Whatever your responsibility, people are counting on you.

CONSIDERATION AND RESPECT

Consideration in a family simply means that every person thinks of the feelings and rights of the others. This can be difficult when you are a teenager trying to cope with growing up. Sometimes you are just careless about other people's needs. From time to time, everyone has to be reminded to think of others.

LOYALTY

Loyalty is believing in others just as you know they will always believe in you. As your family grows, each member comes to trust and believe in the others. You know you can depend on each other in bad times as well as good times. When one member of your family is in trouble or ill, everyone stands by that person. When another family member takes on a difficult job, the rest cheer that person on. Loyal family members are faithful to one another. When they share secrets, they can count on each other not to tell anyone else. When they promise to do something for one another, they keep that promise. From learning what loyalty means within your family, you will be able to build loyal friendships with people outside of the family.

CARING

People in a caring family always seem to feel good about themselves. Just knowing that your family cares about what happens to you can help you feel like a valuable person. This feeling is called *self-esteem.*

If you care about someone, you feel sorry when that person is sad or ill. Likewise, you feel happy when that person has good luck. This feeling is called *sympathy.* If you care very deeply about someone, you may even feel *empathy.* This is a feeling that allows you to imagine yourself in that person's place. The pain that person feels is your pain; that person's joy is your joy.

Getting More Out of Family Talks

Before you complain about not being able to talk to your family, take a look at your own communication skills. Here are some questions to ask yourself about the way you communicate with your family:

• Do you listen to how your own words sound when you talk to family members?

• Do you listen to other family members when they talk to each other and to you?

• How do others react to the things you say?

• How do you react to the things said to you?

• Do you accept each other's feelings as all right to have?

• Do you think before you speak?

• Are you flexible enough to allow others to change their minds or feelings?

• Are you as positive as you can be?

• When you have an argument, do you avoid bringing up past disagreements and concentrate on solving the problem at hand?

• If someone accuses you of something, do you try to give an honest explanation or reply, or do you accuse her or him back?

113

Communication and Cooperation Through a Family Council

Some families gather around a table once a week for a short meeting to talk over anything that affects the family or any of its members.

During the meeting each family member, from the youngest to the oldest, has a chance to speak. Family rules can be set or changed. Vacations can be planned. Complaints can be aired.

If your family decides to try this, here are a few pointers to remember:

• Select a meeting day and time when everyone can be there.

• The very first meeting should last about 15 minutes—just enough time to give everyone an idea of how a family council works.

• Choose someone to call the meeting to order and call on people to speak. Someone else can take notes. Rotate these jobs to different people at each meeting.

• Keep the meetings short and to-the-point.

• Have refreshments and play a game just for fun after the meeting.

• Be patient. The first few meetings may be awkward. But things will get smoother.

It makes sense to call home when your plans change or if you find you're going to be late. This kind of consideration tells your parents that you know how to accept responsibility.

When you were a young child, your parents cared for all your needs. They watched over you when you were sick and when you were playing as well. They cared for you because you were special to them. Now that you are a teenager, they still care about you. They are beginning to allow you to be on your own now and then. However, they still are concerned about you. They worry about whether you are well and safe. Caring is a quality that keeps families feeling good about themselves.

GETTING ALONG

There is no magic formula for getting along with your family. It is a full-time effort for everyone. Talking, listening, cooperating, trusting, and caring are all part of the job. It takes work. Sharing responsibility and showing consideration and respect will keep a family running smoothly. Being loyal to one another gives each person the good feeling of belonging. With all this going for you, you and your family can relax and enjoy each day together.

Helping with household chores means the most when you do it willingly. That's real cooperation.

a quick review

1. What is meant by the saying "Communication is a two-way arrangement"?
2. When you accept someone's feelings or ideas, does that mean you have to agree with that person? Explain your answer.
3. How can you earn the trust of the people in your family?
4. How can learning responsibility within your family be a help to you as you grow up?
5. What does loyalty mean to people in a family?

▶ **Words to Know**

empathy: Sharing another person's feelings as though they were your own; you can almost feel that person's pain or joy yourself.

self-esteem: A feeling that you are a valuable person; belief in yourself.

sympathy: Sharing feelings with someone else; whatever affects that person affects you.

CHAPTER 14
How Children Grow

Children grow and develop month by month and year by year. Their bodies and brains grow. They develop their abilities to move, think, feel emotion, get along with others, and communicate. Helping children grow means understanding their natural growth patterns. That is what this chapter is about.

PATTERNS OF GROWTH AND DEVELOPMENT

Each child is special and different. Yet every child follows a certain *pattern,* or order, of growth and development. Many things can affect the way a child follows these growth patterns. Heredity, nutrition, and surroundings all affect the way children grow. Family love and attention are important factors, too.

Many books have been written and charts drawn up regarding patterns of child growth and development. As you look at any chart showing averages for children, remember these important points:

• Charts are only general outlines of what a child may be able to do at certain ages. Charts are not strict timetables for all children.

• Each child is a separate individual, even with regard to other family members. Each child has a personal growth rate.

• The first two years of a child's life are a time of very rapid growth

The bright colors and interesting shapes in this mobile give the baby something to look at, reach for, and touch. Why is this important to development?

Learning and Newborns
Studies show that babies begin learning actively as soon as they are born. Right away they see and react to people and objects around them. Newborns sense and react to sounds and odors.

During their first few weeks of life, newborn babies are able to see complex patterns. They usually prefer such patterns over solid blocks of one color. When given a choice, a baby will usually prefer to look at a drawing of a face rather than a solid color patch. Then, when shown a drawing of a normal face and one in which the features are jumbled, the baby will usually choose to look at the drawing that looks most like a real face.

What Do You Remember?
Think about your days as a young child. How far back can you remember?
• Did you have a nickname?
• What was your favorite game as a child?
• What were some of your first stories and songs?
• Do you remember your first day of school?
• Did you have a secret hiding place?
• Do you remember losing your first tooth?
• What was the best thing about being a child?

and development. This period is probably more important than any other in a child's life.

• The words *normal* and *average* tell what is true of most people or children in a large group. However, there will always be some individuals who grow and develop more slowly or more quickly than what is considered normal or average.

Physical growth refers to the way the body develops. All children follow the same general pattern of physical growth. However, this growth is never smooth or even. Sometimes when a child is growing in height, weight gain may be slow. Or, while important growth is going on inside the body (heart, stomach, lungs), the outside may look the same.

At birth, babies look top-heavy. Their heads seem too big for the rest of their bodies. Physical growth takes place from the head downward and from the center of the body outward. When a baby is born, the legs, feet, and hands are the least developed. These are the parts of the body that grow the most at first. The head and arms, which are more developed at birth, grow more slowly. Since all their body parts are growing at different rates, babies quickly change in appearance in the weeks after birth.

DEVELOPMENTAL TASKS OF CHILDREN . . .

At 3 months:

- move eyes together
- make fist, both hands
- turn toward bright lights or loud sounds
- grasp rattle or hair
- wiggle and kick both arms and legs
- make cooing sound; smile

At 6 months:

- turn over without help
- reach for and grab large object and transfer to other hand
- look toward any sounds heard
- eat soft foods
- bounce and creep
- recognize and smile at familiar faces or own face in mirror
- babble; repeat sounds
- may be afraid of strangers

At 9 months:

- roll over and sit up
- recognize own name when called
- reach for new pleasing object
- remember objects when out of sight
- eat bits of food with fingers
- imitate many sounds

At 12 months:

- get to standing position without help
- crawl or move forward
- respond to simple directions like "It's time to eat"
- play "peekaboo"
- imitate sounds heard; say "ma-ma" and "da-da"
- try to drink from cup
- like music; show many moods
- begin to understand the word *no*

At 18 months:

- say a few words that can be understood
- bring things to you when you ask
- walk alone
- use hands or fingers to pick up small objects; may scribble with crayon
- pull, push, dump things
- pull off shoes, socks, and mittens; may help dress self
- may perform for home audience; enjoy applause
- point with one finger
- may climb out of crib
- developing sense of humor
- may be negative about things she or he cannot do

. . FROM BIRTH TO AGE FIVE

- can learn simple swimming movements

- begin to use cup and spoon to eat

- point to parts of bodies when named

- imitate adult activities like cooking, cleaning, dancing

- name familiar objects and people

- scribble

- kick a large object

- run; jump; climb stairs

- some self-bathing, front of body

- some self-dressing, tee shirts

- begin feeding self with fork

- may begin to toilet train

- walk sideways, backward

At three years:

- help dress self; use zippers and buttons
- talk in sentences
- listen to and repeat stories
- use circles and copy simple shapes and designs
- simple cutting with scissors, finger painting
- go to the bathroom without help; although accidents will happen
- climb stairs well; hop; skip

At four years:

- balance on one foot; jump from a step
- brush hair and teeth
- show many emotions, often loudly
- ask questions; give answers
- ride a tricycle
- repeat rhymes, songs, stories
- model with clay; paint with brushes; hammer nails; work simple puzzles

At five years:

- draw a body with at least five parts (head, arms, and legs); copy squares and diamonds
- catch a ball
- take a bath without help
- play games with others following simple rules
- tell stories from memory; invent stories

Chubby Baby . . . Overweight Adult?

Years ago, a chubby-faced baby with dimpled knees was considered the picture of health. Mothers often added extra foods to nursings or bottled milk when the baby was still very young. Perhaps they hoped that this would help the baby sleep through the night. It usually did not. But what it did do was help that cuddly, chubby baby become a child with a weight problem and then usually a fat adult. Experts think that early overfeeding may cause infants to build up fat cells or develop the habit of overeating. The result could be a lifelong battle with the waistline.

What a Newborn Baby Looks Like

Have you ever seen a newborn baby? If you have, you know that most new babies are not very good-looking at first. They may look reddish in color and wrinkled. The head may seem a little out of shape with very little chin. There may be little hair or no hair at all. Fingers are curled into tiny fists. Legs may look bowlegged. The stomach may bulge, especially after feeding.

All this may sound somewhat ugly, but it does not last long. (We were all tiny and funny-looking at first.) But wrinkles fill out

(continued)

120

Mental growth refers to the way the mind develops. Mental growth in children is measured by the tasks they can do at certain ages. These are called *developmental tasks.* Walking, talking, and drawing with a crayon are all developmental tasks. Some of these tasks are tied to physical development. Children are able to do them only when both their muscles and their minds are ready to learn the new tasks. Sometimes important skills like walking or talking develop in stages. Walking may begin as crawling. Later the baby may pull himself or herself up to the furniture for several weeks before trying a first step.

Talking may begin with listening. At ten to thirteen months a child may understand several words and even follow simple commands. Yet it may be another five months before the child's jaw and mouth muscles and teeth are physically developed enough to form any understandable words. Until then, the baby's efforts sound like babble. Simple, two-word sentences like "Baby go" and "Want apple" may not come before the age of two. Then the baby's mind is ready to try combining words. At this stage, language ability is likely to pick up speed at a very fast rate, especially if people talk to the baby a lot.

During a child's growing years, there are two periods of very rapid growth, called *growth spurts.* The first growth spurt happens during the first year of life. It begins even before birth. It continues until a child is about nine months old. The rate a child grows in length (height) during these early months is amazing. The child can triple in length during the first six months. A child who kept growing at this pace would at the age of ten be as tall as a fifteen-story building and twenty times heavier!

The second growth spurt happens during the early adolescent years. You are probably going through this one now. This spurt lasts longer for some people than for others. However, the average adolescent growth spurt begins around the age of eleven and lasts about four years. During this period, a child's body changes into an adult's body. Between these two growth spurts, physical development is slower and more even.

During both growth spurts, your body needs extra food. Your appetite is hearty. After each spurt, your appetite slows down. You are likely to tire more easily during a growth spurt. Rapid growth drains your energy. Bones and muscles grow at different rates and times. This can cause you to feel awkward. Coordination of your body seems impossible during a growth spurt. However, all this gets better after the growth spurt ends.

BIRTH TO ONE YEAR OLD

At birth a healthy infant's skills are basically reflex actions. A *reflex* is

PHYSICAL GROWTH FROM BIRTH TO FIVE YEARS

Age	Weight Range	Height Range
Birth	3.2 to 3.6 kg (7 to 8 lb)	51 to 56 cm (20 to 22 in)
6 months	6 to 9 kg (13 to 20 lb)	63 to 71 cm (25 to 28 in)
1 year	8 to 11 kg (18 to 25 lb)	71 to 81 cm (28 to 32 in)
18 months	10 to 13.5 kg (21 to 29 lb)	74 to 84 cm (29 to 33 in)
2 years	10.5 to 14 kg (23 to 32 lb)	81 to 91 cm (32 to 36 in)
3 years	12 to 17 kg (27 to 38 lb)	89 to 99 cm (35 to 39 in)
4 years	14 to 19 kg (31 to 42 lb)	96 to 107 cm (38 to 42 in)
5 years	15 to 22 kg (34 to 48 lb)	102 to 114 cm (40 to 45 in)

Different growth charts may show slightly different height and weight ranges. However, they give an idea of average sizes for most children. There are natural differences in growth rates between boys and girls. Also, children from other countries may grow at different rates.

something you do automatically. For example, when someone taps you below the knee, your leg jerks up automatically. Newborn babies are able to taste, smell, see light, hear, grasp, suck, and cry. These are all examples of reflex action.

In the first four months a baby uses and changes reflex actions for comfort. A baby lets you know of special needs by crying in different ways. Parents soon learn to recognize the baby's different styles of crying. At this age, a baby often seems to be examining nearby objects by picking them up and putting them into her or his mouth. In this way, the baby can feel textures and shapes and taste fla-

and skin color becomes normal in a few days. Very soon fingers uncurl, head and face take shape, and legs get stronger and straighter.

Can We Predict Height?

People who study child growth say that it is impossible to predict adult size from a child's birth weight or length. However, some predicting can be done by the time the child is one year old. A child who is taller than the *median* size (halfway between the shortest and tallest of children that age) is likely to grow up to be taller than the median as an adult. Likewise, a child who is shorter than the median size at age one is likely to be shorter than the median size as an adult.

A person's height is largely inherited from her or his parents, but it is also influenced by the environment. The diet followed during childhood and the teenage years can make some difference.

The average height of people in the United States, the European countries, and Japan has been increasing over recent decades. Specialists in human growth suggest that this increase is linked to higher nutritional, medical, and public health standards in these countries.

Carpentry is a good way for children to practice simple motor skills. Because the tools involved could cause injury, it is an activity that should be closely supervised. Helping a parent with this kind of task can make a child feel important and needed.

and-effect learning. This means learning that his or her actions can make things happen. Shaking a toy rattle makes a noise. A kick at a toy hanging above the crib will make the toy move. Sometimes this learning happens by accident, as when the baby rolls onto a toy that squeaks.

From eight to twelve months of age, a baby begins trying to control nearby objects. For example, a baby that wants a certain object will find a way to get it. One way might be to pull an attached string. If the baby and the toy are both sitting on a blanket, the baby may pull the blanket to get the toy. Another way to get the toy might be to move it with some other object, like a stick.

ONE YEAR OLD

By the age of one, a baby has already learned a great deal through the five senses. She or he can recognize familiar voices even when the person is out of sight. Through the sense of touch, the baby can find a favorite stuffed toy without looking. Familiar objects can be recognized even when seen from a new angle, like upside down. The smell of baking is a sign that something good to eat is on the way. Also, the sense of taste is well enough developed by now to signal the difference between, say, plain toast and toast with peanut butter. A baby expects the world to be a certain way all the time. When something

vors in order to learn more about an object.

From four to eight months of age, a baby becomes interested in cause-

familiar changes, it may cause confusion at first. For example, if the father shaves off his mustache, the baby may not recognize him at first. However, this change will soon be accepted.

TWELVE TO EIGHTEEN MONTHS OLD

From twelve to eighteen months of age, a baby is known as a *toddler*. A toddler is able to move about under her or his own power, whether crawling, climbing, or walking. Because of this, toddlers are explorers. A toddler set free in an interesting room moves from object to object, looking, touching, tasting, smelling, and listening. With everything so new and now easier to get to, a toddler is never bored. The sounds toddlers make are so expressive that they seem to be real questions. Family and others should answer with real answering words.

During this time, a toddler uses the process of trial and error to find new ways to do things. For example, a toddler who cannot get around some large object will try to climb over it or go under it. He or she may also try to move it out of the way.

EIGHTEEN MONTHS TO TWO YEARS OLD

Until the eighteenth month, a baby's developmental tasks involve physical abilities and the senses. From the eighteenth to the twenty-fourth month, mental abilities become more important. Gradually the baby begins to figure things out by thinking. The ability grows to picture things and places in the world outside. Creating new ideas becomes possible, along with pretending. The baby becomes like a scientist doing research. She or he experiments with dropping objects and discovers that they always fall down, never up. There is no realization that this is caused by gravity, but the effect is understood. The baby also learns that when something round is pushed, it rolls. Something square, however, will not roll. Other differences to be learned include those between liquids and solids, soft things and hard things, and hot things and cold things. The baby may even have words to label these different items. During this time, the baby has become even more mobile, crawling, climbing, and walking.

TWO YEARS OLD

After the age of two, the child begins learning the difference between things and ideas. She or he also learns about the *properties* of objects. These properties include size, weight, color, sound, and amount. Playtime may now be spent trying to sort and classify things by their size, color, or other features. This stage is also an emotional turning point for the child. He or she learns that it is impossible to completely control the world. This new knowledge is very frustrating.

Tips for Mealtime with Young Children

• Ask the children to help choose which foods to serve. Offer them a list of nutritious foods and let them have a say in the weekly menu. This may be a good way to slip in a nutrition lesson along with a little fun.

• Keep mealtimes regular. On those days when there are delays, have nutritious snacks on hand.

• Avoid making eating a matter of discipline. If children do not want to eat, excuse them from the table, or at least do not force them to eat. Even if children go to bed hungry one night, their mood usually changes by the next day.

• Introduce children between the ages of one and two to as many new foods as possible.

• Make some meals a celebration of special events—not just birthdays, but also the completion of a family project, the birth of puppies, or the first day of spring.

• Invite the children's friends to dinner sometimes.

• Smile.

Learning how to work with other children is an important part of the preschooler's social growth. These youngsters are working on a soft sculpture made of painted fabric.

The child soon learns that she or he must cope with those things that cannot be changed. This age is a time of pushing for independence, but also of a desire for constant, loving attention. This may explain why some parents call this age the "terrible twos." It is an important stage in a young child's life. Extra patience, understanding, and encouragement are needed from the family. Sometime during this stage, social activities become more important to the child than physical activities. He or she would rather spend time being with you than practicing walking and climbing. The child loves attention and can become quite a family entertainer and imitator when encouraged by applause. However, play still takes place alongside of, instead of with, other children of the same age. This is called *parallel play*. A two-year-old wants to do things on his or her own, even if physical development cannot yet match the task being attempted. The result is often anger and frustration on the child's part. There may even be temper tantrums.

THREE YEARS OLD

The three-year-old child begins to understand *abstract concepts*. These are words used to describe ideas rather than things that are visible or physically real. Examples of abstract concepts are "more," "less," and "soon." The child may also be able to remember qualities of things that are no longer visible. A child whose game is interrupted for lunch may return to that game later and remember exactly what had been going on. He or she had carried a mental picture of that game throughout lunch because of a wish to continue it afterward. Play

Children have three kinds of needs: physical needs, mental needs, and emotional needs. *Physical needs* have to do with the body, *mental needs* with the mind, and *emotional needs* with feelings and personality. Some needs may overlap into all three areas at times. As children grow, their needs in these areas change and grow with them.

CHAPTER 15
Children's Needs

CHILDREN NEED PHYSICAL CARE

When babies cry, they are telling you something. Usually it is that they are hungry, wet, tired, hot, or cold. These are simple physical needs. They are met with food, clean diapers, a place to sleep, and more or less clothing or blankets.

Sometimes babies cry just to hear themselves make sounds. At other times, babies cry because they are lonely and want to be held.

Clothing needs for children begin with diapers and nightgowns in the first few weeks. Soon, these needs change to shirts, overalls, playclothes, and shoes. Safety, comfort, ease of changing, and washability are all important in an infant's clothing. Soft, stretchy cover-ups are practical for a young baby just beginning to crawl. Toddlers and preschool children need clothing suitable for different weather conditions and for these children's activities. Choose clothes that encour-

age children to dress themselves. Children's clothes should fit comfortably. Loose, baggy clothing can cause accidents, especially falls.

Shelter and furnishings are part of every child's physical needs. Babies spend much of their early days sleeping. The first sleeping place can be a basket or cradle. A crib is usually used as an infant grows. The crib should be safely constructed. Consumer laws provide for safe crib design, with side slats close together to prevent a baby from getting stuck between them. Older cribs should be remodeled to make them safe. The crib mattress should be firm and flat. A type of waterproof sheet (usually made of rubber with a flannel backing) goes between the mattress and the surface sheet. This will protect the mattress from stains. Bed coverings should be warm, lightweight, and easily laundered. A child's room should be well ventilated and comfortably warm, but not hot.

Other special furniture for children—a high chair for feeding, a small bathtub, a changing table, a playpen, a stroller, and a backpack carrier—is available, but not always necessary, for meeting a baby's basic physical needs.

Other physical care should be given to a child with some form of regular routine. Babies seem to feel more secure and comfortable when events such as mealtime, naptime, and bedtime each come at about the same times every day.

Children Need a Safe Environment.

Until children have had enough experience to look out for themselves, they need to be protected. A first step is to accident-proof the home. A simple way to do this is to walk from room to room looking at everything from a child's point of view. Remove anything dangerous that looks tempting. Plug or cover up light sockets and electrical outlets. Keep breakable or heavy objects out of reach. Cover sharp table corners. Remove loose rugs, especially on stairways and landings. Check children's toys for possible safety hazards. Loose parts may be small enough to be swallowed. Sharp edges can cut small fingers.

All medicines and poisonous products and plants must be kept completely out of a child's reach. They should be stored behind locked doors if necessary. To be ready for emergencies, keep a first-aid kit that also contains a small supply of *antidotes,* or treatments for poisons. Your doctor or poison-control center can give you more information.

All this protection is needed because children are naturally curious. Sometimes their curiosity leads them into danger. When this happens, older family members must remove them from the dangerous areas. Distracting them in some playful way of-

Good nutrition is important to a child's physical growth. It is also important in beginning good food habits that will last a lifetime.

ten helps keep them from returning to the tempting object. Children over two years of age will understand the word *no* when it has been taught with care. Younger ones will need close watching once they start crawling.

Adults must also protect children from illness and disease. A family doctor or a *pediatrician*—a type of doctor who specializes in child care—can help families to learn basic health care for children. Regular health checkups and immunization programs for children are important. *Immunization* means giving shots to prevent diseases such as polio, tetanus, measles, and diphtheria.

Children Need Good Nutrition. Good nutrition for children begins even before they are born. The diet a mother follows before her baby is born, and even before she becomes pregnant, affects much of the baby's physical and mental development. If the diet of a young child lacks the proper amount of protein and calories, the child's growth may be slowed. Mental development is also affected by nutrition. During the first year of life, the human brain grows to about 70 percent of its adult size. If an infant lacks proper nutrition, it is possible that the brain may not grow to its potential size.

How to Help Children Get to Sleep

Here are some thoughts from the Better Sleep Council to help children get to sleep more easily and happily:

•Realize that children of the same age and weight do not always need the same amount of sleep. Therefore, bedtime should not be a question of age; it should be directed by the child's own body needs.

•Once an appropriate bedtime, based on the child's needs, has been set, make it clear and precise. Stick to it.

•Make the time just before sleep quiet and enjoyable. Books, storytelling, and quiet games can provide a relaxing bridge between the daytime world of motion and the coming silence of sleeptime.

•Help the child "say good night" to toys, pictures, pets, doorknobs, pillows, and whatever else the child likes. This may help make going-to-sleep time seem final.

•Recognize the difference between bedtime and sleeptime. A child may be given a set time to retire to the bedroom and be allowed to stay awake quietly until sleeptime.

Rock-a-bye Baby . . .
Studies show that rocking a baby in a rocking chair or in one's arms has a calming effect. A crying baby who is picked up and put on someone's shoulder is more likely to stop crying. Infants held on the shoulder also open their eyes and look around more than infants who are

(continued)

What children eat during their first few months and years of life is equally important. The nutritional habits children learn while they are young stay with them through their teenage years and beyond. Eating a variety of wholesome foods throughout childhood is the beginning of good food habits.

Newborn babies must be fed often because they are growing and developing so rapidly. Their small stomachs digest feedings quickly, and they are soon hungry again. At first, a baby drinks only mother's milk or a special formula. A mother's breast milk, developed during her pregnancy to match her baby's natural needs, generally agrees with a young infant. It contains all the nutrients a baby needs. Babies also enjoy the comfort of being held close during nursing.

TOYS AND PLAY IDEAS FOR EVERY AGE

Here are some examples of toys and ways to stimulate children of different ages:

Infants

- homemade colorful mobiles to hang above a crib
- a texture pad made of different materials sewn to a square piece of fabric
- small bean bags made at home
- a lightweight basket filled with discarded junk mail or greeting cards
- a music box that plays when the lid is lifted
- you making faces and interesting sounds

Toddlers

- a wagon filled with colorful wooden blocks
- a magnifying glass
- a sandbox or safe dirt pile with cups, pans, and spoons for digging
- a large cardboard box big enough to play inside
- books and a chalkboard and chalk
- you on your hands and knees to serve as a pony for riding
- balloons and old tennis balls

Preschoolers

- pots and pans to stack and nest
- a rope ladder, a balancing/walking board, a crawl-through tunnel, a wading pool
- crayons, paper, safe scissors, and paste
- crayons, trucks of all sizes, rubber animals and people
- put-together building toys like bricks, blocks, and logs
- hand and finger puppets and a stage made from a cardboard box, with towels for curtains
- cutout letters or magnetic letters to stick on the refrigerator door
- puzzles, flashcards, and books on many topics
- homemade musical instruments
- you telling stories (some you let the child finish)

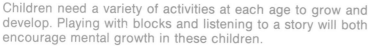
Children need a variety of activities at each age to grow and develop. Playing with blocks and listening to a story will both encourage mental growth in these children.

Some parents choose to bottle-feed their baby with a formula recommended by the doctor. Bottle-fed babies receive good nutrition also. Babies should be held close as they are being fed. This helps them feel secure and loved.

Most babies begin tasting a few solid foods sometime around the middle of the first year. These early foods are usually soft cooked cereals and strained fruits and vegetables. Egg yolks and fine-ground meats may be added later. Baby food, whether commercially prepared or homemade, should be prepared without adding salt or sugar. These two ingredients add no nutritional value.

By the beginning of the second year, most children are eating many foods along with their daily milk. They are learning to drink from a cup and feed themselves bits of food with their fingers. Encourage these efforts on the child's part, even when they seem messy.

Older toddlers enjoy raw vegetables and fruits in addition to cooked foods. These are tasty, and they often serve as good teething materials for children who are cutting new teeth. Whole grain food products like whole wheat bread, crackers, and cereal give children more food value and fiber than white-flour breads and other products.

propped up to a sitting position or left alone in their cribs.

Some *psychologists*—doctors who study behavior—have proved that there is an "optimum rock" for babies. Two doctors tested this theory with a special mechanical rocking chair. The chair could be set at different rocking speeds. Sixty rocks per minute seemed to work best. This is about the same as a person's heartbeat. Do you think this is a coincidence?

131

A New Idea About a Baby's First Hours of Life

Doctors, nurses, and parents are beginning to understand the importance of a baby's first contact with the mother and father during the first minutes and hours after birth. Some experts on child development believe that *bonding*—a strong feeling of belonging to each other—takes place when the newborn baby is held by the mother or father or both immediately after birth. Some doctors believe that the close eye contact and the warmth of touching give the infant a feeling of being loved by his or her parents. This first contact also gives the parents a special feeling of closeness in their new family. Many experts and parents claim that family members never forget this feeling even as the child grows up.

One study discovered that infants who had experienced such early contact with their mothers cried less and smiled and laughed much more than did infants who had not experienced bonding immediately after birth. This study also showed that two years later, the children who had experienced bonding talked more to their parents. At five years of age, these same children had high scores on
(continued)

132

Some foods should be avoided in young children's diets. These include fried foods, rich desserts or highly sugared foods, nuts, popcorn, highly seasoned foods, and strong beverages like tea, coffee, and cola drinks. Many of these foods are difficult or impossible for children to digest.

MENTAL AND EMOTIONAL NEEDS OF CHILDREN

The mental and emotional needs of children are often harder to think of and remember than the physical needs. However, they are equally important. The steps you take to meet a child's mental and emotional needs help the child feel good about herself or himself and about the world.

Children Need a Stimulating Environment. All children, from the one-month-old baby to the fifth-grade student, respond to the stimulating, fascinating things around them. Every day their minds take in all the things they see, hear, touch, taste, and smell. The experiences they have spark learning and creativity. Parents and other family members can bring new experiences into children's lives to help this learning process happen.

Children Need Social Experiences. *Social* means having to do with other people. A baby's smile is one of the first signs of social development. During these early days, the family provides most of the child's social experiences. Family members are vitally important in helping a young child learn to relate to people. Parents and other care givers are a baby's first contact with people. Being held close and cared for lovingly gives an infant trusting feelings about people. Soon a baby begins to recognize faces and voices. Talking to the baby helps with social growth; soon the infant will coo back to greetings. During the first year, a baby who gets this kind of loving attention will play peek-a-boo, wave bye-bye, and often cry when left alone for long.

As babies become toddlers, they learn to express their feelings. As preschoolers, they share games and stories with friends and family members and thus continue their social development.

Families who play with, talk to, and listen to their young children help them learn to communicate with others. Most important, they help the child feel like a valued, loved, and respected person.

Children Need to Play. Play is a child's natural way of learning. Children test and practice new physical, mental, and social skills through play. As the child grows, play gives the opportunity to act out feelings. Play builds a foundation for future learning. It is the way a child learns to concentrate, to imagine things, to try

Making friends is a big part of nursery school. Being around other children in a play situation encourages sharing and taking turns.

new ideas, and to practice grown-up behavior. Today's stacking and counting blocks is tomorrow's math and science lesson. Several afternoons of fingerpainting may open a young mind to creativity in the arts.

You can help a child move into the world of play by providing toys that are safe and fun. Choose objects with different textures to touch. Choose colorful toys with moving parts that the child can move. Raw materials like sand, water, and even mud are also great toys for a toddler. Avoid unsafe playthings that may break or splinter easily. Watch for dangerous, sharp edges or loose parts.

As children reach preschool age, they become interested in playing with other children. Play then becomes a social experience. Games are an important part of playing with companions.

Television can also be a teaching toy. However, television is no substitute for face-to-face play with people. Watch television with the child and talk about the new ideas and words that the child sees.

Play can stimulate a child's imagination. An ordinary cardboard box becomes a spaceship or a kitchen stove through pretending. Children can discover the real world through their make-believe world of play. As they grow in their awareness, children enjoy imitating adults and older brothers and sisters.

language tests plus greater resistance to infections and higher average weight gain.

Even premature babies—who could not be held by their parents immediately after they were born—responded and gained weight better when they were touched and talked to through special openings in their incubators.

These new theories do not mean that all babies who do not experience bonding during the first hours and days of life will feel unloved and be slow to learn. What the theories do show is that doctors and parents are continuing to search for new ways to improve life and family loving for everyone.

About the "Perfect Child"

Fred Rogers of the "Mister Rogers' Neighborhood" television show has this to say:

"When a baby is born, the parents often feel that they would like to give that child a perfect life. It's a very natural feeling, but of course not a very realistic one, especially if 'perfection' to those parents means no trouble, no tears, no fights, and providing for every need, every minute. Every parent soon discovers that that kind of perfection is far from possible (even if it were desirable)."

Tots and Toys: A History

Children have always had toys. In ancient Persia, dolls were buried in children's graves. In Egypt, youngsters played with molded clay whistles. In ancient Greece, they had jeweled dolls, pull-toys, boats, carts, hoops, kites, and wooden horses. In China and Japan, children played with tops, wooden snakes, birds on strings, and paper toys. In ancient Mexico, they bounced inflated animal bladders as balls.

In the fifteenth century, Germany became the toymaking center of Europe, and toymakers formed craft clubs called *guilds.* The first mechanically powered toys were introduced in the seventeenth century. They included moving windmills and animals. By the eighteenth century, many of these toys had become quite complicated, with toy animals and dolls dancing and playing music.

The nineteenth century was the "golden age of toys." The kaleidoscope, china dolls, mechanical toys, and miniature railroad cars were all very popular. The first toy factories were also built at this time.

The twentieth century introduced soft toys, educational toys, and electronic toys. Toy safety

(continued)

Play promotes exercise and coordination for children of all ages, from the baby kicking in the crib to the toddler pushing a wagon to the preschooler riding a tricycle. A doll whose clothes can be changed teaches a child how to use buttons, zippers, shoelaces, and snaps.

Children Need Guidance. To get along in the world, children need some basic guidelines for behavior. Adults have the responsibility to teach children how to behave. Older brothers and sisters help by setting good examples.

Teaching these guidelines should begin as soon as the child begins to move around. At first, safety is the main concern. As a child grows through the toddler months into the preschool years, learning self-control and ways of getting along with others will be added to these safety guidelines. The ability to follow some guidelines usually comes around the age of four, when children can really understand what people say to them.

Behavior guidelines are sometimes called discipline. Both mean teaching. The word *discipline* comes from the word *disciple,* which means "student" or "follower." To teach guidelines successfully, begin with encouragement, love, and praise. Children repeat actions they are praised for and give up any actions that are ignored by others. For example, a parent tak-

ing a child shopping might say, "I enjoyed taking you to the supermarket today because you were so polite and fun to be with. You even helped me load the cart. I hope you will come with me again." A small child will remember this.

Rules are necessary to protect a child from danger and set examples of acceptable behavior. Everyone is more confident and comfortable knowing how to act in a new situation. This is especially true of a growing child, whose world is getting larger every day. A few easy-to-understand guidelines need to be taught to children in a *consistent* way. This means going by the same rules every time. It helps to explain new rules to a child who can understand.

A younger child who is less able to understand language can still be helped to avoid danger. Use the word *no* and move the child away from the hazard and toward something new and interesting. The lesson will need to be repeated again and again. This may take much patient effort.

Children and Independence. One big goal of early learning is to become independent. Children usually want to do things for themselves. They become very proud of their growing independence.

An important part of this process is letting the child know that it is all right to try and fail. Making a mistake is one way to learn. Spilled milk is an example. Show the child how to wipe up the spill and get another glass of milk. Encourage the attempt to drink the milk and encourage the clean-up job. They are more important than the spill.

Almost as soon as children begin wanting to feed themselves, they want to help dress themselves. Even when it takes extra time, children need to be allowed to do as much as they can. At first, they are usually better at undressing than dressing. Clothing designed for self-help, with large buttons and buttonholes, for example, makes this learning easier. As children become good at dressing themselves, they are ready to begin putting away and hanging up clothing. Hooks and dresser drawers should be low enough for their reach.

By the time children are toddlers, they want to begin combing their hair, brushing their teeth, washing their hands, and going to the toilet alone. They also like to open doors and climb stairs on their own. Letting children do as much as they can for themselves every day will help them grow in both self-confidence and independence.

Toilet training is an important stage in a child's growing independence. Most children do not have the nerve and muscle control needed to control their bowel and bladder until they are about two years old. To try to toilet train them before that age is a waste of time and can cause emotional problems.

As children become interested in household tasks, let them join in the cooking, cleaning, and other activities. They can put toys away, empty wastebaskets, and set the table. Their hand coordination will improve and their sense of being a helpful, cooperative person will grow. Along with participating in household chores, children need to be allowed to help make decisions. Whether it be what color shirt to wear each day or how the family will spend its free time, a child can take part. As children learn to be responsible for their own decisions and the outcomes, they grow more confident.

Children Need to Be Touched. Touching is a natural, easy way to show children they are loved and needed. Touching as communication between parents and children is more than hugging and kissing. Touching can be a pat on the shoulder or a gentle poke in the ribs. Children never outgrow their need for the good, secure feelings that come from hugs and touching. Touching begins on the day children are born and placed in their parents' arms. And it should continue throughout their lives.

Children With Special Needs. Some children have physical, mental,

also became an issue for the first time. In 1969 the U.S. Congress passed the Child Protection and Toy Safety Act to protect children from dangerous toys.

Being a Child

Put yourself in a young child's place. Find a small, detailed, printed picture. Use a thick stubby crayon to color it in. Use your left hand if you are righthanded and your right hand if you are lefthanded.

How did it feel to do this coloring? How do the results look?

How might your feelings be similar to those young children experience? Why were you asked to use the hand that you ordinarily would not use? How did the size of the picture you colored compare to the size of a picture young children might be given to color? What have you learned from doing this that relates to the development of young children?

social, or emotional abilities that are different from what is considered normal. These special children may have physical limitations. They may be far more intelligent than others, or they may be mentally slower than the average. They may have problems getting along with others, or they may have emotional problems. Sometimes these children are affected in several areas of development at once.

Special understanding and guidance may be needed to help exceptional children develop as normally as possible. The successful adjustment of these children is determined largely by the attitudes of others toward them. Family relationships that help develop a good self-concept are especially important when there is an exceptional child in the family.

Children Need Love. Children need love in order to grow into healthy, caring, self-confident adults. The love parents and other family members give to babies and young children must be *unconditional*. That means loving them all the time, no matter what they may say, do, or look like. It also means separating what they do from who they are. You can be angry at a child's behavior without making the child feel unloved. Saying to a child "I am angry about what you did" explains your feelings. However, saying "You are a bad child" may be confusing. It doesn't tell the child what you *do* want. And it may be damaging to a child's self-concept. Of all a growing child's needs—physical, mental, social, and emotional—love may be the most important.

a quick review

1. What are some of the early physical needs of children that are provided for by their parents?
2. How does nutrition affect the physical and mental growth of children?
3. How can play help a child learn and grow?
4. How are guidance and independence important to a child from infancy to toddlerhood and preschool years?
5. What is unconditional love for a child, and why is it important?

Picture yourself in the middle of a bright, active kitchen. You are making soup and sandwiches for a preschool boy and his nine-year-old sister. You have just explained a geography question to the nine-year-old as she does her homework at the kitchen table. You have also been carrying their eight-month-old baby sister against your shoulder, trying to comfort her as she fusses about cutting a new tooth. No, you are not a busy father or mother. You are a baby-sitter. Yet what you are doing at this exact moment is just as important as if you were a parent of those three children. You are actually their substitute parent, or *care giver,* while the parents are away. You are fully responsible for the children's safety and well-being. You are an employee hired to do an important job. Your primary task is to keep the children safe, happy, and learning. If you do your job well, you will gain valuable experience and also earn money. And best of all, you will have fun playing with the children and teaching them new things. You will become someone special in their lives.

You are the star of this chapter. In the next few pages you will move through one complete evening as a baby-sitter for the family you have just read about.

CHAPTER 16
Taking Care of Children

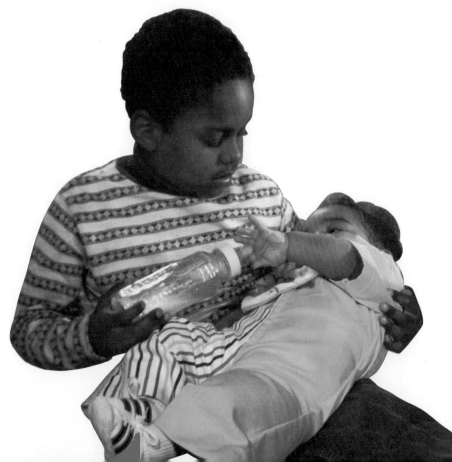

How to Hold a Baby

Young babies' muscles are soft and somewhat weak. Infants cannot hold their heads up without help. To support a baby's head and the upper part of the back, slip one hand under the baby's head and place your other hand and arm under the lower part of the baby's back. Then you can lift the baby safely to your shoulder. The baby's head will be supported securely by your body.

Pick babies up by grasping their entire bodies rather than just their arms. Hold them firmly, either resting them against your shoulder or cradling them in your arms. This gives babies the support that makes them feel safe. Young babies have an inborn fear of falling.

An Evening With You, the Baby-Sitter. Your baby-sitting job actually begins when you receive the call offering you the job. Before you accept it, discuss the following points with the parents:

• what your responsibilities will be
• when you are expected to arrive
• how long the parents will be away
• what transportation arrangements will be made for you
• what your pay will be

Arrive early enough to spend the first few minutes asking the parents for the following information and telephone numbers, which should be written in your baby-sitter's notebook:

• where the parents can be reached
• phone numbers for the family doctor, nearest fire station, police, poison-control center, hospital, and neighbor or relative to call in an emergency
• location of first-aid supplies and any special medication for the children (for allergies or special health conditions)
• any special family emergency plans (see the special feature in this chapter entitled "Accidents and Emergencies Guide")
• location of blankets and room temperature controls
• what and when each of the children should eat, and where the food can be found
• whether the children should be fed or encouraged to feed themselves
• for a baby, any special lifting or handling methods, diapering methods, bathing methods, or sleeping methods
• how much playtime children should be given between the evening meal and bedtime
• the time each child usually goes to bed and anything special about sleeping habits
• the usual routine in preparing for bed—bath, brushing the teeth, using the toilet, taking favorite toys to bed
• what nightclothes to use and if

A story before bedtime gives children a quiet time to settle down. It is easier for a child to get to sleep after a quiet activity than after a more physical activity.

any night-lights are to be left on or windows left open.

Next, you meet the children and talk with them while their parents are present. This is a good time to settle any questions that might cause problems later. You might ask the children if they usually watch television or play music during the evening. You might also ask them to help you remember their set bedtimes or any other special rules their parents may expect to be followed. Once these points are discussed in front of the parents, you will be able to keep a gentle but firm control over the children. They will have less reason to test you or dispute the family rules.

When all these important matters are out of the way and the parents have left, you can begin to get better acquainted with the children. These first few minutes are important ones. Your kind words and caring ways will help the children feel comfortable and safe with you in charge. Your efforts to run things in the ways they are used to will keep them happy and cooperative. How you act at this point may well determine how the rest of the evening progresses.

If the younger children cry when their parents leave, try to catch their attention with something interesting or amusing. Holding, rocking, talking, or singing to young children will help to calm them. Once the moments of missing their parents have passed, you may begin directing their activities toward a fun evening. Now your skills as a teacher and idea per-

Listening is an important part of dealing with whatever problem has caused tears. When two children argue, always listen to both sides of the story.

139

Storytelling

Storytelling is almost as old as the human race. Ancient people told tales of the moon and sun, of gods, of travels, and of wars. Stories were used to explain mysterious happenings and to record history.

Early stories were probably combined with songs and dances. They were passed on from generation to generation. Homer's *Odyssey* and the ballads of the Middle Ages are examples of tales that were passed on by word of mouth.

In the 1400s, with the invention of the printing press, some stories were written down. The Grimm brothers and others wrote folktales and fairy tales.

Small children love Mother Goose nursery rhymes. Who was Mother Goose?

Some say she was Elizabeth Vergoose, a woman who lived in Boston in the 1700s. Her son-in-law is said to have published her rhymes.

Other people believe that the stories are far older. They think that the author was a woman called Queen Goosefoot, or "Goose-footed Bertha," who was the mother of the emperor Charlemagne. Charlemagne ruled much of Europe in the ninth century A.D.

(continued)

son take over. Games, stories, simple crafts, and special activities you have planned will please the preschooler and older child alike. Often, just being in the middle of things, watching and listening, will keep a baby happy.

At suppertime, you need to be well-organized. The two older children may help you prepare their meal while you warm the baby's milk and food. Once the older children are feeding themselves, you may join them at the table. You may hold the baby to feed her yourself, unless she usually sits in a high chair. Perhaps the children usually help with clean-up after meals. If not, you may decide to wait until everyone is in bed before cleaning up. In either case, do not leave a messy kitchen for the parents when they return.

Bath time often follows suppertime in households with young chil-

---

Bath Time for Baby

Get ready: Arrange all supplies within reach. You should have soap, warm water, a soft washcloth, large bath towels, and a clean diaper and clean clothing.

Give a sponge bath: For babies only a few weeks old, bathe by gently washing with a soft cloth. Do not put a newborn in a tub of water.

Give a tub bath: Put warm water into a small tub or sink. Line the tub or sink with a towel or a large sponge to keep the baby from slipping. Wash and rinse the baby as follows:

- Face, hair, and scalp: Use a washcloth. Cradle the baby in your arm.

- Chest, arms, and stomach: Use soap and clear water for rinsing.

- Back and bottom: Wash while turning the baby over on one side. Use one hand to support the baby's head. Put your other hand under the baby's armpit.

- Legs, feet, and toes: Turn the baby over onto his or her back. Lift the baby's legs by holding the ankles with one hand, using your forefinger to separate the ankles.

- Final rinsing: While resting the baby in your arm, rinse all folds and creases on the baby's body one last time.

- Drying and dressing: Pat the baby dry as you wrap her or him in a soft towel. Move the baby to a safe dressing area for diapering and dressing. Keep your moves gentle, slow, and firm.

Diapering a Baby

Place the baby on a flat, clean surface. This might be a changing table, a crib mattress, or a clean pad or towel on a table or warm floor. Remove the soiled diaper, using the front part to wipe away most of the waste, if possible.

Lift both of the baby's legs by the ankles, keeping your index finger between the ankle bones for the baby's comfort. Remove and discard the old diaper in a nearby container. Clean off any remaining waste with a cotton ball or disposable wiping cloth. Still holding the baby's legs up, place the new diaper flat underneath. Lower the baby's legs. Pull the front part of the diaper between the legs and fasten each side in place snugly and comfortably.

If the baby has a diaper rash, you may apply a small amount of ointment or powder to the rash area before fastening the new diaper. If pins are used, keep your hand between the pinpoint and the baby's skin. Use only specially guarded safety pins. If disposable diapers are used, take care not to stick the tapes to the baby's skin.

An infant can roll over and fall in the time it takes you to turn your back and answer the telephone. Never leave a baby alone on a changing table, even for a second.

dren. The baby gets her bath first. She needs your constant attention. Do not leave her for any reason while she is in the bath. This bath will not take long. Then dry her quickly, diaper her, and dress her for bed. Follow the baby's usual bedtime routine as outlined by her parents. Tuck her in, making certain she is comfortable and safe.

By now the older children are probably ready for their baths. You may follow their baths with some quiet playtime, singing or telling a story as they prepare for bed.

Once all the children are asleep, you have time to finish cleaning the kitchen and putting away any toys or games that have been left out. At last the house is quiet. However, you are still in charge. Stay awake and alert to hear the children if they cry out.

If the parents have told you to "make yourself at home," you may choose to read their magazines, listen to the stereo, watch television, or enjoy a snack. But do this only if you have the parents' permission and instructions in advance. Remember that your first responsibility is the children. You are still on the job.

When the parents return, tell them about their children's evening. Tell them what and how much the children ate, when they went to bed, and anything special that occurred. Give a written record of any phone calls.

Before you leave for home, you will receive your pay and possibly the promise of future jobs with this fam-

Some of the Mother Goose rhymes are based on fact. For example, the rhyme "Hey Diddle Diddle" is about real people. Queen Elizabeth I of England, who reigned in the sixteenth century, had a lady-in-waiting called Spoon who stood by her while she ate. She also had a servant nicknamed Dish who served her meals. The two servants eloped: "And the Dish ran away with the Spoon."

How to Talk to Kids

Here are some hints for talking with young children:

• Be natural, and don't talk too much. Really listen to what the child is saying.

• Don't be a phony. Be sure you are really interested in what a child is saying. Children can tell if you are not.

• Ask genuine questions like "How do you feel about this?" "What would you do?" or "Which one is your favorite?"

• Do not talk down to children. Sit or kneel down so that you are eye-to-eye.

• Be honest and direct. If you do not know an answer, or do not feel like talking any more, say so.

• Don't use baby talk, even if the child does. He or she should be learning good speaking habits from you. Speak clearly.

Things to Make for Children for Little or No Money

Finger Paint. You will need soap flakes, liquid starch, and food coloring. Mix the three ingredients until you get the thickness and color you want. Let the children paint on large sheets of white paper. The inexpensive paper used to cover banquet and picnic tables works well. The back side of leftover wrapping paper works, too.

String-together Toys. Collect odds and ends of play materials like uncooked macaroni and thread spools to string together as a necklace. Graduated sizes of paper cups, empty cans, or margarine tubs and lids can be tied together with string to form a pull-toy or wind-chime. This is not an activity for very young children, who may swallow small objects. Be sure that your materials do not have sharp edges.

Flash Cards. Cut sturdy white paper into pieces the size of playing cards (or use 3 × 5 inch index cards). Put alphabet letters on one side and a simple drawing of something that begins with each letter on the other side.

Toy Chests. Cut out pictures from magazines. Glue them onto cartons or packing crates.

142

ily. As a point of personal good business manners, never talk about the the family or their home to outsiders.

You can feel proud of the job you have completed. Your satisfied customers will call you again because of your good work. You may even be on your way to a career in one of the many interesting jobs available in the child-care field.

A bike ride is a good time to explore the neighborhood and learn bicycle safety.

Soapsuds are a fun play material for preschool children. What other play activities can you think of that use kitchen equipment?

THE BABY-SITTER'S BAG OF TRICKS

Bag of Games

Pack a large shopping bag with inexpensive things to take with you to your sitting job.

Who Am I? Fill a bag with items like false beards, mustaches, dark glasses, false noses, wigs, old hats, and wash-off crayons. Let the children create disguises.

Twin Bags Game Bring two small paper bags, each filled with one of two matching things like gloves, marbles, bracelets, and plastic spoons. The children find one object and then try to find its mate, without looking, as they reach into the bag.

Mystery Photo Games Hide a large photo inside an envelope and pull it out one inch at a time until the children guess what is in the photo.

Brown Bag Faces Use paper bags and felt-tip pens to create over-the-head masks. Cut holes for eyes and mouths.

Life-Sized Me Bring a roll of extra-wide paper usually used for covering tables or wrapping packages. One by one, the children lie down on the paper while you trace around them with a felt-tip pen. Then they draw in their own faces and clothes.

Magnetic and Magnified Teach children about these big words by bringing a horseshoe magnet and a large magnifying glass with you.

Thinking and Talking Games

Silly Sentences Start a sentence and let the children finish it with anything they like. For example, you might say, "Yesterday, while I was walking to school I saw..."

Everything starts with B Ask questions that the children must answer with words that start with B (or any one letter).

How Many Windows? Ask the children to tell you, without looking, how many of something are in the room or house. For example, you might ask, "How many buttons are in the room? How many windows are in your house?"

Riddle-Me-Ree Select something everyone can see in the room; then say, "Riddle-Me-Ree ... I see something you don't see, and it starts with K and is red." (Use any other letter and color.)

Pretending Games

Tennis Ball Puppets Make puppets and let the children act out their feelings and ideas. Cut a hole the size of your finger in an old tennis ball or other hollow ball. Draw a face on the ball and decorate it with yarn, and so on. Cover your hand with a scarf and push the tennis-ball puppet over your scarf-covered finger. Let the children do the same, and make up plays with different characters.

Going Out to Dinner If the parents have gone out to a restaurant, treat the children to a special supper complete with handmade menu. Take orders, play music, and give them a bill, letting them use play money to pay and leave tips.

ACCIDENTS AND EMERGENCIES GUIDE

What Can Happen	What to Do
• The child has a simple accident.	• Use first aid. Notify the parents. Never give medicine unless the parents or a doctor directs you to do so.
• The child is bleeding badly, vomiting, or has a very high temperature.	• Apply direct pressure and elevate the wounded, bleeding area. Call a doctor at once. If the doctor suggests taking the child to a hospital emergency room, call the police. They will send an emergency car to take you and the child to the hospital. While waiting for the emergency car, call the parents. Ask a neighbor to come at once to care for the other children.
• The child burns herself or himself.	• Submerge the burned area in cold water until the pain goes away. Cover the burn with a thick, dry, sterile bandage to keep air out. Get medical help and notify the parents.
• The child gets a dangerous substance in his or her eye.	• Wash the eye thoroughly with water for 15 minutes. Hold the eyelid open and pour the water from the inside corner of the eye out. Put a pad over the closed eyelid. Get medical help and notify the parents.
• The child swallows something you think may be poisonous.	• Call the poison-control center or hospital emergency room nearest you for instructions. Have the bottle or label of the swallowed substance in hand when you call. Notify the parents.
• The child chokes on something.	• If the child is breathing, do not try to remove the swallowed item by slapping the back. Ask the child to cough up the item. If necessary, give a sharp "bear hug" by standing behind the child and placing your arms around the body between the waist and rib cage. Tell the child to slump forward while you squeeze him or her with a sudden, strong pressure to force the item out of the throat.
• A fire breaks out in the house.	• Get yourself and the children out of the house immediately. Go to a neighbor's house to telephone the fire department first, and then the parents. Do not go back into the house for any reason.

a quick review

1. What are the primary responsibilities of a baby-sitter?
2. What are some questions a sitter should ask the parent or parents?
3. What are some ways to assure a successful evening when you are meeting the children for the first time?
4. What are some special things to remember when bathing, dressing, or feeding a baby?
5. What should a baby-sitter do during an emergency or accident?

144

Ask yourself the following questions:

- Do you like being with people?
- Are families and children interesting and important to you?
- Do you like caring for, playing with, and teaching children?
- Do you feel you might be good at working with children and adults to solve family problems?

If you answer yes to any or some of these questions, you might enjoy a career related to families and children. This chapter will show you the many possibilities for jobs in this area and how you might get started in one.

CAREERS RELATED TO FAMILIES AND CHILDREN

In the field of careers related to families and children, there are jobs you can do right now. There are also jobs that may take a little training or several years of education. Some jobs take many years of education. You may even wish to try a part-time job in this field while you are still in school. This will give you a taste of a possible future career. Many pediatricians, child psychologists, day-care directors, and social workers began as baby-sitters and camp counselors when they were teenagers. Other people make it their lifetime work to care for children and families as a home-maker's aide or a live-in baby-sitter.

CHAPTER 17
Careers Helping Families and Children

Start a Summer Business

Put your skills as a baby-sitter, housekeeper, lawn or houseplant keeper, or even pet-sitter to profitable use. Organize your own summer business as a family helper. Here are some hints:

1. First make a list of the services you will offer. Set a fair price for each.
2. Write and design an advertising sheet describing your services and prices and telling people how they can reach you. If you have already worked for people, ask for permission to list their names as references.
3. Have the sheet duplicated on a copying machine, which you can probably find at the local post office or library.
4. Distribute copies throughout your neighborhood in person. Talk with people about your skills.
5. Place a classified advertisement in your local newspaper, or post your advertising sheet on the local supermarket bulletin board.
6. Keep a calendar schedule of your job appointments so that you will be on time. Also, keep track of how many hours you work so that you can bill your customers fairly.

Entry Level

Baby-sitter. A baby-sitter cares for children on an hourly basis.

Homemaker's aide. A homemaker's aide assists a busy homemaker with routine housekeeping duties, meal preparation, child care, and entertainment plans. This job can be full-time or part-time work. You can work for one family or through an agency.

Playground assistant. A playground assistant directs the activities of children on playgrounds run by the schools or a community's public park system. This is often a summer job for teenagers.

Clerk in children's store. A clerk gives advice about and sells clothing, shoes, toys, and furniture to parents for their children. This can be a full- or part-time job.

Camp counselor. A camp counselor directs the activities and learning experiences of children attending a summer camp. This is often a summer job for young people.

Some Paraprofessional Training or Licensing

Licensed practical nurse in pediatrics. A practical nurse gives medical care to newborn babies and young children, usually as an assistant to the nursing staff in a hospital or clinic or sometimes in private homes. This can be full- or part-time work. It requires two years of training beyond high school and passing a state exam.

Day-care center aide. A day-care center aide provides care and supervision for children in a professional child-care center. This can be full- or part-time work. Some states require extra training and some centers provide on-the-job training.

Assistant teacher in nursery school or kindergarten. An assistant teacher helps a teacher in learning situations with children, plans lessons, and guides activities. This can be full- or part-time. It requires some training in teacher education beyond high school.

Playground supervisor. A playground supervisor plans and provides for children's activities on one or several playgrounds in a community or school system. This is full-time work during the school year or summertime. It requires training in physical education.

Crisis center counselor. A crisis center counselor is available by telephone or at a special location to offer help and support to people of all ages who may be facing a crisis in their lives, including problems of physical abuse, drug abuse, suicidal impulses, and emotional distress. This may be a volunteer job in some cities, with a variety of hours around the clock. Training is usually given by the crisis center.

Senior citizens' center staff member. A staff member at a senior citizens' center helps to organize and conduct ac-

Playground assistant and camp counselor jobs in the summer are a good way to explore an interest in working with children.

tivities for older people in the community. He or she also possibly offers some counseling about the legal rights of older people and the special resources available to deal with their particular needs. This can be volunteer or paid work. It requires some special classes or on-the-job training.

College Education with a Professional Degree

Supervisor of a day-care center. The supervisor of a day-care center controls all aspects of the center's operation, oversees budgets and expenses, hires aides and teachers, plans activities, and works with parents. This is full-time work. It requires a bachelor's degree in education, business, and/or child psychology.

Dietitian for a nursery school or public schools. A dietitian plans and manages the meals served in schools in order to maintain good nutrition for the children. This is full-time work. It requires a bachelor's degree in home economics with a major in food and nutrition and training and certification in dietetics.

Teacher. A teacher teaches children in nursery school, kindergarten, or elementary school.

Registered pediatric nurse. A registered pediatric nurse provides medical attention for newborn babies and children and assists doctors in a hospital or clinic. This is full-time work. It requires a college degree in nursing.

Sociologist. A sociologist studies the origin, behavior, and interaction of

---

What If Homemaking Were a Paying Career?

A homemaker does not receive a salary the way a secretary, restaurant chef, nurse, laundry manager, accountant, taxi driver, tailor, dietitian, or hotel housekeeper does. Yet the homemaker does many of the same tasks. If the homemaker were paid the 1980 minimum wage for a twelve- to fourteen-hour day, seven days per week, the pay would be $11,607 per year.

If you had to hire people to do homemaking jobs, the cost would be even higher. Here are the hourly wages:

meal planning	$10.00
housekeeping	4.00
cooking	4.00
washing dishes	3.75
laundry	3.75
buying food	5.00
driving	5.00
cleaning	3.75
sewing	5.00
practical nursing	5.00

The average homemaker spends 99.6 hours per week performing these services. At these rates, that would mean a salary of $352 per week, or $18,283 per year. Homemaking is an important career.

147

many groups of people, such as families, tribes, communities, villages, states, cults, professional and business organizations, and others. Sociologists often work for universities and research institutions. A sociologist must have at least a bachelor's degree in sociology.

Anthropologist. An anthropologist traces the beginnings and evolution of the human race through the study of changing physical characteristics and cultural and social behavior. Anthropologists may work for universities, research institutions, or governments or independently as authors of books and magazine articles. An anthropologist must have at least a bachelor's degree in anthropology.

Pediatrician. A pediatrician gives medical care to babies and children and counseling to their parents. This is a full-time job. It requires a bachelor's degree, four years of medical school, and an internship and residency in pediatrics in a hospital.

General/family practice doctor. A general/family practice doctor gives medical care to entire families. This is a full-time job. It requires a bachelor's degree, four years of medical school, and an internship and residency in a hospital.

Child psychologist. A child psychologist counsels, tests, and gives support to children and their families in special problem situations, like learning and emotional difficulties. She or he works through the schools or in private practice. This is full- or part-time work. It requires master's and doctoral degrees in child psychology and clinical experience. Psychologists are often state-certified.

Director for community youth service organization. This kind of worker guides and plans the programs provided for young people through such organizations as the 4-H, Big Brothers, Big Sisters, Scouts, YWCA, and YMCA. This is full-time work. It requires a two-year or four-year college education.

Social worker. A social worker assists people with problems of child care, financial support, and emotional stress. He or she works through state and local government agencies and helps people to use these service agencies to solve their problems. Being a social worker is a full-time job. It requires a college education and the successful completion of a civil service examination.

Family therapist. A family therapist works with families to help them solve varied problems, including conflicts between teenagers and parents, through a hospital, clinic, or social service agency. A job as a family therapist usually requires master's and doctoral degrees and experience working in a clinic.

Family budget debt counselor. This kind of counselor helps families work out financial problems and manage

Hospitals offer many opportunities for work with both children and adults. Volunteer work after school or on weekends requires no experience and may involve talking with or reading to patients. Licensed practical nurses assist the nursing staff in a variety of tasks.

their money successfully. This can be a full- or part-time job. It requires a college education in financial management and accounting.

Careers That Combine Two Interests or Talents

Photographer of children and families. This kind of photographer takes portraits and candid photographs of children and their families in a studio or in their homes. This can be a full- or part-time job. It requires some training and experience as a photographer.

Writer of children's stories and books. This kind of writer writes stories for magazines or books for publishers to sell to children and their parents. This can be full- or part-time work. It requires training or experience as a writer or a bachelor's degree in English or creative writing.

Baby-food specialist. A baby-food specialist tests the nutritional value, taste, and appearance of baby food and plans menus for infants and small children or designs packages for children's food products. She or he can work for the U.S. Food and Drug Administration, the consumer protection and environmental health services, or a food-manufacturing company. This

Places Where People Work With Children

Talk in class about how it might be to work with children in these settings:

- library
- playground
- clinic
- photography studio
- overnight camp
- school lunchroom
- children's theater
- day-care center
- scout troop
- clothing store
- elementary school

How would these job settings be alike? How would they be different?

Plan a Day-Care Center in Your Classroom

As you study careers related to helping children and families, your teacher may let you organize a child-care center. Invite preschool children of neighbors and friends to be your "students." Here are some points to think about as you plan your setup. These are very similar to the legal requirements for professional child-care centers in most states.

The Room. Is the room neat, clean, safe, well-lighted, and well-ventilated? Does it have enough space for play? Is there a place for privacy? A quiet corner for taking naps? Is there a rest room nearby? Is there running water in the room? Is there more than one exit? Is all electrical or heating equipment out of the reach of children?

The Physical Activities. Are there activities that encourage climbing, crawling, balancing, hanging, sliding, and digging?

The Materials for Play. Are there toys that involve reading, art, science, music, water play, dramatic play (dress-up),

(continued)

150

job requires a bachelor's degree in home economics or nutrition.

Designer of children's clothing. This kind of designer designs clothes for children and chooses fabrics and colors and accessories for the clothing manufactured for children by a clothing company or a pattern-making company. This can be full- or part-time or free-lance work. It requires a college education in art and design or on-the-job training and artistic talent.

Illustrator for children's books. This kind of illustrator draws pictures to accompany stories written for children. This can be full- or part-time or free-lance work. It requires talent as an artist or some training at a commercial art school or in college.

Dance teacher for children. A dance teacher trains children to dance, tumble, or perform gymnastics exercises. This can be full- or part-time work. It requires training as a dancer or physical education teacher and talent as a dancer.

A CLOSER LOOK

Here are three people talking about their jobs in the field of child and family care. Perhaps you know people in your community to whom you could talk about similar jobs.

Salesclerk in a Children's Store. Don works as a salesclerk for a large children's store. He spends some of his time selling in the toy department and the rest fitting children's shoes in the shoe department. Don is a junior in high school. His job is part-time, evenings after school and Saturdays. He could work full-time for the store right now, with or without his high school diploma. The diploma is not a requirement for his job. However, Don wants to finish high school, and his boss has encouraged him to combine work and school until he is ready for a full-time job.

"I have always liked to be around kids, at home with my brothers and sisters and when I was a helper at summer camp," says Don. "I got this job by starting out as a stock boy on Saturdays. Now I sell toys and shoes for kids. Last summer my boss paid for me to attend a special training session given by one of our shoe manufacturers. Now I am qualified to fit children's shoes. At holiday time I really love selling toys and watching the kids' faces as they walk through my displays. It took some time to get used to handling cash registers, credit card machines, and special-order forms. Sometimes the hardest part of my job is to keep my cool if parents and kids get into a hassle about which shoes to buy. I don't take sides. I just try to help everybody keep a sense of humor.

"I spend plenty of time on my feet. Some days, I sell a lot of merchandise. Other days, sales are slow. I'm learning a lot about the retail business."

A variety of different professional positions involve family counseling. Social workers, budget debt counselors, and therapists all help families solve different kinds of problems.

How does Don see his future taking shape in this job? Here is what he says: "My boss says I am learning fast. I could be promoted to assistant manager someday. My dream is to be part owner of my own children's store someday. But I could also be pretty happy if I kept on working here, especially if I got to be the assistant manager of the store."

Day-Care Center Aide. "I got my job because they could tell from my interview that I was willing to give a lot to my work. I considered this to be more than just an eight-to-five job," says Marianne, an aide for a day-care center in her community. She got the interview through her high school job-placement office. "I had

been a mother's helper for a farm family when I was fifteen. It was just a summer job, but it gave me the idea that I might like this kind of work full-time. I wanted to do something that would make me feel good," explains Marianne.

What does she like or dislike about her job at the day-care center? Marianne says, "I like reaching out to a troubled child and helping that child feel better and do better because I am a friend. But sometimes I am uncomfortable working with parents. If I believe they are not caring for the child in a way I feel is needed, I have trouble being diplomatic or keeping quiet."

What advice would she give to someone wanting to get into a job

woodworking, simple cooking, and large and small muscle development play?

The Children's Comfort. Are nutritious snacks planned for each day? Are there comfortable resting places? Do you have enough adults to give each child personal, loving attention?

The Safety Plan. Have the adults in charge practiced a plan for getting the children out of the building in a quick and orderly manner? Are there fire extinguishers and first-aid kits in the room? Is someone trained in first aid? Is there a telephone nearby?

The Teaching Plan. Is someone on the staff trained or experienced in teaching and guiding young children? Is there a written plan for activities to help children learn new games and play activities?

Although you may not be able to provide a complete child-care program in your classroom, you may be able to come close. This will give you some idea of how it feels to work in a day-care center. And above all, enjoy the children!

Work With Children

Below are some of the qualities you need to work well with children. Discuss in class what they mean. Ask yourself if you are:

- alert
- cooperative
- flexible
- generous
- healthy
- mature
- organized
- resourceful
- sensitive
- thoughtful
- understanding

Some of these words may already describe you. You may want to work on others.

A Recreation Center Career Ladder

Playground aide
   (entry level)
Playground assistant
   (assistant level)
Playground leader
   (supervisory level)
Recreation leader
   (supervisory level)
Director, recreation center
   (supervisory level)
Recreation supervisor
   (management level)
City Superintendent, recreation
   (managerial level)

What education and experience are needed to begin at each level and to move from one level to another?

Day-care centers and nursery schools employ both paraprofessional aides and college-trained teachers.

like hers? "The best thing is to be interested and read a lot. It also helps to be a people watcher and child watcher. You have to be interested in how children learn and explore. I did not go to school beyond high school. Our center offers continuing education for new employees. Therefore, I learned my skills on the job. Some people go to school for extra classes in child psychology. If you are devoted to your job, you will gain the trust of your employer. I began as a play supervisor and soon graduated to teaching and writing lesson plans for various children's programs at the center."

Child Psychologist. Judy is a child psychologist working in the public schools in her community. She also counsels children in her own office privately. She became interested in the field of child psychology even before she knew it existed. Judy explains, "My mother was always talking to me about the ways people behave. She would ask me, 'Why do you think that person did that?' and I would try to come up with ideas."

After high school, Judy studied psychology in college. Unable to find a job in her field after college graduation, she took a secretarial job with a child psychiatrist, a doctor who specializes in children's mental health. She soon became interested in the doctor's work and helped with some child testing. She took extra courses in related subjects. "Then," she tells, "I went into the U.S. Navy and joined the hospital corps doing personality testing. It was fascinating. When I got out of the navy, I went back to college to earn my Ph.D. degree in the area of children's learning disabilities." Judy has enjoyed a long and successful career and had a family of her own, too.

Are there good things and bad things about her work? She says, "Sometimes it seems like saving a life," referring to helping a child settle a serious emotional problem. "However, spending every day dealing with people's problems can be very sad at times."

A WORD IN CLOSING

You may or may not be interested in a career or job related to families and children. However, learning about how children grow and how families care for them will help you all your life. You will always have children in your life, whether they are your own or those of your friends and family. Knowing their needs will help you bring important guidance into their lives. Understanding children will help you enjoy their own special magic.

a quick review

1. What are some questions you might ask yourself in order to decide if you are interested in a career related to children and families?
2. What are some jobs that are open to people who are interested in children but who have no special training?
3. What are some careers in child care that might be open to someone with some special training beyond high school?
4. What are some job areas that combine an interest in children and another special talent a person might have?
5. What are some part-time jobs you can hold as a student that might prepare you for considering a career related to families and children?

A Day-Care Center Career Ladder
Child Development Aide
(entry level)
Child Day-Care Assistant
(assistant level)
Teacher
(supervisory level)
Center Director
(managerial level)

What education and experience would a person need to begin at each of these levels and to move from one level to another?

▶ **Words to Know**
day-care center: A professionally managed place offering full- or part-time care for children whose parents cannot be with them during the day because of their jobs or other special situations.
nursery school or preschool center: A professionally managed place offering part-time educational programs for young children in the year or two before they start school.
paraprofessional: A person with some special training or experience who assists a professional person or works as an associate in a professional field.
professional: A person with a college education or additional training who works in a special field.

Unit 3
HOME

CHAPTER 18
Homes and Families

The words of popular songs often describe how people feel about home. Feelings may be the best way to describe what home means. A home is also something you can see. It can be a farmhouse, an apartment, a mobile home, or a ranch-style house. For people who travel or move often, "home" is sometimes a feeling they carry inside them from place to place. Whether you think of home as something you feel or see, a home meets many of the same needs for all families. This chapter will explore these needs.

PHYSICAL NEEDS

Homes meet certain physical needs. These are often called *tangible* needs because you can see or touch them. They are shelter, protection, and safety. People need a place to stay comfortably warm and dry. They need enough space for sleeping, eating, and bathing. Some people have extra space for hobbies or family play activities. Others may need special work space for a business at home.

Safety is a need both inside and outside a home. The space and equipment inside a home should be carefully arranged and kept in good repair to prevent inside accidents or fires. Outside walkways, driveways, and yards must be checked for possible dangers. Doors and windows need locks to prevent break-ins.

Home is a place to share a funny story or tell something nice that happened during the day. It is also a place to recover from a bad day.

Careful use of energy in a home is of special importance today. Heating and cooling a home and running appliances all take energy. The energy supply is an important and shrinking resource. Energy-wise families are checking their homes for ways to save energy and money.

EMOTIONAL NEEDS

A home also serves as a springboard for personal growth. A comfortable, safe, carefully managed home helps children grow into healthy, happy adults. Such a home provides a calm, secure place away from the busy outside world. People of all ages need to relax and feel refreshed to keep going and growing.

SOCIAL NEEDS

Each family has different needs for *socializing,* or being with other people. Families meet these needs in a variety of ways. For example, a family whose members like sports may live in an apartment building with an activity room or a nearby park. If that same family were moving to a house, it might be one with a recreation room and a large yard.

Another family may enjoy entertaining with parties at home or invit-

Being Good Apartment Neighbors

Apartment living brings many people close together under one roof. This can be fun. However, there may be times when this everyday closeness makes getting along difficult. Here are some ideas to help apartment neighbors stay good neighbors:

• Try to keep noise down, especially during naptime or late at night.

• Do not let your family's boots, toys, and other possessions clutter the hallways, stairs, and storage areas.

• If your building has a laundry room, remember to take turns using the washers and dryers. Clean up any mess before you leave and report any out-of-order equipment.

• In apartment playgrounds or swimming pools, always share the play equipment and game areas with others. Invite new people to join your games.

• If pets are allowed in your apartment building, be sure yours do not run loose or bother other people.

As a rule, being neighborly simply means thinking about the feelings and needs of the people who live around you.

157

Save Heating and Cooling Energy

Here are some ideas from the U.S. Department of Energy to help you to save energy and the money it costs:

• Insulate your home by putting extra thicknesses of proper materials in the outside walls and the attic to keep out heat in summer and cold in winter.

• Close off unused rooms and shut off their heating or cooling vents if it is possible to do so.

• Use ventilating fans in the kitchen and bathroom as seldom as possible.

• If you have a fireplace, keep the damper closed unless you build a fire.

(continued)

ing relatives and friends to share dinner often. This family may want extra space for fixing and serving meals for many people. They may want room for listening to music and for storing stereo equipment, albums, and tapes.

Compared to years past, many families today have more free time to spend together. Shorter work days and longer vacations make this possible. Family members may gather together in a "family" room. This room can be anyplace in the home. The kitchen may be a gathering place for family conversations. A living room may turn into a family room. An ex-

tra bedroom can be used for family reading or television watching.

AESTHETIC AND SELF-EXPRESSION NEEDS

Aesthetic and *self-expression* needs are part of people's need to have art and beauty around them.

Art can be more than paintings on a wall. At home, art is a way of thinking about how you like the things around you to look, feel, sound, and even smell. The colors, textures, and sounds that you and your family choose to fill your home help meet your aesthetic needs. Bringing them

The time family members spend together is an important part of what home means to them. A "family room" is any room where you and your family gather to relax and enjoy each other's company.

Home is a place to get away from the rest of the world. It can mean having a small corner that is your place to think.

together yourself helps you to meet your needs for self-expression.

Having attractive surroundings in your home is not a matter of money. Families can create beauty in their homes with very little expense. Such simple items as paint, pictures cut from magazines, houseplants, pillows, and recycled vegetable crates can bring the creativity of people to a room. Even favorite music and wild-flowers from the yard help bring a special mood into a home.

Chapter 19, "Design and the Home," has more ideas and guide-lines to help you and your family make your home your own special place.

With the world changing so quickly day by day, everyone needs a familiar place to be. Home can be that place. In addition to shelter, safety, and basic comfort, a home can give you that important feeling of be-longing somewhere. At the end of a busy, hectic day at work or school, home becomes that important place to relax and be yourself.

• When the heat is on, lower the *thermostat* (temperature control) to 24°C (65°F) during the day and 13°C (55°F) at night unless someone is ill or you have a new baby or older person in the home. Dress warmly.
• In cold weather, keep windows near your thermostat tightly closed.
• Use ventilating fans instead of air conditioning wherever possible.
• If you have an air conditioner, clean or replace filters monthly.
• Turn off window air conditioners when you leave the room for many hours.

▶ **Words to Know**
aesthetic: Relating to or dealing with things that are beautiful or artistic.
socializing: Being with other people.
tangible: Able to be seen, touched, or tasted.

a quick review

1. What are some of the physical needs a home can meet for the people who live there?
2. What are some ways to save energy in the home?
3. How are people's social and emotional needs met in the home?
4. What is meant by the words *aesthetic* and *self-expression* when referring to a home?

CHAPTER 19
Design and the Home

In some ways, decorating a room is like putting an outfit together. You want the room to be both good-looking and comfortable. You want the room and the things in it to work for the people who use it. People who design and decorate homes professionally talk about aesthetics and function. *Aesthetics* refers to how a space looks. The aesthetics of a home depend on how color, texture, and line are used in decorating. These factors are called *design elements*. *Function* is how the home is used. This chapter is about combining aesthetics and function in home decorating.

There are no rigid rules about home design. However, there are some important questions to ask before thinking about decorating:

• Who uses the different parts of the home? When and how are these spaces used? The answers tell enough about a family's life-style to help them choose either an informal design or a more formal look.

• In what directions or patterns does the family move around the home? What areas are used most often? The answers should be kept in mind when arranging furniture and choosing floor coverings.

• What kinds of activities go on in the home each day? Do some family members have special needs, like extra work space? What are mealtimes, bedtimes, and morning getting-ready times like? The answers point to the need for special items like a large dining table, a business desk area, a room divider for a shared bedroom, or a place to keep the family's games and sports equipment.

• What colors, textures, or styles in furnishings and accessories do the family members like? The answer will tell them the look they want to create through design.

• Are there any special situations in the home? If the family includes physically handicapped members, small children, or pets, it may be necessary to consider extra safety features or more washable, unbreakable materials in furnishings.

FUNCTION

The *layout,* or overall *floor plan* and individual room arrangements, of a home should reflect the ways it is used. How everyone moves from room to room is called a *traffic pattern.* Traffic patterns follow the layout of a house.

To plan or improve the traffic patterns in your home, first think about the ways your family members come and go all day. If certain pieces of furniture always seem to be in the way, you may be able to find a new way to arrange them. Sometimes something as simple as changing the arrangement of chairs in a room can bring about a better opportunity for face-to-face family talks. The amount of family traffic in a certain area should also be considered when choosing floor covering. Some carpets may wear out quickly in a busy walkway. Or they may need extra padding under them. A practical flooring choice for a high-traffic area might be wood, vinyl, or even tile. Sometimes a protective mat placed in front of a busy doorway can save wear and tear on a carpet for very little expense.

Family traffic can be hectic when everyone is getting ready for work or school at the same time. If you have a traffic problem in your home, try placing extra mirrors in well-lighted places or in each person's bedroom. Busy morning traffic can also spill over into the breakfast area. Sometimes family members eat in shifts that are ten or fifteen minutes apart. The arrangement of the family kitchen can determine whether these busy moments are difficult or easy. How you organize chairs, a table, a snack bar, or countertop work areas for lunch packing or breakfast preparation can make a difference. A careful plan will help keep things moving along smoothly and happily as family members prepare and eat breakfast. Room arrangement involves organizing everything in that room according to a family's needs and wishes. Factors to consider when arranging a room are:

• convenience and use
• safety and comfort

On-the-Move Homes

If your family moves often, you may have discovered ways to make each new house or apartment look and feel like home. Here are a few ideas to help you decorate space when you move a lot:

• Use your favorite useful things as wall decorations. Tennis racquets, hockey sticks, baseball pennants, movie posters, or guitars can add color to your room the day you move in.

• Choose bedspreads, curtains, and pillows that will look good in a room of any color. Avoid colors that are too bright or hard to match. Printed sheets and pillowcases are a good way to coordinate these items.

• In many towns you can borrow framed paintings or posters from the local public library or an art gallery for a small fee.

• Think of things like your radio, record player, record collection, aquarium, or gerbil cage as decorating items. Arrange them in your new room carefully.

• Shelves that hang on the wall with brackets are easy to put up and take down. They make good places to organize and display your favorite things.

• Cork squares can be used to make a bulletin board. They also make good pinup boards next to a family telephone.

(continued)

162

• privacy as needed
• versatility to allow for many activities and purposes

HOW ROOMS LOOK DIFFERENT

Look at rooms in people's houses or in pictures in magazines. What makes one room different from another? Notice that some rooms look larger, and others, smaller. Some seem cooler, and others, warmer. Some look cluttered, and others, uncomplicated. The reasons for these differences are the many ways that people handle the basic ingredients of home and room design. These design ingredients include styles of furnishings and types of room arrangements, along with the design elements of color, texture, and line. How you select and combine these basics is what makes one room look different from all the rest.

Color. Color has a lot to do with how a room looks and feels. It is usually the first thing you notice when you walk into a room. Color is also an important means of self-expression.

Part of choosing colors for a room is deciding what feeling you want the

The floor plan of a house or apartment is an important planning tool. It can help you figure space needs and traffic patterns before you begin moving furniture or choosing floor coverings.

colors to express. Are you an outdoor person who likes sun, sky, and earth colors? Do you prefer an elegant, dressed-up feeling? Is your favorite dream place the beach, the mountains, a lively shopping center, a quiet fishing stream, the circus, or someplace else? Colors can help create any of the feelings these dream places bring to mind.

Combining colors in a room is usually done in two steps. The first step is to choose an overall mood or feeling for the room. This will help determine the room's basic color. This color will be used for the largest areas, such as walls, floors, and large pieces of furniture. The second step is to decide what extra color touches to add to the room. These touches are called *accent colors.* Pillows, pictures, and window coverings are done in these colors. It is helpful to look at paint color chips and scraps of fabric together before making final choices about colors.

Color can also be used to make a room appear larger or smaller. For example, light colors and white tend to make a room look larger. Dark colors close in a room to give a cozy feeling. Bright colors on the short walls seem to shorten a long room. A long, narrow room can be made to seem square if the end wall is painted a darker color and the sides a brighter color. Chapter 38 has more information about color.

Color is a strong design element in this room. The triadic color scheme—red, yellow, and blue—uses these primary colors with neutral carpeting and walls.

Planning colors for one room is usually affected by the colors selected, or already used, in the rest of the home. Some homes, for example, may already have carpets of the same color in every room. All the rooms in an apartment may have been painted white by the landlord. When you cannot change such colors where you live, you add color with your furnish-

• Concrete blocks and smooth boards can be used to build instant bookshelves and desks.

• Each time you move, pack a few of your special personal things in one box. Mark the box "Open Me First." You may feel more at home during the first day in a new place if you see these familiar things.

Walls, Floors, and Ceilings

Designing a room usually begins with the backgrounds—the walls and ceiling. Here are some ideas for wall and ceiling background areas:

• paint—smooth, textured, shiny, or dull
• wallpaper—in many styles
• fabric—bed sheets, canvas, burlap, or muslin
• self-stick vinyl paper, in rolls or squares
• cork tiles
• mirror tiles (too heavy for ceilings)
• self-stick carpet squares (also for soundproofing)
• wood or plastic paneling
• barn wood or other used boards
• roofing shingles
• ceramic or plastic tiles

Here are some ideas for covering floor areas:

• marine paint—deck paint for wood
• natural wood— unvarnished or varnished
• wall-to-wall carpet, in many styles and fibers
• area rugs or room-size rugs
• self-stick carpet tiles
• linoleum or vinyl, in rolls or tiles
• sisal rugs—strawlike woven material
• floor canvas—may be stapled, glued, or painted

ings and with window and floor coverings.

Texture. *Texture* refers to how something feels. In a home, texture appeals to your sense of touch. Surfaces in a room can feel soft, hard, smooth, rugged, fuzzy, or bumpy. Sometimes you do not need to touch things in a room to discover textures. Your eyes will tell you that a chair's surface is hard, a carpet is soft, or a pillow is lumpy or smooth. Lighting in a room can be designed to show off special textures by casting shadows. Likewise, textures can be used to affect lighting and even sound in a room by absorbing them or reflecting them. A variety of different textures helps to make a room interesting.

Shape and Line. Choosing furniture means thinking about function, comfort, and personal taste. It also involves looking at line and shape as they relate to home design.

The shapes and lines you see when you enter a room can create a mood. For example, if nearly all the furniture shapes are curved, the feeling will be soft and easy. Straight lines, on the other hand, may give a crisp, clean, or even hard look to a room. Soft, curving shapes combined with straight, angular shapes can create a casual feeling if carefully planned.

Line is an important design ingredient in a room. *Vertical* (up-and-

down) lines can be created with striped wallpaper, floor-to-ceiling draperies, tall furniture, and long wall hangings. You get more *horizontal* (across) lines when couches and tables are long and low. Whether a room is designed around horizontal, vertical, or even diagonal lines is a matter of personal taste. Some people prefer to combine several different lines or add curved lines to get a certain style and feeling in a room.

Accessories. *Accessories* are those things that say "this is my place" in any room. They can be simple everyday items, such as a lamp, a calendar, a pillow, or a bulletin board. Or they can be special objects to see and touch, such as pictures, posters, trophies, or sculptures.

Accessories can be made from souvenirs you have collected. Seashells in a basket or beautiful rocks in a glass jar may start conversations about your favorite walking places. Collections of various objects can be displayed in an interesting combination on a tabletop.

Accessories can be used to keep a room up-to-date. Most accessories are light enough to be portable. You can move them from room to room to create a new look. If you leave home for a trip by yourself, you might take along one or two of your favorite little things to help you feel less lonely.

Accessories add texture, color, and shape. If a room seems a bit heavy or

SMART WAYS WITH FURNITURE

1. Screens That Organize/Divide. This old screen has been covered with denim. Any sturdy fabric will work. Pockets and giant rings have been stitched to one side of the screen. They hold all the little things you can never find, like scissors, tape measures, and rulers. The screen divides room space or can hide a laundry basket or messy project.

2. Basket Storage. Baskets come in many sizes and shapes. They are a good choice for portable, attractive storage for all kinds of different items.

3. Wall Poster/Pull-Down Desk. This plywood tabletop is hinged to the wall at desk height. Two legs are hinged to the front for support. When not in use, the table is pulled up and fastened to the wall with hooks. When the desk is in the up position, you see another poster glued to the underside. When the desk is down, as shown here, you see the bulletin board.

4. Chair With Pouch. This old chair has been recycled. Bright covers can be made from pillowcases, towels, or old bedspreads. The pouch stitched to the back holds homework or stationery. When the desk is in the up position, the chair is put by the lamp for reading.

5. Nightstand/Desk Supplies Storage. This is made from unfinished pine and has casters on the bottom so it can be rolled closer to the desk or bed as needed.

Desk supplies are stored on the bottom shelf.

6. Guest Bed/Pillow. This large pillow is also a guest bed. It is a large, soft, twin-size quilt with a bed sheet stitched to one side. When company comes, unroll it on the floor and insert a sleeping bag between the quilt and the sheet.

7. Platform Bed/Storage Unit. This easy-to-build bed is made of sturdy, inexpensive plywood. Drawers can be built into the platform for storage. Bright pillows add color to the room.

8. Record and Book Storage. These are old crates or sturdy soft-drink cases. They are covered with vinyl self-stick paper to add color.

Loft Beds Save Space

A *loft bed* is one built as a platform high above the floor. Enough space is left between the platform and ceiling for sleeping. Sturdy wood is used in the supporting leg posts.

A ladder is used for climbing into the loft. A mattress on the platform is used for sleeping. For safety, a railing can be built around the sides of a loft bed. A small shelf to hold books, a clock, a radio, or a lamp can be added. Floor space under the loft bed is left free for use as a play or study area, or for extra storage.

dark, a light accessory, like a brightly colored wicker basket or footstool, provides a lift. If a chair looks a little hard or stiff, a small quilt draped across the back can soften the look. When a room appears small, mirrors may give it a roomier feeling.

Accessories provide great opportunities for the do-it-yourselfer. *Found objects* (things that you find rather than buy) or items rescued from the trash can become something special for your room with a little imagination and work. Polish an old, leaky teapot and transform it into a con-

tainer for dried flowers. Cover an empty coffee can with self-stick paper to make a bright pencil holder. Use the same paper to cover an address book or a wastebasket for a go-to-gether desk set. Ask the local movie house manager to save old movie posters to put up in your home. The possibilities are as wide as your imagination.

Here are some more hints for adding accessories to a room:

• Hang pictures at eye level for people who are sitting.

Look at how the books, plants, and printed fabric give texture and pattern to this room's design. How would you describe the "feel" of this room?

The plants on the shelves in this room are an example of turning a hobby into a decorating accessory.

• For a greater impact, try hanging many pictures together in one large group.

• When displaying small items together, use a contrasting background color to set them off.

• Experiment with new ways to arrange pillows, collections on a tabletop, books, and other items.

• Look for new ways to actually use the accessories you already have. For example, fill an empty basket with balls of yarn. The effect will be colorful as well as useful.

a quick review

1. What questions about the use of space in a home should you ask before decorating?
2. What factors make a room look different or special?
3. How can color and texture affect the look of a room?
4. How does furniture affect the lines in a room?
5. What are some examples of accessories you might place in a room?

CHAPTER 20
Space and Storage

Do you have a Sock Monster in your home? You know, the one that always seems to gobble up one sock out of every pair. Or maybe you have a Math Book Muncher who eats math books and sometimes English books, too. The muncher's appetite for schoolbooks is usually biggest the night before your big test. These monsters and munchers may be the signs of space and storage problems around your home. This chapter will help you get rid of storage monsters. You will find new ways to store things around your home.

GETTING ORGANIZED

Begin the battle against the Sock Monster by getting organized. To start, list all the items you have to store and the places you have available for storage.

Sort through your possessions. Start with clothes, shoes, and accessories like belts, scarves, gloves, ties, and jewelry. Move on to books, games, record albums, and things you collect. If you have not used something in over two years, think about recycling it. Chapter 48 has suggestions for recycling clothing. It may give you some ideas for recycling other items.

After you sort through your things, take a good look at your storage space. List the places you and your family now use for storage.

The open storage areas in this kitchen and living room are both functional and decorative. People often choose this kind of storage because it makes things easy to find and adds interest to the room.

These probably include closets, shelves, and cabinets. However, there may be other places you can use for storage. Here are some ideas to start you thinking about creating new spaces to keep things:

• cardboard suit boxes for under-the-bed storage of shoes or flat items

• empty suitcases for out-of-season clothes

• small cup hooks inside closet doors for belts and neck chains

• walls for hanging sports equipment

• shelves built under stairways for canned goods

• hooks behind bathroom doors for robes and shower caps

• a portable tote box for carrying cleaning products from room to room

• small pillow covers to store your pajamas as a pillow during the day

• a mesh netting bag to hang from the shower head for shampoo bottles

• a small shelf above your bed for an alarm clock, tissue box, or books

Closets. No one ever seems to have enough closet space. However, you may be able to think of ways to reorganize your closet to make more space. If your closet is deep, you can put extra hooks on the back wall for hanging things you do not wear very often. This saves space on the clothes rod and saves your clothes from being

Hang Up Your Clothes!

You have probably heard those words before. Here are some new ways to prevent wrinkles, save ironing, and make your clothes last longer:

• Use plastic-coated hangers to avoid rust.

• Make terrycloth covers for coat hangers from old towels.

• Wrap the bottoms of coat hangers with thick yarn so that they hold pants without slipping or leaving a hanger crease.

• Use pinch-style clothespins to hold skirts on coat hangers.

• Place a towel rack on the back of your closet door to hold the pair of jeans you wear most often.

• Use an inflatable hanger sold at drugstores to dry hand washable clothes.

• Attach several doorknobs to a board. Then hang the board on the back of your room door or closet door. Hang your everyday jackets or hats on these knobs. Make each knob different. Even empty, they make an interesting decoration for your room.

CREATIVE CLOSETS

Here are some smart ways to divide and use every inch of closet space to your best advantage:

1. Tie racks or hooks on the door.
2. A shoe bag for socks and underwear.
3. High shelves for luggage and out-of-season sports equipment.
4. Baskets or covered cardboard cartons for out-of-season clothes.
5. Flat shelf storage for sweaters or T-shirts.

6. Wire or plastic baskets on runners for more flat storage.
7. Multiple hangers and two layers of hanging space for shorter clothes.
8. Floor space for more storage.
9. Longer hanging clothes and garment bag storage.
10. Shelves to keep shoes neat and organized.

crowded or crushed. Hooks can also be placed on the closet door to hold a robe or jacket you wear every day.

You may want to hang a second clothes rod across part of your closet below the main one. This can hold shorter clothes like shirts and jackets.

Shoes often clutter the bottom of closets. This can mean stumbling over shoes each time you open the closet door. There are better ways to store shoes. You can hang a large, flat bag with pockets for shoes on the inside of the closet door. These shoe bags are sold in department stores. Most hold six or more pairs of shoes.

Or you can use the shelves above the clothes rod to hold shoe boxes. Mark the shoe boxes with a felt-tip marker to tell shoe color or style at a glance.

You can build a shoe shelf that slants up from the closet floor. Nail a strip of wood near the top of the shelf to catch the heels of your shoes. Store your shoes leaning against the shelf with their toes down and their heels hanging on the wood strip.

Pegboard can also improve closet storage. *Pegboard* is a special type of wood paneling with small holes all over the surface. Hooks of different sizes and styles fasten through the holes. You don't need nails or screws. Pegboard can be attached to the inside or outside of a closet door. The hooks can hold everything from a belt collection to a laundry bag.

Small racks like those used for spice bottles in the kitchen can go on closet doors to hold lotions and cosmetics. This may help unclutter the top of a desk or dresser. A towel rack fastened to the closet door or inside wall can be used for ties, belts, suspenders, scarves, and anything that folds.

Flat Storage. All over your home you have items that need to be stored flat. Sheets, blankets, photograph albums, sweaters, and tablecloths are some examples. These things are usually kept in drawers, on shelves, and in cabinets.

Drawers are good for storing almost everything, from stamps and envelopes to T-shirts and gym shorts. How you organize a drawer can make the difference between messy or neat drawer storage. Here are some tips for better drawer storage:

• Use small boxes or other dividers to create separate sections for small items.

• Make linings for drawers with aluminum foil, tissue paper, or wrapping paper to help control dust.

• Place a small, unwrapped bar of soap in the corner of a drawer to keep a fresh scent inside the drawer.

• Put a plastic margarine tub or foam egg carton in a front corner of the top drawer of your desk or chest for loose change or small pieces of jewelry.

A Recycling Closet

If you have an extra closet or cabinet in your home, declare it your "recycling closet." Use it to store reusable items such as newspapers, string, gift boxes, plastic food containers, grocery bags, ribbons, fabric scraps, glass jars, coffee cans, and anything else you or your family might use again.

A closet for recycling things might give you new ideas of what to do with things you used to throw away. For example, dip empty mayonnaise or pickle jars up to their necks in a bucket of paint. Let them stand overnight to dry. Your results will be several colorful flower vases or pencil jars for you or for gifts.

A recycling closet is a good place to store clean rags (worn-out T-shirts) for cleaning and polishing the house or car. Put them in a "rag bag" made from an old pillow case.

Store your returnable bottles in your closet until shopping day.

Greeting cards from past holidays and birthdays can be stored for reuse in art projects. They can also be cut apart to use as gift tabs on wrapped gifts.

Create a Storage Wall

Create shelf storage of any size, from a whole wall of shelves to just one corner, with crates. Ask the manager of your fruit and vegetable market or grocery store to save all the old wooden crates for you. Then sand and paint your collected crates. For larger storage walls made of crates, you might build a platform for the bottom and a cap for the top. Your large crate arrangement will hold together better against the wall with these extra connecting boards. You can paint the crates or leave them a natural color. The vegetable and fruit labels can be left on as decoration, too.

• Color-code each drawer of a chest shared by two people.

Shelves around your home provide space for things you can store flat. You can create more shelf space in the following ways:

• Stack several wooden vegetable crates together against a wall. Add color with a coat of paint.
• Use wall brackets to hold bookshelves on your walls.
• Bricks and boards can be combined to create instant shelves resting on the floor.

Containers. Containers of all shapes and sizes can be used to store things around your home. Boxes, baskets, bags, bottles, and bins are some examples. Fishing-tackle boxes can be used to store many things (buttons, coin collections) other than fishing gear. Colorful shopping bags from department stores can be used to store lightweight things. Their handles make them easy to hang on a wall or behind a door. Recycled juice cans, coffee cans, and pickle jars can become containers for pencils, paints, or even flowers.

SPACE AND STORAGE

Now you have some idea of the storage possibilities in your home. The second step in getting organized is to decide where to put various items. Here are three questions to ask before choosing a storage location:

1. Where do I use the item first and most often? Your answer will tell you the best room or place to store that item for easy use.
2. Is the item something I use every day, once or twice a month, or only once a year? Your answer will tell you if the item is something you need to be able to reach easily every day (like shoes, shampoo, or a notebook) or something you can hide away for a whole year (like holiday decorations or ice skates).
3. How can I place the item so the things I need every day are within easy reach? Your answer will tell you whether to place the item

Many newer furniture designs combine several functions or uses. For example, this bed is designed to give you shelf and cabinet storage as well as a place to sleep.

Good storage space in a work area allows you to have everything you need for a project close at hand.

high, low, or near the front or back of a shelf, closet, or other storage area.

"A place for everything and everything in its place" is an old saying. Whoever said this probably had more space than most people do today. Yet the idea is a good one. The amount of storage space you have is not as important as how well you use it. Plan your storage with care and stick to the plan every day. You never know when the Sock Monster may return!

a quick review

1. What are the two steps in organizing your storage?
2. Describe some ways to add storage space in your closet.
3. What are some ways to organize items you store in a drawer?
4. Name some throwaway items you might recycle as containers for things around your home.
5. What are three questions you should ask yourself before deciding where to store an item?

CHAPTER 21
Your Own Space at Home

Everybody needs both time alone and time with other people. You may have days when you really enjoy having people around you. Other times you simply want to be by yourself just to think or dream or read. These are feelings everyone has—children, teenagers, and grownups.

A place to go for being alone can be almost anywhere, from a tree house to the rooftop of an apartment building. Your special place at home may be your own room. Even if you share your room with a brother or sister, part of that room is yours. This chapter will give you a chance to think about your own space at home.

Think about all the things you do in the room or space you call yours. You begin your day using your closet space and drawers when you get dressed. After school you may stretch out on your bed for a nap. Later you may sit on the floor to listen to the radio. After supper your room may become a study area where homework can be spread out. On Saturday afternoon your room may be the place where your friends gather. On Sundays your room can be your hobby workshop for building models. Your personal space at home meets many needs.

A NEW LOOK

What you need from a room changes as you grow up. In part, this is because your daily routine is changing. You may be spending more time caring about your clothes now. Your homework may be taking more of your time and space than ever before. Your room probably needs to be reorganized to allow for such things.

This may be a good time to ask your parents to give you the responsibility for giving your room a new look. This does not mean asking for lots of money or buying any new furniture. You may be able to update your room simply with a new color of paint for the walls and a bulletin board you make to hang over your bed. If you make the choices and help do the work, the room can begin to feel like the new, growing-up you.

Floor Plan. Draw several sketches of your room's floor plan. Try the furniture in different arrangements until you find one that works best for you. If you share your room with someone, you may need to think of a new way to divide the space to create some privacy for both of you.

Have you outgrown some of your childhood furniture? If you need a change of furniture, consider building your own desk or platform bed like those described in Chapter 19. There are more ideas in the third columns of this chapter, too.

Color and Texture. The home design ingredients of color and texture

Your room probably says a lot about what is important to you. If this were your room, how would it be different?

are explained in Chapter 19. You can use these guidelines to help you personalize your own room. *Personalizing* your room means giving the room the look that best fits you. You probably have favorite colors you like to wear or have around you. These colors are part of the way you express yourself. Use them in your room. If you like one special color, put it on your walls. However, if you have many favorite colors, you may want to paint your room walls white. Then use the other colors in pillows, posters, throw rugs, and a bedspread.

Texture can add interesting feelings to your room. If some of your furniture is smooth wood or hard plastic, you may want to add a softer

Be Cold-Weather Energy Smart in Your Room

Here are some tips for smart energy use in your room:

• Dust or vacuum heat vents or radiator surfaces to allow the heat to flow out.

• Keep furniture away from heat outlets to allow the air to move.

• If you have a thermostat in your room, keep it turned way down when you're out.

• Use drapes and window shades to keep heat in and cold air out.

• Try a fabric roll shaped like a bean bag on the windowsill to cut drafts.

• Turn off lights and radios not in use.

175

Free or Inexpensive Room Decorations

Looking for room decorations? Don't overlook those items you may already have around. With a little thought and work, you may be able to turn them into interesting accessories. Here is a partial list to get you started:

- travel posters
- plants grown from cuttings
- rocks or shells in a jar
- a quilt made from scraps
- a kite
- your bike hung on the wall
- record jackets
- fabric on a wooden stretcher frame
- a bulletin board with cartoons and clippings
- special event posters from concerts, plays, or school activities
- hats hung on wall hooks
- a collage, or picture made from fabric scraps, paper, and string
- storage cans covered with paper or fabric scraps
- family photos

texture with a fuzzy pillow or a leafy plant in a basket. Hanging paper or fabric on one wall can also add texture to your room. Decide how you want your room to feel and look the minute you walk in. Then choose colors and textures to make it happen.

Accessories and Displays. Accessories are the finishing touches you give your room. More than anything else, accessories say, "This is my place." They can be simple items like framed photos you took yourself. They can be special things like a mobile you put together out of driftwood you found at the beach. Perhaps you like experimenting with color, light, and sound. You could place some colored lights around your room to create a special mood or show off your record album covers.

Displays of things you collect will personalize your room and give your visitors many things to talk about. These can be seashell collections, team pennants, or stamp albums. You might display travel posters of places you have been or dream about. Your display area can be a shelf on the wall or a tray on a tabletop or windowsill. Cork tiles placed on a wall can hold a changing display of postcards or ribbons you won running a race.

All of these choices you make about how your room looks will tell the world all about who you are and where you are going.

SHARING A ROOM

When two people share a room, two different personalities are involved. Here are some ways to let two people express their own personalities and enjoy a feeling of private space:

- If a room is small with high ceilings, build a sleeping loft for one person.

- Build a platform for half the room so one person's space is a step up from the other's.

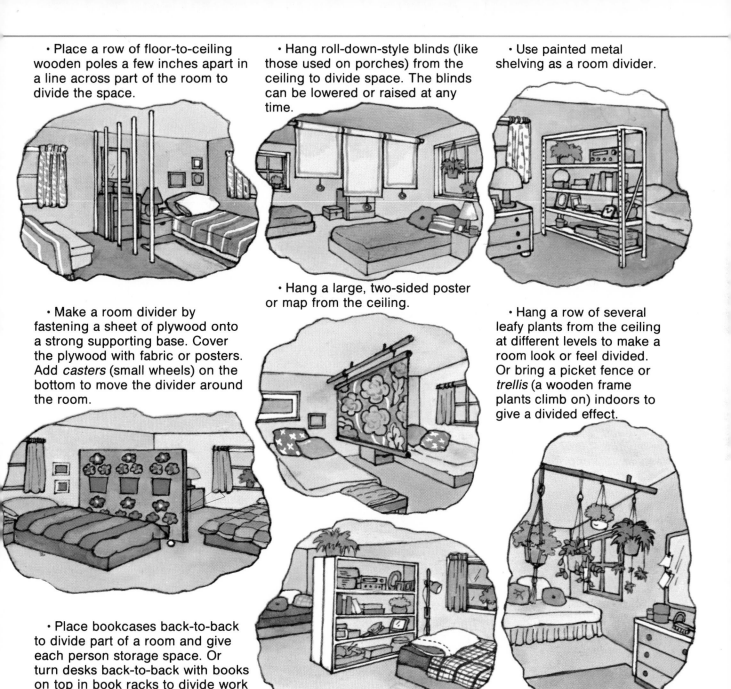

- Place a row of floor-to-ceiling wooden poles a few inches apart in a line across part of the room to divide the space.

- Hang roll-down-style blinds (like those used on porches) from the ceiling to divide space. The blinds can be lowered or raised at any time.

- Use painted metal shelving as a room divider.

- Hang a large, two-sided poster or map from the ceiling.

- Make a room divider by fastening a sheet of plywood onto a strong supporting base. Cover the plywood with fabric or posters. Add *casters* (small wheels) on the bottom to move the divider around the room.

- Hang a row of several leafy plants from the ceiling at different levels to make a room look or feel divided. Or bring a picket fence or *trellis* (a wooden frame plants climb on) indoors to give a divided effect.

- Place bookcases back-to-back to divide part of a room and give each person storage space. Or turn desks back-to-back with books on top in book racks to divide work space.

Your Room Grows Up With You

Your room at home reflects the many ways you change as you grow up. As you become a teenager, you may want to show some of your new interests in your room. Here are some ideas to try:

• *Your bed.* Try making your bed look more like a couch by pushing it against a side wall and adding large toss pillows to lean against.

• *Your play table.* Convert it to a desk or work table with longer legs or extra shelves added.

• *Your storage.* Add a cardboard or metal file cabinet (two-drawer type) for organizing your school papers and notebooks.

• *Your floor covering.* If your floors are bare wood or vinyl, you may want to add carpeting or a rug for comfort and soundproofing.

• *Your windows.* You may want to add blinds for more privacy.

• *Your lighting.* You may want to soften your bright lights to create a denlike mood. Be sure to add good, sturdy lamps for your desk and over your bed.

• *Your accessories.* By now you are collecting many things that are valuable and meaningful to you. Think of careful ways to display and use them.

(continued)

A foam mat with a cover that you make can be used for exercising or as a guest bed. It can be stored out of the way when not in use.

TAKING CARE OF YOUR ROOM

Although your room is your space, it is also part of your family's home. How you care for your room has a lot to do with the way your entire home looks and feels. Perhaps you believe you can let your room get messy if you keep your door shut. However, this only works for so long, and you usually end up in a mess. Keeping your room clean is a task that does not have to pile up on you. Room care can be an easy 15-minute routine like this:

4:00 P.M.: Hang up clothes you wore that day.

4:03 P.M.: Put dirty clothes into the laundry basket.

4:05 P.M.: Make your bed (if you didn't do it in the morning).

4:08 P.M.: Dust your furniture and straighten desk, chest, and tabletops.

4:11 P.M.: Vacuum or sweep the floor.

4:15 P.M.: Take a moment to admire your room.

Some of these jobs, like dusting and sweeping, can be done once a week. So your daily routine might take only 10 minutes. You feel good about yourself and your own personal space when it looks neat and clean.

SHARING SPACE AT HOME

Sharing space is part of family life. You and your family share nearly every room in your home at one time or another. Bathrooms get busy when everyone needs to leave at the same time in the morning. People get into each other's way in the kitchen just before suppertime. Two people may want to watch different television programs. Sharing space can be handled in the same way you handle other family matters.

Respect for each other's feelings and needs should come first. This often means compromise. *Compromise* happens when each person gives in a little so that everyone can have things go his or her way once in a while. For example, a morning schedule that gives each person equal time in the bathroom may be a compromise a big family makes.

Here are four ways to help everyone in a family enjoy home space:

• Knock on the door before entering someone's room.
• Respect each person's quiet time.
• Put things back in order after you use them.
• When guests come to visit, let them share your space.

Now that you have read and thought about your own space at home, take those ideas one step further. A part of your room at home will always go with you wherever you may go. Someday you will be ready to move away to a place of your own. Some furnishings from your room will probably move with you. These familiar things will carry memories of the feelings you developed about yourself growing up in your own space back home.

• *Your colors and textures.* You may want to change your childhood sheets for some bright new prints or stripes in sheets and pillowcases for your bed. These can also be used to make new curtains for your room. A new coat of paint in a color you feel is more grown-up may be a good idea.
• *Your favorite things.* If you simply cannot part with your stuffed animals or baseball cards, think of a new way to display them.

▶ **Words to Know**

compromise: A method of solving a disagreement among people by having each person give and take a little until everyone feels fairly treated.

personalize: To design your space or room with your personal choices of colors, textures, furnishings, and accessories to reflect your own personality.

personal space: A room or part of a room in your home that is totally yours to use as you like.

shared space: Rooms and spaces in your home that are shared by every member of your family at one time or another.

a quick review

1. What is meant by the phrase "Everyone needs both group time and time alone"?
2. Describe some ways you can personalize your room at home.
3. What is the difference between personal space and shared space in a family home?
4. Describe some ways to divide a room for privacy when two people must share the same room.
5. List some ways to help everyone in your family enjoy both shared space and personal space.

CHAPTER 22
Home Care

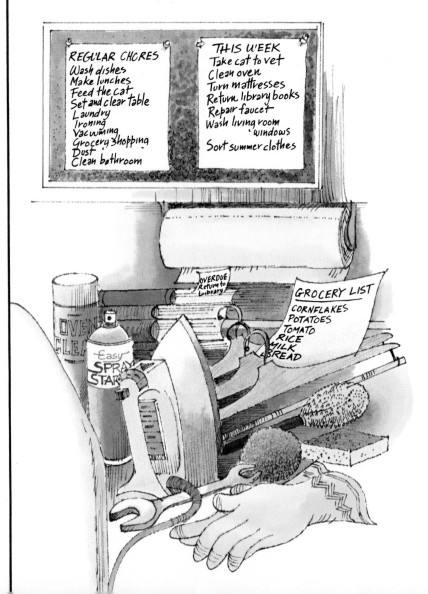

REGULAR CHORES
Wash dishes
Make lunches
Feed the cat
Set and clear table
Laundry
Ironing
Vacuuming
Grocery shopping
Dust
Clean bathroom

THIS WEEK
Take cat to vet
Clean oven
Turn mattresses
Return library books
Repair faucet
Wash living room
    windows
Sort summer clothes

GROCERY LIST
CORNFLAKES
POTATOES
TOMATO
RICE
MILK
BREAD

To run smoothly, a home needs to be managed well every day. Part of home management is home care. Each family has its own way of dividing home-care jobs. However, in most families everyone helps in some way.

The words *clean* and *neat* mean different things to different people. One family may prefer a lived-in look, with belongings scattered casually about. Another family may like everything neatly in place all the time. Nobody expects your home to be perfectly spotless all the time. The important point is for your family to feel comfortable, to stay healthy and safe, and to be proud to live in your home.

GETTING ORGANIZED

Smart home care means planning how best to use a family's energy, time, and money. A plan or schedule of jobs to be done helps keep things rolling along smoothly and fairly for everyone. Without some kind of plan, the work can pile up until no one wants to do it. This is unfair to everyone and hard on the home.

One kind of home-care plan is a schedule of jobs—a calendar or chart of things to be done on certain days of the week. This way a family can plan the work load for good use of everyone's abilities and time. Job responsibilities can be shared so that all family members help and still have

Dividing home chores can be part of a family meeting. This family sits down together once a week to talk about each person's schedule of activities and to assign home tasks.

free time for themselves and each other. Some flexibility is important, too. This means being able to bend the schedule to allow for trading jobs under special situations.

A household work schedule helps your family in two ways. First, it helps everyone see what has to be done and when. Second, it is a checklist to see how things are going and whether changes need to be made.

Of course, some jobs must be done every day. Picking up clutter, preparing meals, and washing dishes are examples of daily work to do. Some of these jobs you just do as you go along. These jobs are probably never written on a chart. For example, you put things away after you use them.

You store things in their usual place so they are easy to find the next time. You hang up your clothes or toss them in the laundry when you take them off.

Work will take all the time you have if you let it. Do not let it do that. Look for ways to do two jobs at once. Wipe countertops while your dinner cooks. Iron shirts while doing laundry. Straighten books and magazines while you dust. Prepare meat loaves two at a time, placing one in the freezer for another meal.

HOME CARE ROOM-BY-ROOM

There are several ways to manage and schedule caring for your home.

Home-Care Schedules

Make a job schedule chart for your own family. Here is a list of jobs to get you started:

- preparing meals
- washing dishes
- setting the table
- making beds and changing bed linens
- doing laundry
- ironing clothes
- cleaning the bathtub, sink, and toilet
- feeding the pet(s)
- vacuuming carpets
- mopping or sweeping floors
- shopping for groceries and other needs
- taking out trash
- hanging up clothes
- dusting furniture
- caring for children

Home-Cleaning Tools
- broom and floor brush
- brushes (scrub brush and bowl brush)
- buckets (at least two)
- carpet sweeper (hand or electric)
- polishing cloth (chamois)
- dishcloths and dustcloths
- dustpan
- mop (sponge- or string-type)
- sponges and rubber gloves
- scouring pads (nylon, copper, plastic, and steel wool)
- stepladder
- vacuum cleaner
- window squeegee

Home-Care and Repair Tools
- screwdrivers, wrenches, and pliers
- clean-out auger for drainpipes
- hammer and saw
- plunger for clogged drains and toilets
- adhesives (glues and tapes)
- nails, screws, washers, nuts, and bolts
- hand drill
- electric fuse
- measuring rule or tape measure
- utility cutter (razor-blade edge or mat knife)

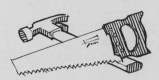

One way is the room-by-room method. Each room or area of your home is given one day each week for a top-to-bottom cleaning. For example, Monday is cleaning day for the kitchen; Tuesday is for the bathroom; Wednesday is for the bedrooms; Thursday is for the living room or family room area, and so on. Another way is to do light cleaning each day and heavy cleaning on the weekends. How you manage home care is up to your family.

The Kitchen. Keeping your kitchen clean is fairly easy because water is handy and most kitchen surfaces are hard and shiny. While a thorough cleaning may be done only once a week, kitchen care is something you do each time you use the room.

The Bathroom. Most of the surfaces in your bathroom are hard and shiny. These include toilets, sinks, tile walls, countertops, bathtubs, and shower stalls. Keeping them clean and sanitary is a daily job. Each member of the family can share this job.

Living and Sleeping Areas. The living room, family room, and bedrooms of your home serve many purposes. These are all rooms that become cluttered quickly throughout a busy day. You and your family can

Room care means both picking up and cleaning. Putting things away as you use them makes both these jobs easier.

There are many different brands and types of cleaning products on the market today. Read labels and evaluate products carefully before you buy.

help by picking up and straightening things as you come and go all day.

Your Room.   Your idea of a clean room may differ from someone else's. If you like things kept neatly in place and you share a room with someone who leaves clothes on the floor and never makes beds, you may need to ask for a compromise. Sharing the cleaning jobs will help this along.

Because there is usually not much time in the morning, especially on school days, it is easier to straighten your room before going to bed. Clothes that need washing can be put in the laundry basket. Other clothes can be hung up or put away. When

there is a special place for everything in your room, it will always be easy to find things. Chapter 21 has more ideas about your room.

Caring for Storage Areas.   Storage areas in your home also need routine care. Closets for clothes and linens are more useful when they are well organized and kept free of dust and dirt. Getting dressed in the morning is less of a scramble when clothes hangers are untangled and all turned the same way on the clothes rod. The family medicine chest should be cleaned and checked often to remove out-of-date medicines and to keep shelves neat and sanitary.

Home Care Out-of-Doors

If you live in a house with a yard, you and your family also have outdoor home-care jobs to do:

- Care for plants or window boxes.
- Rake up plant trimmings, leaves, and grass cuttings to discard or store for *mulch* (natural fertilizer).
- Sweep sidewalks and driveways (clear away snow or ice in winter).
- Clean and repair doors, shutters, windows, railings, fences, and gutters.
- Put away yard tools, toys, and hoses.
- Pick up litter.
- Water and care for the garden areas and yard as needed.
- Fertilize the lawn as needed.
- Cut the grass and trim lawn edges around walks and curbs during summer.
- Pull weeds and treat trees and plants for any pests.

You can organize outside jobs in the same way as indoor home-care jobs. Decide which jobs must be done each day, which may be done only once a week, and which are to be done on a seasonal basis.

Pet-Care Tips

Nearly 55 percent of the households in this country have at least one pet. Many have more than one. Dogs and cats are the most common household pets. However, some families have birds, fish, turtles, gerbils, and many other types of pets.

Pet care is a shared job in many families. A pet may belong to one person in the family, but others may help in the feeding, exercising, and grooming at times. Most young children are ready for this kind of responsibility by age eight.

Here are some tips for living with pets:

• Clean up any accidents at once by mopping with a paper towel and rinsing with vinegar and water.
• Brush your dog or cat often, especially when the pet is shedding.
• Check for fleas often. When fleas appear, do a thorough housecleaning. Fleas are hard to get rid of and carry diseases.
• Keep your pet's feeding and drinking area and bowls clean and out of children's reach.

Storage areas in an attic, basement, or cellar need to be checked often for fire hazards and water damage.

If you have a garage, you may store garbage cans there until trash is collected. Be sure trash can lids are tightly in place. Wash cans often to prevent odor and health problems. Check other items stored in your garage, like lawn- and garden-care tools, chemicals, and fertilizers. They need to be stored safely out of children's reach. Be certain equipment is clean and in good working order at the end of seasonal use.

Controlling Household Pests. Nobody likes flies, cockroaches, mosquitoes, ants, mice, rats, bedbugs, or other household pests. Pests can carry germs that may make people sick. They can get into food and spoil it. Some may ruin clothing. Keeping the whole house clean is the first step in pest control. Pests need food, water, a way to get into the house, and places to hide. Control these and you will be able to control pests. Here are some guidelines:

• Always wipe up spilled foods immediately.
• Do not leave dirty dishes and pans unwashed.
• Keep boxes and bags of dry food tightly sealed.
• Get rid of garbage, scraps of cloth, and other wastes that pests like to eat.

The old saying "Many hands make light work" may be the best statement on family home care. All the methods, schedules, tips, and gadgets in the world will not get household care jobs done unless everyone in the family cooperates.

a quick review

1. What are some ways for a family to organize household care jobs?
2. List some household jobs that usually need doing every day.
3. List some household jobs that usually need doing every week.
4. Name some kitchen surfaces and suggest ways to keep them clean.
5. How can every family member help keep the bathroom clean and sanitary?
6. Describe ways to control household pests or get rid of them.

Millions of people are involved in household accidents every year. Not every accident causes death. However, many accidental deaths and thousands of injuries can be avoided if basic home safety rules are followed.

In this chapter you will learn about ways to prevent home accidents. You will also learn ways to prevent illness and how to handle health problems and emergencies in your home.

CHAPTER 23

Health and Home Safety

HOME SAFETY

The three most common household hazards are falls, fires, and poisonings.

Falls. Falls are the leading cause of accidental deaths at home in this country. Surprisingly, people often fall on level surfaces. Problems like improper lighting, poorly fitting shoes, lack of handrails on stairways, poorly waxed floors, broken steps, and uneven sidewalks cause falls.

Fires. Fires are the second leading cause of accidental death in the United States. Most fires are caused by carelessness. People toss away lighted matches or drop cigarettes into seat cushions or beds. They leave matches and lighters where children can find them. They overload electrical circuits. No home is completely fireproof.

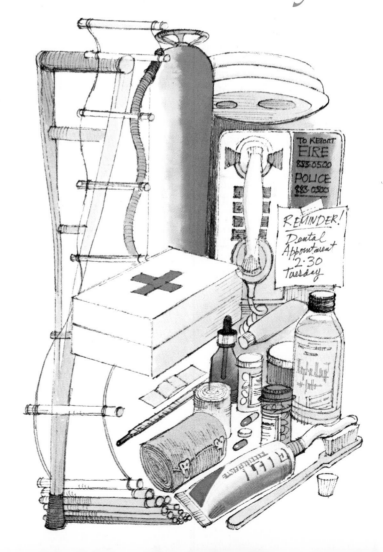

To Prevent Falls

• Be sure you have good lighting indoors and outdoors.

• Place light switches where you can reach them before entering dark rooms, stairways, closets, and storage areas.

• Use night-lights.

• Use nonskid bath mats or strips in tubs and shower stalls.

• Use grab bars on the wall beside the bathtub.

• Never place a throw rug near a stairway.

• Use rugs with nonskid backings.

• Replace worn or loose carpeting on stairways or in hallways.

• When washing floors, polish them over and over until you get a hard, dry, safely polished finish.

• Do not clean and wax with the same mop or sponge. Oil left by the cleaning product will soften the wax and create a slippery surface.

• Always use a sturdy ladder or footstool when climbing to reach things.

To Prevent Poisonings

• Keep detergents, polishes, and cleaners on high shelves or locked up.

• Keep medicines, ointments, laxatives, hair-care products, and shaving products out of children's reach. Never tell a child that medicine is candy.

(continued)

186

Accidental falls in and around the home are very common. How do you think this boy broke his arm? What are some ways to prevent falls at home? The third column on this page will give you some ideas.

Poisonings. The third leading cause of accidental death in the home is poisoning. Small children are often the victims of accidental poisoning. Almost every room in your house contains something poisonous—from medicines to houseplants.

Make home safety improvements a family project. Spend an hour walking through your house together. List any fire hazards to remove or fix. Remove toys and other objects blocking the halls and stairways. Put away poisonous products and medicines.

Sit down as a family group to talk about what to do in case of fire. Write a list of emergency telephone numbers and place it beside each telephone in your home. Point out each possible *escape route* (way out). Teach everyone how to break open a window safely, clear away the glass, and climb out.

For any major safety hazards you were able to find in your home, call in professional repair people. These might be an electrician, a carpenter, a plumber, a brick mason, a gas or electric company representative, or even a local firefighter. Go back to recheck these problems often and look for any others. Make this home safety checkup a year-round habit.

ILLNESS

Some illness in a family is normal. Even with a good general health program, sooner or later each family is likely to experience illness. Many childhood diseases like measles, mumps, and chicken pox happen in spite of efforts to prevent them. These diseases are *communicable* (passed from one person to another). Children can catch them while playing or going to school with others.

Cold water is good first aid for a kitchen burn. Never use butter or any kind of grease on a burn. What are some ways to avoid burns when you are cooking and working in the kitchen?

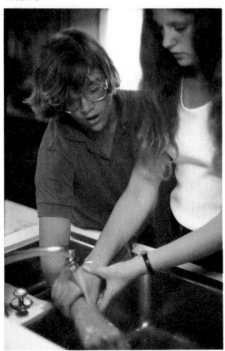

Colds and influenza are also communicable illnesses for all ages.

People who are seriously ill are usually cared for in a hospital. However, many minor illnesses are treated at home. Also, the *patient* (sick person) may return home from a hospital while recovering from a serious illness or surgery. In either situation, every family member should know how to care for the sick person.

Here are some ways you may expect your family life to change when a family member is sick:

• Time usually spent on other jobs and activities will be used to take care of the patient.

• Each family member may have to accept extra duties.

• Extra effort must be made to keep a home clean and sanitary. Germs can spread quickly in dirty kitchens, bathrooms, and laundry rooms.

• All members of the family must be careful to have clean clothes and eat nutritious meals. Simple-to-fix foods and easy-care clothing will help make these jobs easier.

• Extra quiet may be necessary. Use a quiet carpet sweeper, broom, or mop instead of a noisy vacuum cleaner. Keep the volume low on a radio, television set, or stereo record player.

Here are some jobs that might be shared by the family to help a sick member recover:

• Do not allow children to chew painted woodwork, furniture, or old toys. The paint may contain lead, which is poisonous.

• Check for poisons in your laundry room, workshop, garage, and yard. Always store items such as bleach, turpentine, paint, varnish, pesticides, dyes, fuels, and car-care products in their original labeled containers.

• Plants can be poisonous. Teach children not to put any part of any houseplants or yard plants into their mouths.

• Keep the telephone numbers of your local poison-control center and hospital emergency room next to your telephone.

What to Say When You Call a Poison-Control Center

If someone in your family has swallowed something poisonous, keep calm and act quickly. Call your local poison-control center or hospital emergency room and be ready to tell:

• what poison was swallowed

• how many or how much was swallowed

• the weight or approximate age of the person who swallowed the poison

• where you are located

Follow the directions you are given.

187

To Prevent Fires

• If there are smokers in your house, make a rule that no one smokes in bed or while napping in a chair.

• Be sure cigarettes and matches are cold, even wet, before they are emptied into trash cans.

• Remove trash from the attic, basement, closets, garage, and storage areas.

• Discard oily rags or keep them in tightly covered metal containers.

• Choose *fire-resistant* (will not support a flame) fabrics for draperies, curtains, rugs, and furniture coverings.

First Aid Kit for Your Medicine Chest

The following items will help you prepare a basic first aid kit for your family:

• roll of adhesive tape
• *sterile* (germfree and clean) gauze dressings
• old bedsheet, clean and folded, for bandages, slings, or splints
• cotton-tipped swabs or cotton balls
• rubbing alcohol
• calamine lotion
• syrup of ipecac (to cause vomiting after poison is swallowed)
• petroleum jelly
• adhesive bandage strips
• spirits of ammonia (for fainting)
• aspirin or aspirin substitute

(continued on page 190)

188

• Keep the sickroom clean, neat, and cheerful as well as quiet and comfortable.

• Store medicines and sickroom supplies on a tray near the patient or in a nearby bathroom—but separate from household items.

• Give the patient special attention at mealtimes. Special food may be recommended by the doctor. The patient may have a poor appetite. Arrange the food to please the eye as well as the taste.

EMERGENCIES

Family health and safety emergencies come in all shapes and sizes. They can happen anytime and anyplace and to anyone in your family. Some emergencies are related to the safety of your home. Others concern your family's health. Your family will be better prepared to react to either type of home emergency if plans are made in advance.

If someone in your family has a special health problem, such as epilepsy, diabetes, heart disease, or a drug allergy, have that family member join Medic Alert, a nonprofit organization that provides medical identification worldwide. Members pay a small fee and wear a bracelet identifying their special needs. Write to Medic Alert Foundation, Box 1009, Turlock, California 95380.

Learn first aid. *First aid* is immediate and temporary care given to the

SAFETY CHECKUP FOR A HOME

1. Floors and Stairways:

• no loose rugs or broken steps
• handrails on stairways
• good lighting
• no tripping hazards on steps

2. Kitchen:

• all appliances and wiring in safe condition
• poisonous products and knives safely stored
• pot handles turned away from stove front
• grease, water, and food spills wiped away
• sturdy stepstool handy
• fire extinguisher handy
• refrigerator kept tightly closed
• exhaust fan free of dust and grease buildup
• iron cord in safe condition; iron stored when cool

3. Laundry Room:

• appliances clean and in safe condition
• soaps, detergents, and bleaches safely stored

4. Basement:

• furnace in safe condition
• flues and ducts clean
• oily rags thrown away
• fire extinguisher handy

5. Bathroom:

• nonskid mat or strips in tub
• hand-grab bars in tub or shower
• medicines and cosmetics safely stored and childproof

- doors can be unlocked from outside
- unbreakable plastic or paper cups used

6. *Living Room/Family Room:*

- furniture arranged for free movement
- carpets and rugs with nonskid backing
- television and stereo sets with enough space for air to circulate around them

- electrical circuits not overloaded
- unused outlets plugged with childproof covers
- extension cords in good condition and not under rugs
- mesh screens across front of fireplace; safe space between fireplace and rug

- sliding glass doors clearly marked at eye level

7. *Bedrooms:*

- no one smoking in bed
- light switch or lamp located near bedside and door
- crib meets legal safety standards
- toys put away at night
- plastic bags over clothes out of children's reach
- chain or rope ladder available for fire escape from second story

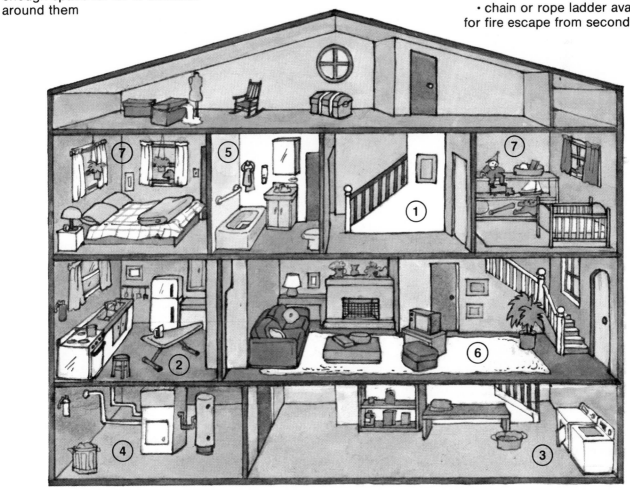

First Aid Kit
(cont. from page 188)
- mild antiseptic
- thermometer
- tweezers
- scissors
- tongue depressors
- a list of common household poisons from a poison-control center
- a first aid manual

▶ **Words to Know**

American National Red Cross: The United States part of a worldwide organization that voluntarily helps people in time of need, disaster, and personal tragedy.

childproof: Incapable of being opened by a child or of doing harm to a child.

communicable: Capable of being passed from one person to another, as a disease.

fire extinguisher: An appliance containing fire-stopping chemicals to spray onto a fire.

fire-resistant: Able to keep from burning or flaming for a long time.

first aid: Immediate and temporary care given to the victim of an accident or sudden illness until the services of a physician can be obtained.

hazard: A dangerous item or situation.

patient: Any sick person.

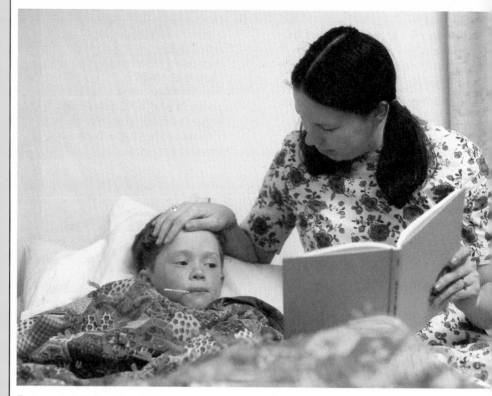

Being sick is no fun. Having someone read to you can help.

victim of an accident or sudden illness until a doctor arrives. Some hospitals offer first aid courses. Schools supply first aid instruction through home economics, health, and physical education classes, or through student organizations. The Red Cross offers complete courses in first aid.

a quick review

1. What are the three leading causes of accidental death in homes in the United States?
2. What are some ways to prevent falls around your home?
3. What are some ways to prevent fires around your home?
4. What are some ways to prevent poisoning around your home?
5. Describe five steps a family may take to maintain good family health and avoid illnesses.

Housing careers involve many different and varied fields. Many building contractors and architects gained early practical experience working on summer construction crews. Home economists often gain firsthand experience in 4-H Club work or as teachers' assistants in high school. Whatever your interest or experience may be, there are many part-time or summer job possibilities in career areas related to the home.

HOME DESIGN AND CONSTRUCTION CAREERS

Entry Level

A *construction worker* usually begins as a member of a *crew,* a group of workers working together, helping to build homes or apartments. On-the-job training and experience in construction can lead to higher wages and supervisors' jobs.

A *painter* may be in business alone or may work as a member of a paint crew. Painters sometimes specialize in painting the outsides or interiors of homes and other buildings.

Paraprofessional Training or Licensing Required

Plumbers install and repair pipes that are needed for water, air, and steam. They may be self-employed or work for plumbing contractors.

Electricians work with the electrical systems in homes or in industry.

CHAPTER 24
Careers in Housing

Interior Designer
Pat Capewell:

"When I was in high school, my favorite courses were the ones in art. I especially enjoyed the design projects. One of those projects was the design of any room in a house. I designed my own room, using my furniture. I had such fun. I changed the colors completely and totally rearranged the furniture. After I had sketched the design, I liked it so much that I talked my parents into letting me put my plan into action. I took everything out of the room, painted it, made new curtains, and rearranged the furniture. It looked like a new room. And my friends thought it was just marvelous.

"One of my neighbors heard of my project and asked if I'd like to talk with her about her job as an interior designer. I didn't know what a designer was, but I quickly became interested. She showed me her shop and asked if I'd like to visit a client with her. I did. And I followed that project by talking with her often. I knew then that I wanted to be an interior designer.

"After high school I went to design school for three years and then took a job as an assistant interior designer in a large

(continued)

192

They install, repair, and inspect the electrical equipment.

Carpenters or cabinetmakers work with wood. Some build kitchen cabinets or remodel old ones. Others specialize in floors or furniture.

Plumbers, electricians, and carpenters are usually trained in vocational or apprentice programs. In most states they must pass a test and be licensed.

Home-security experts sell and install burglar alarms, fire alarms, locks, or safes for the home.

Lighting specialists are employed by lighting manufacturers, engineering firms, and theaters. They may prepare educational materials on lighting, or test new products and designs.

College Education with a Professional Degree

Architects design houses or other buildings. They draw plans or scale drawings that show where every door, every window, every wall, and even every electric outlet will be. They also produce *elevations,* or drawings that show what the outside walls of the house will look like, and they specify building materials.

Landscape architects plan outdoor areas. They may design parks or the outside grounds of shopping centers, resorts, or hotels.

A *kitchen planner* designs kitchens to meet the specific needs of the client or customer. This job involves working with people such as whole-

Carpentery is a skilled craft that requires great accuracy.

An aide's job offers entry-level on-the-job training in many areas related to housing and home furnishings.

salers, retailers, manufacturers, architects, contractors, and the public.

INTERIOR DESIGN AND HOME FURNISHINGS CAREERS

Entry Level

An *aide's* job involves helping someone else do his or her job. It is often a way of learning on the job. In this career area, slipcover and drapery-maker's aides are examples. The aide works with a person who has more training and experience. Other possibilities include appliance and equipment aides and accessories and home furnishings aides.

Training or Experience Required

Drapery and slipcover sewers are craftspeople who work in this home furnishings area. They may work with a furniture company or store or have their own business.

Interior designers work with clients to help them select furnishings, accessories, wall treatments, and flooring appropriate for their homes. Training at a design school is necessary for a career in interior design.

The *home furnishings coordinator* for a department store consults with clients about their selection of furnishings. He or she may assist the customers in their selection of fabric or draperies.

department store. I loved working with clients to decorate their homes the way they wanted them to be. After a few years I became an interior decorator with the same store. Shortly after that promotion, I began working with a client who was opening his first office. Decorating an office was quite different from decorating a home. We were now interested in making the space interesting and attractive to a great many people. I became very interested in office and industrial decor.

"When I had completed my first office project, I went into business for myself. The first year was very slow, but eventually I found my first commercial client. I was to decorate the lobby of the new bank in town. I've been a commercial interior designer now for ten years, and there hasn't been one boring day."

An Institution Maintenance Career Ladder
Cleaner (entry level)
Janitor (assistant level)
Supervising Janitor (supervisory level)
Head Janitor (managerial level)
Chief Janitor (managerial level)

Construction Company Manager

Harold Byers:

"My uncle owned his own construction company, and as I was growing up I used to love to listen to his stories about his projects. When I was very young, he took me to visit only the finished projects. But as I got older, he started showing me his projects during construction. I'll never forget the first day I put on a hard hat and walked around the construction site of the Anderson Municipal Building. I was in the seventh grade, and that was when I knew I wanted to work on building projects.

"In high school, I took every woodworking course that was offered. I also took math courses and mechanical drawing. When I turned seventeen, my uncle got me a summer job with a construction crew that was building an apartment building. That first summer I just assisted one of the other crew members, but I learned a lot. When I went back the next summer, I was a regular member of the crew. Each day I got my assignments from our crew chief. We spent all day at the site. Only when it rained hard did we have to quit.

(continued)

A CAREER FOR YOU?

There are many different kinds of careers related to housing and home furnishings. Not all of them are discussed in this chapter. You can use this chart to find career areas that involve the things you like to do.

Work with People

Antique Dealer	Community Planner	Housing Teacher
Appliance Dealer	Furniture Showroom	Interior Decorator
Architect	Receptionist	Paint Dealer
	Home Economist	

Work with Aesthetics

Color Analyst	Home Furnishings Editor	Photographer
Florist	Interior Designer	Textile Designer
Furniture Designer	Landscape Designer	Wallpaper Designer

Work with Things

Appliance Repairer	Engineer	Mover
Cabinetmaker	Gardener	Nursery Worker
Carpenter	Hardware Buyer	Plumber
Carpet Installer	Janitor	Refinisher
Drapery Maker	Lathe Operator	Telephone Installer
Electrician	Loom Operator	Wallpaper Hanger

Work with Information and Data

Bookkeeper	Chemist	Engineer
Builder	Contractor	Shipping Clerk
Building Inspector	Drafter	Tax Assessor

Work Out-of-doors

Firefighter	House Painter	Sanitation Worker
Forester	Mason	Surveyor
Gardener	Pool Cleaner	Tree Surgeon
Horticulturist	Roofer	Trucker

Buyers for stores must evaluate many different products.

Many *photographers* specialize in photographing furniture displays for books, magazines, or brochures. This career requires photography skills, artistic skills, and creativity.

College Education with a Professional Degree

A *buyer* for a department store or home furnishings store is responsible for purchasing merchandise. Purchases are made either from the manufacturer or the wholesaler. The buyer decides what and how much to buy. Buyers must be aware of the latest trends. Many of the large stores have their own training programs for those persons with a college degree who are selected for the program.

A *consultant* in a large architectural firm meets with clients to discuss their needs. He or she discusses the alternatives for building materials with the family and then explains the needs of the family to the architect. The consultant also explains the builder's concerns to the family. This kind of consultant often has a degree in home economics and has taken specific courses in architecture, construction, and drafting.

HOME MAINTENANCE CAREERS

Entry Level

A *housekeeper* goes into a family's home for a specified amount of time

"After high school I signed on with my uncle's firm. I continued working with the construction crew for many years. In the winter we weren't able to do a lot of work because of the weather, so I picked up some college courses in business.

"As I became more interested in business, I began asking questions about the office procedures of the firm. And in my spare time, I used to assist the office workers and study the business records. Eventually my uncle began discussing deals with me.

"When my uncle retired, he asked me to manage the firm. It's a lot bigger now, and I have plans for it to continue growing."

An Interior Design Career Ladder

entry level:

- Apprentice drafter
- Aide in upholstery, drapery making, furniture finishing

assistant level:

- Junior designer
- Commercial drafter
- Upholsterer, drapery maker, furniture finisher

professional/managerial level:

- Interior design educator
- Interior designer
- Home furnishings buyer

195

Real Estate Broker

Johnson Breuer:

"When I was in high school, I wasn't sure what I wanted to do for a career. I always just assumed I would go to college, so in high school I took all the academic courses. My father was a chemical engineer, and he had always wanted me to become one. When I entered college, I did so as a chemical engineering major.

"After college my first job was with a large chemical company on the East Coast. My assignments in the beginning mostly involved monitoring the equipment on the lines. Whenever any of it malfunctioned, I had to fix it or arrange to have it fixed. Of course, many of the problems happened at night, and I would be called into the plant.

"After a few years of monitoring equipment, I began to design equipment to do particular tasks. That involved travel to various other plants. After designing the equipment lines for several new plants and considerable travel away from my home and family, I requested a transfer to the central engineering division.

"In that position I was supervising several engineers and not doing as much traveling. I continued

196 *(continued)*

each week to clean and perform other household chores.

A *resident manager* lives in the apartment complex that he or she manages. The manager is responsible for the daily operation, maintenance, or care, and rental of the apartments.

Maintenance workers are often part of a crew that goes into a home and thoroughly cleans it. Each member may have a specific job, such as cleaning carpets or washing windows. Maintenance workers learn on the job. This job can lead to supervising the crew or owning the business.

CAREERS IN REAL ESTATE

Paraprofessional Training or Licensing Required

A *real estate salesperson* finds homes to be sold and people to buy the homes. Real estate salespeople must take a course and pass an examination to qualify for a license. This license is required in all states.

A *broker* is an independent business owner who, in addition to selling real estate, sometimes rents and manages properties. A broker must pass a comprehensive examination to qualify for the broker's license. All real estate salespeople must work for a broker.

COMMUNICATIONS AND TEACHING

College Education with a Professional Degree

Some *home economists* who teach in high schools and colleges specialize in housing and interior design. These teachers have a college degree in

Work with an appliance manufacturer may involve writing, product testing, advertising, or public relations.

A housing and home furnishings editor keeps up to date on the latest design trends and newest products. Her magazine is an important source of this information for the public.

home economics and special course work in these areas.

Extension home economists work through the Department of Agriculture and a state college to provide information about the home. The work can include teaching, writing, and appearing on radio or television.

A home economist employed by an equipment company may teach sales representatives how to use a new piece of kitchen equipment. The job can also include answering consumer questions and preparing the care and use information that accompanies a new piece of equipment.

Some *writers* and *editors* specialize in areas relating to the home. They usually have a college degree in journalism or home economics. They may work for newspapers, magazines, or book publishers. Or they may be in companies that sell consumer products related to the home.

in that position for five years. While there, I began taking some night courses in real estate. Then I began selling real estate. I liked it so much that I resigned from the chemical firm and went into real estate full time. I was lucky. I sold my first house two months after I started. And after that, it seemed easy. Oh, I put in a lot of hours, but it was fun.

"I continued taking courses and in two years passed my broker's exam. A year later I went into business for myself. I now have five agents selling for me, and business looks good."

▶ **Words to Know**

consultant: An expert in a particular field who advises others about a project.

contractor: A person who builds or supervises the building of homes or industrial buildings.

design: A creative or imaginative plan.

maintenance: The upkeep or care of a home or industrial building.

manufacturer: The person or firm that makes a particular product.

paraprofessional: A person with some training or experience in a particular field who assists professional people working in that field.

a quick review

1. List five careers that are related to housing that do not require a college education.
2. List five entry-level careers that are related to housing.
3. Describe the jobs of three different designers.

197

Unit 4
RESOURCES

CHAPTER 25
Setting Goals

In a game, whether it is soccer or checkers, the goal is the aim or objective you try to reach. You have goals for your life, too. In life you make plans to help you reach those goals. When you were little, you may have said, "When I grow up I want to be President or the first person to go to Mars." Those were definite long-range goals. You would have had to set many short-range goals in order to reach them. And if you did reach them, you would continue to set more goals. Even Presidents and astronauts do. In the course of living, you set not just one goal for a lifetime, but many goals.

Knowing what you want is not always easy, but setting goals can help you. If you think you would like to dance with a ballet company and climb a mountain and open a restaurant, you have to make some choices. You cannot do all three at the same time of your life. (Perhaps you could manage to do them one after another, but not all three at once!) In the meantime, you can plan toward goals you can reach *now* as you work toward your larger goals.

SHORT-RANGE GOALS

A short-range goal is one that can be reached in a brief period of time. If you want to lose 5 pounds, catch up on letters to friends, strengthen your backhand drive, or paint your room, you can do so in a short amount of time. The end is in sight even as you begin.

There are often many ways to work toward a short-range goal. Anna, Carlos, and Kurt are running for the office of class president. They each campaign in the way that suits them best. Their campaign posters reflect their personalities, and the issues they support reveal their special interests.

• Anna favors a dialogue between students and the administration. She is looking into past issues of the school newspaper for background information. She explains her point of view in interesting articles that she writes for the paper.

• Carlos feels that the greater part of the school's sports program should be extracurricular. He is talking to coaches in other schools in his county to hear their opinions on the subject. Carlos is lining up all the school's athletes to campaign for him.

• Kurt thinks the conditions in the cafeteria are the most important issue and is polling the students and their parents to learn their present feelings. Kurt meets and talks to as many people as he can.

Each of these young people has the short-range goal of winning the election, but each looks at the office from a different viewpoint and uses different methods.

Setting realistic goals helps you get what you want in life. Short-range goals are reached quickly. Long-range goals are reached step by step.

Advice from the Cheshire Cat

When Alice in Wonderland was deciding where to go, she asked the Cheshire Cat, "Would you tell me, please, which way I ought to go from here?"

"That depends a good deal on where you want to get to," said the Cat.

"I don't much care where," said Alice.

"Then, it doesn't matter which way you go," replied the Cat.

201

WHERE WILL YOU BE IN TEN YEARS?

What do you think you might be doing five and ten years from now? Thinking about what you would like your life to be like may help you form specific goals. Then you will be able to start planning how to get the training or experiences you need to reach those goals. Darrell and Pam each gave some thought to their futures. Here are some of their ideas:

Darrell W.

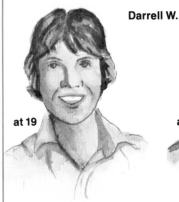

at 19

- attending junior college
- working at a part-time job
- saving up for my own car
- meeting lots of people

at 25

- probably married
- starting a family
- doing a good job as a programmer
- owning my own car
- owning a house

Pam B.

at 19

- working at a job with room for promotion
- living in my own apartment
- owning my own car
- having fun on weekends— going places

at 25

- advanced in my career— more pay and responsibility
- traveling a lot
- owning a condominium
- driving a nicer car

Long-Range Goals: Set Early or Found Later?

Many famous people set out early in life toward their chosen goal. Some people show special interest and talent as youngsters. Examples include the composer Mozart, the baseball player Babe Ruth, the circus producer P. T. Barnum, and the scientist Marie Curie. But many other famous achievers did not set out to do the particular thing for which they are now famous. They began with strong interests

(continued)

LONG-RANGE GOALS

Most often, long-range goals are related to your future work. In order to keep up the effort needed to reach a long-range goal, you must feel that the goal is important. If baseball means little to you, you will probably not aim to be a sports announcer or team manager. Think of people you admire when you consider what you want to do with your life. Who does things that you feel are interesting and worthwhile? Look into the various kinds of jobs related to what interests you. Your school counselor and librarian have many books and pamphlets about the kinds of jobs related to certain interests. If you know someone doing the kind of work you would like, ask that person about her or his job. What kind of training was useful? What about the job is enjoyable? What about it has turned out differently than expected? Look into as many sources of information as possible to help you select your work goals.

Next, consider your abilities. Where do your talents lie? Suppose you have a strong interest in live theater but find it impossible to memorize a script. You could paint or design scenery, direct lighting, do makeup or costuming, advertise the play, or write plays. In some way, you can use *your* special abilities.

Long-range goals are easier to consider if they are broken into smaller steps. Gina's long-range goal is to be a dental assistant. She finds out that the junior college in her city offers a two-year dental assistant program for high school graduates. She will need certain courses in high school so she can enroll in the program. In particular, she needs math and science courses. As a result, to gain her long-range goal she has the short-range goal of studying well in her high school math and science courses.

But that is only part of the picture. Suppose Gina does so well in the dental assistant program that she finds she is able to do far more than she had first planned. She might then decide to become a dentist, which is a change in her long-range goal. On the other hand, she may find that although she does well in her efforts to achieve her first goal, her hobby of photography is developing into another career opportunity. Her studies in math and science have helped her in this field, too. She is seriously considering the possibility of changing her goals to something very different from what she had first planned.

It is best to be open to the possibility of change without losing sight of your original plans. A long-range goal gives direction to your choice of short-range goals, but it should not prevent you from being flexible. There may be changes in your life or your interests that make it desirable to alter your original plans. Or there may be new opportunities that lead you to change your choice of career or life-style. Whatever your future brings, the habit of setting short-range goals in order to reach long-range goals will help you.

a quick review

1. Explain what a goal is. How does having goals for the future help you?
2. Give three examples of how short-range and long-range goals differ.
3. Name three things that can help you set a long-range goal.
4. Why is it necessary to be flexible in setting long-range goals?
5. Choose a short-range goal for yourself, and then list three things that could happen to cause a change in your plans. Give three alternate plans to allow for these changes. Is it still possible to reach the original goal?

that determined certain early goals. Reaching these original goals helped them set new goals that led them on to further success. Here are some famous people who started off in one job and then switched to something very different:

- Thomas Paine: corsetmaker to famous pamphleteer
- Henry David Thoreau: pencil maker to writer
- Carol Burnett: usher to actress
- Harry Truman: hatmaker to President of the United States
- Bob Hope: boxer to comedian
- Desi Arnaz: bird-cage cleaner to musician
- Perry Como: barber to singer
- Sean Connery: bricklayer to actor

▶ **Words to Know**

long-range goal: A goal that will take a fairly long time to reach.

pamphlet: A very slim book with a paper cover; a booklet.

realistic goal: A goal that is possible to reach.

short-range goal: A goal that will take a short time to reach.

CHAPTER 26
Decisions for Everyday Living

Every day you face many decisions. Most of these are simple choices with little need for deep thought. "Will I have chocolate milk or orange juice?" "Do I want to watch this television program or that one?" "Will I buy the pen with the blue ink or the one with black?" On the other hand, there are times when it is necessary to solve a problem. As the word *solve* hints, some thought and consideration are necessary. "Should I use my savings to buy the bicycle I need for a paper route?" "Could I be on the soccer team this year even though I was sick a lot last year?" "What can *I* do to really help cut down pollution in my town?" Whether you are making an easy decision or solving a serious problem, how you approach it is important.

DECISION-MAKING STYLES

There are four ways of approaching decision making that are well known and easily recognized. Can you see yourself in any of the following examples?

• Deciding by not deciding is one of the most common ways to "make a decision." Can't-Make-Up-My-Mind Mary does this well: "I'd really like to, but . . . I don't know. Maybe it's not such a good idea. But I know I'd enjoy it." She puts off deciding until the opportunity has passed and the choice is no longer hers.

CAN'T-MAKE-UP MY-MIND MARY | **HYSTERICAL HARRY** | **IN-A-RUT RUTH** | **I'LL-GO-ALONG -WITH-YOU JOE**

• Deciding under self-made stress is second nature to Hysterical Harry. He rushes into a decision simply to get it over with, anxious about having to choose. He acts on impulse. He is not always happy with his decisions, but he gets them out of the way.

• Deciding by force of habit is letting one past choice set the pattern for all future choices of the same kind. Even though you change and your tastes and interests change, that old standby decision is usually used. In-a-Rut Ruth has little variety in her life. No matter what it is, if she made a choice about it in the past, she will do just the same this time.

• I'll-Go-Along-With-You Joe decides by using other people's decisions: "Whatever you want to do is all right by me. I don't care one way or the other. What does everybody want to do?" He does not weigh the pros and the cons or even his own likes and dislikes. The decision is out of his hands—by his own choice.

You can learn to make decisions in a thoughtful, intelligent way. On the following page is a sensible, step-by-step approach to decision making that will help you work out the problems you face. Try using this approach the next time you have a problem to solve.

True or False
1. Every decision has a "cost." Making a choice limits other choices.
2. Real freedom to choose cannot exist without rules and laws.
3. Decision making is only a matter of "good common sense."
4. Sometimes a poor decision is the best teacher.
5. The more decisions a person makes, the better the decisions will be.
6. If you are afraid of making the wrong decision, you should not make any decision at all.

205

Below you will find a list of decisions that a teenager might have to make.

For each pair, list all the possible results of the two choices. Consider every possibility you can think of.

• Do homework right after school or visit with friends?
• Eat a hot fudge sundae or an apple after school?
• Practice the piano or play baseball with friends?
• Watch television or ride your bike with friends?
• Go to basketball practice or stay home?
• Rake leaves or go shopping with friends?
• When baby-sitting, play outside with the children or watch television with them?
• Bring lunch from home or eat the school lunch?
• When baby-sitting, help the children with their homework or play a game with them?
• Clean your room or leave it messy?
• Wash your hair tonight or tomorrow morning?

How can looking at the possible results of a choice help a person make a decision?

STEPS IN PROBLEM SOLVING

When you think about solving a problem, you must consider certain things in a certain order.

1. The first thing to do is to *state the problem*. What exactly is it that is troubling you? Try writing it down. Be as specific as you can—even if it means making a list of the parts of the whole problem. You might ask a friend to listen to you "think out loud," then "feed back" to you what she or he thought you said. Suppose you are having trouble getting along with your friend Robbie. Robbie's not fun to be with anymore. He often seems to be in a bad mood. Is the problem not having much in common anymore, or just a temporary bad mood? If you can clearly define what is wrong, you are already on the road to the solution.

2. *Collect all facts* you will need to solve the problem. What do you need to know about the situation? Try to be specific. Try to avoid what "somebody told somebody who told you." One of your friends may think that you envy Robbie's basketball award, but if you know that you have really lost interest in basketball, then that friend's "opinion" does not tell you anything you need to know. If you know for a fact that Robbie's schedule during basketball season is very full, you could try to find out if he's been getting enough sleep or is worried about his grades. This might explain a bad mood in a person who is usually even-tempered.

3. *Consider alternative solutions.* There is usually more than one way to solve a problem. You might ignore the difficulty in the hope that it is temporary. You might openly go to Robbie and discuss your feelings. Whatever the difficulty, there is likely to be more than one side to it.

4. *Consider the possible results or consequences.* What do you hope to achieve with your solution to the problem? Will the action you take affect others? Is it possible that Robbie is not aware how his attitude is affecting your friendship? It may help to clear the air if you show your concern. Possibly Robbie may feel you are criticizing him. How do you express your feelings? Do you know your own motives? If you decide not to say or do anything at this time, will things get worse instead of better?

5. Having completed the first four steps, you are at the point of actually deciding. Yes, *make the decision*. If it helps make things clear in your own mind, write out your decision—you can even put a date on it! Do not let circumstances decide for you.

6. When you have made up your mind what to do, *act on your decision*. Do it. This may seem too obvious to mention, but often people make a decision in their mind, yet fail to actu-

ally do what they have carefully decided on. Your decision has no strength until you act upon it.

7. An important part of the problem-solving process is to *evaluate, or judge, the results.* If you take notice of how things turn out this time, it will help you in your next effort. You may find that you were skilled and *tactful,* or able to speak without hurting his feelings, when you talked to Robbie about the problem. You may find a need to be more careful in gathering your facts. Evaluating the results of your problem solving helps you build confidence. It makes problem solving something that you are able to take in your stride.

PROBLEMS WITH PROBLEM SOLVING

As you practice making a decision or using the steps in problem solving, you may have to *cope* with, or deal with, attitudes that can cause problems of their own. Some people may find it difficult to take advice or face up to a problem. Others may have trouble taking action because they are afraid of making a mistake.

Refusing to Face a Problem. It is important to recognize that refusing to face a problem will not make it go away. There are usually signs that tell you that a problem lies ahead. If you start second-year French thinking that

Evaluating a Decision
Evaluate a decision you made in the last two months.

1. Were you able to clearly understand the problem?
2. Are there facts that you did not know at the time?
3. Did you have problems choosing or taking an action?
4. What consequences resulted from your action? Did you expect them?
5. Would you take the same action now?
6. Would the steps for problem solving have helped you?

Refusing to face problems makes the present problem worse. It also prevents you from strengthening your problem-solving skills.

Risk-Taking Behavior

People's personalities differ in regard to how much risk they are willing to take. For example, suppose it's Thursday and you must decide whether you will go on a hike this Saturday. You love to hike, but you don't like to hike in the rain. You find out that the chances of rain on Saturday are 2 in 10. That means there is a 20 percent chance of rain. Would you go?

Would you go if the chances were 5 in 10? How about 9 in 10? At what point would you decide that the fun of hiking wasn't worth the risk of getting wet?

Your willingness to take risks may be different according to what you

(continued)

Most kinds of problems are not new! Whatever your problem is, there is a good chance that a parent or another adult knows something about it. It makes sense to consider advice from others.

you will do well just because you got a good grade in first-year, you may become careless about studying. Then you may find yourself getting low marks on tests and having trouble answering questions in class. These are clear signals that you have a problem. If you ignore it until midterm, it will not go away. It will get much worse. Be alert for signs of *any* problem and face the problem before it gets out of hand.

Being Afraid of Making Mistakes. It is normal to be afraid of making mistakes. But every normal human being *does* make them. If you choose the wrong solution to a problem, do not let it discourage you. It is more important that you make the effort to solve the problem. Being aware of what went wrong will help you be better prepared the next time. Gerry gave up piano lessons after taking them for four years. She felt she needed more time for friends and school. However, after a few months she realized that her problem with having time for her studies and her friends was due more to poor study habits than anything else. She also realized that she needed more practice in gathering facts for decision making. You will find that you will make fewer mistakes as you keep on practicing problem-solving techniques.

Being Unable to Take Action. Some people feel that they "just can't" take action. Even though they can decide on a certain course of action, they seem unable to make themselves act on the decision. When you don't take action, circumstances act for you. Isn't it much better to step forward and do what *you* choose? Remember, you have given careful thought to deciding how best to solve your problem.

Taking Advice. A final point to be aware of in problem solving is the value of accepting advice. Often people reject advice because accepting it would mean sharing with someone the credit for solving the problem. Keep in mind that the main goal is to solve the problem. If someone else's advice is helpful, you learn from it and are better prepared for the next time. Of course, not all advice is helpful or accurate. To find out what is helpful, you need to listen, then evaluate. Refusing even to consider advice means that you may miss out on a new *insight,* or new way of viewing the problem.

a quick review

1. Describe a problem and solution that shows one decision-making style. Suggest a different solution. What points did you consider in changing the original solution?
2. What are the seven basic steps in problem solving?
3. Show how the seven problem-solving steps may be used to solve a problem that is common to teenagers.
4. What happens when you refuse to face a problem? Give an example.
5. Why should you consider the consequences that your decisions may have for others? Can you show how *not* considering these consequences can be hurtful for you as well as others?

might gain or lose. At what chance of rain would you still go if:

a) completing the hike gave you a desired award—like a Scout badge, or the chance to see a sight you've wanted to see?
b) you have a $10 bet on your ability to finish?
c) the odds were for a hurricane rather than rain?

▶ **Words to Know**
circumstances: The present situation, or events that are taking place.
consequences: The results of a decision or action.
cope: Deal with or overcome a difficult situation.
evaluate: To judge, or to decide what something is worth.
impulse: A sudden urge or idea.
insight: Knowledge of the true nature of a situation.
tactful: Able to say or do what you want without hurting people's feelings.

CHAPTER 27
What Is a Resource?

When you have a job to do, a problem to solve, or a goal to reach, you use resources. A *resource* is anything that can help you accomplish what you set out to do. It could be something you can touch—such as tools, books, or materials—or something you cannot see or feel. Abilities, family, friends, intelligence, and the environment in which you live can all be resources, too. What resources do you have?

YOU

You have youth, a fresh outlook on life, enthusiasm, and the prospect of your future. You have a high energy level—the ability to be "on the go." You have special abilities and talents. You have experiences that help shape your judgment. You have skills that enable you to perform an amazing variety of actions. You are unique and can offer what no one else can.

YOUR FAMILY

Your family supports you by filling your basic needs. The family gives you the food and shelter that you need for life. It gives you the love and emotional support that cannot be found anywhere else. Despite the ordinary conflicts that every family has, your family can be counted on to care about you as a special person.

The family is unique in human relationships. It is the basis, or foundation, for your self-identity and self-image. In other words, families teach you who and what you are. How you relate to others is established in your family relationships. How you accept yourself and others as human beings is a process begun in the family.

YOUR SCHOOL

At school there are teachers and coaches to help you learn. They try to guide your abilities and help you develop as a whole person. Your guidance counselor shares in these concerns and can help you connect your various worlds—home, school, and career. There are social opportunities at school that give you a chance to be a part of the human community. You begin to see yourself as part of a group larger than your immediate family. You meet people who have their own way of looking at life, which may be different from yours. You begin to understand the responsibility of participation. You realize the support you can offer as a citizen.

There is also the opportunity to achieve and discover in your studies. You have the chance to reach to the limit of your abilities. You can find other interests from those you have always known.

YOUR COMMUNITY

Beyond the "community" of your school are the communities of your

A resource is anything that can help you accomplish what you set out to do.

city, county, and state. There are many people who serve the community. Some are volunteers, and others are elected. Some are employed by the government and others, by private companies. Their jobs are to serve you. There are many *cultural resources* in the community, such as libraries, museums, parks and play areas, theaters, concert halls, historical buildings, gardens, and even zoos. They all add to your choice of resources. They offer you ways to enrich your leisure

Boosting Teen Earnings
What teens earn for mowing the lawn or baby-sitting has not changed much in the last ten years. Why not offer *references*, or recommendations from other people? Suppose you have already worked at a plant nursery on Saturdays or at a day-care center as a volunteer. You would then have experience and skills. With these advantages, you could reasonably ask for a higher wage.

211

Your school is an important resource for increasing your knowledge and know-how. School also offers a chance for friendship with other teens.

Your community offers you both commercial resources and cultural resources.

time. They can help you understand yourself as part of a community.

There are also *commercial resources* in your community. There are stores where goods can be bought—tools, books, and materials—to help you. If you have the hammer, nails, saw, wood, and directions, you might make a table yourself. There are also services to be bought. You might buy the wood and hire someone to use his or her tools and plans to make the table. You can reach beyond your own limited experience by using the resources of your community.

TIME

This period of your life is one in which you have free time to use. You have more free time than most working adults. Because the greater responsibilities of family and career lie ahead of you, you have more freedom for change and development. You are free to make trade-offs with your time. Will you choose to spend time developing your talent in playing the guitar, or will you get a part-time job in the record shop? Will you try out for the track team or for the award-winning drum and bugle corps?

MONEY

Money as a resource is a useful tool. You exchange your money, which you spent *your* time and ability to earn, for someone else's goods or services. As a young teen you are limited in how much you can earn. This limitation is due mainly to the lack of work opportunities for people your age, the kinds of work available to you, and the wages offered for these kinds of work. You probably give careful thought to how you acquire your money and how you spend it.

MANAGING RESOURCES

What you choose as a resource and how you manage it reflects what is important to you. For example, Karen had been wanting to learn to play her guitar for some time. She had to consider her resources at home and in the community. She had to consider her time, money, and abilities. Then she had to choose how she would use all these resources.

Karen had seen an advertisement in a magazine for lessons by mail. She sent away for more information about the lessons and their cost. While waiting for the information, she got a book from the library. The book had written instructions, photographs, chord charts, and songs. This gave her a better idea of what she would be expected to do on her own. A friend told her about a group class to be given at the local high school in the evening. The fee was to be paid at the beginning for ten weekly lessons. Her brother mentioned that the public television service was going to broadcast a series of lessons for 30 weeks. For a small fee, they would send a record and a book to go along with the televised instructions. Karen also considered private lessons and found out the cost by telephoning several music stores that advertised that service. The classified section of the newspaper had advertisements from people who would come to her home to give her lessons. These lessons would have to be paid for weekly. Karen had to decide how much time she could spend, how much she could pay, and how much she wanted to do on her own.

In this unit you will learn about managing your resources of time, school, community, and money.

a quick review

1. Name five resources you can see and touch. How can they help you?
2. Name five resources you cannot see or touch. How can they help you?
3. Give an example of how you can make a resource trade-off.
4. Do you think you can trade your resources for those of other people? If so, tell how it would work out. If not, explain why not.

Zero In on Resources

• Think of one of your human resources that has been or could be used to benefit your entire family. Have you used it to best advantage?

• Think of a famous person who had very little money as a resource. What other resources did this person use instead?

• Think of a resource that you share with another person. How often do each of you use it? Do you use it in different ways? Does one of you get more out of it?

• What would you do if you had twice as much of a resource? For example, suppose you had a library that was twice as big, or the ability to speak Spanish *and* French. How would "twice as much" change your goals?

▶ **Words to Know**

commercial resource: A resource that can be bought or sold.

cultural resource: A resource that enriches your life and reflects the nature of your community.

references: Recommendations from other people.

resource: Anything that can help you accomplish your plans.

trade-off: Using one resource in place of another.

unique: One of a kind.

CHAPTER 28
Who Has Time?

Time is one resource that everyone has in equal amounts. Robin may seem very busy rushing around and still not get very much done. Gale easily takes care of one job after another. They each have the same twenty-four hours every day. What's the difference?

Time has always been a part of your life, so it can seem strange to think of it as a *resource,* something helpful you can use. It is not tangible, not something you can see and touch. You cannot store it the way you can store food, books, or money. If you "run out of time," where can you get more? You will find that the only way to *save* time is to spend it wisely.

Planning how you will use your time makes it more likely that you can do what you have to do *and* what you want to do. You will find yourself enjoying more freedom and self-confidence. Planning your time will also help prevent many frustrations you might otherwise face if you let time slip away from you.

MANAGING YOUR TIME

How do you use *your* time resource to get the most out of twenty-four hours? A schedule can help you manage your time instead of letting circumstances take control. A *schedule* is a written plan for how you will spend your time.

My Week

	Monday	Tuesday	Wednesday	Thursday	Friday	Saturday	Sunday
7 a.m.	Get up – Catch bus	Get up – Catch bus	Get up – Catch bus	Get up – Catch bus	Get up Catch bus	Sleep late	
8 a.m.	School starts.	School starts	School starts	School starts	School starts	Go shopping	Church
9–10 a.m.							
11 a.m.		Lunch	Lunch				Dinner
noon	Lunch			Lunch	Lunch	Lunch at Joe's	Start reading book for English report
1 p.m.							
2 p.m.					School's out	School's out	Home
3 p.m.		School's out	School's out	Chorus Practice	Home		Fix food for party
4 p.m.		Home	Home	Home	Ball Practice	Ball game with South Valley	Phone Grandpa
5 p.m.		Ball Practice	Homework			Call Lee	Snack Homework
6 p.m.		Supper Call Lee	Supper Call Lee	Supper Mork & Mindy channel 8		Supper at restaurant	Watch T.V.
7 p.m.					Study for test	Shower, wash hair Press shirt	
8 p.m.		Homework	Watch T.V. special for science channel 11	Call Lee	Call Lee	Babysit for Joe Cooper	
9 p.m.						T.V. movie	Party
9:30 p.m.		Bedtime	Bedtime	Bedtime	Bedtime	Bedtime	Bedtime

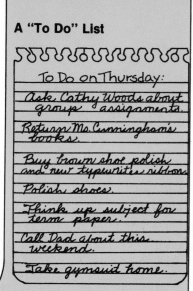

A "To Do" List

To Do on Thursday:

Ask Cathy Woods about group assignments.

Return Ms. Cunningham's books.

Buy brown shoe polish and new typewriter ribbon.

Polish shoes.

Think up subject for term paper.

Call Dad about this weekend.

Take gymsuit home.

Making a Time Schedule. Spend a few minutes making up a schedule for a week in your life. Start on a weekend afternoon or evening by jotting down what you expect to be doing for the coming week. You could write in pen all the things you have to do, such as sleeping, eating, school, music lessons, part-time job, chores at home, or club activities. Then, with a pencil, add those things you want to make time for, such as reading magazines, taking a hike, window-shopping, watching television, telephoning, or visiting a friend.

It will be to your advantage to leave some time open, with no special activity planned. Allow time for unexpected things to happen. You could also circle the "want-to-do" items that could be done some other week. Doing these things makes your schedule more *flexible,* or easily adjusted, and more *elastic,* or easily expanded. Than you can handle changes as they arise.

As you make up your schedule, it may seem that there are so many "have-to-do" items that there is no time for you to just be yourself. You need to do things that make your life more fun and interesting. Include leisure activities as you plan, so that you have time for a favorite hobby, a new friendship, or a "do-nothing" break from your studies. These are important activities. They allow you to return to your busy week refreshed and ready for whatever is ahead.

Take a moment on the next weekend to review your practice schedule. Compare it to the way you actually did use your time. You will probably find that you spent more time than you thought you would on some things, and less on others. Perhaps there were things you thought you would do that you never got around to. By comparing your plan for spending time with your actual time use, you are evaluating your schedule. You are learning how to be more realistic in your future planning. And you are learning something about yourself and the way you operate.

When someone is late for team practice, the whole team loses time. Group members need to be considerate of each other's time.

Keep a Working Calendar and a "To Do" List. Once you have made a schedule to get the "big picture," you may want to use two more tools that will help you use your time well no matter what the week holds. These two tools are a working calendar and a "to do" list.

A calendar with squares large enough for notes can improve communication between you and your family. You can write on it the activities you have scheduled, such as your afternoon club meetings or sports practices, the day the big game takes place, or your baby-sitting jobs. Your family can then take note of them. They, in turn, can fill in important activities that you may not want to miss, as well as family responsibilities that you must consider.

A "to do" list will help you set *priorities,* or put your activities in the order of their importance to you. You might give highest priority to those activities that you *must* do and mark them "A." Those you *should* do have the next highest priority and can be marked "B." The ones you would *like* to do can be marked "C." You can more easily choose between two activities if one has a higher priority than the other. You can trade one activity for another if both have the same priority. This kind of choosing gives you more control over how you use your time.

VALUING OTHER PEOPLE'S TIME

Many of the decisions you make about your time will also involve the use of other people's time. As a part of a family, a club, or an athletic team, you cannot always choose the timing that would work best for you. The needs of the whole group must be considered.

When you have a meeting, a date, or a business appointment, your planning involves other people's time as well as your own. To be late or to break an appointment without telling the other person in advance causes that person to lose her or his time resource. It is as if someone borrowed a record from you and returned it with a scratch on it. Even though the scratch may not have been the other person's fault, you would be annoyed at such careless use of a resource that was not that person's own. The more skilled you become in managing your own time, the easier you will find it to be on time. This will not only please others, but will also give you more confidence in yourself.

TAME THE TIME-WASTERS

Three of the most troublesome time-wasters are procrastination, disorganization, and little pieces of time. You can begin to tame them by understanding what they are and how they steal your time.

Procrastination. Why do people put off doing something, or deciding something, until the choice is made by circumstances? Most people tend to put off what is unpleasant. For example, Maida has an important history test on Thursday, but studying for a five-chapter test is not her favorite activity. Also, Maida feels that unless she can make a very high grade, studying is not worth the time she will have to spend. So why start now? People like Maida, whose standards are high, may procrastinate out of fear of falling short of their standards. Or maybe five chapters is more than Maida thinks she can handle in three days. If a job seems too big, it is easy to feel overwhelmed and take no action.

Do a mental check the next time you find yourself procrastinating. Are you putting off something important just because you don't enjoy it? Are you delaying out of fear of not doing a first-rate job? Are you doing nothing because the task seems too large or too hard?

A good way to keep from procrastinating, for whatever reason, is to divide a task into small pieces. "Today I will study history for 20 minutes," decided Maida. "I don't have to do any more than that." The next day she again studied for 20 minutes and then stopped. The following day she planned to study for 20 minutes, but she ended up studying for 30 minutes.

She was able to study for 20 minutes a day for a week. It worked because she only had to study for a short time. And the more she studied, the less overwhelming it was. After the fourth day, she was almost positive she would do well. She studied for 1 hour the night before the test. That was the longest time she spent studying. Maida got an A.

Disorganization. The first thing to do in any task is get your tools together. For example, when preparing for a test, your tools may include a comfortable chair, pencils, notes from class, textbook, paper, and a determination to concentrate. Imagine two people who are going to wash identical cars. The one who gathers the necessary equipment before beginning will probably finish first. The other will have to go back to the house for the sponge after bringing out the bucket of soapy water. When the car is ready to be rinsed, there will be a search for the nozzle end of the hose and a struggle to bring it to the driveway. Then there will be another trip back into the house for rags to dry off the car.

The second thing to do is to decide in advance how you will approach the problem. Should you wash the car roof first, or the hood? When you have a test coming up, should you study vocabulary first, or review your notes? Sometimes there is a way to order steps that makes a task easier. Sometimes the order itself doesn't matter. In that case, deciding what you will do first, next, and last helps you cover the entire task without forgetting steps.

Little Pieces of Time. In one minute there are 60 seconds that can quickly add up to opportunity. There are many things that can be done in less than 300 seconds (5 minutes). Try timing yourself. Once you develop the habit of making use of those little pieces of time that are usually lost, you will be surprised at what you can do without much extra effort. Look at the third column on page 218 for examples.

STARTING AND FINISHING

Sometimes a certain task turns out to be different from how you thought it would be. It may be harder or take longer than you expected. When this happens, you may begin to wonder if the task makes good use of your time.

Why does this happen? Perhaps the priority was not high. Or maybe you have had doubts about how important it was for some time. Maybe you set the goal too high or are not well prepared.

If it is a job to which you have given a high priority, you should probably stay with it. If you keep at it, you will have a sense of achievement when you finish.

The job might involve participation in an organization, such as the basketball team or the drama club. In that case, it may help to talk with the sponsor or your parents.

As you practice scheduling your time and setting priorities, you will

Inch by Inch
Explain the meaning of the expression "Inch by inch, it's a cinch. Yard by yard, it's really hard." Think of a time in your life when you found this saying to be true.

When a project takes a long time, ask a friend to help. Finishing the project will give both of you a sense of achievement.

Don't paint yourself into a corner with an impossible schedule.

piano lessons, working part-time, or raising tropical fish to sell.

Sometimes it makes sense not to finish a job. Thinking carefully about a task and then deciding not to go on with it is not the same as being a quitter. A quitter gives up without good reason, for selfish reasons, through laziness or fear of not living up to someone else's expectations.

You might ask yourself some questions about what you hope to achieve through a task. Remind yourself of your original goals. Ask yourself, "Is this activity the best way to reach my goal? Could I reach the same goal another, better way? Is the goal specific enough for me to accomplish it in the time I have set? If I stopped at this point, would I be satisfied?"

There are times in life when you learn from such decisions. If you can decide when to quit—or when not to—you will be better able to make good decisions in the future.

be better able to judge whether you should stay with something or let it go. This applies to specific tasks, such as washing the car on a cloudy day, for example, or building a new bookcase. It is also true for ongoing activities such as continuing in the scouting program, taking another year of

a quick review

1. What does it mean to use time as a resource?
2. Describe a tool of time management mentioned in this chapter. Tell how it is used.
3. How does your time involve other people's time? Give an example.
4. Select one of three time-wasters and tell how you would tame it.
5. Before you begin an activity, think about whether you are likely to finish it. How does thinking this way relate to using time as a resource?

The question "Where do you live?" usually has two answers. Home is the house or apartment in which you live. Home is also your *community*, your city or town.

Your community is more than a place to live and go to school. Think of all the different groups and buildings and businesses that make up your community. Many of them can be important resources for you.

Each community is different. But any community provides you with resources. Pretend you are a tourist visiting your community for the first time. You will probably be pleasantly surprised. You may have known about the playground, the newspaper, and the library, but not about the visiting nurse service, the antique store, or the zoo. You may be surprised at the number of places where you can listen to live music, see a piece of history, or buy fresh eggs.

People are also one of a community's resources. There may be someone nearby who can teach you a craft. Or you may find someone with a job like the one you want someday.

To take advantage of these resources, you have to know what they are, where they are, and how to use them. You must become *resourceful,* or "good at thinking of ways to do things." The more resourceful you become, the more satisfying and interesting your life will be.

CHAPTER 29
School and Community

There are programs and activities in your community offered to you by your school, local government, religious organizations, and service clubs. Make it a point to find out what is going on around you. Getting involved gives you insight into yourself and other people. It is a positive way to spend time, have

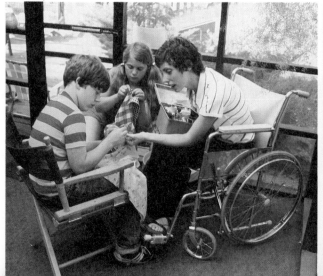

fun, and feel that you belong. Allow your community to give you what it has to offer.

As you learn more about community organizations, you will find out that many depend on volunteers. *Volunteers* are people who work without pay. You may find a group with whom you would like to work as a volunteer. If you are able to do it, you will have a valuable experience. While you are helping an organization that you feel is important, you will also be

- helping yourself and the people who live nearby
- learning more about an area that interests you
- getting to know people who share your interest
- finding out how members of a group work together

Volunteers can work with children or old people, beautify the community, help out the handicapped, start a conservation project, or build a park.

Strange as it sounds, you can make a major contribution to the attractiveness of your community by doing nothing! Do nothing to either spoil or destroy the community. People who cause damage for no reason are called *vandals*. A building or public object destroyed by vandals is ugly, and it makes everything around it look less attractive. Littered sidewalks and streets have the same effect. Remember, the community is your home—inside and out.

Schools offer a wide range of programs. Although most take place within the school building, some use the resources of the community. Find out not only what courses are taught in your school, but also how they are taught. You may be in for some surprises. For example, you may discover that there is a biology class that meets at a hospital lab one day a week. Or there may be a class that spends part of its time working in a nursery school so that it can study child growth and development.

When you are deciding which courses you are going to take, keep in mind that this is a time to explore new worlds as well as to learn more about familiar ones. Take a course on

a subject about which you know very little. It may turn out to be a course that you find fascinating. One way to prepare for the rapid changes going on in our society is to introduce yourself to unfamiliar ideas.

a quick review

1. What makes up a community?
2. How do communities differ? How are they alike?
3. Why do some people choose to work as volunteers in the community?
4. How can you contribute to your community by "doing nothing"?
5. How do some school classes use community resources?

CHAPTER 30
The Money Maze

Dana is surprised to see her younger sister Staci ride up on a new ten-speed bike that Staci has just bought with her own money. Dana is surprised because she knows that she and Staci get the same allowance. Dana also knows she makes more money delivering papers than Staci does baby-sitting. How can Staci afford to buy a bike when Dana has to borrow money to buy Mom a birthday present? In fact, Staci always seems to have plenty of money!

IT IS EASY IF YOU PLAN

How can you get money? One way is an allowance. But there are also three other ways you may not have thought about: earnings from a job, interest from savings in a bank, and money gifts. Some income you can count on, while other income is unexpected. Here is how the kinds of income differ.

You Can Count on Your Allowance. If you receive an allowance, it is an earning you can count on in exchange for responsibilities you hold at home. It pays for things such as school expenses, entertainment, and sometimes even clothes. It is an earning that can increase as you grow older and assume more responsibilities.

A Job Is Yours for the Looking. To earn money from a job, you of course first have to find one. You can start by looking around for a job that already exists, like delivering groceries or newspapers. Or create your own job! Begin by asking yourself, "What do I already know how to do? Am I good with children? Do I have a green thumb? Am I handy with a hammer? Am I a champion cookie baker?" Next, turn your skills into a job by thinking about who would pay for your services. Consider your family, friends, and neighbors.

Earn Interest While You Save. When you put money into a bank, the bank pays you for the right to use that money until you withdraw it.

The fee the bank pays you is called *interest*. As long as your money is in the bank, you earn interest.

Money Surprises from Family or Friends. Gifts are usually unexpected, but they are still important earnings to consider. Money gifts come at various times, such as holidays, birthdays, or graduation.

SPEND SMART . . . SAVE SMART!

Are you often broke and in need of money? Do you rarely have money left for savings? Then you are probably a spender, not a saver. If you are a spender, you need a *spending plan*. A

A WEEK'S EXPENSES

THE BIG DIFFERENCE

Staci packed lunch most days; Dana always bought lunch.

Staci walked to school in good weather; Dana always slept to the last minute and had to catch the bus.

Dana bought a snack every day; Staci usually snacked at home.

Dana went to two movies; Staci saw one movie and spent another evening with friends.

Staci planned ahead and made Mom's present; Dana bought a present at the last minute.

Staci had money left to save; Dana ended up borrowing.

	Staci	Dana
Lunch	$1.80	$3.00
Transportation	.50	2.50
Snacks	1.00	2.00
Entertainment	3.50	7.00
Mom's present	1.50	2.50
A Week's Expenses	$8.30	$17.00

Create Your Own Job!

Here are a few ideas to get you started.

Jobs with children:
- Baby-sitting or helping with child care.
- Walking younger children home from school.
- Helping at a children's party by decorating, organizing games, and so on.
- Tutoring.

Jobs with plants and gardens:
- Growing and selling plants, herbs, flowers, vegetables.
- Gardening, mowing lawns.
- Watering plants when owner is away.
- Shoveling snow, raking leaves.

Jobs with pets:
- Pet sitting, pet grooming, dog training, dog walking.

Recycling jobs:
- Collecting newspapers and aluminum cans for recycling.
- Making fireplace logs from newspapers.

Food jobs:
- Baking your specialty: cakes, cookies, pizza.
- Grocery shopping.

Handy-helper jobs:
- Repairing and painting fences.
- Washing cars, washing windows.

227

You can control how much you spend for items such as movies.

Let Your Goals Guide You. Every successful spending plan is based on clearly defined goals—things you want very much. Such goals can be short-term wants such as a new pair of flashy shoes, contact lenses, or a vacation with your best friend's family. Goals can also be long-term ones, such as a college education, your own plant store, or your own car. Whatever your goals are, they probably require more money than you have right now. That is why you design a spending plan. Decide which goals are most important to you and work toward them first.

Examine Your Expenses. Expenses fall into two categories: fixed and variable. *Fixed expenses* are those that you must pay regularly. Payments usually vary little in amount from one payment to the next. Many of your fixed expenses are for basic needs such as lunch or transportation to school. When you become an adult, you will find that basic needs like food, clothing, and shelter make up the most important parts of your plan. *Variable expenses,* on the other hand, vary greatly from week to week and from person to person. These expenses are for items you want, not those you need. Such items include, for example, records, movies, vacations, hobbies, even savings. Since these items are wants, not needs, you can control how much you spend.

What Is Interest?

If you have $100 in the bank and the bank pays you 5 percent interest, at the end of the year you will have $105. You have earned $5.

$100.00 (money in the bank)
×.05 (percent of interest)
$ 5.00 (interest, or money the bank pays you)

228

spending plan is simply a "road map" for using the money you have so that you can get the things you want. Designing a plan for yourself is not difficult. It simply takes a little time and thought. You must know your needs, evaluate your wants, decide on your own personal goals, and examine your expenses.

DESIGN A SPENDING PLAN THAT IS RIGHT FOR YOU

Now you are ready to make your own spending plan. Try it out for a week or so. Then evaluate it and revise it until it works just right.

What Is Your Present Spending Pattern? First, chart your present spending pattern for a typical week. List your income. Remember to include unexpected items such as gifts of money. Next, enter all your week's expenses: the fixed ones like school lunches, the variable ones like a movie ticket, and your regular savings. Add up your expenses and compare them to your income. If your expenses are more than your income, decide how you can either lower them or earn more money.

Once you know your spending habits, plan your spending for next week. If you need extra income, create an extra job. If your expenses are too high, see where you can cut them. Now begin charting your expenses and your spending week by week. Compare what you actually spend against your plan. You may be surprised. Chances are, you will discover money you didn't know you had!

The Best Plans Always Include Savings. When you design your budget, remember to include savings. Then, save regularly. That is the only way to be sure you will have enough money to reach your long-term goals. Also, you need savings for unexpected expenses, such as having your bike repaired.

A well-designed spending plan and a savings account at a bank put you in control of your money.

Record Your Expenses

Keep a record of your income and expenses for a month. Use the outline below or develop one of your own.

SAMPLE EXPENSE RECORD

1. *Income*
   Allowance
   Earnings
   Gifts, loans, others
   Total Income

2. *Fixed Expenses*
   Lunch
   Transportation
   School Supplies
   Clothes
   Club dues
   Total Fixed Expenses

3. *Variable Expenses*
   Recreation
   Snacks
   Personal grooming items
   Bicycle repairs
   Hobbies
   Gifts
   Contributions
   Sporting goods
   Books and magazines
   Others
   Total Variable Expenses

4. *Savings*

BEYOND THE PIGGY BANK

The amount of interest you can earn on savings of $75.00 depends on where you save and for how long.

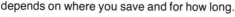

	Piggy Bank	Commercial Bank	Savings and Loan Association	Checking Account	One-Year Savings Club
Interest Rate	None	5%	5¼%	None	4½%
After 1 year:	$75.00	$78.75	$78.94	$75.00	$78.38
After 5 years:	$75.00	$95.72	$96.87	$75.00	

Opening a Savings Account? Ask These Questions:
  • How much do I need to open a savings account?
  • How much interest will I earn?
  • Can I withdraw my money any time I want?
  • Do I need the name of a parent or guardian on the account?

Watch Your Savings Grow. To be a successful saver, you must find a special place to keep your savings. You will want your money to be far away so that you will not be tempted to spend it. A piggy bank just will not do! It is too easy to borrow money from a piggy bank. You intend to pay it back, of course, but you probably will not.

So instead of a piggy bank, find an official spot for your savings, like a bank savings account or some other type of savings plan. Your savings will be harder to reach, and they will earn interest, too. There are many kinds of savings plans, and one will work for you.

Your Own Passbook Savings Account. One way to save money and earn interest is with a passbook savings account. Commercial banks, savings banks, and savings and loan associations all offer this kind of account. These businesses differ, however, in the amount of interest they pay you. Under federal government rules, savings banks and savings and loan associations can pay you ¼ percent more interest than commercial banks.

When you open a *passbook savings account,* you receive your own passbook. Every time you put money in the bank (make a *deposit*) or take money out (make a *withdrawal*), the bank records the amount in your passbook. The bank also records in the passbook all the interest you receive on your savings. Passbook savings accounts have several advantages. You can open an account with just $5 or $10. You can make a deposit at any time. You can also withdraw money just by taking your passbook to the bank. And you earn money in the form of interest by allowing the bank to hold your money for you.

Savings Clubs. Savings clubs are great ways to save for special occasions. There are Christmas Clubs, Vacation Clubs, or clubs for special goals. Most clubs are one-year plans that work in the following way:

1. You decide in advance how much you want to save. Say that it is now June and you want to save $300 for a trip next summer.
2. You go to your local bank and ask to open a Vacation Club account. Your banker will tell you how often to make payments into the account. Club payments are usually due every two weeks.
3. The amount of each payment is based on your making 25 equal payments a year. For example, say you wanted to save $300. Dividing 300 by 25 gives 12. So the amount of each payment would be $12.
4. At the end of one year you get all the money you put into the club plus interest. Say the bank is offering 4 ½ percent interest. Over the year you have saved $300. Multiplying 300 times 0.045 gives 13.5. So you have earned $13.50 in interest. The bank pays you your $300 plus your $13.50 interest, or $313.50. Have a nice trip!

a quick review

1. What are the four sources of income listed in this chapter?
2. What is interest?
3. What are the fixed expenses in your spending plan?
4. Are wants a fixed or a variable part of your spending plan?
5. If you wanted to save $100 for one year, which method would you choose?

231

CHAPTER 31
Your Consumer Buying Power

Just who are consumers? A *consumer* is anyone who buys goods or services. *Goods* are any items for sale. *Services* are tasks that other people do for you, such as repair work or handling your telephone calls. Long ago, people made at home many of the things they needed and wanted. They therefore knew exactly the quality of these goods. Today, however, the situation is different. Now we are mainly consumers of goods and services provided by others. These goods and services are sold by individuals and companies that compete for your business. You need a great deal of information to make wise buying decisions. You need to know what a product is made of, how long it will last, and what it can do.

Many Things Say "Buy Me!" Every day you see, hear, and even smell things around you that make you want to buy. The "trigger" may be a label on a pair of jeans, a commercial with your favorite football star, the smell of cookies baking in a cookie shop, a colorful store display, or a bargain you can not pass up. Whatever the reason, you decide to buy.

Status Symbols. You have probably heard the expression "keeping up with the Joneses." It means buying the same things as your neighbors to show you are as well off as they

ADVERTISING IS ALL AROUND YOU
Can you count the advertising messages in these two scenes?

are. You may want to "keep up with" the most popular students in your school by buying the same things they have. Or you may want to impress others by buying items that no one else has. Items that you buy for these reasons are called status symbols. For many people, clothes are status symbols. For example, people may want a particular designer's name on their jeans. Other status symbols are a school letter jacket or a club pin. They deliver the message "I made the team" or "I'm in the club." Places can be status symbols, too. Your status can show in where you live, where you eat, where you shop. You might enjoy a special feeling when you carry a shopping bag from an "in" store. The bag is a status symbol.

Advertisements. Advertising is all around you. Turn on the television, listen to the radio, read a magazine, open your mail, or drive down a highway. In all these places, products are advertised. Advertising may appeal to your emotions, give you information, or offer you a free gift or a chance to win something.

Emotional advertising gives you very little information. It is not help-

Displays in stores are designed to make you stop and buy.

234

ful for making a good buying decision. For example, an ad might convince you that everyone will like you if you use Shampoo X. An informational ad tells you about the product: what it costs, where to buy it, or how to use it. Many ads today combine these approaches. Some talk not about a product but about the company that made it. These ads tell you that Company A is concerned about your community, the quality of the products you buy, and the life you live. And since the company is so concerned about you, its products must be the ones for you! Another kind of advertisement encourages you not to use too much of the product. An electric company may suggest you use less electricity. Credit card companies may tell you how to use your credit card more wisely.

Displays That Demand Your Attention. When you walk into a store, you are immediately surrounded by tempting things to buy. Stores spend a great amount of time planning the most appealing way to display goods in order to get you to stop and buy.

Impulse Purchases. Impulse purchases are those things you buy on the spur of the moment, without advance planning or thought. Certain kinds of products are likely to be impulse purchases. You will usually find them without having to look for them—in the front of the store, near the cash register, or at the end of an aisle. For instance, cosmetics and gift items are always on the first floor, and candy or gum are near the cash register. *Planned purchases,* on the other hand, are things that you usually make a trip to buy. They are often placed near the back of the store or on the top floor where you have to seek them out.

The next time you are in a store, notice what is displayed with what. Pants are often displayed with the perfectly matched sweater, the right pair of shoes, or an attractive jacket. The reason is simple. The store wants you to buy more than just the pants—maybe even the whole outfit!

Store owners realize that the longer you stay in a store, the more you will buy. So many of them create attractive surroundings, play the latest music, and even provide pleasant places to rest or eat.

SUPER SALES AND BARGAINS

Everyone loves a bargain! That is why stores always seem to be holding a sale of one kind or another.

1. The *end-of-the-season sale* is held to make room for the next season's merchandise. Sales on ski clothes often take place in February; swimsuit sales happen in July. These sales are a good time to buy, provided you know you will still like and use the items the next year.

2. The *off-season sale* is usually timed for a period when people are less likely to shop. For instance, January sales are an attempt to perk up business after Christmas. Beach towel sales may be held to improve business in the summer.

3. *"Seconds,"* or imperfect merchandise, make ideal sale items. Stores buy slightly damaged goods from a factory at low cost, then offer them to you at a low price. "Seconds" are real bargains if the flaws are few, hard to notice, and easily mended.

4. *Annual sales* are once-a-year opportunities to buy certain items on sale. Look for "white sales" of sheets in January, sewing machine sales in March, and coat sales on Columbus Day.

A word of caution: nothing is a bargain if you do not need it. Before you become a bargain buyer, ask yourself, "Would I buy it if it were not on sale? Do I really need to have it? Is it in good condition? Is this sale price really less than the regular price in another store?" If your answer to

235

Implied Warranty

"This umbrella had better be guaranteed!"

No worry! Every product sold carries an *implied warranty*. That means that if you buy, say, an umbrella that does not serve the purpose it was sold for, you do not have to keep it. Instead, you have the right to ask the store or the manufacturer for another umbrella or a refund!

Sample Limited Warranty for a Color Television

XYZ Company guarantees to the first retail purchaser that if anything goes wrong with your XYZ set within 90 days from the day you buy it—and it is our fault—we will pay your local XYZ Authorized Servicenter its regular labor charges to repair it. Additionally, we will make available new or, at our option, rebuilt replacements for parts that become defective within these time periods from the date of purchase: picture tube, two years; all other parts, one year. After the 90-day labor warranty

(continued)

these questions is yes, then your bargain is truly a bargain.

PROTECTING CONSUMERS

Today's marketplace offers you so many things to buy in so many different stores that you have a great many choices to make. With so much to decide, you will probably at some point buy something that is not what you expected. Even a familiar and famous brand can disappoint you. When this happens, you can take action. Fortunately, there are many people to guide you, agencies to write to, consumer information to help you, and even laws to protect you.

Laws Protecting Consumers. Most businesses are reliable. But some are not. The government has passed hundreds of laws to help protect you from dishonest business practices, or *consumer fraud*. A few of the laws you should know about are:

• *The Consumer Product Safety Act* protects you against the making and selling of unsafe goods. If a product is unsafe, the manufacturer must stop selling it. The manufacturer may even have to ask customers who bought it to send it back so it can be fixed or replaced. This is known as a *recall*.

• *The Truth-in-Advertising Act* protects you from unfair, false, or misleading advertisements. For example,

a manufacturer must prove that a product will perform as promised. Also, dealers cannot charge a higher price than advertised.

• *The Care Labeling Act* requires clothing manufacturers to attach to each garment a permanent label that tells you how to clean it.

Other important laws are the Fair Packaging and Labeling Act and the Child Protection and Toy Safety Act. All of these laws are enforced by powerful federal agencies such as the Food and Drug Administration, the Federal Trade Commission, and the U.S. Office of Consumer Affairs in Washington, D.C.

Warranties. A *warranty*, or guarantee, is a manufacturer's promise to you. It states what the company will do about repairing or replacing the product if it does not perform as you were led to expect. It may even promise to return your money if you are not satisfied. Any product that costs over $15.00 must carry a written warranty. This warranty must be simple to read and available to you before you buy. The law also requires that a warranty include the following:

• the name and address of the manufacturer

• what the warranty covers and what it does not cover

• where you can have your product repaired

Warranties for the same type of product may differ. Compare warranties carefully. Sometimes it is wise to pay more money for a product with a better warranty.

Will Your Complaint Be Heard?   A complaint is not a simple matter! Some complaints get fast, satisfying results. Others get no reply at all. What makes the difference? Study Bob's and Michael's letters on the next page. What did Bob do?

• He wrote only to the store. When that did not work, he gave up.
• He addressed the complaint to the store. Therefore, his letter may never reach the right person.

• His letter did not give enough information.
• His letter was emotional, angry, and threatening.

What did Michael do?

• First he went in person to the store. When that did not work, he wrote to the manufacturer.
• He wrote to the company's director of consumer relations by name. (He got the name by telephoning the company and asking for it. If that had not worked, he might have checked a business directory at a local library.)
• His letter included the following information:
    —what he bought
    —where he bought it

expires, labor charges for installing replacement parts are your responsibility. To obtain in-home warranty repairs, you must call an XYZ Authorized Servicenter and present the warranty registration card when repairs are completed

XYZ Company
250 Pioneer Avenue
Everywhere, U.S.A.

Warranty #58762

Kelly can't decide. Should she buy one record, as she planned? Or should she buy both? How do you make on-the-spot consumer decisions?

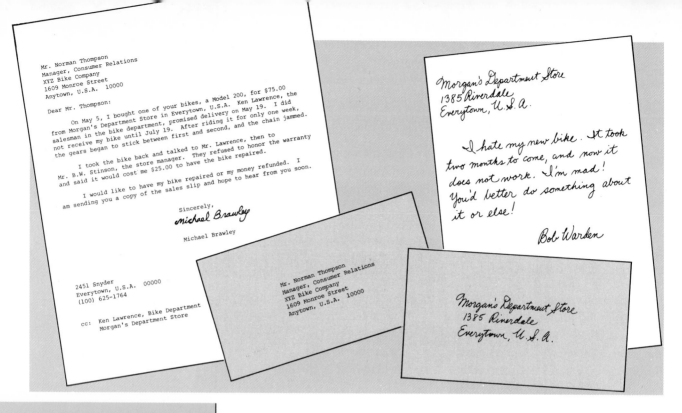

Mr. Norman Thompson
Manager, Consumer Relations
XYZ Bike Company
1609 Monroe Street
Anytown, U.S.A. 10000

Dear Mr. Thompson:

On May 5, I bought one of your bikes, a Model 200, for $75.00 from Morgan's Department Store in Everytown, U.S.A. Ken Lawrence, the salesman in the bike department, promised delivery on May 19. I did not receive my bike until July 19. After riding it for only one week, the gears began to stick between first and second, and the chain jammed.

I took the bike back and talked to Mr. Lawrence, then to Mr. B.W. Stinson, the store manager. They refused to honor the warranty and said it would cost me $25.00 to have the bike repaired.

I would like to have my bike repaired or my money refunded. I am sending you a copy of the sales slip and hope to hear from you soon.

Sincerely,
Michael Brawley
Michael Brawley

2451 Snyder
Everytown, U.S.A. 00000
(100) 625-1764

cc: Ken Lawrence, Bike Department
    Morgan's Department Store

Morgan's Department Store
1385 Riverdale
Everytown, U.S.A.

I hate my new bike. It took two months to come, and now it does not work. I'm mad! You'd better do something about it or else!

Bob Warden

Mr. Norman Thompson
Manager, Consumer Relations
XYZ Bike Company
1609 Monroe Street
Anytown, U.S.A. 10000

Morgan's Department Store
1385 Riverdale
Everytown, U.S.A.

—when he purchased it
—how much he paid for it
—what was wrong
—whom he had already complained to
—that person's reaction
—what he wanted done
—a copy of the sales receipt (do not send the original)
—his own name, address (with zip code), and phone number

• Michael sent a copy of his letter to the manager of the store where he made the purchase.

a quick review

1. What is a warranty?
2. Name ten items of information you should include in a letter of complaint.
3. Name three consumer agencies that may help you resolve a complaint.
4. What are the two main types of advertising?
5. Where should you send a letter of complaint?

Salesclerks often ask, "Cash or credit?" They want to know whether you are paying with cash or a credit card. Learn to think before you answer. It is a very important decision!

Of course you probably know all about paying with cash. But what about credit? Credit is simply a promise to pay in the future for what you buy or borrow today. Buying with a credit card is called *charging*. Credit buying can be good or bad. It depends on you!

Charging goods or services lets you use and enjoy things while you are paying for them. In other words, you can buy an item today and pay for it later. For example, you can ride your new bike while you are still paying for it. You can take advantage of special sales. You do not need to wait until you have the money saved up. Instead, you sign an agreement stating how you plan to pay. If you have a good record of paying your bills on time, the credit will be approved and the bike will be yours!

THE CREDIT CRUNCH

Saying "Charge it, please!" is easy, and buying many things at once is fun. But if you use credit too often or without thinking, you may be in a credit "crunch" at the end of the month. In other words, you may find that you have more bills to pay than

CHAPTER 32
Paying Now or Later

SHOPPING AROUND FOR CREDIT

Ann has finally found the right stereo turntable. But there is one problem. It costs $150 and she only has $100. She decides to "buy on credit." If you were Ann, which credit plan would you choose?

	March 1	April 1	May 1	June 1	Total Cost	Advantages	Disadvantages
Cash	Earns and saves $50.	Buys turntable			$150	Pays only $150	Does not have turntable for 1 month
Layaway	Puts turntable on layaway. Pays $100 down	Pays $25	Pays final $25 and takes turntable		$150	Pays only $150 Has turntable on reserve	Must wait 2 months for turntable
Thirty-Day Credit Card	Charges turntable	Pays total bill within 30 days			$150	Pays only $150 Has immediate use No finance charge	Must pay interest after 30 days
Revolving Credit	Charges turntable. Pays $15 per month plus interest for next 10 months	Pays $15.00 Interest 2.25 Total $17.25	Pays $15.00 Interest 2.03 Total $17.03	Pays $15.00 Interest 1.80 Total $16.80	$162.40 (through January)	Small monthly payments Has immediate use	Must pay interest on unpaid balance (costs $12.40) Must make payments for 10 months

cash to pay them with. This happens often to impulse buyers. If you are that kind of shopper, then credit is not for you. But if you always plan carefully before you shop, then credit can be a way to have something new that costs more than you can pay at the moment. That is a credit "plus" that you can really enjoy.

Using credit almost always costs more than paying cash. Unless you pay the full price of your purchase within a very short period of time, you have to pay a kind of interest, called a *finance charge.* This charge is the fee you pay for the privilege and convenience of buying on credit. It is normally a percentage of the purchase price. The size of the percentage varies from bank to bank, store to store, and credit plan to credit plan. For this reason, it is important to study credit plans to find one that meets your needs. As a rule, the longer you take to pay, the more the credit will cost. However, if you stretch your payments over many months, each payment can be small. You end up paying more overall because of the high credit cost, but that might be a trade-off you are willing to make.

Thanks to a law called the Truth-in-Lending Law, a store or bank must tell you three things about your credit plan: the cost of the finance charge in dollars and cents, the percentage of interest you pay per month, and the percentage of interest you pay per year, called the *annual percentage rate.* For instance, think about the purchase of a stereo turntable. If the purchase price is $150, the finance charge is $1\frac{1}{2}$ percent per month, and you take twelve months to pay, you figure the total cost of the stereo as follows:

1. List the purchase price:
   $150.00
2. Find the annual percentage rate ($1\frac{1}{2}\% \times 12$ months):
   18%
3. Find the total finance charge ($18\% \times \$150$)
   $27.00
4. Add this charge to the purchase price to find the total cost of the stereo:
   $177.00

Credit Cards. Many businesses offer the most common type of credit, the credit card. A credit card from a store or a gas company allows you to charge goods and services in that specific place. A travel credit card allows you to charge such things as meals, plane tickets, and gifts. A bank credit card allows you to withdraw a limited amount of cash just by presenting your card at a member bank. You can also use it to charge items at participating stores. In all cases, once you own one of these credit cards, you can charge continually—provided you pay your bill regularly. A good way to handle credit cards is to set a monthly

Lost Your Credit Card?

Don't panic! Instead:

• Report it immediately! You will not be held responsible for charges made on it if you do.

• Is it a bank or a travel card? Call 800 555 1212. Ask the operator for the 800 number of the company that issued the card. Call immediately!

• Is it a store credit card? Call the local branch of the store.

• Follow up on your calls! Send a letter confirming your call. Or better yet, if you received a self-addressed, stamped form when you opened up your account, send it in.

• For safety's sake, keep a list of your credit card numbers handy.

Credit Is Not New

As early as the 1880s, you could "buy now, pay later." That was when Isaac Singer invented the installment credit plan to encourage people to buy his new invention, the sewing machine.

"Under Eighteen": Is Credit For You?

To have a charge card or installment plan, you must sign a legally binding contract. To do this, you must be eighteen or more years old. However, many stores may let you use your parents' credit card as long as you have their permission!

limit on your credit card purchases. Then make sure you do not go over this limit!

The Installment Plan. When you want to purchase something major, like a car or furniture, consider an installment loan. This kind of loan lets you pay for the item over a period of years. On the installment plan, you must first pay a certain sum, called a *down payment.* Then you make monthly payments, which include interest, until the total purchase price is paid. Every time you want to purchase a new item on the installment plan, you have to reapply for credit. A word of caution: when paying for an

item on the installment plan, the item is not really yours until you have completed all of the payments. If you miss payments, the store has the right to take the item back. You lose the item as well as the money you have already paid for it.

Loans. If you ever need money for college tuition or perhaps to open up a small business, ask your banker for a loan. The banker will do an in-depth credit check to see if you are a good credit risk. If you qualify, you will be asked to sign an agreement describing how much you will pay each month and for how many years. Then the money is yours! A word to

Even if now you pay only with cash, you need to know how credit works.

the wise: interest rates on bank loans vary greatly. So shop around for the best plan. Be sure to check the interest rate and the annual percentage rate you will pay.

DO YOU RATE CREDIT?

Your *credit rating* is simply a record of your past performance in paying what you owe. Your credit rating will be checked when you apply for a charge account, buy something on an installment plan, or try to borrow money from a bank. The store or bank contacts an office called a credit bureau. A *credit bureau* is a business that keeps a detailed record of how people pay their bills. It can report how you have paid your bills starting from the very first time you bought something on credit. If you keep a good credit rating, your new charge accounts or loans will be readily approved. A good credit rating is one of your most valuable possessions!

Ask for credit at a store or bank and you will be asked to fill out a *credit application.* This is a form with questions designed to find out if you are a good credit risk. The following are a few questions you will usually find on a credit application: Do you have a job? If so, what is it? How long have you had it? What is your salary? Where do you live? How long have you lived there? How much do you already owe? Your answers will help the business to decide if it will give you the credit or loan. You should not find any questions regarding your race, age (provided you are over 18), or marital status. Under the terms of a law called the Equal Credit Opportunity Act, businesses cannot ask such questions or consider such information when making their decisions. Most stores allow shoppers under eighteen to use their parents' credit cards provided that the parents have signed a release in advance.

a quick review

1. What is credit?
2. What is the law that requires creditors to tell you exactly how much the use of credit will cost you?
3. What are the advantages and disadvantages of credit?
4. Ann wants to buy a new turntable. She has only $50 cash but has $20 left each month after paying her fixed expenses. Which type of credit arrangement would be best for Ann to use to buy a turntable?
5. What should you do if you lose your credit card?

▶ **Words to Know**

annual percentage rate: The cost of a loan over a full year. It is always described as a percentage.

credit: An agreement that allows you to pay in the future for something that you are buying or borrowing today.

credit application: The form you fill out when you apply for credit.

credit bureau: An agency that keeps your credit rating.

credit rating: The record of how you have borrowed and repaid your debts.

down payment: The first and largest payment in an installment plan.

finance charge: The fee paid for using credit. Also called *interest.*

installment: A purchase plan with monthly payments for a long period of time.

layaway: A payment plan by which the store reserves an item for you in exchange for a deposit. The store holds the item until the full purchase price is paid.

CHAPTER 33

Natural Resources

A natural resource is something provided by nature that people can use. Everything we need for living begins with a natural resource. In this chapter we will look at three groups of resources. The first group, resources for survival, are often not considered resources at all. We tend to take them for granted. The second, renewable resources, are items that can be replaced or that replace themselves in a reasonable amount of time. The third group, nonrenewable resources, are materials that cannot be replaced. Once they are used, they are gone forever.

RESOURCES FOR SURVIVAL

Each of us has basic needs. Without oxygen from the air we breathe, we would die in minutes. Without food, our bodies would waste away. Without water, we could survive for only a few days. We also need shelter and clothing to protect us.

Beyond just surviving, we also try to make our lives pleasant. Eating many different kinds of food makes nutrition enjoyable. Attractive, well-built homes add pleasure to our lives. We enjoy green lawns, clean city blocks, and well-planned gardens. We spend our free time in well-kept parks or at beaches or other resorts. And most people value wilderness areas for their natural beauty and peace.

244

RENEWABLE RESOURCES

A *renewable resource* is one that can be replaced within a reasonable period of time. For example, forests are renewable resources. Each tree produces seeds that can grow into new trees. With careful planning, there can be enough trees each year to meet the need for wood products.

Farmers and ranchers provide us with food from two other natural resources, water and soil. By managing their crops and herds, they are usually able to ensure fresh food supplies each season.

Natural disasters, such as drought or floods or fire, can destroy these resources. Human-caused disasters can, too. Most forest fires are a result of human carelessness. Poor judgment by humans can slowly destroy resources. Overgrazing can ruin grasslands. Poor field management can destroy crops.

Water, a Special Resource. Water is a renewable resource. It is used but not used up. The natural water cycle circulates water in patterns around the planet. There are about nine million billion tons of water on Earth. Less than 1 percent of it is fresh water that we can use.

Think of all the ways that you use water. In a typical home, about 40 percent of the water is used for flushing the toilet and 38 percent for washing and bathing. About 6 per-

cent is used for cooking, 5 percent for drinking, 4 percent for laundry, and the rest for gardening and other uses.

The water supply is linked to other resources, too. These resources include forests, farmlands, and soils. Fires and erosion affect the local water supply. Pollution also threatens the water supply. Adding raw sewage or chemicals to water can make it unsafe for use. Using water to cool industrial machinery is another way of polluting water. The heated water

Water: An Important Tool
More water is used to irrigate farmland than for all other uses together. About 10,000 liters (2650 gallons) of water are needed to grow and process the animals, grains, fruits, and vegetables that make up a person's healthy diet for one day. Industries use water, too. The production of one automobile requires 100,000 liters (or 26,500 gallons) of water.

Although water is a renewable resource, it can take 10 to 50 years to restore a polluted stream.

Oil, like most other fuels, is a nonrenewable resource. The world's oil supply is getting smaller as the need for oil grows.

How Are Natural Resources Distributed?

Some countries are rich in natural resources. Others are not. Choose a few natural resources. Find out which countries *export,* or sell, them. Which countries *import,* or buy, them?

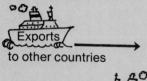

Exports
to other countries

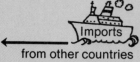

Imports
from other countries

may harm the natural plant and animal life in the area where it is released.

NONRENEWABLE RESOURCES

Nonrenewable resources are resources that cannot be replaced or can be replaced only very slowly. Soil, minerals, and fossil fuels are nonrenewable resources.

Have you ever thought of soil as a resource? Without soil, the plants and animals we know could not exist. The United States loses billions of tons of good soil each year. One way soil is lost is by erosion when soil is blown or washed away. Soil is also lost through land development. Land that is covered by new roads and buildings is no longer a useful resource.

The minerals in rocks are used in making steel, aluminum, and other building materials. Minerals are mined from ores. Some minerals are abundant. Others are scarce. At one time, the mineral copper was used to make water pipes for home plumbing. Because copper is scarce and expensive, pipes are now usually made of other materials.

Coal, oil, and natural gas are known as *fossil fuels.* They were formed from the remains of plants and animals buried in the ground millions of years ago. Not many years ago, fossil fuels were abundant and cheap. That is not the case today. Many scientists believe that we will run out of easy-to-obtain oil and natural gas in the near future. The coal supply will probably last longer, but burning coal produces pollution. Many people do not favor the use of coal as our primary fuel.

The talk of an *energy crisis* has caused many people to think of how they use energy from fossil fuels. Take a moment to make a list of the ways you and your family use energy. Your list probably includes gasoline for the car and fuel for heating or cooling your home. Did you include electricity on your list? Most of the electric power plants in this country burn fossil fuels. Did you include all the plastic items in your home? Plastics are made from materials in oil and natural gas. Did your list include articles of clothing? Synthetic fabrics are made from petroleum. Did you list your record albums and roller skates? How about cosmetics, medicines, salves and creams, ink, rubber, paint, candles, chewing gum, polystyrene cushions, detergents, cleaning solutions, and disinfectants? All these things and many more are made from oil and natural gas. As you can see, we depend upon fossil fuels for many of our needs.

The Energy Situation: Sources of Energy. The world's supply of easy-to-obtain oil and natural gas is getting smaller. What is in our energy future? You may believe that scientists will solve the energy problem. You may be right, but it will take time. Today, scientists and industry are studying methods of releasing oil from oil-rich sand and rock. These processes are very expensive. It seems certain that the oil taken from sand and rock will be costly. Scientists are also looking for *alternate sources of energy.*

Nuclear power is one alternative to fossil fuel. In today's nuclear reactors, atoms of uranium are split to release heat energy. This energy can be used

Energy Use

How is energy used in the United States? Look at the picture below. Industry is the biggest user of energy. Transportation uses the second biggest amount. Stores, schools, offices, hospitals, and public buildings are third. Houses and apartments use the least.

Each one of us uses energy in all these areas. For example, when you buy an item at a store, you are paying for energy used to make the item (industry), to ship the item to the store (transportation), and to display the item (commercial). When you take it home, you may need energy to enjoy the item.

The solar collectors on top of this house gather enough solar energy to heat the house and to provide hot water.

247

Endangered Species

Extinct means gone forever. Since 1600 two hundred kinds of animals have died out. Seventy percent of these have disappeared in the last one hundred years. By the year 2000, many more may be gone.

Some of these animals have become extinct because of natural changes in the environment. But most of the losses have been caused by human activity.

In 1914 passenger pigeons became extinct because people caught them, hunted them, and collected their eggs. Heath hens disappeared in 1932 because building on the Atlantic Coast destroyed their *habitat,* the place where they lived.

When an animal is in danger of becoming extinct, it is put on the Endangered Species List. In the past fifteen years, many animals have been added to this list due to hunting and the destruction of their habitats. These include:

Animal	Year Listed
Whooping crane	1967
Finback whale	1970
Cheetah	1970
India tiger	1972
Green sea turtle	1978
Elephant	1980

(continued)

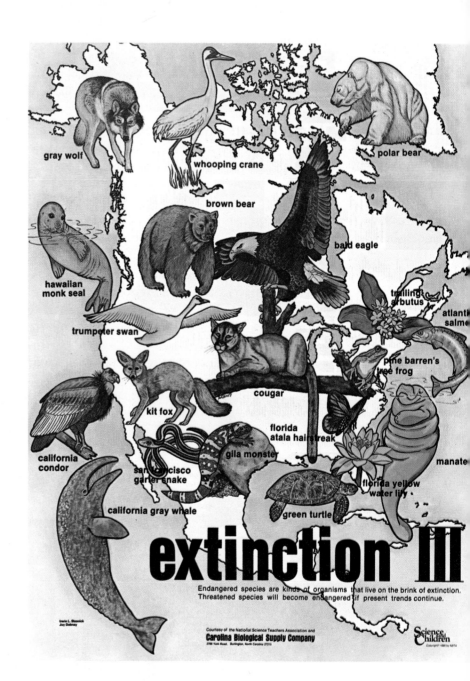

extinction III

Endangered species are kinds of organisms that live on the brink of extinction. Threatened species will become endangered if present trends continue.

gray wolf

whooping crane

polar bear

brown bear

bald eagle

hawaiian monk seal

trailing arbutus

atlantic salmon

trumpeter swan

pine barren's tree frog

cougar

kit fox

florida atala hairstreak

california condor

gila monster

manatee

san francisco garter snake

florida yellow water lily

california gray whale

green turtle

Irwin L. Slesnick
Joy Dabney

Courtesy of the National Science Teachers Association and
Carolina Biological Supply Company
2700 York Road, Burlington, North Carolina 27215

Science and Children
Copyright 1980 by NSTA

to produce electricity. Nuclear power supplies about 13 percent of our electricity today. Like all the alternatives, there are good things and bad things about nuclear power. One gram (0.04 oz) of uranium releases as much heat as three tons of coal. But, like fossil fuels, the supply of uranium is limited. And many people feel that nuclear power is dangerous. Nuclear power plants may give off radiation that can be harmful to humans. The reactors in use today also produce waste products that could be dangerous if they are not stored properly. Nuclear scientists are working on safer reactors. They are also working on reactors that do not give off radioactivity.

Many people believe that solar energy can solve some of our energy problems. Solar energy can be used for heating and producing electricity. Have you noticed how hot the air inside a car gets when it is in the sun with the windows closed? Some of the sunlight entering the car is turned into heat. Scientists call this the *greenhouse effect.* The greenhouse effect can be used to heat or cool your home. By opening shades on the south side of a house, you let sunlight enter to warm the house. To keep the house cool, draw the shades and close the windows on the south side of the house during sunny hours. Soon homes may be designed with most windows on the south side to take advantage of the greenhouse effect. However, in most areas of the United States the greenhouse effect will not provide enough heating for healthful living all year round.

Another way to get energy from the sun is to have *solar collectors* on roofs of homes. Solar collectors capture the sun's energy. The energy is transferred to a storage tank and then to a transport system for use throughout the house. The energy can be used for heating the home and for heating water.

Solar energy is clean and does not pollute air and other resources. Its use saves our other energy resources. But there are some problems with solar heating. Solar energy is not constant. During the night or during cloudy or cold periods, a backup system is needed. Also, today's solar heating systems are still expensive.

You may have heard of other methods of producing energy. *Geothermal* energy refers to the heat energy locked up under the ground. Methods of tapping this energy are being developed. The wind that drives a windmill can be turned into electricity. *Hydroelectric* power uses the energy produced by falling water to make electricity. People are looking for ways to use tides and the temperature differences in the ocean waters to produce electrical energy. Others are exploring ways to turn grain or trash into gasohol. Gasohol

Many *conservationists*—people who want to save the environment—are concerned about these animals. They are working to prevent extinction by controlling hunting and protecting habitats. Why not join them? For information, write to these addresses:

National Audubon
  Society
950 Third Avenue
New York, N.Y. 10022

National Wildlife
  Federation
1412 16th Street, NW
Washington, D.C. 20036

For General Information on Conservation, Write to:
Conservation Consultants
417 Thorn Street
Sewickley, Pa. 15143

Citizens Energy Project
1110 6th Street, NW
Suite 300
Washington, D.C. 20005

Reynolds Aluminum
  Recycling Company
6601 West Broad Street
Richmond, Va. 23261

Worldwatch Institute
1776 Massachusetts
  Avenue, NW
Washington, D.C. 20036

U.S. Forest Service
P.O. Box 2417
Washington, D.C. 20013

SAVING ENERGY AT HOME

Did you know that the amount of water in 2 baths equals 3 showers?

So what can *you* do?

1. Take short showers rather than tub baths. It takes 114 liters (30 gallons) of water to fill a tub, but just 76 liters (20 gallons) for a 5–minute shower.

2. Check the temperature on your hot water heater. Unless you have a dishwasher, your family will have enough hot water with the heater temperature control set at 50°C (112°F).

3. Use cold water for household cleaning and laundry whenever possible.

4. Repair leaky faucets right away. Ninety drops of water per minute from a leaky faucet equal 3800 liters (1000 gallons) in a year.

Did you know that a fluorescent bulb gives as much light as five incandescent bulbs for the same amount of electricity?

So what can *you* do?

1. Use fluorescent lights whenever and wherever you can.

2. Turn off lights any time that they are not being used.

3. Use low-watt light bulbs in places that do not need much light.

4. Use dimmer switches and three-way light-bulbs in any part of your home where you can. These devices can be switched to lower brightness and thus save energy.

Did you know that toasting bread in an oven takes three times as much energy as toasting bread in a toaster?

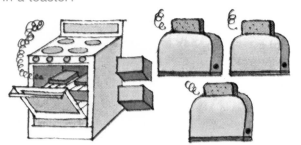

So what can *you* do?

1. Use small appliances when they save energy. For instance, cooking in a small, countertop toaster oven uses less energy than cooking in a full-size electric oven.

2. Do not run dishwashers or washing machines unless you have a full load. You need the same electricity for a full load as for a single item.

3. Turn the dishwasher off after the final rinse to let dishes air dry. This can reduce dishwasher energy consumption by one-third.

4. Use the dishwasher or clothes dryer during the day in cold weather and at night in hot weather. This can help heat the house or help keep it cool.

is a substance that may one day be widely used instead of gasoline. Electric and solar cars are also being developed. Alternate fuel sources would free some oil for other uses.

You Can Affect the Energy Crisis. A large part of the energy crisis is a result of the way we waste energy. Wasting energy takes many forms. Conservation can take many forms, too. *Conservation* is protection and wise use of natural resources. Energy conservation is wise use of energy.

We can all help conserve energy. For example, does your family's car need a tune-up? A well-tuned car uses less gasoline than one that needs a tune-up. And how is your car used? It is more energy efficient to do two or more errands in one trip than it is to make two or more trips. Can buses or trains take you where you need to go? You will conserve energy by leaving the car at home. Can you form a car pool? Sharing a ride is a good way to get to know your neighbors and conserve energy at the same time.

A lot of energy is wasted every day in American homes. Have you ever left your radio on all day while you were at school? Do you turn off the lights and the television when you leave the room? Some people think that energy conservation means they must give up their appliances. This is not so. You can conserve energy by using your appliances only when needed. Homes with insulation in the walls and attics save energy. Closing doors quickly when you enter and leave the house saves energy, too.

Another way to conserve energy is to *recycle* waste materials. When something is recycled, it is used again in some way. Recycling aluminum cans, for example, saves energy needed to mine and refine aluminum. It also saves some of the energy needed to turn aluminum into cans. It even helps conserve our mineral resources.

There are many ways that you can conserve energy. Conservation takes thought and, sometimes, extra time or effort. But every little bit helps.

a quick review

1. Compare the availability of renewable resources with that of nonrenewable resources.
2. List three uses of water.
3. Name five items made from fossil fuels that can be found in the kitchen.
4. How does recycling save resources?
5. Name three alternate energy sources.

CHAPTER 34
Looking Beyond 2000

In the past, people used tea leaves, cards, even the stars to predict the future. Today, *futurists* (people who study the future) use science, technology, and creative ideas to understand what resources will be available in the year 2000 and beyond. Of course, no one can predict exactly what the future will bring. But futurists are trying to present us with the possibilities of what tomorrow may be like.

A TYPICAL AFTERNOON IN TOMORROW

It is the year 2000. Paul Edler is close to thirty years old. It is Wednesday. He has the day off, since "weekends" are now scattered throughout the week. His job is to repair robots, and he works only thirty hours a week. He is still single. So are most of his friends. The average age for marriage is now thirty-two.

Paul lives in a "condomaxium," a huge skyscraper city that contains apartments, stores, offices, and parks. Eighty-five of every one hundred people in the United States now live in cities, so he is not unusual.

He puts on his digital jogging shoes and takes the solar-powered elevator to the 289th floor for a run around a small lake. His jogging clothes change temperature as he exercises. The temperature and humidity of this "park-in-the-air" are also computer-controlled. So are the numbers on his jogging shoes, which now tell him that he's run his daily distance.

Now Paul hops on a moving sidewalk and goes to buy a "fishsicle," a frozen protein pop. He doesn't pay cash. Nobody does. Instead, he pulls out a "money card" and places it in the "pay machine." The cost of the pop is instantly subtracted from his bank account.

He calls up a friend on his television-phone and invites him for dinner. He reads the day's news on a video screen, plays a game of chess on his home computer, and watches some robotball on his wall-sized television screen. Meanwhile, Roto, Paul's robot, makes soyburgers in the kitchen.

This is just one of many possible descriptions of a typical afternoon in the future. It may prove to be correct. It may not. Many things could change between now and the year 2000.

Welcome to the Computer Age. The Computer Age is already here. There are computers in government. There are computers in business. And more and more, there are computers in the home.

What is a computer? It is an electronic "brain" that stores millions of facts and figures in its "memory." Humans must feed it *data,* or information, because the computer cannot

think on its own. At least it cannot do so yet.

The first electronic computer was built in 1946. It took up an entire room. Today all the information that computer contained could be stored on a computer chip the size of your fingernail. By the year 2000, computers will be the largest business in the world.

And what will your home computer do? Your computer terminal, or hookup, will remind you about appointments, make ticket reservations, reserve library books, and order groceries. With a home computer, you may even be able to vote without getting out of your easy chair.

Computers will make your life more *convenient,* or easy. But widespread use of computers may cause new problems Someday data banks— huge computer networks—may have the ability to store information on each citizen. Such "banks" might keep "files" on your grades, who your friends are, what you spend, and maybe even what you say. Many people are worried that this would take away their privacy.

Lasting Youth and the Perfect Tooth: Medicine in the Twenty-first Century. Imagine a world where you could eat five ice cream sundaes and not gain an ounce, where a shot could smooth away wrinkles, where you could grow new arms or legs.

Future Foods

Did you know that we eat only 4 percent of the world's edible plants? Are you aware that although 70 percent of the Earth's surface is water, we get only 1 percent of our food from the sea?

In the year 2000 there will be less farmland and more people to feed. New protein sources may have to be found and new tastes developed. You may eat less meat, fewer dairy products, more vegetable protein, and six to seven times as much ocean food. You may even eat worms, insects, and artificial foods. And you may like all three!

The following foods may be added to your grocery list: cocoyam (a potato substitute), krill (a shrimplike sea animal), and squid. All are rich in protein.

Possible Menu for Tomorrow:

Appetizer: chilled krill

Soup: squid chowder

Main course: wormburger, cocoyam fries

Salad: seaweed and kiwi fruit

Dessert: algae ice cream

Beverage: vegetable "milk" or soybean soda

ROAD MAP of the FUTURE

LET COMPUTO PLAN THE PERFECT VACATION JUST FOR YOU!

FISH FARMING

HOUSES UNDERGROUND (DIRT CHEAP)

NEW FABRIC BUILDINGS

OPEN HOUSE

1982
- Anti-fat drug
- First home data banks
- Sewing with sound
- Garbage burned to produce oil
- Bacteria used to eat oil spills

DACRON DOME

PLAID PALACE

1985
- Immediate hair-strand diagnosis
- 2-way TV
- Accurate earthquake and tidal wave predictions
- Shots to slow aging
- Lie detector wristwatches
- Electronic hearing and sight for blind and deaf

1990
- 3-D TV
- 50% of homes have computers
- Regrowing of lost limbs
- No more tooth decay
- Mental exercises to "unlearn" illness

2000
- 30 nations have nuclear power
- Voting at home
- Widespread ocean mining
- First space "travel —
- "Tubecraft" travel begun go across U.S. in

JET FLYING BELTS

Hello?

PORTABLE POCKET PHONE

WELCOME TO **FUTURVILLE**
POPULATION: 7,638,291,432 AND COUNTING

SOLAR HOMES GALORE

Predictions That Did Not Come True

No one can exactly predict what the future will bring. In fact, over the years, many people have been wrong in their predictions:

• In 1878 a British science committee said electric lights would never be possible. The next year, the light bulb was invented.

• At an exhibit about the future at the 1939 World's Fair, a professor claimed that television would never catch on. It did.

• In 1941 a scientist predicted that by the 1980s cars would run on liquid air. They don't. Another said that slums would be gone. They aren't.

• In 1945 a famous admiral predicted that the atom bomb would never

(continued)

Imagine going to a "drill-less dentist" or taking "electric aspirin." These breakthroughs may be just around the corner.

In the year 2000 and beyond, the doctor's house call may be electronic. You may visit her or him by two-way television-phone. By feeding a saliva sample or a strand of hair into your home computer, you might even get an instant diagnosis.

With new medical techniques, people will be living longer, too. One way to slow down aging might be to take some of your white blood cells while you are young, freeze them, and then inject them back into you when you are older.

Someday EM, or electromagnetic medicine, may be used to regrow lost arms or legs. Electricity is already used to help heal broken bones. With EM, rats have regrown parts of missing feet.

There will be new sprays, pills, and shots of all kinds to help with medical problems. By 1990 you may be able to spray away tooth decay! There may be a pill you can swallow daily to prevent cancer. There may also be non-habit-forming drugs to fight fear and fat, too. Run out of ideas? Someday you may even be able to take a "creativity shot."

Solar Cottages and Dome Homes: Housing in the Year 2000. Today there are over 4 billion people in the world. By 2000 there will be 7 billion. Where will they all live?

Paolo Soleri, an architect in the United States, thinks he has a solution. He has already started building a high-rise city in the Arizona desert. It is called "Arcosanti." Its towers will rest on a giant greenhouse where food will be grown for the city's thousands of residents. The roof will collect the sun's power to heat and cool the city year-round.

Buckminster Fuller, a well-known engineer, has another idea. He has drawn up plans for a 300,000-family city to be built under a single dome. Another of his city designs, known as Tetra, calls for skyscrapers floating on the ocean.

Jacques-Yves Cousteau, a French ocean explorer, set up the first undersea work station in 1962. The first underwater city has not yet been started. But architects are thinking about it.

Dr. George O'Neill of Princeton University says that during the twenty-first century we may have colonies in space. Each would be solar-powered and pollution-free. And each would house 10,000 people.

If you were planning to build a single-family dwelling, what kind would it be? You might build a solar house with solar panels or a greenhouse. You might choose to live underground, where heating costs are low. Or you might buy a submarine home. The "modular" house is already available. Your family could start with a small house and add new rooms one by one onto the house any time that you need them.

Mining Asteroids and Flying with "Bird Belts": Work and Play in the Year 2000.

By the start of the next century you will probably work only four days a week for five or six hours each day. You will get thirteen weeks of vacation. With home computer hookups, you may even be able to do your job at home. And you may retire at the age of forty to begin a second or third career.

Robots may take over boring or dangerous jobs. People will have other work to do. You may work at mining on the ocean floor or at aquaculture, which is "farming" in the sea. You might build solar-powered homes or design new cities. You might even become a "space miner," collecting ores from *asteroids,* which are small planets floating around in space.

What will you do with all your free time? At home you will play many computer games. Video discs—plastic discs projected by computer onto a television-like screen—will bring entertainment into your living room. Holograms—three-dimensional

The house of the future may look much like this modular dome unit. It may be designed to use the wind and sun, rather than petroleum or natural gas, as energy sources.

work. It was exploded a few months later.

• In 1955 a group of scientists predicted that in twenty years there would be a cure for the common cold. Achoo!

• In the late 1950s a group of researchers said that a space station would be built by 1970. They also said that oil prices would stay low. Untrue!

Why not see if your predictions come true? In a shoebox, place your forecasts for the year 2000. Include predictions about population, computers, food, cities, transportation, medicine, work, and play. Remember to open it on New Year's Day, 2000.

Tomorrow's City

The city of the future will have many shapes. Try "shaping" one such city right now.

Divide into small groups. Each group should design or sketch one of the following: a skyscraper city, a floating city, an underwater city, an underground city, or a space city. Be sure that your city includes homes, schools, shops, offices, parks, food-growing areas, and a transportation system.

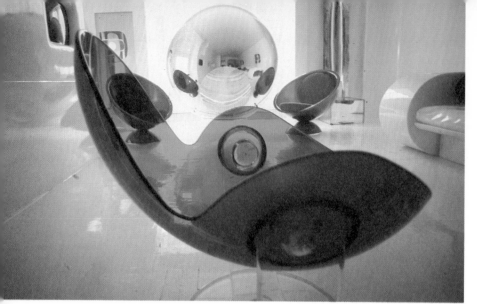

Homes of the future will use new materials and easy-care designs. Can you think of the advantages and disadvantages to this "room of the future"?

There will be new recreational resources outside the home, too. Would you like to retrace the steps of Marco Polo? Artificial adventure environments will help you to relive the past. Underwater exploring will become more popular. So will new forms of travel. Are you tired of skateboarding? You may someday be able to fly across town with a small "jet-belt." Do you need a vacation? One airline has already taken thousands of reservations for the first commercial flight to the moon.

Tomorrow's House

The house of the future will have to be energy-efficient. To achieve this, houses will be smaller. Architects think that the house of the future will have a "great room," combining living room, dining room, den, and kitchen in one area.

films projected with lasers—will "bring" museum sculptures into your home, too. And you may spend time creating computer art or electronic music.

▶ Words to Know

condomaxium: A skyscraper city of the future.

diagnosis: Identifying a disease from tests and symptoms.

electronics: Using electricity or its principles to do work.

technology: Putting the principles of science to use.

The Most Important Resource. People will always be the most important resource, no matter what the future holds. How people feel about themselves and each other and how they act on these feelings will really determine what life will be like in our world in the year 2000 and beyond.

a quick review

1. How will computers affect your future?
2. If you were a real estate salesperson in the twenty-first century, what kinds of homes might you sell?
3. What will a doctor's job be like in the year 2000?
4. Describe a typical workweek and weekend of the future.
5. If you were a restaurant owner in the year 2000, what kinds of food might you serve your customers?

You live in a changing world, with many resources around you. These resources include the people in your community, money, your time and other people's time, and natural resources such as gas and water. Some of these resources are plentiful today, but some may be very scarce in the future. As resource supplies change, the careers connected with the resources change, too. Therefore, new careers are born every year.

CAREER QUIZ: ARE YOU ESPECIALLY INTERESTED IN YOUR COMMUNITY?

1. Do you like working with children?
2. Do you like to help others?
3. Do you enjoy getting involved in community activities?
4. Are you good at helping other people solve their problems?
5. Are you a good listener?
6. Do you like working outdoors better than in a schoolroom or an office?

If you answered "yes" to any or all of these questions, then helping to make your community a better place to live may be the career for you!

CHAPTER 35
Careers in Managing Resources

A Real Person in a Real Job

Sherry Golden has always been a people person! Today she is a consumer affairs director. She is also a speaker, a manager, and a writer. Here is how she describes her career:

"Experimenting with food and being with all kinds of people have always been my 'loves.' These brought me to earning a bachelor of science degree in home economics as a food major, then a master of advertising degree a few years later.

"After graduate school I traveled throughout the United States as a consumer information specialist for a major equipment company. How I loved demonstrating delicious party-food ideas using our cookware at large women's club gatherings, on television shows, and in newspaper photographs!

"Today I am still communicating with millions of people—now as the consumer affairs director of a major consumer products (packaged goods) company. Some of our products are food products, so that is perfect for me! As director, I supervise a staff of twelve consumer specialists who talk and
(continued)

Community Careers: Entry Level

• *Teacher's Aide.* A teacher's aide assists a teacher with activities like checking homework, grading tests, keeping classroom records, and working with students on projects. This is full-time or part-time work with on-the-job training opportunities.

• *Library Assistant.* A library assistant helps a library's professional staff by checking books in and out, sorting and shelving books, and answering questions. This can be full-time or part-time work.

• *Hospital Nursing Aide.* A nursing aide answers patients' bell calls, delivers messages, serves meals, feeds patients unable to feed themselves, bathes and dresses patients, and assists patients with walking. This can be part-time or full-time work with on-the-job training opportunities.

Community Careers: On-the-Job Training or Paraprofessional Training Needed

• *Extension Paraprofessional.* An extension paraprofessional assists the county extension agent in preparing programs. The paraprofessional often helps train volunteer leaders, presents special-interest programs, and helps at county fairs. This can be part-time or full-time work.

• *Community Help Line Worker.* This kind of worker gives a listening ear to those who call a special "help line" or "hot line" number. The work involves talking to callers about their problems with drugs, alcohol, child abuse, rape, or thoughts of suicide. This is usually part-time work.

Community Careers: College Education with a Professional Degree

• *Librarian.* Some librarians help you find books. There are also acquisition librarians who select and order books, classifier librarians who classify materials by subject, and catalogue librarians who prepare information for the card catalogue. This is all full-time work.

• *Extension Home Economist.* An extension home economist conducts homemaker programs, works with 4-H Clubs, and often presents radio and television programs on household concerns. This is full-time work.

• *Fund Raiser for Community Help Programs.* This kind of fund raiser works for groups like the United Fund to determine how much money they have and how much they are going to need. She or he also helps develop plans to raise contributions. This is full-time work.

• *Urban Planner.* An urban planner analyzes a community's future needs for housing, transportation, economic development, and business and industry locations. A planner also plans for future needs of the community, such as improved mass transit or pollution control. This is full-time work.

This urban planner creates landscape designs for towns, cities, and other communities.

CAREER QUIZ: DO YOU ENJOY BEING A GOOD CONSUMER?

1. Are you a good shopper? Do you read the label before you buy a product?
2. Do you like to teach others?
3. Do you like to write?
4. Do you like talking with all types of people?
5. Are you a self-starter?
6. Do your friends often ask you to settle an argument?

If you answered "yes" to any of these questions, there may be a career in the consumer field for you!

Consumer Careers: Entry Level

• *Consumer Survey Assistant.* This kind of worker conducts surveys either person-to-person or over the telephone to see if a company stands behind its products, manufactures products with the consumer in mind, and produces products that perform well. This can be full-time or part-time work with on-the-job training.

Consumer Careers: On-the-Job Training or Paraprofessional Training Needed

• *Consumer Service Representative for the Airline Industry.* An airline repre-

write to hundreds of consumers each day.

"I act as the voice of our consumer—in meetings, at conventions, and in written communications to our management. How our consumers use our products, what they think of our advertisements, and what they find unsatisfactory with our products are all my major concerns.

"My career is perfect for me. It allows me to meet all kinds of people, help them, and write a lot, all at the same time. That is what being a consumer affairs director is all about!"

A Real Person in a Real Job

Jean Parmer is a lending officer in a bank. She is also a home economist. Here is how she describes her career:

"I started my career in a high school in a small town as a home economics teacher. Marriage led me to move to a large city. So, I found my first job in business—as an administrative assistant to the director of education of a large pattern company.

"In that job, I not only worked with home economics teachers, but also handled countless details and even had to balance our department's budget. To my surprise, I loved the numbers part of the job! So gradually, as my responsibilities grew, I began working on my master of business administration degree. Soon I found another career—in finance.

"Today I am a lending officer for a bank. But my career in banking is much more than just working with numbers. It is working with people, too.

"Every day I talk with people in specific businesses assigned to me, then work with other people within my bank to give my clients the best service possible. As a loan officer, I
(continued)

262

sentative answers questions from travelers about flight information, aids handicapped travelers, and helps passengers find their way. This is full-time work with on-the-job training opportunities.

• *Consumer Correspondent.* A consumer correspondent answers consumer product complaints and tells consumers how to use products. He or she works for a product manufacturer, a consumer magazine, or the state or federal government. This is full-time work with on-the-job training opportunities.

• *Consumer Product Tester.* A product tester judges products "right off the production line" to see if they meet quality standards. She or he works with scientific testing equipment. This is full-time work with on-the-job training opportunities.

Consumer Careers: College Education with a Professional Degree

• *Consumer Advocate.* A consumer advocate acts as mediator between companies and consumers to help solve consumer problems. She or he usually works for a state or federal government consumer agency. This is full-time work.

• *Advertising Claim Specialist.* An advertising claim specialist tests products to see that they meet advertising claims of product performance. He or she usually works for the Federal Trade Commission, a television net-

work, or the National Advertising Review Board. This is full-time work.

• *Consumer Affairs Director.* A consumer affairs director manages a consumer affairs department of a company or a federal government agency. He or she conducts consumer communications programs, advises companies of the latest consumer trends, and resolves complaints. This is full-time work.

• *Lawyer: Consumer Issues.* This kind of lawyer offers legal advice and services in consumer cases, which involve consumer products or consumer rights. She or he works as a partner in a law firm or as a lawyer for a product manufacturer. A law degree with an emphasis in consumer law is required. This can be full-time or part-time work.

CAREER QUIZ: DO YOU ESPECIALLY LIKE TO WORK WITH FIGURES?

1. Are you especially good with details?
2. Are you accurate and careful?
3. Do you like to work with figures?
4. Can you look at a list of facts and figures and draw conclusions?
5. Are you good at keeping track of your money?

If you can reply "yes" to any or all of these questions, then the field of money and finance may hold the career for you.

Money Careers: Entry Level

• *Collection Agent.* A collection agent contacts people who have not paid their bills. He or she determines why the bills have not been paid and helps arrange a payment plan. This can be part-time or full-time work.

• *Bank Clerk.* A bank clerk in a small bank sorts checks, totals deposits and withdrawals, and prepares monthly account statements. A bank clerk in a large bank operates advanced machines to perform similar duties. This is full-time work with on-the-job training opportunities.

• *Credit Bureau Research Clerk.* This kind of worker investigates the credit ratings of customers who seek credit. She or he evaluates the "credit risk" of customers and reports it to the store or credit card company. This is full-time work.

Money Careers: On-the-Job Training or Special Licensing Needed

• *Bank Teller.* A teller helps the bank customer by cashing checks, handling deposits or withdrawals, and selling savings bonds. This is full-time work.

• *Retail Credit Manager.* A retail credit manager helps store customers fill out credit applications and gives guidance on the kind of credit the customer should choose. He or she works for a bank or a retail store. This is full-time work with advancement opportunities.

Money Careers: College Education with a Professional Degree

• *Consumer Money Management Specialist.* A money management specialist writes consumer materials on budgets, credit, and "how to manage your money." She or he works for a newspaper, a magazine, a bank, or some other financial institution. This is full-time work.

• *Accountant.* An accountant prepares and studies financial facts. He or she provides up-to-date information to aid in making financial decisions. Accountants can work for businesses or for individuals. This is full-time work. It offers many opportunities for advancement.

• *Loan Officer.* A loan officer works for a bank to evaluate loan applications. She or he determines if individuals or businesses will be able to pay am the main contact between that business firm (my 'client') and my bank. So communicating with people becomes very important.

"Naturally, the 'numbers part' of my job is important, too. I decide whether or not to lend a business money, as well as how much we should lend. For other clients, I watch over their checking accounts, take care of their investment needs, even arrange for their employees to get paid.

"Traveling to these businesses is usually a big part of any loan officer's job. Since I am combining my career with raising a family, I chose a regional bank rather than a national one so my travel would be local, close to my home."

Many consumer careers involve careful testing of products using scientific methods.

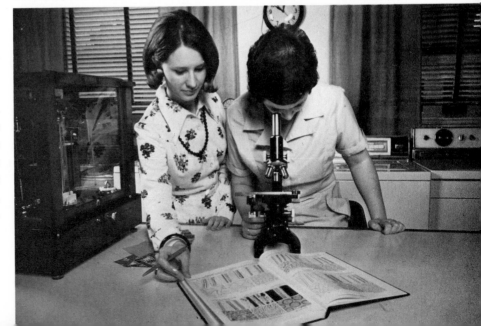

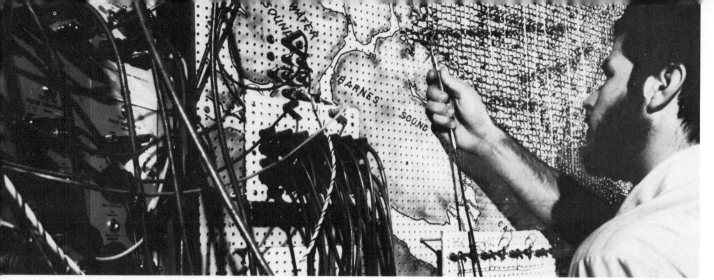

One important environmental career is water management.

A Real Person in a Real Job

Ed Waight is a tree-care specialist just starting his own business. Here's how he developed his career path:

"When I was in high school, I started to work after school for a neighbor down the road who had a tree service business. I like to work outdoors, so this part-time job was great. I made good money, too. By the time I graduated from high school, I was working 20 hours a week. The day after graduation I just went to work full-time.

"It's a relaxed job. The hard work comes in spurts. In between, you need time to observe and to make good judgments.

"Lots of people love trees. They get upset when something is killing a tree

(continued)

264

back a loan. This is full-time work. This job has opportunities for advancement.

• *Financial Planner/Counselor.* A financial planner/counselor helps people manage their money by analyzing expenses and helping design budget and savings plans to support family goals and life-styles. This is full-time work.

CAREER QUIZ: ARE YOU CONCERNED WITH THE ENVIRONMENT?

1. Do you make a special effort to keep your room clean?
2. Do you keep up to date with the national news about natural resources like water and petroleum?
3. Do you enjoy solving problems?
4. Do you frequently ask questions?
5. Do you like to work with scientific equipment?

A "yes" answer to any of these questions may mean that a career relating to natural resources and the environment is for you!

Environmental Careers: Entry Level

• *Environmental Plant Worker.* This kind of worker helps run a solid waste disposal plant, a water treatment facility, or an air pollution check station. This is full-time work with on-the-job training opportunities.

• *Waste Water Treatment Plant Operator.* This kind of worker operates equipment that removes industrial and domestic waste from the water supply or treats the water to make it clean and safe. This is full-time work.

Environmental Careers: On-the-Job Training or Paraprofessional Training Needed

• *Soil Technician.* A soil technician tests soil samples to determine the physical, chemical, and biological characteristics of soils. This is full-time work with on-the-job training opportunities.

• *Energy Conservation Center Guide.* This kind of worker receives visitors at an energy conservation center and shows them how energy can be saved by energy-conscious consumers. This can be part-time or full-time work.

• *Solid Waste or Water Inspector.* This kind of worker works with engineers to conduct field surveys to determine if waste or water environmental regulations are being met. This is full-time work with on-the-job training opportunities.

Environmental Careers: College Education with a Professional Degree

• *Geophysicist.* A geophysicist studies the makeup and structure of the earth. She or he examines rocks, minerals, and water resources and searches for oil and mineral deposits. This is full-time work.

• *Conservation Planner.* A conservation planner plans and conducts studies about animals, plants, and other natural resources. She or he works to preserve the quality of life in a specific location. This is full-time work.

• *Waste Systems Engineer.* This kind of engineer specializes in designing methods to collect, get rid of, and use solid waste materials from industries and communities. This is full-time work with good advancement opportunities.

a quick review

1. What are some careers that would let you work with young people in the community?
2. Let's assume that you enjoy writing and helping others. Name some consumer-oriented or community-oriented jobs that combine both of these interests.
3. Name some careers that would allow you to work with facts, figures, and money more than with people.
4. What are some part-time careers that involve working for your community?
5. Which careers allow you to carry on scientific experiments and protect the environment too?

that is part of their surroundings. Trees make everything look alive.

"Once all the Norway maples along one street began to die, one after the other. My boss took samples to send to the university lab. He and I found out it was a combination of a soil-spreading virus and a leaky gas pipe. We stopped the disease from spreading. I felt great about that.

"After three years I was managing one of the crews. People from two counties over used to call us because there was no tree service there. One night I told my boss about an idea I had to set up a service base in that county. He said he didn't want to take on any more business because he wanted to retire in five years. But he offered to sell me one of the older trucks and to keep me working half-time for him while I got started there. I've been working up a business in the new county for a year now, and it's just beginning to take off. In another year I figure I'll be on my own."

▶ **Word to Know**
paraprofessional: A trained aide who assists a professional person.

Unit 5
CLOTHING

CHAPTER 36
You and Your Clothes

You choose your own clothes for many different reasons. You want your clothes to feel comfortable and to look nice on you. Or you may have a favorite color in clothes. You also choose your clothes to match your activities.

WHY PEOPLE WEAR CLOTHES

You can see that people choose different clothes for different times and places. However, the basic reasons *why* people wear clothes do not change. These reasons include modesty, protection, status, identification, and decoration.

Modesty. Small children often feel fine about running outside without clothes. They have not yet learned *modesty.* Modesty is the need to cover the body according to what is considered proper. Every *society,* or group of people, has its own ideas about what is proper or modest. These ideas can change over time. For example, in the 1920s both men's and women's bathing suits covered almost the whole body. Today, much briefer bathing suits are accepted.

Protection. People also wear clothes to protect their bodies. Sometimes they need protection from the weather. A cold climate means that warm clothes are necessary, especially outdoors. Gloves, hats, scarves, boots, and heavy coats are all clothes that keep you warm. People who live in hot or warm climates need clothes that help them stay cool and comfortable. White or light-colored garments are common choices. So are loose-fitting clothes. Many parts of the United States can be either warm or cool depending on the season. This calls for both hot-weather and cold-weather clothes.

Some sports activities call for protective clothes. Helmets and shin guards help prevent football and field-hockey injuries. Some people need special clothes at work. For example, firefighters wear clothes that protect them from water, smoke, and fire.

Status. Clothes are also worn for *status*. People choose certain clothes to impress others. Often, status clothes are expensive, or they cost more money than other, similar clothes. Designer jeans are an example. So are special running shoes or sneakers. Many status clothes go out of style quickly.

Identification. Clothes are also worn for *identification*. They show that a person belongs to a certain group. A group of friends or club or team members may all wear a certain jacket. This identifies them as part of the group. What kinds of special clothing do groups in your school wear?

Uniforms are another kind of clothing worn as identification. Some people, like police officers and airline personnel, wear uniforms at work. This helps others to recognize them easily.

Decoration. Decoration may be the most enjoyable reason for wearing clothes. People like to choose and wear things that look nice on them. Clothes have been used in this way since ancient times. People also use clothes to say something about who they are.

Making an Impression. Your clothes are part of the impression you make on other people. Sometimes clothes have much to do with what people think of you when they first meet you. You can probably think of people you did or did not want to get to know because of their clothes.

Having your clothes say good things about you is easy. It does not mean spending a lot of money on clothes. It has more to do with being neat and well groomed. It means knowing what you are comfortable wearing. It also means choosing the right outfit for the occasion. The feature on the next page tells more about clothing impressions.

Deciding What to Wear. Matching your clothes to your activities can be fun. It is also a challenge to find something you enjoy wearing that

All About Jeans

Do you have five denim pant legs? If you do, you are average. The average person in this country has two and one-half pairs of jeans.

Traditional jeans are pants made of *denim,* a coarse, shrink-and-stretch cotton twill. A *twill* is a tight weave.

The word *denim* comes from the French phrase *de Nimes.* This refers to the city of Nimes in France where the cloth was first made. The word *jeans* comes from "genoese," a cotton cloth made in Genoa, Italy.

In the past, jeans were worn mainly by cowboys and workers who needed *durable* (lasting and strong) clothes. Some college students wore them in the 1940s, but jeans did not really catch on until the 1950s, when two movie stars, Marlon Brando and James Dean, made them popular.

In the 1960s blue jeans were worn by young people, often as a way to show their political and social ties. In the late 1970s the jeans scene grew to include people of all ages in all parts of the country. At the same time, jeans created by famous designers came into fashion.

The space suit is a good
example of clothing worn
as protection.

The typical space suit of
the 1970s had four layers.
The first layer (closest to
the skin) had a nylon liner
for comfort. It also allowed
for water to circulate. The
second layer was made of
coated nylon to make the
suit airtight and to keep the
right inside air pressure.

(continued)

will please others. However, it is not
always easy to know what to wear.
Here are a few hints:

In school, if you have a written
dress code, you have a good idea
about what you are expected to wear.
If not, there are probably some un-
written rules to follow. Neatness is
the key to school dressing. Comfort is
also important. Pants or a skirt with a
shirt or sweater are good choices. If
you want to wear something a little
dressier, add a blazer or a jacket.

For sports, choose clothes that are
comfortable and that allow free movement. Cutoff jeans, shorts, and sweat-
pants and tops are good all-around
sports clothes. The clothes you wear
also depend on the sport. Hiking calls
for clothes that cover and protect
most of your body. Running calls for
a pared-down outfit like shorts and a
light top. If you are going canoeing
on chilly waters, you will want warm,
waterproof clothes. Whenever an outdoor activity is planned, find out ex-

actly what you will be doing and then choose your clothes accordingly.

At a job interview, you will want to make a good impression because usually you don't get a second chance. Therefore, it is best to wear your nicest school outfit or something a little dressier. Jeans are too casual for an interview, even if you plan to wear them to work later. Once you have a job, see what the people you work with are wearing. This will give you an idea of what is accepted.

Comfort is usually the most important factor in choosing clothes for relaxing. Think about the clothes you like to relax in. What makes them comfortable?

WHAT DO YOUR CLOTHES SAY?

Clothes tell a lot about what you think of yourself. They also help others decide what to think about you. Of course, no one would be comfortable in dressy clothes all the time. Everyone needs casual clothes.

Real maturity is knowing how to dress for different occasions. Look at the four outfits the teen on the left is wearing. What impression do you get of him in each outfit? Where do you think he might wear each of these outfits? In what situations would each of these outfits look out of place?

With your friends, what you wear depends on your group. For casual gatherings, you can usually wear comfortable or even old clothes. For more important occasions, girls may wear nice school clothes or a dressier outfit. Boys may wear a good sweater and tie or a sports jacket and tie on important occasions.

With your family, sometimes you dress very casually. At other times, your parents may want you to dress up a bit. Family parties or visits to relatives are times when your parents want to be especially proud of you. Since you make your own clothing choices most of the rest of the time,

The third layer was a link net lining that kept astronauts and their clothes from exploding from the vacuum of space. The fourth layer was of nylon aluminized to withstand high temperatures and to protect against small objects flying through space.

Fitting the space suits was done by covering the astronaut's body with strips of wet tape. When these dried, they were cut away from the body in large pieces. Then the mold was used to shape the suit.

▶ Words to Know

identification: A means, such as a way of dressing, by which a person can be known or recognized as a member of a group.

modesty: A sense of what is right and proper in dress and behavior.

society: The people of a country, or any part of it, who share certain goals and beliefs and are thought of as a group.

status: Rank or standing in a group, especially high rank or position.

Some jobs and hobbies require special clothing to protect the body. Others call for something to keep regular clothes from being stained or dirtied. What other hobbies or occupations require protective clothing besides football and woodworking?

these special occasions are a nice time for you to go along with your parents' wishes. Most of the time this only means being a little neater or a little less casual than you usually are.

Clothes mean different things to different people. This unit will help you think about your own clothes. It will help you in choosing, buying, making, and caring for clothes.

a quick review

1. What are the five main reasons why people wear clothes?
2. Which of your clothes do you wear for protection? How do they protect you?
3. How are clothes a part of the first impression that people make?
4. What kinds of clothes do you think are worn for status reasons?
5. What guidelines are there for choosing school clothes where you live?

272

What do you think of when you hear the word *fashion?* Do you think of famous designers? Or does the word remind you of the latest styles in the fashion magazines? Maybe you think of the racks of new clothes in the streets of New York's garment district. These things are all part of fashion. The world of fashion includes the designing, making, and selling of clothes. It also includes you because you choose and wear clothes.

HOW CLOTHES CHANGE

If you look at an old fashion magazine, you will see that the clothes are in some ways different from what people are wearing today. For example, the shape, or *style,* of jackets may have changed. Jackets may be loose one year and more fitted the next. The width and shape of collars and lapels may have changed. Skirt lengths may have shifted. The width of pant legs changes; so does the use of cuffs. Clothing styles change for several reasons.

People who study fashion use several terms to describe types of clothing styles. A *classic* style is one that is always around. Classics do not change much from year to year. Men's business suits are fashion classics. Shirtwaist dresses and trench coats are also classics. Blazers are classics, too. They all stay in style for a long time.

CHAPTER 37
Fashion

Fashions for the Foot

The first shoes were probably fur wrapped around cold feet. Since then, shoes have been made in many different styles and for many different reasons. Shoes are worn for decoration, warmth, work, warfare, or sport. Below are some facts about the "twins on your toes":

- Egyptians were wearing sandals by 3700 B.C.
- The ancient Chinese wore shoes with wooden soles as well as cloth soles. Some Asian shoes were connected to stilts up to 15 centimeters (6 inches) high.
- In the Middle Ages, when the Crusaders brought back tales of Asia, shoes became more decorative. Men in the 1300s wore *crackowes.* These shoes had toes so long that they had to be attached to the knee with a chain so the wearer would not trip.
- European women of the sixteenth and seventeenth centuries had shoes so thick they had trouble walking. Some of these *chopines* were up to ½ meter (1½ feet) high.
- The English *duckbill* of the 1600s had a toe up to 23 centimeters (9 inches) wide.
- Native Americans were not the only ones to wear

(continued)

When classic styles change, they change very slowly.

A fashion *fad* is an extreme or unusual version of style. It does not stay in fashion for very long. Fads are often started by the fashion industry to encourage people to buy more. Sometimes clothing fads are part of more general style fads. One such fad was the disco look of 1980. People tend to get tired of faddish clothes quickly. They stop wearing them long before they give up classic clothes.

The way in which clothing styles change over the long run is called a *fashion cycle.* The same styles come and go over and over again. A style may have a new look each time it comes back, but it is basically the same shape. For example, in the spring of 1980, designers showed the *chemise.* This loose-fitting dress had been stylish about twenty years earlier, in the 1960s. It had also been popular still earlier, in the 1920s. Now it was back with a new look.

A *trend* is the direction in which a fashion is going. That is, whether it is just becoming popular or is fading. One way to spot fashion trends is to look at new designer clothes in newspapers and fashion magazines. These clothes are often very extreme. Few people really wear them. The styles are toned down by the time they reach the stores. But they give you an idea, for example, of whether pant legs will be wide or narrow. Another way to spot trends is to watch what people are wearing. If you watch fash-

A fashion fad is often started by a famous person. Coonskin hats were worn by Davy Crockett fans in the 1950s. Espadrilles were popular in the 1970s. Name three recent fads begun by famous people.

SPRING & SUMMER 1894.

M. BORN & Co.
CHICAGO

Men's clothing styles do not usually change as quickly or as often as women's. How do the clothes above compare with today's styles?

ion trends, and are careful to buy mostly classics and only a few fad clothes, you will get the longest wear for your clothing dollar.

WHY CLOTHES CHANGE

Fashion is a big business. Without new styles each year, people would probably buy less clothing. Often a

275

You can tell a lot about a society by looking at the clothes people wear. It was not until the late 1800s that active sports became acceptable for women. Even then, bathing dresses like the one you see above were not really made for hard swimming. Compare this with women's swimsuits today. What can you say about how times have changed?

Wrapping and Cutting Up

The first clothing was probably animal skins that people wrapped around themselves. Those people were cold and wanted to be warm. Fashion was not important.

Ancient Egyptian, Greek, and Roman clothing was *draped* instead of wrapped. That is, it hung on the body. These clothes were for physical protection, too,

(continued)

style becomes popular because it is the only one people can find in the stores.

As consumers, we influence the fashion industry as much as it influences us. Clothing manufacturers watch what people are buying. If a certain style or fabric sells well, they make more of it. For example, during the 1960s people began to buy a lot of clothes made of synthetic fabrics. These fabrics are easy to care for. Clothing made of these fabrics could be washed and dried by machine and needed little or no ironing. As a result, clothing manufacturers began producing more and more of these easy-care clothes.

Clothing also changes because the world changes. If clothes designers worked apart from the outside world, clothes might change less. But they do not. Designers are creative people who live in the same world you do. *Creative* means able to find new ideas and ways of doing things.

Designers get their ideas in many ways. They do many of the same things you do. They see movies and plays. They go to art shows and read newspapers. They watch television. All these things give them ideas for clothes styles. These same things also make you want changes. When the world around you is changing, your life will change too. And clothes are one easy way people have found to change.

Designers are not the only ones who set styles. Almost anyone can set a style. For example, blue jeans are a style that started among ordinary people. Some kinds of workers had worn jeans for years. But then large numbers of young people began wearing them, and jeans became *chic,* or high-fashion. Now all kinds of people wear jeans. Designers have even begun to design special ones. This kind of fashion is fun. You can watch it all around you. You can also be part of it if you want to. In your own school you may have seen someone wear something unusual that everyone else soon started wearing. Have you ever worn something that other people copied?

Technology also causes clothing styles to change. *Technology* is the way science and inventions are put to work in our everyday lives. Technological changes that happened in the middle of the 1800s helped to bring about the fashion industry. Until that time, people sewed clothes by hand. Most sewing was done at home. Then in 1846 the sewing machine was invented, and clothing began to be made in factories. From then on, many copies of the same garment could be produced. Clothes made in this way soon began to appear in but they also served another purpose. A draped dress bordered with gold paint, beautiful embroidery, or silver thread sent the world an extra message—that the wearer was important, wealthy, or at least in fashion.

Modern clothing is made from combinations of wrapping, draping, sewing, and cutting. And people wear clothing for more than just to keep warm or to avoid embarrassment. The clothes that you wear may tell the world what you do, where you are from, what you have, what you think about yourself, and maybe even what you believe.

The blazer is a fashion classic for both men and women. It does not change much from year to year.

Not all fashions are started by a few designers. The popularity of jeans is an example of a fashion that was inspired and made popular by ordinary people.

► **Words to Know**

consumer: A person who buys goods or services.

designer: A person who develops ideas for clothing styles.

fad: A style that comes and goes very quickly. It is usually extreme.

fashion: Current style or custom, manners, or behavior.

fashion classic: A long-lasting style. Clothes of this kind can be worn for many years.

fashion cycle: The way that fashions come and go and sometimes return again in slightly different form.

quality: A degree of excellence; in clothing, the sense that an item is made well and will last for a long time.

ready-made: Already made according to a set pattern and ready to wear as bought in a store.

style: The shape of a garment. A fashionable look in clothes. Something "in style" follows the popular way to dress.

synthetics: Fabrics that are created, or made, out of something other than plant or animal materials.

technology: The way that ideas are put to work in our everyday lives.

trend: The direction in which popular taste is changing at a given time.

stores all over the country. These clothes are called *ready-made* because you buy them already made rather than sewing them yourself. In this century, scientists have learned to make new fabrics. These fabrics are called *synthetics* because they are made from chemicals, not plant or animal products. You can read about synthetic fabrics in Chapter 41.

CLOTHES FOR THE FUTURE

The clothes you wear next year or even five years from now will probably be different from what you have on today. In part, this is because of the fashion changes you have been reading about. It is also related to changes in the way we live.

Life in this country has become more casual than it used to be. People want clothes that are comfortable and practical. Also, clothes are more expensive than ever before. And people have less to spend. Because of this, shoppers look for clothes that are made to last. People also want clothes that go together or are coordinated. Then they can mix and match. Such clothes are useful because with just a few of them, a person can make many different outfits.

What we wear in the future will also be affected by the natural resources available to us. Already, as high fuel prices make us turn down our heat and air conditioning, we are starting to dress differently. For example, many people are wearing more layers of clothing in cold weather instead of turning up the heat. Fabrics may be different, too. Some fabrics may not be available in the future or they may be very expensive. As a result, scientists will be looking for new fibers and fabrics for clothes of the future.

a quick review

1. What is technology?
2. Describe how technology has contributed to the kinds of clothes we wear today.
3. What is the difference between a fashion classic and a fad? Give examples of both.
4. What are the two ways that a style may get started?
5. What are fashion cycles? Why are they important?
6. In what ways are the clothes you will wear in the future likely to differ from the clothes you wear now?

What clothes are you most likely to pull out of your closet on a rainy day? Do you reach for something in a bright color? Or do you want to wear something that is especially warm and soft? Are there some clothes you like to wear when you are in an especially good mood? Maybe the colors are as cheerful as you feel.

Your choice of clothing is only partly related to your mood or to the weather outside. It also has a lot to do with the clothes themselves. Whether or not you like a garment depends very much on its color, texture, pattern, and lines. These factors are called *design elements.* The way that these elements work together in any one garment has much to do with how that garment looks on you. And the way a garment looks on you has a great deal to do with how much you want to wear it.

LOOKING AT COLORS

Color in clothing is important. It can make you look larger or smaller, healthy or unhealthy, or even happy or unhappy. Color can change the look of your skin. It can also change the look of other colors you wear. Try putting blue next to red. Both colors will look slightly different from the way they look alone. To understand how color works, you need to know something about the language used in talking about color.

CHAPTER 38

Design Elements

Looking at Color

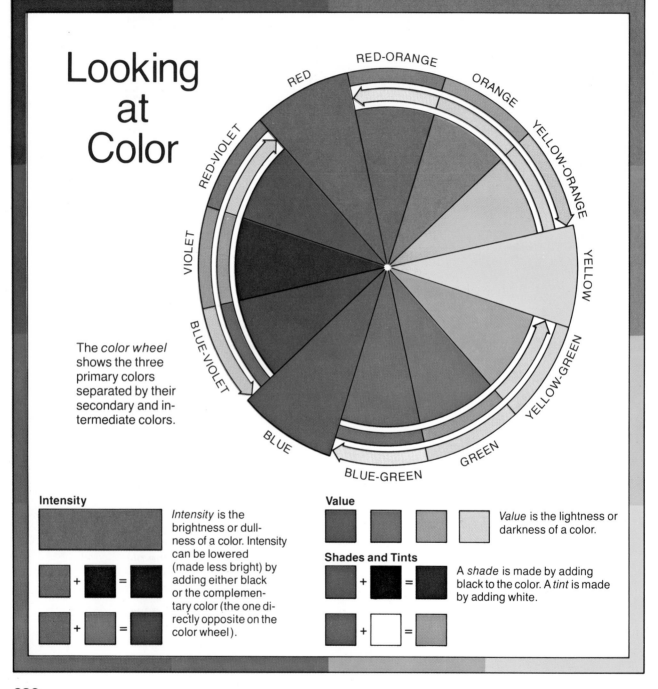

The *color wheel* shows the three primary colors separated by their secondary and intermediate colors.

Color wheel labels: RED, RED-ORANGE, ORANGE, YELLOW-ORANGE, YELLOW, YELLOW-GREEN, GREEN, BLUE-GREEN, BLUE, BLUE-VIOLET, VIOLET, RED-VIOLET

Intensity

Intensity is the brightness or dullness of a color. Intensity can be lowered (made less bright) by adding either black or the complementary color (the one directly opposite on the color wheel).

Value

Value is the lightness or darkness of a color.

Shades and Tints

A *shade* is made by adding black to the color. A *tint* is made by adding white.

The name that is given to a color is its *hue*. There are three primary colors, or hues: red, yellow, and blue. All the other colors are made by combining these hues. Red and yellow are considered warm colors. Blue is considered a cool color. Look around you at objects that have these colors. Blue is the color of sky and water. Yellow and red are colors in the sun. This helps to explain why these colors are considered warm or cool.

One way to arrange colors is on a color wheel. Look at the color wheel on page 280. First find the primary colors. Then look for orange, green, and violet. These are called *secondary colors*. Secondary colors are made by combining equal amounts of primary colors. Red and yellow, for example, combine to make orange. Blue and red make violet. And yellow and blue together make the third secondary color, green. Secondary colors can also be combined with primary colors to make *tertiary*, or *intermediate*, *colors*. For example, blue and green combine to make blue-green. Yellow combines with green to make yellow-green. In a tertiary color, the name of the primary color is always used first.

Still other words are used to describe colors. The word *value* describes how light or dark a color is. If a color has a light value, it is called a *tint*. If a color has a dark value, it is called a *shade*. Navy, for example, is a shade of blue. Pink is a tint of red.

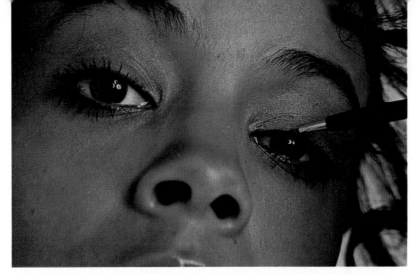

Like clothing, makeup should be chosen with skin tone and hair color in mind.

Intensity is the term that tells how bright or dull a color is. Navy blue, dark brown, and rust are dull colors; light blue and pale peach are bright colors. Black is the presence of all colors. White is the absence of color. The shades and tints of black and white are considered neutrals. They do not appear on the color wheel.

Various colors are used together to make *color schemes*. Color schemes are combinations of colors that you might wear or use to decorate a room. The color wheel is useful for making up color schemes. Any three colors that are the same distance from each other on the wheel form a *triadic color scheme*. Blue, yellow, and red are a triad. Colors that are next to each other on the wheel and have a hue in common form an *analogous color scheme*. Blue-violet, blue, and blue-

Colorful Expressions
People often use color words to describe feelings or situations. Here are a few common phrases using colors:

seeing red: being angry
a red-letter day: a good day
in the red: in debt
feeling blue: feeling sad
once in a blue moon: once in a long while
in the pink: in good health
yellow-bellied: cowardly
green with envy: jealous
still green: still young and inexperienced
in the black: making a profit
born to the purple: royal

Can you think of any others?

281

Lines in Clothing

These drawings help explain the ways that lines are used in clothes.

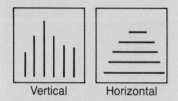

Vertical   Horizontal

What happens to your eye when you look at the vertical lines? Can you feel your eye moving up and down? Lines that go up and down make a person look taller and slimmer.

The horizontal lines, on the other hand, make your eye move from side to side. Clothes with horizontal lines make a person look shorter and wider.

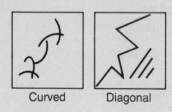

Curved   Diagonal

The curved lines shown above make your eye keep going around. Curved lines in clothes suggest softness and easiness.

Diagonal lines like the ones shown above have a lot of energy. They take your eye neither up nor down. If cut right, a garment with diagonal lines can be very flattering.

green are an analogous color scheme. Colors that are directly opposite each other on the color wheel, such as green and red, are *complementary* colors. A color scheme built around one color and the values and intensities of that color is called *monochromatic*.

CHOOSING YOUR BEST COLORS

People often avoid one color because they have been told they cannot wear it. For example, for many years redheads were told not to wear the color pink; it was thought to clash with red hair. Today, people recognize that a particular color is not so important as the shade or tint of the color that you choose. If you cannot wear bright yellow, you may still look good in a light tint of yellow. Or you might look good in a very dark shade of yellow.

Colors are usually chosen to flatter the skin tone. Skin also has a wide variety of shades, but most people have either a red or a yellow undertone. If your skin has a red undertone, certain shades and tints will flatter you. If your skin has a yellow undertone, then a completely different set of shades and tints will flatter you. Wearing the wrong shade or tint may make your skin look dull. It may also make it look more red or yellow than you really look. The only way to know which colors look good on you is to try them out. Hold colors next to your face and see which ones flatter you. You can use clothes or pieces of fabric or even colored paper.

Generally, complementary colors tend to *intensify* each other. This means that if your skin has yellow undertones, it will look even more yellow when you wear violet and other related colors. People with red undertones will only play them up by wearing greens and blues. On the other hand, if your skin has only a slight undertone, you can play it up by wearing a related color. Bright yellow, for example, will emphasize light-yellow skin; pink will bring out reddish skin undertones. You will learn through experience that various intensities of colors also affect your skin tone.

How you combine colors in clothes is also important. A bright color can be used to lessen the dullness of another color. For example, you might wear a red belt with black or dark-brown slacks. Colors also play tricks with your body size. Dark colors make people look smaller, and bright colors make them look larger. Wearing all one color tends to make a person look taller, and wearing two or more contrasting colors makes a person look shorter. An accent color can be used to highlight your appearance. An accent color is a small area of color, such as on a scarf, that contrasts sharply with the main color c the rest of your clothes. Accent color attract a lot of attention, so you may want to choose them to match your hair or eyes or some other good feature.

CHOOSING TEXTURES AND PATTERNS

The textures and patterns of fabrics are closely related to color. *Texture* refers to the way a fabric feels. It may feel nubby or have small loops of fabric sticking up all over it. Or it may feel smooth and soft. As you walk through a fabric shop, you can see how many different textures there are.

There are also many different *patterns.* Stripes, large or small prints, and plaids are all patterns. Colors can be combined in many different ways to make various patterns.

Texture and pattern can make your body look smaller or larger just as colors do. For example, rough textures tend to make a body look larger. Smooth textures make it look smaller. A heavy person will look slightly less heavy in chino slacks than in corduroy slacks. A very thin person might choose a rough texture in order to add some bulk. Texture can also be used to add interest to a color. For example, a dark, dull color may be greatly enhanced by the addition of an interesting texture. A bright color might seem overpowering if an unusual texture were added to it.

Patterns also change the way the body looks. A very large person may look slightly larger wearing a huge plaid. A very small person might be

The texture, weight, design, and color of fabric all influence the total appearance of a finished garment. What type of garment would look best in each of these fabrics?

Lines in Clothing

All the squares below are the same size, but the shapes the lines form make some squares look larger than others.

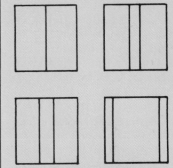

When you look at the squares above, your eye goes up and down. What would a garment with these lines do to a person?

In the bottom two squares the spaces between the lines look larger and more important. A garment with lines that are far apart will make a person look large. Your eye focuses on the spaces rather than on the lines.

You can also use lines on just a part of your body to make it look larger or smaller. Which spaces look smallest in the squares below? What effect would horizontal lines have?

283

The angular lines in the design of this woman's suit convey a certain message. How would a flowered blouse alter the look? How do the lines of this man's outfit affect his physical appearance? If he wanted to appear tall and slim, would this be a good clothing choice?

overpowered by a large plaid. A tall, average-shaped person, though, might wear a large plaid quite well. And a medium-sized plaid might look just right on a small person who wants a plaid look.

CHOOSING LINES

The last element that influences how a garment looks on you is *line.* Lines help to create the shape of garments, and the shape of garments has much to do with your shape. Lines also help to create the mood of a garment. Lines are either straight or curved. Straight lines tend to look more severe and strict. It is no accident that men's and women's business suits are composed mostly of straight lines. These create a sense of authority. On the other hand, a woman may choose to wear a blouse with soft lines, such as a curved collar. Or a man may select a tie in soft colors. How do you suppose this changes the look of each suit?

Lines can also be *vertical* (up and down) or *horizontal* (across). Vertical lines make a person look taller; horizontal lines lessen height. Diagonal lines can make a person look either slimmer or heavier, depending on the direction of the lines.

Lines can be used for structure or design in a garment. *Structural* lines are the main lines of a garment. For example, a skirt can be A-line or straight or full. *Design* lines are smaller, such as the shape of a neckline or hem. Both kinds of lines can also change the way your body or face looks. You have already read how vertical or horizontal lines can make a body appear different, but a V-shaped neckline can also be used to make a face seem slimmer. And a square face can be made to look softer by curved lines near it.

All the general rules discussed in this chapter can be used to change how your body looks. The best way to know what colors, textures, and lines especially flatter your body and face shape is to try on garments. Choose as many different shapes, textures, and colors as you possibly can. Be aware of how each one looks. Decide what looks nice on you. Gradually you will develop a good sense of the right colors and lines for you.

a quick review

1. What are the three primary colors? What are the three secondary colors?
2. Describe the three basic color schemes that are used to make attractive combinations in clothes and room decorations.
3. What does the undertone of your skin have to do with the colors you choose? Can everyone wear all colors? Are there some colors certain people should avoid?
4. What is texture? How does it change a fabric? How does pattern change a fabric? What should you keep in mind when choosing a texture or a pattern?
5. What do the lines of a garment have to do with its overall look? How do the lines change the way people see your body or face shape?

▶ **Words to Know**

analogous colors: Two or three similar colors that are next to one another on a color wheel.

complementary colors: Two colors that are across from each other on a color wheel.

design elements: Aspects such as line, color, texture, and pattern that combine to create the style of a garment.

hue: The name of a color family.

intensity: The strength or weakness of a color.

line: The outline of a garment.

monochromatic color scheme: A combination of various values and intensities of a single hue.

pattern: The design created by the colors or textures in a piece of fabric. Prints and checks are examples of patterns in fabric.

shade: A dark value of a color.

texture: The appearance or feel of the surface of fabric.

tint: A light value of a color.

triadic or *intermediate colors:* Three colors that are equally distant from one another on a color wheel.

value: The lightness or darkness of a color.

285

CHAPTER 39
Building a Wardrobe

Do you ever feel that you have many clothes but nothing to wear? A wardrobe that is really usable is the result of planning. This chapter will help you put together a wardrobe that works for you.

WHAT DO YOU NEED?

Forget for a minute the clothes you already have. The first step in making a wardrobe plan is to make a list of the kind of clothes you need. Think about all your activities. What kind of clothes do they call for? Here are some questions to think about:

• What kind of climate do you live in?

• Do you need special warm-weather or cold-weather clothes?

• Do you go to a school where you must wear a certain type of clothes? If not, what is the right thing to wear in your school?

• Do you have any special activities that require certain types of clothes? Some examples might be basketball, swimming, dancing, or hiking.

• Are there ever special occasions in your family, community, or school for which you might need dressy clothes?

Now you are ready to draw up your wardrobe plan. It helps to work with a chart. You may want to use the one on page 289 as a sample. From the answers to the questions

As people change, their clothing needs do, too. When you analyze your wardrobe, try on each item. Does it fit? Does it fit the image you want to present? Does it go with your other clothes?

you have just read, you now have an idea of the clothes you need. Write your activities across the top of the chart. Then write the various types of garments down the left side of the chart. You would include, for example, shirts or blouses, trousers or skirts, and sweaters.

WHAT DO YOU HAVE?

The next step is to take a *wardrobe inventory*. This inventory is simply a list of the clothes you now own. Take everything out of your closet and dresser drawers. Look carefully at each of your clothes one by one. Then sort them into the following five categories:

- clothes you like and wear
- clothes that need repair
- clothes that you have outgrown or worn out
- clothes that do not go with anything else you own
- clothes that you just do not wear for one reason or another

Now you can put the clothes you like and wear back in your closet or dresser drawers. As you do so, list each garment in the appropriate boxes on your chart. Remember that many of your clothes can be listed in more than one box because you use them for more than one activity. For example, some jackets are suitable for both school and dressier occasions.

Do you see any blank spaces in your chart? Look through the pile of clothes that need repair. Add to the chart any of these garments that will fit a need. In Chapter 47, "Clothing Care," you will learn how to make these clothes wearable again.

Anything you do not think can be repaired should go in the "outgrown or worn out" pile.

Travel Wardrobes

If you and your family travel a lot, you want clothes that are good travelers. Here are some tips:

- Mix-and-match separates let you bring fewer pieces and still have several outfits.
- Lightweight clothes mean less suitcase weight to carry.
- Clothes made from synthetic fibers are easier to care for when you are on the road.
- Outfits with one color theme make it easier to plan for shoes, jackets, and accessories.

Cool Clothes for Hot Weather

To feel cooler in hot weather:

- Wear loose-fitting styles.
- Choose absorbent fabrics.
- Wear white and light-colored clothes.
- Choose cool colors.
- Wear open shoes.
- Wear fewer layers.
- Choose lightweight and open-weave fabrics.
- Use water-repellent rainwear that "breathes."
- Wear a hat in the sun.

CLOTHES THAT WORK TOGETHER

Clothes that really work for you usually have three things in common. First, they are clothes you like wearing. Second, they are clothes that you can wear for several different activities. Third, they are clothes that go with, or look well with, a lot of your other clothes.

As you sorted through your closet you may have discovered some things about yourself and your clothes. There are probably some clothes that you wear a lot and always feel good in. Think about what these clothes have in common. It may be color or style or fabric or all three. Remember this common feature when it comes to adding new clothes.

A WARDROBE PLAN

Now look at your chart again. Do you have too much of one type of clothing and not enough of another? For example, do you seem to have a great many shirts that only go with jeans? Or do you have too many clothes that are dressy? Are there categories for which you have nothing at all?

Part of creative wardrobe planning is finding new uses for clothes you thought had only one purpose. Try again to see if you can find clothes that will work in more than one situation. You probably have more than you think. For example, you may

A good wardrobe is made up of clothes that you like and need. Before analyzing your wardrobe, weed out anything that is unwearable or unuseable. These clothes can be recycled to younger members of the family, friends, or a local thrift shop.

wear a pair of dressy corduroy pants with a dressy shirt for a party. Why not try those same pants with a sweater for a football game, or with a shirt and vest for school? Now you have three different places to wear one garment. Add your new ideas to your wardrobe planning chart. Look again at the "do not wear" pile. Can you add anything more to your chart now?

Now you know what clothes you have and how to put them together. By looking at the blank spaces left in your chart you can see what, if anything, you need.

This is your chance to plan ahead and make sure that all your clothes will work together. Begin by looking for basic colors. Choose two or three of your favorites. Think in terms of colors that go together. Look for *neutral colors,* such as tan and navy, that go with many other colors. If most of your clothes are already in those colors, you can add other colors for contrast.

Think about fabric choices also. You may need some light clothes for warm weather and heavy ones for colder times. Think also about fabrics that you can wear all year. These really stretch your wardrobe. To be useful all year, a fabric should be medium to light in weight. It can be made of either a natural fiber (cotton, wool, silk, linen), a synthetic fiber (polyester, nylon), or a blend of fi-

accessories that will go with many items in a client's wardrobe.

"My clients are people who are too busy to shop, or who don't like to shop, or who don't have the confidence or ability to coordinate their clothes. I go to their homes, analyze the clothes they already have, talk with them about their life-style, and then advise them about what clothes to buy. For an additional fee, I also do the actual shopping for a client."

PLANNING YOUR WARDROBE

	School	Casual	Work	Dressy	OK	Repair Or Alter	Need	Approx. Cost	Plan
SLACKS	⊘✗	✗	✗	✗	✓				
SKIRTS				✗			✓	20$	
SWEATERS		✗		✗	✓				
SHIRTS	✗	✗		✗	✓				
JACKETS		✗←——→✗			✓				
ACCESSORIES	✗	✗		✗	✓				

MIX AND MATCH
Smart planning means clothes tha[t]
work together to make many outfit[s]

Warm Clothes for Cold Weather

To feel warmer in cold weather:

- Wear soft, bulky fabrics.
- Choose warm colors.
- Wear darker-colored clothes.
- Choose natural fibers.
- Use thermal underwear.
- Plan layered outfits.
- Cover your head.
- Choose close-fitting styles.
- Keep your feet warm.

bers. For example, you could wear a pair of navy cotton gabardine pants in the summer with a light shirt or T-shirt. Then in the spring or fall you could wear them with a sweater, and in the winter you could wear them with a sweater and shirt. Some all-season fabrics to watch for are challis, duck, flannel, and khaki.

A BUYING PLAN

If you decide that you need some new articles of clothing, set up a buying plan. Do this no matter how much or how little money you have to spend. Here are some guidelines to follow:

- Decide how much you can spend on each item.
- Put the most money toward the garments you will wear most.
- Avoid buying items that aren't in your plan. An item you only wear once is a waste of money.
- Consider sewing. If you have the time and skill, sewing saves money because you do the work.

Your wardrobe should also take into account your family's overall budget. Talk with your parents about your wardrobe plan. If you are not able to buy the clothes you need now, you may be able to make some of

n each of the wardrobes shown
ere, the items can be combined to
make forty different outfits. How
many can you find?

them. Or you may have to choose between what you can buy now and
what you will have to put off buying
until next season or next year.

a quick review

1. What are some questions to ask yourself before deciding what kind of clothes you need?
2. What is a wardrobe inventory? How do you go about taking a wardrobe inventory?
3. How do style and color make a difference in getting the most out of your clothes?
4. What are some all-season fabrics? How do they help you build your wardrobe?
5. What are some hints for setting up a buying plan? Why is it important to talk with your parents about it?

CHAPTER 40
Buying Clothing

Most people have a mistake or two hanging in the closet. It may be a shirt in a great color that doesn't go with any other clothes. Or it may be something bought on sale that never really fit right. Do you have any shopping disasters in your closet? Everyone makes these mistakes once in a while. The trick to avoiding them is to plan ahead and to be a smart shopper.

MAKE A PLAN

If you have read the chapter before this one, you already know about wardrobe planning. Your shopping trip begins at home with your plan. Use your plan to decide

- what garments you need
- what styles, colors, and textures will go with the clothes you have
- how much you can spend

Make a list of exactly what you need to buy. In it, include any information that will help you in the store. For example, you may want notes about what colors to look for or which clothes you will wear with your new garment.

You can get a preview of what is in the stores by looking at advertisements in magazines and local newspapers. These advertisements will also help you decide where to shop. Different stores and different departments within stores carry different clothes. You will find differences in both style and cost. Try to find the stores that carry the styles you want in the price range you need. This will save you time going from place to place.

Ready-made clothes come in different sizes. The sizes, in turn, are divided into different groups based on shape. Three of these groups are *junior, petite,* and *husky.* There are special groups for children, girls, boys, young adults, and adult men and women. Within a particular group you may find several different sizes that fit you. It usually depends on who made the garment. For example, two companies may both make size 5 junior jackets. But one company's jacket may fit better on tall, thin girls than on short ones. You may wear one manufacturer's size 5 and another's size 7. The only way to know what size you need is to try on clothes in your size range.

CHECK FOR FIT AND QUALITY

Once you have found your size, see if the garment fits. The only way to do this is to try it on. Holding a garment up to you will not give you a true idea of how it fits. The box on page 294 shows what to look for when checking a garment for fit.

Quality describes how well something is made. As a general rule, the more you pay for something, the bet-

People often shop in boutiques for one-of-a-kind items, for gifts, and for special occasions. Department stores and large retail chain stores offer a greater variety of items, usually at lower cost.

CHECKING FOR FIT

Never buy a garment without first trying it on. If it does not fit well in the dressing room, you will probably never be comfortable wearing it. Here are some fitting checkpoints:

• Does the collar fit smoothly, close to the neck but loose enough to allow freedom of movement?

• Does the garment fit smoothly across the chest and back? Lean forward and stretch to be sure there is room to move easily.

• Are armholes loose enough so you can move your arm in all directions?

• Do shoulder seams hit you at the shoulder?

• Are sleeves long enough for you to bend your arm easily?

• Does the top hang straight and without binding the body?

• Are closings the same length?

• Is the garment loose enough at the hips so you can sit and walk and run easily?

• Is the crotch of the garment nonbinding and wrinkle-free?

• Is the waist comfortable, yet tight enough to hold up the skirt or slacks?

• Does the skirt or pair of slacks fall straight and fit smoothly?

• Is the shirt or blouse long enough to stay tucked in if that is how it will be worn?

• Is the length right? Is the hem even?

ter made it will be. But even if you cannot spend very much money on a garment, you can still learn to look for quality. One way to learn about quality is to study how expensive clothes are made. Then go to a store or department where less expensive clothes are sold. Choose clothes that have as many signs of quality as you can find.

Here are some quality points to check in a garment before you buy it:

• Look at how the fabric is cut and sewn. Is each piece cut straight, that is, on the grain of the fabric? If it is not, the garment will wrinkle in funny places and may never hang straight.

• If the fabric is a plaid, print, or stripe, be sure the pattern of the fabric matches at the seam lines. The better the match, the better the quality. More time and fabric have been used in making the garment.

• Check the stitching. It should be straight and carefully sewn.

• Look at the seams. Are they neatly sewn? Do they look as if they will hold together under stress? If the fabric ravels easily, then the seams should be finished to prevent this.

• Consider the buttons. Are they right for this garment? Will they last? Study the buttonholes to be sure they are neatly sewn and will hold up.

• Check the other closings. Are zip-

Take the time to look for quality in the clothes you buy. Knit goods should be checked for snags or runs.

For the Clothing Consumer

Many laws have been passed to protect the clothing consumer. Among these are:

• *The Wool Products Labeling Act of 1939.* This law states that labels on wool products must tell you the fiber content by percent and the exact kind of wool used.

• *The Fur Products Labeling Act of 1951.* This law states that each fur item you buy must show the name of the animal, its country of origin, and whether or not the fur is colored with natural or artificial dyes. This law protects you from getting opossum when you pay for mink.

• *The Textile Fiber Products Identification Act of 1958.* This law covers products not covered in the Wool or Fur Acts. It states that manufacturers must tell the percentage of each fiber included in the clothes you buy.

Look for Care Labels

The law requires manufacturers to put labels in clothes to tell how to take care of them. Always read the care label before you buy. You should know what it says before going ahead with your purchase.

You can read more about care labels in chapters 41 and 47.

Where to Buy?

Where you go to buy clothing depends on:

- what kind of clothes you are looking for
- how much you plan to spend
- what kinds of stores are located in your area
- the type of store you enjoy shopping in

The importance of these factors may vary from purchase to purchase.

Here are the main types of stores:

- *Department stores* sell all kinds of clothes for men, women, boys, and girls. You can also buy other products in them.
- *Specialty stores* such as boutiques often sell only one kind of clothes. Examples are shoes, women's clothes, or baby clothes. Some just have clothes for certain kinds of customers, such as athletes or people who want the very latest styles. Specialty stores are often more expensive than the other kinds.
- *Discount stores* sell clothes for less money than many other stores. They may have clothes from manufacturers who have produced more than they can sell. They may also have clothes that have something slightly wrong

(continued)

296

pers smoothly sewn in? Are they strong enough to hold up under heavy wear? Are hooks and eyes sewn neatly? Will they hold up? Do the closings fit smoothly without puckering or wrinkling?

- Study the trimmings. Do they go with the overall look? Will they last?
- Look at the inside of the garment. Are facings large enough so they will stay tucked in? Are they neatly sewn?
- Check the hems. They should be even. Make sure the stitching does not show through.
- Read all the labels carefully. Make sure that all the fabrics in the garment can be washed if the garment is washable or dry-cleaned if that is what is called for.

CONSIDER UPKEEP

Think about how much a garment will cost to maintain. Consider both time and money. If you are buying a shirt that you plan to wear a lot, then it will be less expensive to launder it than to dry-clean it. But if the shirt has to be washed by hand, remember that you will have to take the time to do this every time you want to wear the shirt.

SMART TRADE-OFFS

Few people can spend as much money or time as they would like on clothes. But they can make trade-offs. A *trade-off,* or *compromise,* is giving up a little in one area in order to gain

something in another. For example, you may want to buy clothes of very good quality. But you cannot afford them. You can compromise by buying fewer of these clothes than you might otherwise. You could buy a few quality garments and make sure that they are ones you can wear a lot.

Clothes are made from a wide variety of fibers, fabrics, and finishes. Each has very specific care requirements. They are often listed on hangtags. Pay attention to the manufacturer's suggested care instructions to get the longest life from a garment.

Hand Wash Or Machine Wash In Warm Water Do Not Twist Or Wring Reshape Dry Flat Do Not Dry Clean

STYLE 2728A
SIZE 8
100% PURE SILK
Dry Clean Only
RN NO. 53511

COST PER YEAR

One way to evaluate a garment or to compare two different garments is to figure out *cost per year*. This is the purchase price plus the total maintenance and cleaning costs divided by the number of years you can wear the garment. Here are some sample garments and their cost per year.

Garment	Price	Cleaning Cost	Expected life	Cost per Year
Wool blazer	$120.00	$36.00	4 years	$39.00
Polyester blazer	65.00	18.00	2 years	41.50
Silk shirt	58.00	49.00	3 years	37.67
Cotton shirt	28.00	0.75	3 years	9.58
Polyester shirt	22.00	0.75	2 years	11.38
Wool slacks	50.00	10.40	3 years	21.47
Polyester slacks	25.00	0.50	2 years	12.75

• Why is the cheapest garment not necessarily the most economical?
• Machine-washable fabrics are often less expensive to maintain than silk and wool. Why do you think some people still prefer silk or wool?
• If you are still growing, what effect does this have on a garment's expected life? How will it affect your decision?

You can also look at less expensive clothes and find ways to make them better. If a hem is not right, maybe you can resew it. If the buttons look cheap, you might put on a new set. If you dislike a belt, you can buy another one or use one that you already have. Often, if you spend a little time or money on improving a garment, you can have a good-quality piece of clothing at a relatively low cost.

There are some areas where you cannot compromise, however. These include fit and comfort. If a garment

with them but are still wearable.
• *Factory Outlets* are usually factories or warehouses where you buy directly from the manufacturer. The quality varies. Some clothes are *first quality* (no defects). Some have flaws like holes or pulled threads. Usually only the clothes of a single manufacturer are sold, although this may include several types of clothes made by one company.

Quality in Jackets and Coats
Do they have
• smooth, unbroken shoulder lines?
• a collar that fits close to the neck?
• lines that hang straight from the shoulders without wrinkling?
• a smooth fit about the hips?
• neatly rolled lapels?
• well-fitting sleeves 75 to 125 millimeters ($\frac{1}{4}$ to $\frac{1}{2}$ inch) shorter than those of long-sleeved shirts?
• a well-shaped and neatly finished lining made of fabric that can be cleaned in the same way as the outer fabric?
• Tailoring that will withstand wear and cleaning?

Quality in Sweaters
• Does the sweater fit smoothly at the neck, shoulders, and through the back and chest?
• Are the sleeves a comfortable size and length?
• Is any ribbing firm but elastic?
• Is the sweater of a fiber and knit that will be likely to hold its shape?
• Is the sweater of a fiber and fabric that can be easily cared for?

▶ **Words to Know**
garment: Any item of clothing.
grain: The direction in which the threads or yarns in a fabric run.
preview: See something ahead of the time it would normally be presented.
price range: The highest and lowest amounts charged for an item over a period of time.
quality: A degree of excellence; in clothing, the sense that an item is made well and will last a long time.
ready-made: Already made according to a set pattern and therefore ready to wear as bought in a store.
trade-off: Give up one thing of value in order to get another when it is not possible to have both.

Comfort is no place to compromise when you're choosing clothes for active wear. What qualities would you look for in running clothes?

does not fit you in the store, it will not fit you at home. And a garment that is uncomfortable is always difficult—and sometimes painful—to wear. Try not to compromise in these important areas. Never buy a garment thinking you will lose or gain weight to fit into it.

a quick review

1. How do you use a wardrobe plan to make a shopping plan?
2. What do you look for to make sure a garment fits you well?
3. What are some points of quality in clothing?
4. In what areas can you compromise on quality? What are some of the ways you cannot compromise?
5. Why should you consider upkeep before you buy a garment?

Think of your own clothes and the different fabrics they are made of. Some may be strong, *durable* (lasting) fabrics like the denim in your jeans. Others may be fabrics that keep you cool or warm or even dry There are fabrics in all kinds of weights, textures, colors, designs, and prices.

Every fabric has different characteristics. These are what make a fabric better for one use than for another. For example, if you were making a hammock for your room, you would use a heavyweight, closely woven canvas. However, you would not use this canvas to make a bathrobe. Also, different fabrics are cared for differently.

FIBERS

If you pull a piece of fabric apart with your fingers, you can see how it started out. Fabrics begin with *fibers*. A fiber is a fine hairlike substance. Each fiber has its own characteristics. The first fibers used in clothing were taken from plants or animals. Today many fibers are made from chemicals. They are called *synthetic* fibers.

Natural Fibers. The four basic natural fibers are cotton, linen, wool, and silk. *Cotton* fibers come from the cotton plant. *Linen* fibers come from the flax plant. *Wool* fibers are sheared from sheep. Sometimes the hair from other animals is also used. *Silk* fibers are strands spun by silkworms.

CHAPTER 41
Fibers and Fabrics

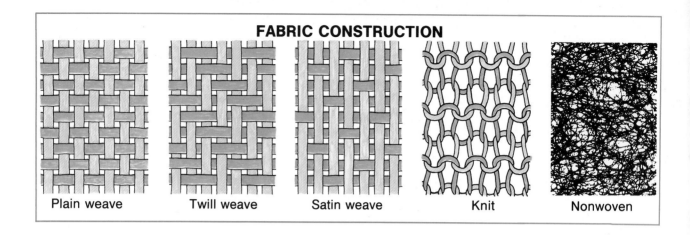

FABRIC CONSTRUCTION

Plain weave   Twill weave   Satin weave   Knit   Nonwoven

Vegetable Dye

Some of the first fabric dyes were made from vegetables. Vegetable dyes are made from flowers, berries, bark, roots, grasses, and leaves. Indigo (blue), madder (red), and fustic (yellow) are some plants used for dyes. These colors can be combined to make other colors.

A disadvantage of vegetable dye is that the colors tend to *bleed*. This means that the color comes out in washing. Chemicals are added to most natural dyes to prevent bleeding. These chemicals react with the dye and with the fabric fibers to "fix" the color.

You can make some dyes of your own from fruits and vegetables. Experiment on unbleached muslin or natural yarn. Many Cooperative Extension Service offices have information on dyeing.

Synthetic Fibers. In the late 1800s scientists discovered that synthetic fibers could be made from chemicals. *Rayon* was the first fiber made this way. It is called *semi-synthetic* because it also includes *cellulose,* which comes from natural wood pulp. Just before World War II, nylon was developed. Nylon is a complete synthetic fiber made from petroleum and chemicals. Since then many other synthetic fibers have been developed.

Blends. The textile fiber chart on pages 304-305 lists the characteristics of each fiber. Natural and synthetic fibers each have their advantages. By blending two or more fibers you get the best *properties,* or characteristics, of each. A *fiber blend* fabric performs most like the fiber that makes up the greatest part of it. A blend of 65 percent polyester and 35 percent cotton has the wrinkle resistance and easy-

care features of polyester. It will also be cool and absorbent because it contains cotton.

FROM FIBERS INTO FABRICS

To make most fabrics, fibers are overlapped and then spun into *yarn* by twisting. Then the yarn is made into the fabric. Fabrics are made in three different ways: weaving, knitting, and matting fibers together.

Woven Fabrics. To weave a fabric, two sets of yarns are used. The *warp* set is held tightly on the loom. The *weft* set, or filling set, is passed over and under the warp set from side to side. The technique is the same one you may have used to weave potholders when you were younger. Many different fabric constructions can be made by changing the number of yarns that the weft passes over or under during weaving.

300

Modern methods of printing fabrics are fast and economical. In the method shown here, dye is forced through a pattern of holes in a screen. The cylinder is then rolled over the cloth, leaving a colorful print.

Weaving is done on a machine called a *loom*. The loom can be a simple hand loom or a complicated mechanical one. One great advantage of woven fabrics is their strength. They also hold their shape better than knitted or nonwoven fabrics.

Knitted Fabrics. Knitting is done by interlocking loops from a single yarn. Fabrics that have been knitted are called knit fabrics, or knits. Knit fabrics stretch more than woven fabrics. They are comfortable, versatile, and require very little care.

Nonwoven Fabrics. Some fabrics are neither woven nor knitted. *Nonwoven* fabrics are made by wetting the

Understanding the terms shown here will help you work with fabric grain when you begin your project.

Generic and Trade Names

Synthetic fabrics have two names. The *generic* name tells what fiber family a fabric belongs to. For example, *nylon* is the generic name for a family of fibers that share a particular set of characteristics. Many fiber manufacturers produce nylon fibers. Each, however, calls the product by a different *brand* name. Often these are the names used in advertising. Some examples of nylon brand names are Cantrece, Enkalure, and Actionwear. These nylon fibers may each be manufactured slightly differently, but they are all nylon.

Clothing Allergies

Do you itch every time you put on your favorite sweater? Maybe you are allergic to it. An *allergy* is a physical reaction like sneezing or coughing or a rash. Many different things can cause allergies.

Cotton and linen, which are unprocessed vegetable fibers, do not usually cause allergies. But wool or silk, which are protein fibers, sometimes cause people to itch or break out in a rash. The result can be a skin condition called *dermatitis*. Dermatitis can also be caused by the finishes or dyes used in particular fabrics.

fibers, pressing them together, and heating them. Felt is made this way. Felt is often used for decorative trims that are applied to other fabrics. A nonwoven fabric will not fray or ravel when you cut it. *Bonded* materials are another type of nonwoven fabric. They are often used inside garments to give shape or support. The material used to make disposable diapers is bonded.

Leather and fur are natural fabrics that are not made of fibers. They come from animals and are used mainly for outerwear.

FABRIC COLOR AND DESIGN

Most fabrics start out a grayish color. They are given other colors by dyeing and printing. Thousands of colors can be created with dyeing. Dye can be added at several stages. Adding it at the fiber stage is called *solution dyeing.* Adding dye to yarn is

called *yarn dyeing.* Yarn dyeing is considered the best method. You may see this term on a label or hangtag. Adding dye to the fabric is called *piece dyeing.*

Printing is another method of decorating fabric. Block printing, silk screen, and batik are all printing processes used with fabrics.

FABRIC FINISHES

Special finishes also change a fabric. They can change its look, feel, or performance. Here are some of the fabric finishes you may want to look for when buying fabric or ready-made garments. The kind of finish used is usually noted on the hangtag.

Surfaces of smooth fabrics can be *napped* to give them a soft, airy look. Velvet is a napped fabric. A starch called *sizing* can be added to poorer-quality fabrics to make them look better. *Durable press* and *permanent press* finishes keep garments smooth and

A fiber's content, construction, and finish are important to consider when choosing fabric for a garment.

Calling All Clothes: Fabric Names

Did you ever wonder where some of the strange names of fabrics came from? Here are the stories behind the names of some famous kinds of fabrics.

Mohair comes from the Arabic word *mukhayar,* meaning "fabric from the hair of goats."

Damask is named for Damascus, the Syrian city long a center of East-West trade. The word originally meant any richly decorated silk cloth.

Burlap comes from the Danish *boenlap,* the name for any very strong rubbing cloth.

Corduroy means "cord of the king." This kind of fabric was long favored by the kings of France.

Chenille, the name of a fluffy or fuzzy material, comes from the French word for "caterpillar."

Poplin, called *popeline* in French, is a cloth used to make church robes.

Wool comes from *wolle,* the German word for "fleece."

Calico is named for Calicut, the Indian seaport where the cloth was first made.

Linen comes from the Latin *linum,* meaning any yarn made of flax fibers.

Gabardine comes from *gabardina,* a Spanish word from the Middle Ages that meant "protection against the elements."

Gingham comes from *gin gam,* the word for a fabric of the East Indies.

Percale comes from *pargalah,* a cotton cloth from Persia.

Gauze is named for Gaza, the city in the Middle East where the cloth was first made.

Madras is named for the Indian region where the fabric is made.

Cashmere is named for Cashmere or Kashmir, the region in the Himalayas in Asia where the goat fleece is gathered.

---

wrinkle-free. They also reduce shrinkage. *Soil- and oil-repellent* finishes keep dirt from attaching to a fabric. This type of finish is usually applied when a fabric is made. You can also buy this kind of finish and apply it yourself to garments and home furnishings.

Some fabrics attract dirt more easily than others. *Soil releasants* treat the fibers so that dirt can be removed easily. Water-repellent and waterproofing finishes help fabrics resist water.

Antistatic finishes stop fabrics from collecting static electricity.

Flame-retardant finishes are applied to fabrics so that they will not burn quickly. A law called the Flammable Fabrics Act requires that certain products, such as children's sleepwear, carpets, and mattresses, be treated with flame-retardants.

Recently much research has been done to develop naturally flame-retardant fibers. New fibers are being tested in firefighting gear.

Fabrics of the Future

Here are a few of the fabrics you may be seeing and using in the future.

Hollow fibers. These are tubelike filaments that are found naturally in the "floating fibers" of milkweed. They can be smaller than the eye can see or as large as plastic tubing. They are made synthetically out of materials like nylon, rubber, and glass.

Soon hollow fibers may be used in mattresses, cushions, and carpets. Since they respond to temperature changes, they may also be used some day to make *thermostatic* clothes, which change temperature for you.

Artificial kidneys are already made from these hollow fibers, and the fibers may soon be used in artificial lungs.

"Pseudo-silk." Goodbye silkworm? Textile manufacturers have recently learned to produce synthetic fibers that resemble real silk. Until now, such artificial fibers have been unsatisfactory. They have either dissolved in liquid, been chemically unstable, or been too weak.

Now, using one of the twenty amino acids that make up protein, Japanese scientists have created long fibers that strongly resemble natural silk.

TEXTILE FIBERS

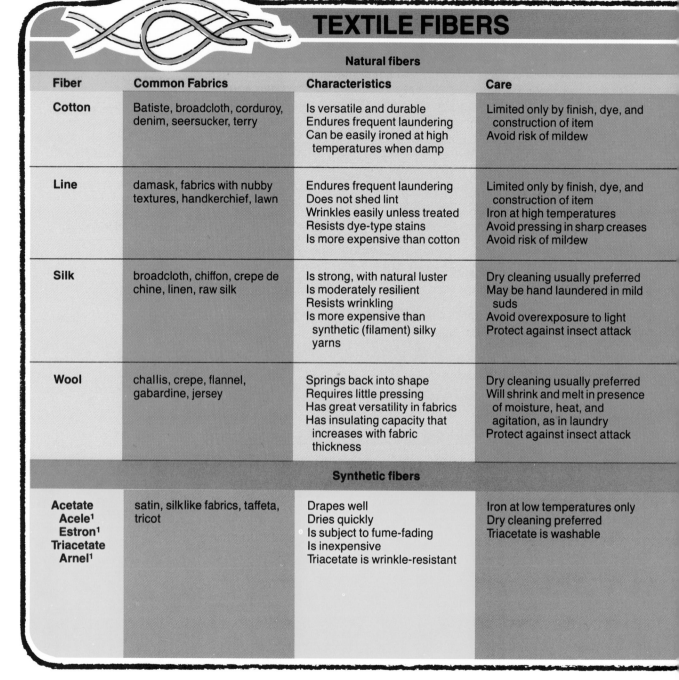

Natural fibers

Fiber	Common Fabrics	Characteristics	Care
Cotton	Batiste, broadcloth, corduroy, denim, seersucker, terry	Is versatile and durable Endures frequent laundering Can be easily ironed at high temperatures when damp	Limited only by finish, dye, and construction of item Avoid risk of mildew
Line	damask, fabrics with nubby textures, handkerchief, lawn	Endures frequent laundering Does not shed lint Wrinkles easily unless treated Resists dye-type stains Is more expensive than cotton	Limited only by finish, dye, and construction of item Iron at high temperatures Avoid pressing in sharp creases Avoid risk of mildew
Silk	broadcloth, chiffon, crepe de chine, linen, raw silk	Is strong, with natural luster Is moderately resilient Resists wrinkling Is more expensive than synthetic (filament) silky yarns	Dry cleaning usually preferred May be hand laundered in mild suds Avoid overexposure to light Protect against insect attack
Wool	challis, crepe, flannel, gabardine, jersey	Springs back into shape Requires little pressing Has great versatility in fabrics Has insulating capacity that increases with fabric thickness	Dry cleaning usually preferred Will shrink and melt in presence of moisture, heat, and agitation, as in laundry Protect against insect attack

Synthetic fibers

Fiber	Common Fabrics	Characteristics	Care
Acetate Acele[1] Estron[1] Triacetate Arnel[1]	satin, silklike fabrics, taffeta, tricot	Drapes well Dries quickly Is subject to fume-fading Is inexpensive Triacetate is wrinkle-resistant	Iron at low temperatures only Dry cleaning preferred Triacetate is washable

Fiber	Common Fabrics	Characteristics	Care
*Acrylic **Acrilan**[1] **Creslan**[1] **Orlon**[1] **Zefran**[1] **Zefkrome**[1]	double knits, fleece knits, pile fabrics, wool-like fabrics	Resists wrinkling Has high bulking power Can have wool-like texture, if desired Is very resistant to effects of sunlight	Remove oily stains before washing Waterborne stains easily removed Washable or dry-cleanable Iron at medium temperature only
*Nylon **Antron**[1] **Cantrece**[1] **Enka**[1]	tricot, two-way stretch knits (swimwear), velvet, wetlook cire	Has exceptional strength Has excellent elasticity Retains shape Woven fabrics are often uncomfortable in contact with skin; textured yarns are less so	Remove oily stains before washing Wash with care to maintain whiteness; washes easily Press at low temperatures May be dry-cleaned
*Polyester **Dacron**[1] **Fortrel**[1] **Kodel**[1] **Trevira**[1]	cotton-, silk-, and wool-like fabrics, crepe, double and single knits, gabardine, jersey	Has sharp pleat and crease retention Some are spill-resistant Has exceptional wrinkle resistance Reinforces cotton in durable press	Remove oily stains before washing Wash with care to maintain whiteness; washes easily Needs little ironing or pressing Use steam iron at warm setting
Rayon **Avril**[1] **Bemberg**[1] **Coloray**[1] **Nupron**[1] **Zantrel**[1]	challis, linenlike fabrics, matte jersey	Is absorbent Lacks resilience; wrinkles easily Is flammable in brushed or napped fabric Is inexpensive	Dry-clean if required Can be laundered Tends to shrink and stretch unless proper chemical finish is applied Washable

*These fibers have the following general characteristics:

Have moderate to high strength and resilience
Are abrasion-, moth-, and mildew-resistant
Are sensitive to heat in ironing
Resist stretching and shrinking
Are completely washable

Tend to accumulate static electricity
Are nonabsorbent; easy to wash; quick-drying
Resist nonoily stains, but body oils penetrate the fiber and are hard to remove
Hold pleats because of thermoplastic qualities

[1] Trademark name

► **Words to Know**

allergy: An illness caused in some persons when they eat certain foods, breathe dust or pollen from plants, or touch animal hair or clothing fabric.

blend: A mixture of two or more different fibers in one yarn or of different yarns in one fabric.

bonding: Holding fabrics together with a sticky substance rather than by weaving.

fabric: Material made by joining fibers together.

fiber: Any of a variety of natural or synthetic hairlike substances that are joined together to make fabrics.

knit: A fabric made by interlocking loops from a single yarn.

nap: The soft surface texture of fabrics like corduroy or velvet.

natural fiber: A fiber that comes from plants or animals.

nonwoven: Not produced by weaving.

sizing: A starch used to finish poorer-quality fabrics to make them look better.

synthetic fiber: A fiber made from chemicals rather than from plant or animal products.

yarn: Natural or synthetic fibers joined in strands and used to make fabrics.

Yarns are made of many fibers twisted together to form one single strand. These fibers may come from natural sources or from synthetic sources manufactured in a laboratory. Fabrics are then made when the yarns are woven or knitted together.

CARE

Fabric manufacturers are required by law to provide labels describing the proper care of home sewing fabrics. These labels also tell you the fiber content and any special finishes that were used. Be sure to ask for a label whenever you buy a fabric.

a quick review

1. What is the difference between a natural fiber and a synthetic fiber? Name several examples of each.
2. What is a fiber blend? What are the advantages of fiber blends?
3. What are the three ways of making fabrics from fibers? Explain each.
4. How are fabrics colored and decorated?
5. How do special finishes change a fabric? Name three special finishes and tell what they do.

Now you are getting ready to begin a sewing project. This is an exciting part of learning how to sew. No matter how much you read about sewing, the "doing" always seems like more fun. This chapter will help you choose your project and pattern.

CHOOSING A PROJECT

There are a few things to keep in mind as you decide on your sewing project. First, choose something you like and will enjoy making. Then the hard parts will not seem so hard. Also, choose something you can really use. Your project may be something to wear or use at home. Or it may be a gift for someone in your family.

You should also think about your own sewing skills. If you are a beginning sewer, you will want a project that you can both learn from and succeed with. The more success you have, the more likely you are to feel good about what you have done.

Finally, think about how much time you have. It takes time to sew well. You will not want to feel rushed as you work.

Your teacher may select a project for you, especially if you are a beginner. If you are making a required project, it has probably been chosen with these factors in mind.

CHAPTER 42
Choosing a Pattern

Difficult Patterns

Here are some factors that make a pattern difficult to sew with. This list can help you judge how hard a pattern will be to make up.

- many pattern pieces
- fly-front zippers
- pleats and tucks, especially when there are a lot of them
- cuffs
- *plackets,* which are special closures set into the body of the garment
- *gussets,* which are triangular or diamond-shaped pieces of fabric sewn into the main pattern pieces
- topstitching
- unusual collar
- a great many darts
- any kind of pocket other than a simple patch pocket

Sizing Guidelines

What do you do when your measurements don't match any standard size? Relax. This happens to many people. In fact, very few people fit into a pattern size perfectly. Here are some guidelines:

- For a shirt or jacket, select the pattern size that is closest to your chest or bust measurement.
- For a shirt or pants, chose the pattern size that is the closest to your hip measurement.

PATTERN SIZING

When making something to wear, there is a middle step between deciding what to sew and choosing a pattern. This middle step is finding your pattern type and size. Commercial patterns, like ready-made clothes, come in *types,* or groups. Each type is designed to fit a certain body shape. *Boys, Teen-Boys, Girls,* and *Young Junior/Teen* are some of the types you will find. Within each type, there are patterns for a number of specific sizes. All of the body-shape types recognized by clothing manufacturers are described on pages 309 and 310. After you measure yourself, you can choose the type and size that are right for you.

TAKING MEASUREMENTS

Because there are so many pattern sizes to choose from, it is important to measure yourself accurately. A *tape measure* is used for this measuring. A tape measure is a long piece of plastic or cloth marked off in centimeters or inches. You will also need a pencil and paper to write down the measurements as you take them. Before you measure, remove jackets, sweaters, or other bulky clothes. Ideally, you should wear underwear or leotards. You can also take accurate measurements over smooth-fitting clothes.

Work with a partner if you can. It is easier to measure someone else than it is to measure yourself. Here are some other tips:

- Stand very straight and look straight ahead while your measurements are being taken.
- Place the tape around the part of the body to be measured. Hold the tape measure snugly in place. It should not be tight, but it should not be loose, either.

You'll need to know your body measurements to choose the correct pattern size. For the most accurate results, wear lightweight clothing and stand in a relaxed, natural posture. It's easier to take measurements if you work with a partner.

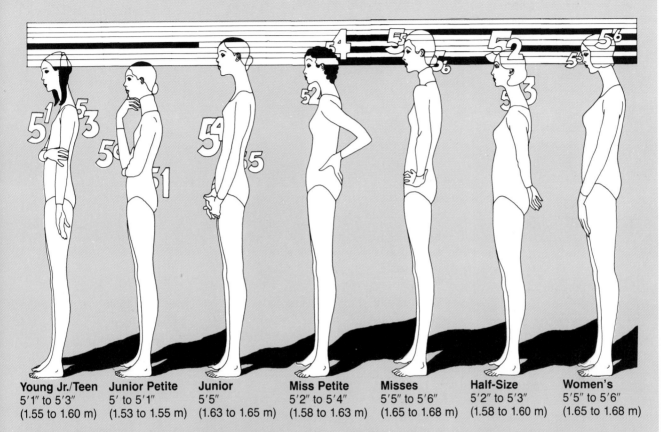

Young Jr./Teen
5′1″ to 5′3″
(1.55 to 1.60 m)

Junior Petite
5′ to 5′1″
(1.53 to 1.55 m)

Junior
5′5″
(1.63 to 1.65 m)

Miss Petite
5′2″ to 5′4″
(1.58 to 1.63 m)

Misses
5′5″ to 5′6″
(1.65 to 1.68 m)

Half-Size
5′2″ to 5′3″
(1.58 to 1.60 m)

Women's
5′5″ to 5′6″
(1.65 to 1.68 m)

Young Junior/Teen designates the developing teen and pre-teen figure which has a very small, high bust with a waist larger in proportion to the bust.

Junior Petite is a short, well-developed figure with small body structure and a shorter waist length than any other type.

Junior is a well-developed figure slightly shorter than a Miss in waist length and in overall height.

Miss Petite is a shorter figure than a Miss with a shorter waist length than the comparable Miss size, but longer than the corresponding Junior Petite.

Misses is well-proportioned overall and is the tallest of all figure types. This type can be called the "average" figure.

Half-Size is a fully developed shorter figure with narrower shoulders than in the Miss. The waist is larger in proportion to the bust than in the other mature figure types.

Women's is a larger more mature figure about the same height as a Miss. The back waist length is longer because the back is fuller, and all measurements are larger proportionally.

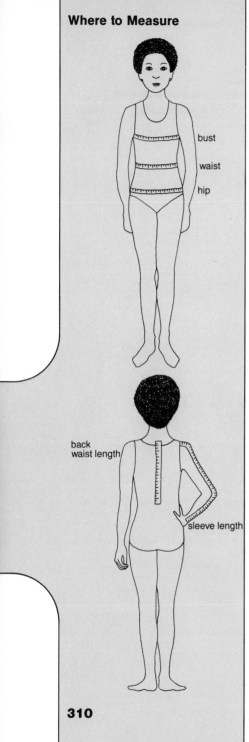

bust

waist

hip

back
waist length

sleeve length

Teen-Boys' 5'1" to 5'8" (1.55 to 1.73 m) *(left)* Teen Boys' patterns fit young men whose sizes fall between Boys' and Men's sizes. Comparable to Young Junior/Teen sizes.

Men's 5'10" (1.78 m) *(right)* Men's patterns are sized for men of average build about 5'10" (1.78 m) tall without shoes.

• Be sure the tape measure goes straight around the body or straight along the line being measured.

• Write down each measurement after you take it.

The drawings on page 310 and 311 show where to measure. Girls' measurements include height, bust, waist, hip, and backwaist length. Boys' measurements include height, chest, neck, waist, sleeve length, hip, and outseam (from the waist to the point where pants end).

LOOKING FOR A PATTERN

Once you know your pattern size and what you want to make, you are ready to look for a pattern. A *pattern* is a package of directions. In some ways, it is like a blueprint for a woodworking project. The pattern envelope contains the actual paper pattern pieces you will use to cut out your fabric. It also includes a sheet of instructions. This sheet has both written directions and small drawings that show you what to do.

To find a pattern that is right for you, look through the commercial *pattern catalogues.* These are books showing pictures of the patterns available from each pattern company. Like fashion magazines, they contain most of the latest styles.

There are two questions to ask yourself as you look at patterns. The first is "How hard will this garment

7255 MENS CAFTAN **7 PIECES**

Very loose-fitting, floor length, pullover caftan has round neckline, center front opening (no buttons on View A), pockets in side seams, side hemline slits and narrow hem. Full-length sleeves are cut-in-one with yoke front and back. Sleeves may be worn rolled up to desired length (NOTE: Wrong side of fabric will show). VIEW A has contrast pointed collar-on-band (cut-in-one) and contrast front facing. VIEW B has front-buttoned standing collar. Topstitching.

BODY MEASUREMENTS	Inches			
Chest	34-36	38-40	42-44	46-48
Waist	28-30	32-34	36-39	42-44
Hip (Seat)	35-37	39-41	43-45	47-49
Neckband	14-14½	15-15½	16-16½	17-17½
Shirt Sleeve	32-32	33-33	34-34	35-35

BODY MEASUREMENTS	Metric			
Chest	87-92	97-102	107-112	117-122 cm
Waist	71-76	81-87	92-99	107-112 cm
Hip (Seat)	89-94	99-104	109-114	119-124 cm
Neckband	35.5-37	38-39.5	40.5-42	43-44.5 cm
Shirt Sleeve	81-81	84-84	87-87	89-89 cm

CHEST	34-36	38-40	42-44	46-48
SIZE	Small	Medium	Large	X-Large
	34-36	38-40	42-44	46-48

CHEST	87-92	97-102	107-112	117-122 cm
SIZE	Small	Medium	Large	X-Large
	34-36	38-40	42-44	46-48

CAFTAN A

	Small	Medium	Large	X-Large
35" **	4¾	4⅞	5	5⅛
44/45" **	4¼	4⅞	5	5⅛
54" *	2⅞	3⅜	4	4⅛

CAFTAN A

	Small	Medium	Large	X-Large
90cm **	4.40	4.50	4.60	4.70 m
115cm **	3.90	4.50	4.60	4.70 m
140cm *	2.70	3.40	3.70	3.80 m

CONTRAST COLLAR AND FACING A

	Small	Medium	Large	X-Large
35" **	⅝	⅝	¾	⅞
44/45,54" */**	⅝	⅝	¾	¾

CONTRAST COLLAR AND FACING A

	Small	Medium	Large	X-Large
90cm **	0.60	0.60	0.70	0.80 m
115,140cm */**	0.60	0.60	0.70	0.70 m

INTERFACING A
18,21,25" Fusible

	Small	Medium	Large	X-Large
	⅝	⅞	⅞	⅞

36" Non-Woven

	⅝	⅝	¾	¾

INTERFACING A
46,53,64cm Fusible

	Small	Medium	Large	X-Large
	0.60	0.80	0.80	0.80 m

90cm Non-Woven

	0.60	0.60	0.70	0.70 m

CAFTAN B

	Small	Medium	Large	X-Large
35" **	4⅞	5	5⅛	5⅜
44/45" **	4¼	4⅞	5	5⅛
54" *	2⅞	3⅞	4	4¼

CAFTAN B

	Small	Medium	Large	X-Large
90cm **	4.50	4.60	4.70	5.00 m
115cm **	3.90	4.50	4.60	4.70 m
140cm*	2.70	3.60	3.70	3.90 m

INTERFACING B
18,21,25" Fusible

	Small	Medium	Large	X-Large
	⅝	⅝	¾	¾

36" Non-Woven

	⅜	⅜	⅜	⅜

INTERFACING B
46,53,64cm Fusible

	Small	Medium	Large	X-Large
	0.60	0.60	0.70	0.70 m

90cm Non-Woven

	0.40	0.40	0.40	0.40 m

Width at lower edge

Caftan A,B	55	59	63	67

Finished back length from base of neck

Caftan A,B	57	58½	60	61½

Width at lower edge

Caftan A,B	140	150	160	170 cm

Finished back length from base of neck

Caftan A,B	145	149	152	156 cm

NOTIONS: Caftan B: Three ½" (line 20) Buttons.

NOTIONS: Caftan B: Three 13mm Buttons.

* with nap, shading, pile or one-way design.
** without nap, shading or pile or with a two-way design.

Obvious diagonal fabrics are not suitable. For one-way design: use nap yardage and nap layout. Allowance for matching plaid and stripes not included in yardages given.

FABRICS: Soft or crisp fabrics such as Broadcloth, Chambray, Pongee, Crepe de Chine, Gauze, Muslin and Lightweight Wool.

A

B

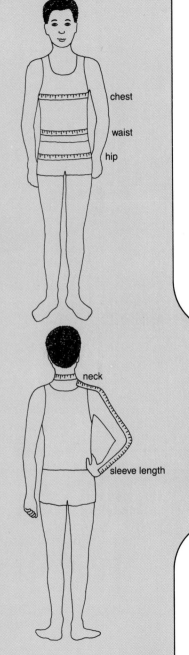
chest
waist
hip
neck
sleeve length

be to make?" The third column on page 308 lists the factors that make a pattern hard to follow. You can also look for phrases like "easy to sew" or "very easy" to find simple patterns. The second question to ask is "How will the garment look on me?" Choose a style that you have enjoyed wearing in ready-made clothes. Or if you want to try a new style, try on a similar garment in a store to see how it looks.

When looking for a pattern, keep in mind your skill level and the time you have to work on the project. Be sure to choose something you will enjoy making.

you in buying the fabric and supplies for your project. Here is what you will find on the envelope:

• drawings showing how the finished pattern will look for each completed *view,* or version, of the garment

• a description of the finished garment that tells more about its style or details than you may be able to see in the drawings

• the pattern number, brand name, and price

• the size and type of the pattern in the envelope

• the number of pattern pieces and a sketch of each piece

• the kinds of fabric to buy

• a chart showing the amount of fabric to buy for each size

• a list of *notions* (small items such as zippers, thread, and buttons) needed to complete the garment

• a chart showing body measurements

▶ Words to Know

catalogue: A book or pamphlet that lists a company's products and describes them.

pattern: A diagram used as a guide in cutting cloth and joining the pieces to make a garment.

tape measure: A strip of cloth or plastic marked off in centimeters or inches and used for measuring.

THE PATTERN ENVELOPE

The outside of the pattern envelope tells you a lot of important information. This information will guide

a quick review

1. What three factors should you keep in mind as you choose a sewing project?
2. How do you go about finding your pattern type and size?
3. What are the guidelines for taking accurate measurements?
4. What is a pattern? What does it include?
5. What important information is given on the pattern envelope?

Choosing fabric is fun. Take some time to walk through a fabric store. Before your shopping trip, you may want to review the information on fabrics in Chapter 41. Look at and touch all the different types of fabric. Your goal is to find the perfect fabric for your sewing project.

The first thing you think of when you see a fabric is whether or not you like it. Your feeling is important because you will be spending a lot of time with the fabric as you work on it and later as you wear it. In this chapter you will learn about the other points to remember as you choose your fabric.

IS THE FABRIC RIGHT FOR THE PATTERN?

The qualities of the fabric should match the design elements of the pattern. For example, if the garment will be loose-fitting, the fabric might be soft and flowing. If the pattern has many details, such as topstitching or a large number of pieces, choose a fabric that is somewhat simple so that it will show off the details. Heavy fabrics are not suitable for details. The material gets bulky as you sew them in. Your pattern envelope will tell you what kinds of fabric will look good with your pattern. Be sure to bring your envelope along as you shop.

CHAPTER 43
Choosing Fabric and Notions

Try to choose a fabric that is sturdy. Fabrics undergo some wear and tear while you sew on them, and even more as you wear them. Since you are going to put so much effort into this project, it is important to choose a fabric that will wear well.

IS THE FABRIC RIGHT FOR YOU?

How will the fabric look on you? Is its color one that you wear well? If you are slim, you can buy a slightly bulkier fabric than a heavier person might. If you are a large person, your fabric can have a larger print than a smaller person's. Use the guidelines in Chapter 40 on choosing ready-made clothes. These guidelines also apply to choosing a flattering pattern.

Is the fabric right for the occasions when you plan to wear it? Some fabrics are definitely dressy or formal. These include silks, satins, velvets and velveteens, metallic fabrics, and brocades. Cotton and many synthetics and blends, on the other hand, are wonderful all-purpose fabrics. If you plan to wear the garment for active sports, be sure to get something that will move with you. Also consider the climate or season in which you will wear the garment.

When choosing a fabric, consider upkeep just as you would if you were buying a ready-made garment. If a fabric requires dry cleaning or hand washing, it will cost you more in the long run in time and money. If you want to wear the garment often, look for a machine-washable fabric.

The cost of the fabric will be an important factor. Fabrics come in a wide range of prices. You will probably not want to spend a lot of money on your first sewing attempt, but you should not choose a cheap fabric. A cheap fabric may be hard to sew with and will not wear well.

The cost of the fabric is probably the greatest expense in sewing. Look at this cost in relation to the number of times you hope to wear the garment. If you plan to wear it often, then it makes sense to spend a little more on the fabric. The cost per wearing will not be very high. But if you are planning to make a dressy

Read the information on the back of the pattern envelope before choosing a fabric. Fabrics most suited to the design are given there. Follow these suggestions for best results.

BUYING FABRIC

You have a lot to think about when you go to buy fabric. You want a fabric that is good for you and for the pattern. You want the best quality you can get for your money. In addition, you want to make sure you buy the right amount of fabric for your pattern. Here are some areas to check:

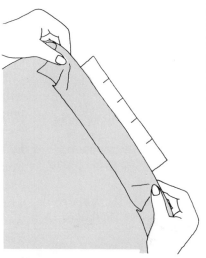

Wrinkling (*right*): Crinkle the fabric in your hand and hold it for about 30 seconds. Then release it. A wrinkle-proof fabric will return to a smooth shape. A fabric that stays wrinkled will wrinkle easily when you wear it.

Stretch recovery. (*above*): When choosing a knit, use the knit gauge on the pattern envelope to make sure the fabric is right for the garment. At the same time, watch to see if the fabric *recovers*, or returns to its original size after stretching. A knit fabric that does not recover may stretch out of shape when you wear the garment.

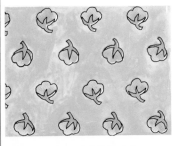

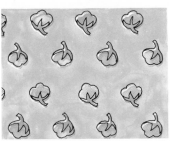

Coloring (*left and bottom*): A fabric should be evenly dyed. Plaids or other designs that are printed on the fabric should be neat and unblurred. Check carefully for this.

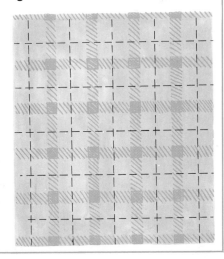

Special layouts. (*right*): For some fabrics, you need to buy more than the normal amount of fabric because of special pattern layout requirements. Some examples are napped fabric, plaids, stripes, large or border prints, and one-way designs. If your pattern does not give you this special yardage information, your teacher can help you figure it.

Difficult Fabrics

Even experienced sewers sometimes think twice before choosing a difficult fabric. The more difficult the fabric is to sew with, the more time and skill you need to work with it. Here are some kinds of fabric that can cause problems. Inexperienced sewers should avoid these fabrics.

• Stiff, bulky fabrics are hard to cut out and hard to sew.

• A very tight weave may look like the perfect beginner's fabric, but it is not. Pin marks and ripped-out seams will show on this kind of fabric.

• Nylons, acetates, some polyesters, silks, and satins are slippery. This makes them hard to cut and sew.

• Loose-woven or looped fabrics such as mohair or terry cloth snag easily or get caught in the sewing machine.

• Stripes and plaids need to be matched. This task takes patience and experience.

• Large prints do not need to be matched, but they create another kind of problem. The print must be balanced evenly over all the pattern pieces.

garment or a fad item that you will not have many chances to wear, you should look for a less expensive fabric or a good quality fabric on sale.

Finally, consider what the fabric will be like to work with. Some fabric unravels the minute you cut it. Others are very slippery to handle. A bulky fabric is harder to cut patterns from than a lightweight one. And no one likes to work on a fabric that wrinkles a lot. Choose a fabric that you will feel confident handling. Your teacher may also have fabric suggestions for you.

BUYING THE RIGHT AMOUNT

The amount of fabric you need is listed on the pattern envelope. Fabric is sold either in meters or yards. You will find a chart for converting metric and customary measures on page 317. The width of the fabric will affect how much you need. Also, be sure to check the right amount for your size and for the view you are making.

For some fabrics, you must buy extra amounts. For example, if you select a plaid, you need extra fabric for matching the plaids at the seams. You will also need extra fabric if the fabric has a *nap*. A nap is a soft, hairy finish on a fabric. Corduroy is a nap fabric. All the nap should run in the same direction, which is why you will need extra fabric. Another reason you might need extra fabric is to allow for shrinkage. Be sure to ask whether or not a fabric has been preshrunk and by how much. If the label says the fabric will not shrink by more than 2

When you buy fabric, always ask for a care label.

When you know	Multiply by	To find
inches	2.5	centimeters
feet	30	centimeters
yards	0.9	meters

percent, you will not need any extra fabric. Try to buy fabric that is preshrunk.

CARE LABELS

Just as the law requires care labels in ready-made clothes, it also requires that such labels be available for fabrics. If the salesperson does not offer labels, be sure to ask for them. You can read more about taking care of your clothing in Chapter 47.

CHOOSING NOTIONS

Notions are all the small items you need for sewing a specific pattern. Try to buy all the notions when you buy the pattern and fabric. That way you will have everything you need when you start to sew and at each step along the way.

One common notion that many garments need is interfacing. *Interfacing* is a type of firmly woven or matted fabric that is cut to fit some of the parts of a garment. It helps to shape the garment by adding body. Interfacing is often used in collars and cuffs. The pattern will tell you the kind of

interfacing to buy, the amount, and how to use it.

Other common notions include zippers, threads, seam bindings, and hem tape. If you plan to make a belt, then you need to buy materials for it. If you plan to use buttons, you need supplies for making covered buttons or buttons that coordinate with the garment. Most of the notions you need are listed on the pattern envelope. Usually anything needed for closures—zippers, buttons, hooks—is listed. You may have to remember to buy matching thread or hem tape.

Notions should match or coordinate with the fabric you have selected. Threads, zippers, binding tapes, and hem tapes all come in a wide selection of colors. Choose one that matches or is slightly darker than the fabric. Also choose these notions to match the fiber content of your fabric. Hooks and eyes and snaps come in black and a light color. Choose the shade that goes with the fabric.

Buttons should match the fabric and the style of the garment. If you are unsure about what kind of button

Threads

A good thread is one that is right for the fabric you have chosen. It must be strong and yet flexible or elastic enough to give with the fabric as you sew with it. A good thread is one that does not tangle easily.

The kind of thread you buy depends on the fabric you have chosen. Use a mercerized cotton thread on cottons and linens. Use silk thread on animal fibers such as wool and on silk. Synthetic threads are excellent for synthetic fabrics. Cotton-wrapped polyester thread works well with most natural and synthetic fabrics.

Mercerized cotton threads are numbered according to their weights. Size 50 or 60 is fine for most sewing, and size 40 is used for heavy-duty sewing. Sizes 80 to 100 are used for lightweight, delicate fabrics.

Silk threads are also marked according to their weights, but letters are used. Silk thread in size A is suitable for most fabrics. Silk size D is a buttonhole thread.

Synthetic threads are so strong and elastic that they are made in one size only.

Fabric Under Fabric

Many garments use one fabric under another.

Underlining gives support and shape to an entire garment. An underlining fabric should be lightweight, and the color should blend with or be the same as that of the fabric.

Interfacing is used to shape a garment in specific places. It is used in collars, cuffs, waistbands, and lapels.

Interlining makes a garment warmer. It is often
(continued)

to choose, look at a similar ready-made garment to see what buttons were used. Remember, buttons serve two purposes. They are part of a closure, but they are also often meant to be decorative or design elements.

The *loop-and-pile fastener* is a new kind of closure device. The name commonly used for this fastener is the trade name Velcro. It consists of two pieces of rough tape. When they are pressed together, they hold securely until they are pulled apart again. The loop-and-pile fastener is too bulky to use on lightweight fabrics, but it is excellent on jackets and coats. Loop-and-pile fastening is often used on slipcovers and pillows.

Notions are a lot of fun to choose. Looking for just the right trim or belt material is just like searching for the perfect belt to wear with a ready-made garment. Notions help you to create a one-of-a-kind garment.

Shop for notions when you go to buy your fabric. Buying everything you need at the same time makes it easier to match thread, zipper, tape, and buttons to the fabric.

Some fabrics need to be handled carefully as you sew with them. This fabric ravels very easily, so directional cutting and stitching are important.

used inside jackets and coats.

Lining gives a neat appearance to the inside of a garment. It can also make the garment easy to put on and take off. A lining fabric should be lightweight, and the color should blend with that of the fabric.

▶ **Words to Know**

closure: A device for closing an opening. Examples in clothing are buttons, hooks and eyes, and the like.

convert: To change into or exchange for something else.

cost per wearing: The purchase and upkeep costs of a garment divided by the number of wearings.

design elements: The color, texture, pattern, and lines of a garment that determine its overall look.

interfacing: A firmly woven or matted fabric sewn inside parts of garments to add shape and body.

nap: The soft surface texture of fabrics like corduroy or velvet.

notions: Small items such as zippers, threads, buttons, and the like needed for sewing and finishing a garment.

a quick review

1. What does the pattern envelope tell you about the fabric you need to make the pattern?
2. Why is it important to choose a sturdy fabric for a beginning sewing project? What might happen if you do not choose a sturdy fabric?
3. What cost factors are important when you are looking for fabric? How might you have to compromise?
4. When might you need to buy more fabric than is called for on the pattern envelope?
5. What common notions are you likely to need to make a garment? What should you keep in mind as you shop for them?

CHAPTER 44
Sewing Machine and Equipment

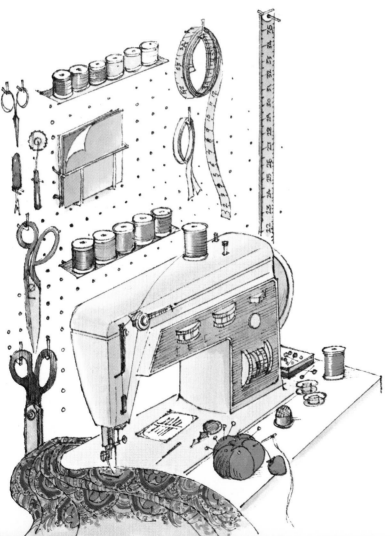

Every trade or craft has its own special tools. For example, an auto mechanic has wrenches and drills that are unique to that trade. A cook has utensils and pans specially designed for cooking. Sewing, too, has special tools. The most important one is the sewing machine. This chapter will help you learn to use and care for a sewing machine. It also includes information about other sewing equipment.

THE SEWING MACHINE

The sewing machine uses thread from two sources. The *top thread* comes from the spool that sits on top of or behind the machine. A smaller spool, called a *bobbin,* holds the bottom thread. The bobbin fits into a special *bobbin case.* It is filled from the top thread.

To make stitches, the machine needle takes the top thread down to the bobbin. The bobbin thread is looped over the top thread. The machine then pulls the threads together to create the basic stitch, called the *lock-stitch.* The different parts of the sewing machine—needle, bobbin, feed dog, tension controls, and presser foot—all work together with exact timing to make the machine sew. The drawings on page 322 show you all the parts of a sewing machine and what they do. Check the machine manual to identify these parts on the machine you are using.

Sewing-machine needles come in different sizes and types for different fabrics. The general rule is the thicker the fabric, the heavier or larger the machine needle should be. The most common needle sizes are 11, 14, 16, and 18. There are sharp, pointed needles for woven fabrics and special needles with rounded points, called *ballpoint needles,* for knit fabrics.

A car has special features such as power steering and automatic transmission. Many sewing machines also have built-in extra features. These enable you to make special stitches that are usually both useful and decorative:

• *Zigzag stitch.* The zigzag stitch is a back-and-forth stitch. It is used to finish seams and edges, to sew seams in some fabrics, and to make buttonholes.

• *Stretch stitches.* Stretch stitches are specially designed to be used on knit fabrics. The machine moves the fabric in a forward-reverse motion while the needle zigzags. This type of stitching can sew and finish the seam at the same time.

• *Buttonholer.* A buttonholer is often a built-in feature of zigzag machines. With special controls, the machine forms a buttonhole of any size, using the zigzag stitch.

• *Blind stitch.* The blind stitch is a combination of straight and zigzag stitches. It sews "invisible" hems by machine on straight edges.

• *Decorative stitches.* Some machines have special decorative stitches built in. On other machines, *cams,* or disks, are inserted into the machine to make the special stitches. Flowers, animals, curves, geometric patterns, and other interesting designs can be sewn with these stitches. Decorative stitches are good as garment trims and can also be used in place of topstitching.

In addition to built-in features, a sewing machine usually has *accessories.* These are usually special *feet* used in place of the standard presser foot. The *zipper foot* is used to put in zippers. It can be moved to the right or left side of the zipper teeth. It is also used for sewing piping and cording. A *buttonhole attachment* is a handy item to have if your machine has no built-in buttonholer or if you find the built-in one difficult to control. The attachment makes buttonholes in different sizes and shapes. A *seam guide* is an accessory that attaches to the machine with screws or a magnet. It helps guide the fabric as you sew so that the seam is straight. A seam guide can be adjusted to different seam allowances; it is also a big help for topstitching.

Other accessories and attachments include a quilting foot, a roller foot, an even-feed foot, a cording foot, a

New Ways to Sew

When Elias Howe made the first sewing machine in 1846, his invention was very advanced. Now there are new and even more surprising developments in sewing.

There are now sewing machines on the market that use the principles of computers. One such machine has an electronic "memory." When you push a button, the machine's "brain" remembers one of fourteen programmed stitches. Lights indicate correct stitch length and proper stitch speed. The machine's control panel also lights up if the machine is not operating properly.

There are also ultrasonic sewing machines on the market. *Ultrasonic* means "beyond sound." This type of machine sews by vibrating at a sound beyond the range of the human ear. The high-speed vibrations produce heat, which melts two pieces of fabric together to join them.

There are other advantages to this type of machine. The seams that it makes are as strong or stronger than those joined by thread. And since the welding is colorless, there is no need to spend time or money buying or matching thread.

Basic Parts of the Machine

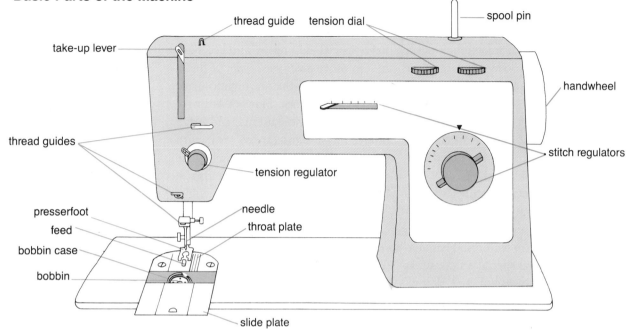

- thread guide
- tension dial
- spool pin
- take-up lever
- handwheel
- thread guides
- tension regulator
- stitch regulators
- presserfoot
- feed
- bobbin case
- bobbin
- needle
- throat plate
- slide plate

The sewing machine you see here may not look exactly like the one you use at home or school. Each brand and model of machine is a little different. However, all sewing machines have the same basic parts. These parts are shown here. Look at the box on the next page for a description of what each part does. For more information on the machine you are using, look in the machine operating manual.

How a Stitch is Formed

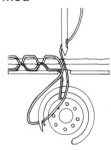
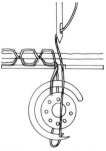
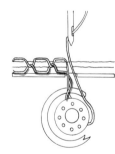
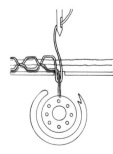

1. The needle moves down through the fabric, bringing the top thread near the bobbin.

2. As needle moves back up, the top thread forms a loop that is caught by the shuttle hook.

3. The shuttle hook moves the thread loop around and under the bobbin case.

4. The top thread loop slides off the hook around the bobbin thread.

5. Both threads are pulled up by the needle. This makes a lock stitch.

What Each Part Does

Head: The machine piece containing most of the sewing parts.

Handwheel, or **balance wheel:** The wheel on the right side of the head. It controls the movement of the take-up lever and needle.

Bobbin: The spool that holds the lower thread in stitching. It fits into a **bobbin case,** or **shuttle.** The bobbin thread tension is regulated here.

Slide plate: The metal plate covering the bobbin case, or shuttle.

Spool pin and **thread guides:** Pieces that guide the upper thread.

Needle: A thin metal shaft with an eye and a point at one end. It is held with a clamp. It carries the thread through the fabric.

Presser foot: The piece that holds the fabric in place as you stitch. It is raised and lowered by a lever called a presser-bar lifter. For stitching, the presser foot is lowered gently, with the fabric in place. After stitching, it is raised and the fabric is removed.

Throat plate: The metal plate directly under the machine needle.

Feed, or **feed dog:** The toothlike part located under the presser foot. It moves the fabric along toward the back of the machine as you stitch.

Stitch regulators: Dials and levers that set the machine for different stitch lengths, widths, or patterns.

Take-up lever: The lever through which the upper thread passes. It moves up and down as the machine is operated.

Tension regulator: The device that controls the looseness and tightness of the stitch by controlling the pull on the upper thread.

ruffler, a hemmer, double needles, a binder, and an edge stitcher. Check the machine manual to find out which accessories are available for your machine.

SETTING UP TO SEW

When you sew in class, you probably have a machine assigned for your use. If you have a sewing machine at home, set it up on a sturdy work surface. Find a stool or straight-backed chair that is right for your height. You should not have to bend over the machine. Make sure that the room in which you are sewing is well lit. If you use a lamp, the light should come over your left shoulder as you sit at the machine.

At the machine, sit back in the chair or stool. Lean forward slightly, but keep your back straight. Keep your feet flat on the floor. Check your machine manual. It will tell you how to use the knee- or foot-control pedal.

Before you begin to sew, make sure the machine is plugged in. Turn on the machine light and, if the machine has one, the machine power switch. Fill the bobbin. Then thread the machine according to the directions. Now you are ready to sew. If you are a beginner, practice with the machine unthreaded first. Sew on lined paper, guiding the needle along the lines. This way you will learn how to handle and control the ma-

Correct Tension

The right *thread tension* means that there is the same amount of pull on both the top and bottom thread. When the tension is adjusted correctly, the stitch is in balance, top and bottom. It is easy to adjust the top tension. Most tension problems are solved this way. Bottom tension adjustment requires an expert.

Correct Tension Adjustment:

When both tensions are in adjustment, the needle and bobbin threads are locked in the center of the fabric.

Tight Upper Tension:

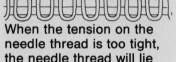

When the tension on the needle thread is too tight, the needle thread will lie straight along the upper surface of the fabric.

Loose Upper Tension:

When the tension on the needle is too loose, the bobbin thread will lie straight along the under side of the fabric.

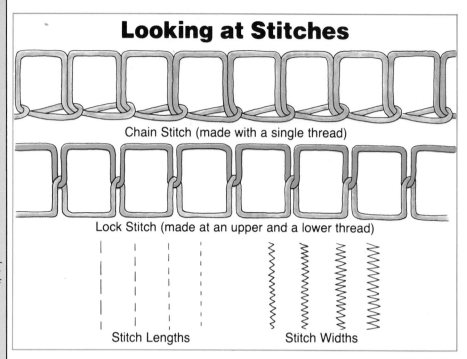

Looking at Stitches

Chain Stitch (made with a single thread)

Lock Stitch (made at an upper and a lower thread)

Stitch Lengths   Stitch Widths

chine. Start slowly and gradually increase your speed as you feel more comfortable.

As you sew, keep the fabric to the left of the needle. Watch the right edge of the fabric. Direct it along the seam guidelines or along the seam guide. If your machine does not have guidelines, place a piece of tape on the throat plate 1.5 centimeters ($\frac{5}{8}$ inch) from the needle.

SEWING EQUIPMENT

The tools of the sewing trade also include some important smaller pieces of equipment. These tools are used for cutting, marking, measuring, pressing, and sewing the fabric. Try to find quality tools whenever you can. They make the job easier and your work better.

Cutting Tools. *Bent-handled shears* with 18- or 20.5-centimeter (7- or 8-inch) blades are the easiest to use for cutting out the fabric. Keep them sharp. *Pinking shears* are handy for an instant seam finish. Never cut out a pattern with them, however, because you'll lose an accurate seam allowance. *Trimming scissors* about 15 centimeters (6 inches) long are good for clipping, trimming, and grading seams. A *seam ripper,* like the eraser on your pencil, is for correcting mistakes. Use the seam ripper to cut

Solving Your Machine Problems

Problem: Thread breaks.

Check: √ Size of needle—too big or too small. √ Type of thread—too thin, knotted, or uneven. √ Type of needle—may be wrong for the fabric. √ Machine threading—may be incorrect. √ Tension—may be too tight.

Problem: Skipped stitches.

Check: √ Type of needle—may be wrong for the fabric. √ Stitch length—may be too long. √ Condition of needle—may be dull or bent. √ Machine threading—may be incorrect. √ Needle position—may be wrong.

Problem: Needle breaks.

Check: √ Tension—may be too tight. √ Needle position—may be wrong. √ Presser foot—may not be tight. √ Fabric—too many layers or too thick.

Problem: Seams pucker.

Check: √ Tension—may be too tight. √ Needle—may be too big or dull. √ Thread—may be too coarse. √ Stitch length—may be too long.

Problem: Fabric jams in machine.

Check: √ Thread ends—may need to be held at start of stitching. √ Needle—may be too big. √ Throat plate—may need round hole plate.

Problem: Machine jams.

Check: √ Bobbin threading—may be incorrect. √ Thread—may be knotted or too coarse √ Bobbin case—threads may be caught there. √ Needle position—may be wrong. √ Machine threading—may be incorrect.

Machine-Care Checklist

Any sewing machine will work better if you take care of it. Here are some tips:

• Use a small brush to remove lint from around the bobbin and upper thread tension.

• If the machine is noisy or stiff, it probably needs oil. A drop or two in the right places will keep it running smoothly. Check your machine manual for the spots that should be oiled. After oiling, sew on a scrap of fabric to pick up any extra oil.

• Many older machine motors need internal lubrication. This can be done at a repair center. Check your machine manual.

• Check your needle often. Never sew with a dull needle.

• Wipe the outside of the machine with a damp (but not dripping) sponge.

---

stitching between layers of fabric or to cut open a stitch every 2.5 centimeters (1 inch) or so along one side of the seam. Then pull out the thread from the other side in one long length.

Marking Equipment. *Tracing paper* and a *tracing wheel* are used to transfer pattern markings onto the fabric. Tracing paper comes in different colors. Choose a color that will show up on the fabric without being too dark. Tracing wheels are either smooth, for flat, thin fabrics, or toothed, for textured and bulky fabrics. A wheel with blunt teeth works well with light- and medium-weight fabrics. Use trac-

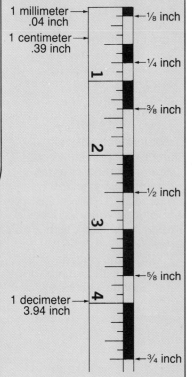

ing paper only on the wrong side of the fabric. *Chalk* for marking fabric comes in different forms. A chalk pencil is good for drawing lines. Tailor's chalk is a square piece of chalk in a refillable holder. The markings made by a chalk pencil and by tailor's chalk can be easily brushed off most fabrics.

Measuring Tools.   A *measuring stick* is used for drawing long, straight lines. It is also used to check grain lines and to measure hems and fabric. A ruler is used as a guide with the tracing wheel when marking fabric. A measuring stick is also called a *meterstick* or *yardstick,* depending on how it is marked. You may be able to find the type that has inches on one side and centimeters on the other. A *tape measure* is used in taking body measurements and later in actual construction. Try to find one made of plastic that will not stretch. It is also helpful to have inches on one side and centimeters on the other. A *sewing gauge* is a handy little 15-centimeter (6-inch) ruler with a sliding marker. It is useful for measuring seams and pockets and for turning up hems.

Pressing Equipment.   An ironing board, or other padded surface, and a steam iron are basic necessities for sewing. Good pressing as you go along adds to the professional look of

your garment. A *press cloth* protects fabric from the shiny marks an iron may make. A press cloth can also be used to add more moisture if needed. Press cloths come in different types. A thin, see-through (often disposable) cloth and cheesecloth give you minimum protection from the iron. Drill cloth is used for extra protection. Wool press cloths prevent the iron from flattening the surface texture of fabrics. Muslin is often used with fusible interfacings.

   A *tailor's ham* is a firm cushion shaped like a real ham. It is used to press curved and shaped seams and darts. The ham helps you shape the garment as you press. A *press mitt* is a smaller version of a tailor's ham. It fits over your hand and is used for small rounded or hard-to-reach areas. A *seam roll* is a long cushion shaped like a tube. It is used for pressing seams open so the seam allowance does not cause lumps on the right side of the fabric. A *sleeveboard* is a small, two-sided ironing board for pressing flat areas. It is used to iron small pieces of a garment during the construction process.

Small Sewing Items.   There are several small items that are helpful for both machine and hand sewing. *Straight pins* hold layers of fabric together for cutting and sewing. They are made of brass or stainless steel. You can get sharp pins for woven

SMALL SEWING EQUIPMENT

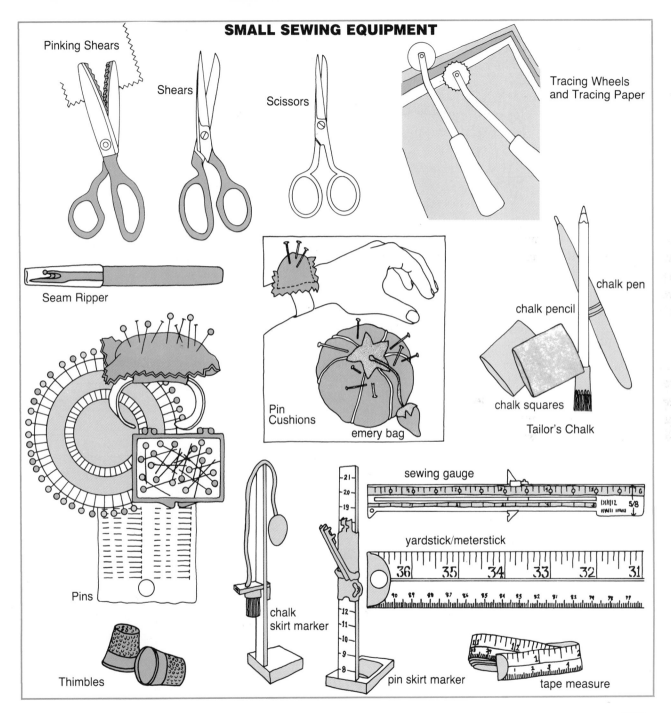

Pinking Shears

Shears

Scissors

Tracing Wheels and Tracing Paper

Seam Ripper

Pin Cushions

emery bag

chalk pen

chalk pencil

chalk squares

Tailor's Chalk

Pins

Thimbles

chalk skirt marker

pin skirt marker

sewing gauge

5/8

yardstick/meterstick

tape measure

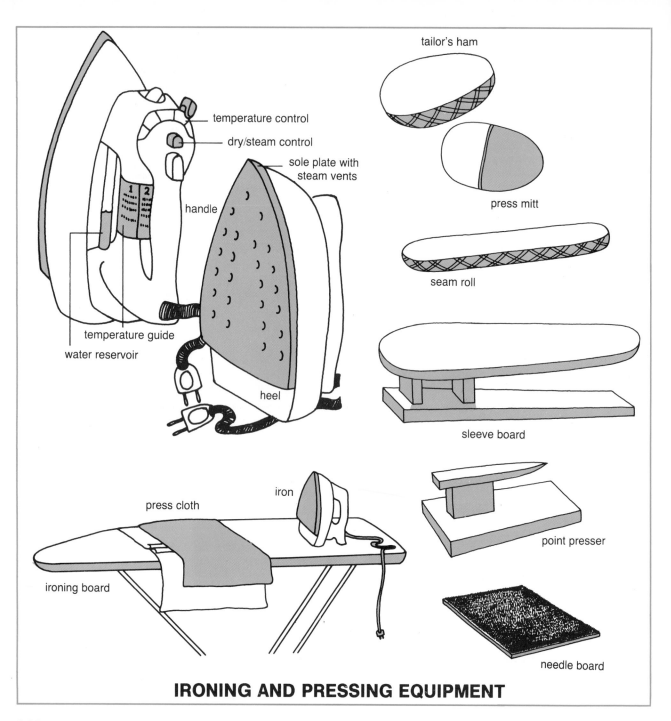

temperature control

dry/steam control

sole plate with steam vents

handle

temperature guide

water reservoir

heel

tailor's ham

press mitt

seam roll

sleeve board

press cloth

iron

ironing board

point presser

needle board

IRONING AND PRESSING EQUIPMENT

fabrics and special ball-point pins for knits. Pins may have either metal or plastic heads. *Needles* for hand sewing come in a variety of sizes and lengths. There are sharp needles for woven fabrics and ball-point needles for knits. Needles vary in size from 1 to 12. The smaller the number, the larger the needle. For most hand sewing, needles in sizes 7 or 8 are a good choice. Experiment with different sizes to find the needle that is most comfortable for you. Generally, the thinner the fabric, the smaller the needle should be.

Basting tape is a narrow tape that is sticky on both sides. It may be used instead of pins to hold layers of fabric together or to hold zippers in place for sewing. Your teacher may not want you to use basting tape until you are more experienced. If you do use it, take care not to sew through it, because it can leave a sticky residue on the needle. *Beeswax* keeps thread from tangling when you are doing hand sewing. A *pincushion* is a place to store your pins. It also allows them to be picked up easily. A wrist pincushion is often convenient to use. A *thimble* protects your finger in hand sewing. It can be either metal or plastic. A thimble should fit snugly on your middle finger. You use it to push the needle through the fabric. A *point turner* has a wedge-shaped end for pushing out the corners of collars, cuffs, and other enclosed seams. Some also serve as rulers.

Thread comes in different fibers, thicknesses, and colors. Use the type of thread most suited to your fabric. Cotton-covered polyester thread can be used on almost all types of fabrics. Cotton, silk, and polyester threads are also available. Choose the same color or a shade slightly darker than your fabric. Look for extra-strong thread for sewing on buttons and special thread for topstitching and quilting.

a quick review

1. How does a sewing machine form stitches?
2. Why is thread tension so important on a sewing machine?
3. Name the common sewing accessories and explain their use.
4. Why are good sewing tools important?
5. Imagine you are setting up your own sewing room or corner. What would you need, and why?

CHAPTER 45
Preparation for Sewing

The time and care you take in preparing your project for stitching will show in the quality of the finished product. Your work now will make each step in the sewing process go more quickly and easily.

The *instruction sheet* inside your pattern envelope is a step-by-step guide to help you construct your garment. This sheet also contains directions for laying out and pinning the pattern on various widths of fabric, a guide to pattern symbol markings, and some other general instructions. Read your instruction sheet completely through at least one time. That will give you a good overall idea of the project. Refer to the sheet often as you work. Some instruction sheets even have boxes to check off as you complete a step.

Before you begin work, set some goals for yourself. Decide how much time you will need to complete each step. Be realistic. Your teacher can help you plan out your work time. If you are not rushed, you will be able to feel a sense of accomplishment as you finish each task. Finally, organize all of your sewing needs, such as your fabric, pattern, notions, and tools, before you begin.

FIRST STEPS

Prepare to lay the pattern on your fabric by following these steps:

1. Study the instruction sheet to

find the suggested layout for the size, style, and fabric width you are using.

2. Circle the layout you have selected so you can spot it quickly each time you want to refer to it for help.

3. Take out the pattern pieces you will need. Return unneeded ones to the pattern envelope.

4. Put your name on each pattern piece, on your instruction sheet, and on the envelope.

5. Press wrinkled pattern pieces smooth and flat with a slightly warm iron.

6. Check the grain on woven fabrics and straighten if needed. Straighten the ends of knitted fabrics. The box on page 332 has information on how to do this.

7. Read the fabric label carefully. If necessary, preshrink your fabric, lining, and other trims that have not already been preshrunk.

8. Press the fabric or trims if they are wrinkled or creased.

CHECKING PATTERN FIT

Before you cut into your fabric, you want to be sure that your pattern fits you exactly. Go back to your list of body measurements. Compare them to the measurements of your pattern pieces. Measure from seamline to seamline. Never measure the seam allowances on the pattern pieces. Also, any garment should be slightly larger than your body measurements. You need this *ease* allowance, or extra room in your clothes, to get them on and to move around in them.

The chest or bust measurement should include at least 7.5 to 10 centimeters (3 to 4 inches) of ease allowance if you are using a nonstretchable woven fabric. For example, someone who measures 80 centimeters (32 inches) around the fullest part of the bust needs a garment that measures 90 centimeters (36 inches) in that area. Stretchable knitted fabrics require less ease allowance. Add at least 5 centimeters (2 inches) to the hip measurement. Add an extra 2.5 centimeters (1 inch) to the waistline measurement. These added measurements provide for comfort and body movement.

Most people are not standard pattern sizes. If your size is very different from the standard, you may need to make adjustments. For example, the pattern may well be too long or too short for you. To adjust it, simply pin tucks in the pattern pieces to make them smaller or insert paper strips to make them larger. The drawings on page 333 will show you how. So will your teacher.

LAYOUT AND PINNING

The *pattern layout* shows the best way to arrange the pattern pieces with as little fabric waste as possible.

Taking Care of Your Pattern

- Write your name and class period on the pattern envelope.
- Remove the pattern and check the pieces with the guide sheet to be sure all the pieces are there.
- Write your name and class period near the center of each pattern piece.
- Before attaching the pattern to fabric, press all wrinkles from the pattern pieces with a warm—not hot—iron.
- Handle the pattern pieces carefully so you won't tear them.
- Try not to tear the pieces as you mark the garment.
- Mend torn pattern pieces with cellophane tape.
- Keep the pattern and the guide sheet in your sewing box during the construction of your garment.
- Place related pattern pieces together immediately after use, and fold them together smoothly and neatly to fit inside the pattern envelope. Store them in the pattern envelope.
- Store the pattern with other patterns to use again.

PREPARING YOUR FABRIC

There are several steps you may have to take to prepare the fabric before you pin and cut the pattern. These include preshrinking, straightening the grain, and ironing.

Preshrinking means shrinking the fabric before the garment is made. Check the manufacturer's label to see if your fabric has been preshrunk. Fabric is usually preshrunk the same way it is cleaned. For example, if the fabric can be machine washed and dried, washing and drying it in an automatic machine will preshrink it.

Straightening your fabric is necessary if it is *off grain,* or not straight. A fabric that is off grain may be difficult to cut out and sew. A garment made from off-grain fabric may hang wrong when you wear it.

Use one of the methods shown below to see if the grain is straight.

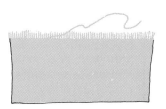 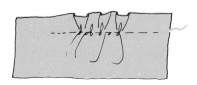 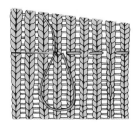

Finding the Grain. Find the crosswise grain by unraveling the cut edge until you can pull a thread all the way across without it breaking or by pulling a thread across the width of the fabric and cutting off the uneven edge above it. (*center*).

To find the grain of a knit, mark stitches across and down the fabric near the edges. (*right*).

Once you have found both grainlines, fold the fabric in half lengthwise. The lengthwise and crosswise grains should meet at right angles. If the corners will not meet without wrinkling, the fabric is off grain. If necessary, use one of the methods below to straighten your fabric.

Straightening the Grain. To straighten fabric that is slightly off grain, pull the opposite ends of the fabric until the crosswise grain is straight (*left*).

If the fabric still does not lie flat when folded or the corners are not square, pin the edges together. Begin steam pressing from the cut edge and work toward the fold (*right*). Smooth the fabric with your hands while the fabric is still hot.

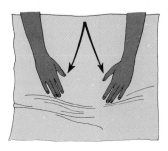 

There are special layouts for directional stripes or prints or napped fabrics. Follow the layout sketch carefully so that you do not end up with two right trouser legs or, worse yet, not enough fabric. You have already circled your correct layout. Refer to this sketch and follow these tips for laying out and pinning the pattern pieces on your fabric:

1. Fold the fabric as shown on the layout with right sides together.
2. Place the pattern pieces in position on the fabric.
3. Check that pattern grainline arrows are going in the correct direction. When you have all pattern pieces in their proper positions, start pinning.
4. Pin pattern pieces located on the foldlines first.
5. For other pieces, start by placing a pin at one grainline arrowhead. Make sure the arrow is on the straight grain of the fabric by measuring from the pinned arrowhead to the fabric edge or selvage. Move the pattern so the other grainline arrowhead is the same distance from the edge. Pin.
6. Smooth the pattern and pin each corner inside the cutting line. Place pins at right angles to the

What's the Right Side?

Pattern instructions often say, "place the right sides together." The *right side* is the side that will show or be on the outside when the garment is completed.

Finding the right side of the fabric is often confusing. In satins and polished cottons, the shiny side is the right side. In napped fabrics, look for the raised surface. Cottons are usually folded right side out. Sometimes a design is printed only on one side. That is the right side.

Make all pattern alterations and adjustments before cutting. Be sure to cut along the thick black cutting line. The broken line marks the sewing line.

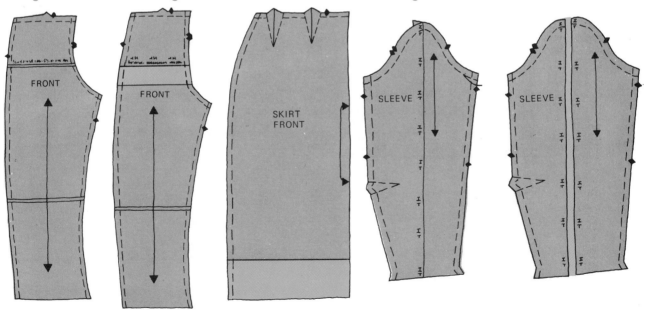

CONSTRUCTION MARKINGS

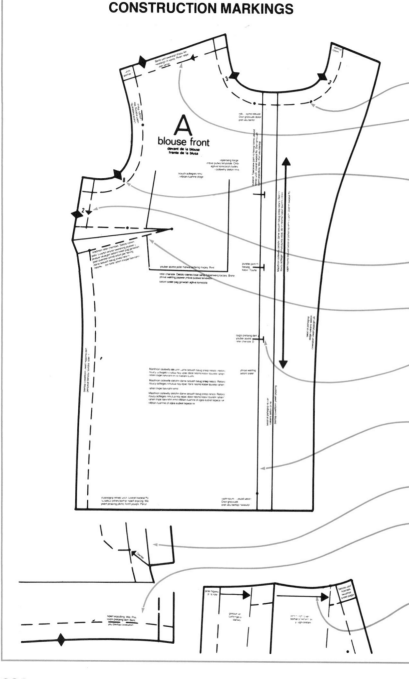

Construction markings are the guide posts for putting together and sewing your garment. Some patterns have many of these markings, others have only a few, depending on the design details of the style.

Dots are aids for matching seams and other construction details.

The seam line (stitching line) is indicated by a broken line. It is usually 1.5 cm (⅝″) from the cutting line, but it can vary in certain areas.

Notches are V-shaped symbols along the cutting line which aid in joining pattern pieces. Two or more notches may be grouped together to form a block for easier cutting.

Arrows on the seam line indicate the direction in which the pieces should be stitched so as not to distort the fabric grain.

Darts are indicated by two broken lines for stitching and a solid line at center for folding.

Buttonholes are indicated by a solid line having a short line at right angles to one end when horizontal or at both ends when vertical.

Solid lines are used also to indicate center fold lines, some hemlines, placement for pockets and trimmings that go on the outside of the garment.

"Clip" with a short arrow indicates where to clip into the seam allowance to release it.

Gathering or **easing** is indicated by a broken line similar to a seam line, but labeled 'gathering line" or "ease." Usually, you gather or ease between two points on the pattern.

Pleats are usually indicated by an alternating solid and broken line. Arrows show the direction of the pleating with the instruction "fold along solid line; bring fold to broken line."

stitching line approximately every 15 to 20 centimeters (6 to 8 inches) around the pattern piece. Recheck the layout sketch. Be sure that all the pattern pieces fit on the fabric before you begin to cut.

7. Check your finished layout with your teacher.

CUTTING OUT

Always cut your fabric with the grain by cutting in the direction of the stitching line arrows. Cutting this way is called *directional cutting.* Cutting directionally places less pull on the grain of the fabric.

Use sharp shears. Take long, even strokes to cut along straight areas. Use the points of the shears to cut corners, curves, and small details. As you cut, keep the bottom of the shears touching the table. Keep the fabric flat on your cutting surface at all times. Be careful not to cut off notches. Cut away from the pattern around the notch. Cut double and triple notches as if they were one big notch.

TRANSFERRING PATTERN SYMBOLS

Each pattern piece is marked with lines, arrows, dots, and notches. These are called *pattern symbols* or *construction markings.* They show you how to place the pattern on the fabric, where to cut, where to match, where to alter, and where to sew. Look at the illustration on page 334 to see what these symbols look like and how they are used.

Look at the illustration on page 334 to see what these symbols look like and how they are used.

Hand Sewing Tips

Sometimes a project needs some hand sewing in addition to machine sewing. Hand sewing may be needed to hold a hem in place or to attach snaps, hooks and eyes, or buttons. Sometimes a zipper needs to be hand basted in place. Here are some guidelines to follow for any type of hand sewing:

• The needle is easier to thread if you cut the thread with scissors.
• Use a short thread, about 45 to 60 centimeters (18 to 24 inches) long, so it won't tangle.
• Use a single thread unless you are sewing on snaps, hooks and eyes, or buttons.
• Use thread that matches your fabric unless you are basting.

Directional fabrics require a special layout. Pattern pieces must be placed so that all pieces are heading in the same direction. Is the pattern layout below suitable for the directional fabric shown?

Selvage edges

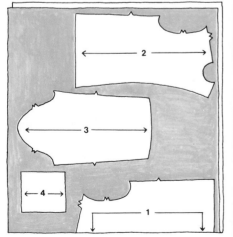

Fold of fabric

Why Sew?

People sew for a lot of different reasons. Their projects range from very simple to very complex. One person may choose to sew a chef's apron while another may decide to reupholster a chair. Some of the reasons people sew are:

• for enjoyment and satisfaction
• to have better-made clothing for the same price
• to have more individuality in their clothing
• to have more variety and color in their wardrobe
• to have clothes that fit properly
• to develop a skill that could be job-related
• to develop a skill that can be used in making smart purchases of ready-made clothing
• to make articles for their room or home
• to make gifts that are individual and inexpensive

PINNING AND CUTTING

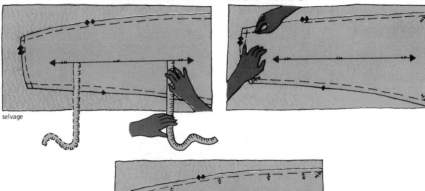

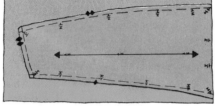

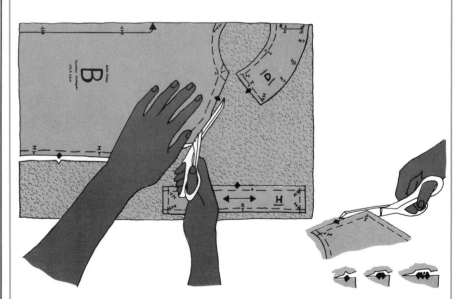

Check to see that each pattern piece is on the straight grain by measuring from the grain line to the edge of the fabric (*top*). Smooth the tissue and place pins in the corners. Then pin around the rest of the pattern (*center*). Leave the pattern piece flat while you cut (*bottom*).

Marking with Tailor's Tacks

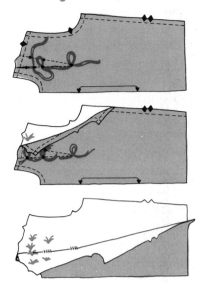

There are several ways to transfer these markings to your fabric. The fastest and easiest way to do it is to use the special carbon tracing paper and tracing wheel described in Chapter 44. Remove enough pins from the pattern to slide the colored side of the tracing paper against the wrong sides of your fabric. Make sure both fabric layers are flat. Run the tracing wheel along the marking lines. The color from the tracing paper will be transferred to the wrong sides of the fabric. Do not mark the right side of fabric. Never use this method on light-colored, sheer, heavily napped, or loosely woven fabrics. Always test-mark a scrap of your fabric first.

You can also transfer markings by using *tailor's tacks* or a tailor's chalk

Working with Knits

Knit fabrics often need to be treated differently from woven fabrics in the construction process:

• The seam must be able to stretch with the fabric in the finished garment or the stitches will break. Use a special stitch or technique that allows for this. Ask your teacher about other special techniques to use. Knits that curl at the edges may need overedge stitching.
• Handle knits gently so they won't stretch.
• Use ball-point needles.
• Put strips of paper under the seam allowance when pressing to avoid making marks on the right side.

Marking with Tracing Wheel and Paper

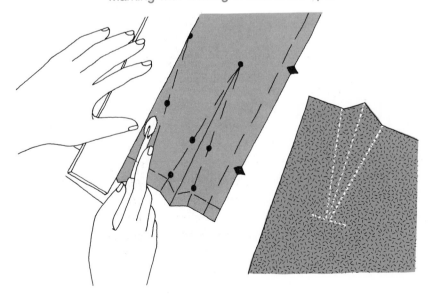

construction markings: The symbols on a pattern that show how to place the pattern on the fabric, where to cut, where to match, and where to sew.

directional cutting: Cutting fabric in the direction of the grain.

ease: Extra room in a garment that allows for body movement.

grain: The direction in which the threads in a fabric run.

pattern symbols: Another name for construction markings (see above).

preshrink: To shrink fabric before making it into a garment so that the finished garment will not shrink later.

seam allowance: The amount of fabric that is between the cutting line and the stitching line for a seam, as marked on a garment pattern.

seamline: The line on a pattern that shows where to stitch a seam.

and pins. Tailor's tacks are long, loose hand stitches made with an unknotted double thread. You make a tailor's tack at each marking point. This method is good for light-colored, sheer, or heavily napped fabrics.

A tailor's chalk and pins are useful for marking fabric quickly. Push pins through the fabric and pattern at the points you want to mark, then chalk-mark both wrong sides of the fabric. This method is not very permanent since the pins can drop out easily, but it is good for alterations.

At this point you have completed all of the preparations for sewing. However, you are not quite ready to sit down at the machine. Take some time to reorganize. Begin by gathering up all but the tiniest scraps of fabric. You can use these scraps for testing machine tension and for tracing paper colors. Make sure unused pattern pieces are put back into the envelope. These pieces will be easier to use the next time if you fold each one separately so that the pattern style number, size, and pattern piece letter show. Neatly fold any large pieces of leftover fabric. These pieces will be useful for repairs or for making accessory items. Gather up all notions and tools that you will not be using immediately. Put them in their proper places so they are ready the next time you need them. Now you can get down to the actual business of sewing.

a quick review

1. Describe the instruction sheet that comes with a commercial pattern. How will it help you with your project?
2. How do you check your pattern for fit?
3. What do you do before you place your pattern on the fabric?
4. What are the steps for laying out and pinning your pattern pieces?
5. What is directional cutting?
6. Explain how to transfer pattern symbols to your fabric.

After all your fabric is cut out and marked, you are ready to begin putting the pieces together. This process is called *construction*. The construction of a garment may look hard or even mysterious until you know how to do it. It is really just a series of basic steps. You will probably be using the *unit method* of construction. In the unit method, the different sections of the garment are assembled one at a time. As each section is completed, it is pressed. When several or all of the sections are completed, they are joined together to make the garment.

Take out the pieces of fabric you have cut out. It is a good idea to keep them attached to the pattern pieces until you are ready to work with them. Also, take out your instruction sheet. It gives you the directions for your project.

Once you have learned the few basic skills required to construct a garment, you will use them over and over in different combinations. As you gain self-confidence, you can go on to learn more advanced skills. The basic methods you will read about in this chapter give you everything you need to know to make most garments.

CHAPTER 46
Construction

Completing Facings

After a curved facing is attached, graded, and clipped, it is usually understitched. *Understitching* is a line of machine stitching through the facing and the seam allowances. It helps facings look smoother and lie flatter.

To understitch, smooth the facing and seam allowance edges away from the rest of the garment. Then stitch on the right side of the facing as close as possible to the seam. You will be sewing through three layers of fabric.

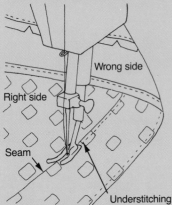

The raw edge on a facing needs to be finished so that it won't ravel. One way to do this is to fold the edge under and stitch. This is called *clean finishing*. It can also be done using a zigzag machine stitch.

CONSTRUCTION METHODS

Staystitching. Staystitching is done on the raw, cut edge of fabric to help prevent stretching. It is especially important on bias edges, which are cut diagonally to the fabric grain, and on curved edges. The pattern directions tell you where to staystitch. To staystitch, machine stitch 1.3 centimeters (½ inch) from the cut edge. Stitch through one layer of fabric only.

Darts and Tucks. Darts and tucks are small folds stitched into fabric. Tucks can be made in various shapes. Examples are folds or small pleats on the front of pants or a skirt. Tucks can be used on the inside or outside of a garment. Some are just for deco-

The arrows on these pattern pieces show which direction to follow as you cut and sew.

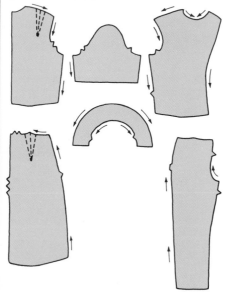

ration. Darts, on the other hand, go on the inside of a garment. They are used to take in and remove fullness. Darts are pointed where fullness is needed, and they are wide where fullness is to be removed. For example, darts are often sewn into the waist area of a shirt. They remove the fullness and taper the waist area. Darts come to a point. Some darts are pointed on both ends. The positions of darts are marked on pattern pieces. Directions for sewing them are given in the pattern instructions. More on sewing darts can be found in the third column on page 341.

Directional Stitching. Stitching joins two pieces of fabric. When two pieces are stitched together, they make a *seam*. There are many ways to make seams, but directional stitching is the most common. Directional stitching means stitching in the direction of the grain of the fabric. This kind of stitching makes seams that are smooth and flat. It also helps prevent stretching and puckering. In a shirt, directional stitching normally goes from the bottom to the top. Most pattern instructions tell you which way to do directional stitching. If they do not, stitch from the wide end to the narrow end.

When you cut out the pattern pieces, you also cut out small notches on their outer edges. To join two pieces of fabric to make a seam, first match the notches.

Facings. Facings are small pieces of fabric attached to the main fabric pieces at the edges. Facings cover interfacings, which are discussed below, and they also help to shape the garment. Facings are usually made from the same fabric as the garment itself. However, if the garment fabric is bulky or scratchy, another fabric may be used. There are three basic kinds of facings. The first is the *fitted facing.* It is shaped to the curve of the garment. Fitted facings are used mostly on collars and armholes.

The second kind of facing is the *bias facing.* It is cut diagonally across the fabric. Because of the way it is cut, it stretches easily and can be used to fit around curved seams. Bias facings are used on sheer fabrics where a wide facing would show through. They can also be used anywhere that you do not want to have the garment fabric against your skin.

The third kind of facing is the *extended facing.* Unlike the other facings, it is not a separate piece of fabric. An extended facing is part of the main fabric piece that is folded under to create the facing. Extended facings are most often used along the fronts of shirts and jackets.

Interfacings. Interfacings are used to add firmness and shape. They are made of special fabric (either woven or nonwoven). Interfacings usually go between the garment and the facings. An interfacing is first sewn to the fac-

ing. Then both are joined to the main section of the garment.

Finishing Seams. How you finish a seam depends on the kind of seam it is. Directional seams are often simply pressed open. The raw edges on facings and other seams can be finished in several ways. Two finishing methods are *clean finishing* and *understitching.* The third column on page 340 will explain both of them.

PRESSING

Pressing is as important as stitching when you are sewing. It helps to shape the garment and smooth out its lines. The result is that your sewing looks more professional. Never skimp on pressing when you are sewing. Think of it as one of your most important steps.

How do you know when to press as you sew? Here are the times when pressing is especially important:

• Press each section when you have finished stitching it together.

• Press darts before they are stitched through to join seams. Press shoulder and waist darts toward the center of the garment. Press underarm darts downward.

• Press shoulder, underarm, and side seams after they are stitched.

• Press main seams before joining the top and bottom of a garment.

• Press the hem in place before you stitch it.

Darts

There are three simple steps in making a dart. First you mark it. Then you pin it. Finally, you stitch it. Darts can be either single- or double-pointed. Study the drawings below carefully to see how to sew a dart.

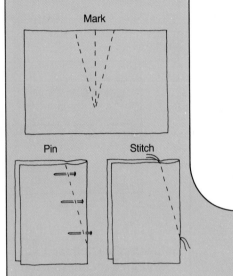

Mark

Pin   Stitch

Backstitch at the widest point of a dart to reinforce it. To finish a dart, leave about 5 centimeters (2 inches) of thread at the ends. There is no need to backstitch or tie off the threads if they will be sewn over to make a seam or to attach a waistband. If the threads will not be sewn over, however, the points should be neatly tied off.

TYPES OF SEAMS

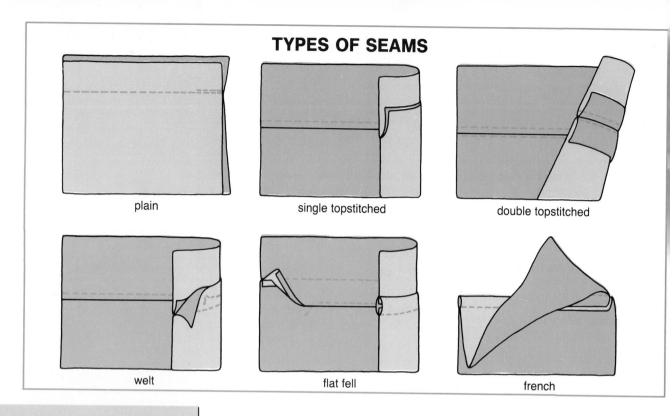

plain   single topstitched   double topstitched

welt   flat fell   french

• Give the finished garment a final pressing.

Remember that pressing is not the same as ironing. In *ironing,* pressure does the work. In *pressing,* steam does it. To press, lay the hot steam iron lightly on the section you are pressing. With a dry iron, use a wet press cloth. Lift the iron and move it forward about 15 centimeters (6 inches). Keep it close to the fabric. This is when the steam does its work. Lower the iron again on the garment. Continue this process until you have pressed the entire seam or section of the garment you are working on.

SPECIAL SEWING METHODS

Once you have sewn together the basic pattern pieces, you may want to hurry up and finish your project. However, now you will be attaching or working on parts that show, such as collars, closures, sleeves, and pockets. Therefore, it is important that you work slowly and carefully. Take your time and be sure to sew each part as well as you possibly can. Here are some tips:

Closures. Closures should be stitched as neatly as possible. Directions for inserting a zipper are given

PRESSING A FINISHED GARMENT

Pressing is an up-and-down motion as shown here. Steam and a press cloth are important aids to getting good results. You can read more about pressing on page 353.

SEAM FINISHES

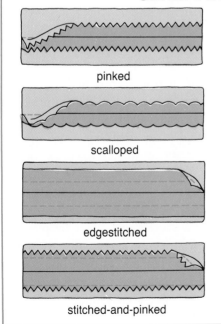

pinked

scalloped

edgestitched

stitched-and-pinked

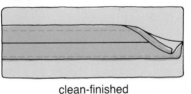

clean-finished

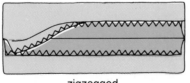

zigzagged

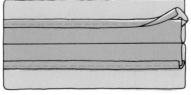

bound

Trimming and Grading

Many seams need further treatment after being stitched. This is true of seams that cannot remain flat or pressed open. Trimming, grading, and clipping are all used to treat seams.

To *trim* a seam, cut off about half of the seam allowance. Cut through both thicknesses. This will reduce the bulk in the seam when the facing is turned to the inside.

trimming:

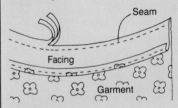

To *grade,* or layer, a seam after it has been trimmed, cut off half of the remaining seam allowance on the facing side. Cut through only one thickness of fabric. Do not cut too close to the stitching. Leave at least 3 to 6 millimeters ($\frac{1}{8}$ to $\frac{1}{4}$ inch) of seam allowance or the seam may unravel.

grading:

343

Clipping and Notching

Curved seams need clipping or notching to make them lie flat.

clipping:

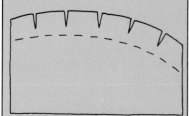

On a seam that curves outward, the raw edge forms a larger arc than the stitching line. To clip, cut slits into the trimmed seam allowance. Do not cut into the stitching line.

notching:

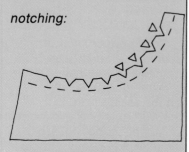

On a seam that curves inward, the raw edge forms a smaller arc than the stitching line. To notch, cut tiny triangle-shaped pieces out of the trimmed seam allowance at 1.3-centimeter (½-inch) intervals.

Curved seams are often found in the shoulder, sleeve, chest, waist, and hip areas of garments.

344

A clothing construction course is the time to try more difficult sewing projects. If you have problems, there is someone there to help.

in pattern instructions and with the zipper package. Use whichever directions you find easiest to understand. Your teacher may recommend a certain method. Instructions for sewing on buttons, hooks and eyes, and snaps are also included in pattern instructions. Special hints are provided on pages 347 and 348.

Collars. Complete directions for making collars are given in the pattern instructions, but here is some extra help:

• Be sure to allow 1.5-centimeter (⅝-inch) seam allowances. These will help the collar, neck edge, and facing to fit together well.

• Understitch the part of the collar that lies next to the garment to help it lie smooth and flat. Refer to the third column on page 340.

• To join the collar to the body of the garment, first pin it to the neck edge. Start by pinning each end of the collar in place. Then find the center of the collar and pin that in place. Next match and pin the notches. You may discover that one seam of the collar seems longer than the other. To join these two seams evenly at this point, you use a method called *easing.* You can ease a longer seam into a shorter one either by pinning or by stitching. For a collar, you will probably pin. Spread the fabric evenly and pin it in the center. Repeat this process and keep pinning until you have pins about every 1.2 centimeters

(½ inch) along the part of the seam that needs easing. Sew the eased seam with the easing on top. To stitch a seam that needs easing, staystitch along the seamline using slightly longer stitches (3 to 4 per centimeter or 8 to 10 per inch). A seam may ease with less trouble if the piece with the fullness is on the bottom.

• Clip the seam allowance of the collar or facing to make the collar lie flat. If the collar is smaller than the neckline, clip the seam allowance of the collar every 2 to 2.5 centimeters (¾ to 1 inch) down to the line of staystitching. If the collar is larger than the neckline, clip the neck of the garment instead.

Sleeves. Sleeves are fairly easy to put in if you follow directions carefully and understand what you are doing. Below are the basic steps in sleeve-making. You can find more information in your pattern instruction sheet.

• Make two rows of machine basting 9 and 12 millimeters (⅜ and ½ inch) in from the top of the sleeve. Sew from notch to notch. Leave the end threads about 5 centimeters (2 inches) long for easing the seam.

• If the lower edge of the sleeve will be finished with a hem, staystitch it 6 millimeters (¼ inch) in from the edge and clean finish it (see the third column on page 340).

• Put the right sides of the fabric together and match the notch at the top of the sleeve to the notch at the shoulder seam. Match the other notches. Pin the top edge of the sleeve to the edge of the armhole.

• Ease the sleeve into the armhole by pulling gently on the basting stitches. Pin in place, adjusting the easing evenly.

• Stitch the sleeve to the garment, keeping it on top as you stitch. The sleeve should fit smoothly, so keep the easing evenly adjusted as you sew. The easing should not create puckers.

• Take special care to match the sleeve seam with the garment seam at the underarm.

Patch Pockets. Although there are many kinds of pockets, most beginning sewers start with *patch pockets.* A patch pocket is sewn directly on the outside of the garment. The pattern instructions will tell you how to make a patch pocket. There will also be markings on the pattern to show you where to place it on the garment. Here is how to attach a patch pocket to the garment:

• If topstitching is needed, do it before the pocket is attached.

• Place the pocket right side out on the right side of the garment, exactly where it is to be stitched. If the pocket will go on a curved area of the garment, such as a hip, then pin the pocket while the garment is resting on a curved surface.

• Baste the pocket in place. Check

THREE WAYS TO PRESS A SEAM

1. Press seam flat (*right*). Press the seam area flat without a one-way direction. This method will blend stitches and shrink in fullness. It prepares seams for the next pressing step. Use this method for sleeve seams and the curve of pants seat seams.

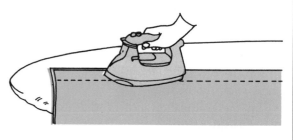

2. Press seam open (*left*). Press the seam flat. Press the seam allowance open, using your finger or the tip of the iron to open the seam allowance completely. This method is for straight and curved plain seams.

3. Press seam to one side (*right*). Press the seam flat, then open. Press the seam allowances to one side. This method is for waistlines, yokes, some collar and cuff seams, and for topstitched and special seams.

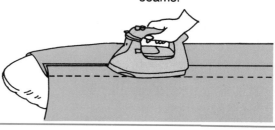

to be sure that it is straight on the garment and aligned with the other pocket if there are two.

• Stitch the pocket in place. Remove the basting.

Hems. Usually the last step in making a garment is the hemming. Hems are needed at the bottoms of gar-ments and at the ends of uncuffed sleeves. The most important thing about a hem is that it should not show on the outside. There are many ways to hem a garment. With any method, the raw edge is first finished. The most commonly used hemming method is to fold the fabric up and sew it in place with small, invisible

STEPS IN SEWING ON HOOKS

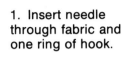

1. Insert needle through fabric and one ring of hook.

2. Bring thread under point of needle. Loop the thread in the same direction for each stitch, and pull tight.

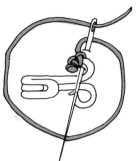

3. Take two or three stitches in bill of hook.

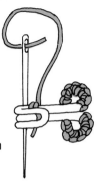

STEPS IN SEWING ON BUTTONS

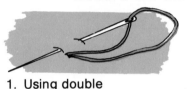

1. Using double thread, take one or two small stitches at the point where the button will be attached.

2. Hold a pin across the top of the button. Take a stitch over it.

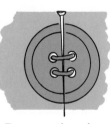

3. Take several stitches over the pin and through the fabric.

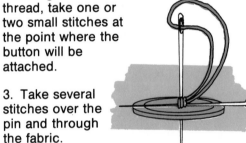

4. Remove the pin, and bring the needle and thread through the fabric.

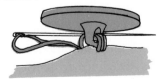

5. Wind the thread around under the button several times to make a thread shank. Fasten the thread on the underside of the fabric.

6. For a button with a shank, take several stitches over the shank and through the fabric. Fasten.

iron used with steam to smooth and shape a garment during construction.

ravel: Loosen the threads at the raw edge of a fabric.

seam finishing: Treating the raw edges of a garment to give a finished appearance and to prevent raveling.

staystitching: Regular-length machine stitching within the seam allowance to keep the edges of the fabric from stretching.

tuck: A small fold or pleat stitched into a garment to give shape.

understitching: Stitching through the facing and seam allowances to keep the facing from turning to the right side of the garment.

unit method: A construction method in which the parts of a garment are put together one at a time.

STEPS IN SEWING ON SNAPS

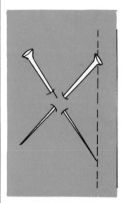

1. Mark location of snap, using two pins.

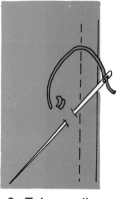

2. Take small stitch in position to be covered by snap.

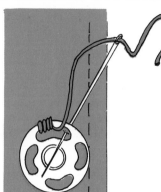

3. Stitching closely, go over the edge of the snap and into the fabric several times. Do not let stitches show on right side.

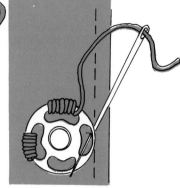

4. Insert needle under snap and into the next hole. Keep stitching. Fasten thread on wrong side under snap when finished.

More Safety in the Lab

• Use a slow speed while learning to use the sewing machine.

• Locate the electric cord so that no one will stumble over it. Disconnect the cord from the wall or floor outlet before disconnecting it from the sewing machine.

• Close the sewing machine carefully to avoid damaging the machine or the electric cord.

• Keep the drawers or door of the sewing machine closed to avoid accidents.

• Never run in the clothing lab.

handstitches. Hemming tape may be used. If it is, sew it to the end of the garment, fold the garment up, and then stitch the hem by hand. A hem should be the same depth all the way around.

a quick review

1. Describe the unit method of construction. What are its advantages? What are some disadvantages of this method?
2. What purpose does staystitching serve? How does it help protect the fabric while you work on it?
3. Describe the difference between a dart and a tuck. Use examples on classmates' clothes to show the difference.
4. Why is directional stitching important?
5. How are facings and interfacings used? Why are they often used together?
6. What is the difference between pressing and ironing? Why is pressing important in sewing?

Do you ever feel that you have nothing to wear? Often the problem is not a lack of clothes. It may be a broken zipper, a missing button, or a stain from last week's pizza. The way you take care of your clothes affects the real size of your wardrobe. A regular clothes-care system will keep your clothes in top shape. This system includes routine care, cleaning, ironing, and seasonal care. Organization and know-how are the keys.

CHAPTER 47
Clothing Care

THINKING AHEAD

Laundry day is not the only time clothing care is important. Think about care needs before you buy your clothes. Many fabrics need less care than others. Consider the time, money, and effort it will take to keep a garment looking its best. An acrylic sweater, for example, is machine washable. A wool sweater needs hand washing or dry cleaning. Use common sense when choosing an outfit for a day's activities. A rainy-day football game or an art class is probably not the time to wear your best blazer.

Think about care as you wear your clothes. Try not to use your pockets for carrying heavy or bulky objects. Protect clothes from stains when you are cooking, eating, or working on messy projects. Look before you sit down. Straighten slacks or a skirt

Laundry Products

There are many types of laundry products. Each has a certain job to do. Laundry products come in several forms—powder, liquid, concentrate, and spray. Here are the most common ones:

- *soap:* A cleaning product made from animal and vegetable fats; works best in soft, hot water.
- *detergent:* A cleaning product made from chemicals; works in cold or hard water.
- *bleach:* A product that whitens, disinfects, and removes some stains, but does not clean. Be sure to use the right type for the fabric.
- *enzyme:* A product used to break up stubborn stains like meat juices and blood.
- *water softener:* A product used to soften *hard water,* which contains minerals; allows soap to dissolve more easily.
- *fabric softener:* A product that makes fabrics soft and fluffy; prevents static; added to the final rinse or in the dryer.
- *starch:* A product that adds stiffness and body to fabrics; provides some oil resistance; can be added to rinse water or used in spray form when ironing.

when you sit to prevent wrinkles. Put on and take off clothes carefully to avoid ripping seams or hems.

ROUTINE CARE

Routine tasks are those you do all the time. For example, brushing your teeth is part of your morning routine. It is a habit. Here is a checklist for routine clothing care:

- Air clothes after you wear them.
- Brush off any lint or dust.
- Check for anything that needs repair or spot removal.
- Put dirty clothes aside for cleaning.
- Hang clothes straight on hangers, with buttons and zippers closed, or fold them carefully for drawer or shelf storage.

Spots and Stains. Try to treat spots and stains on clothes immediately. The longer stains are left untreated, the harder they are to remove. Some stains, like perspiration or soft drinks, can become permanent. Stains can also weaken a fabric or encourage insect damage.

Certain stains can be removed with water or spot removers. Spot removers are available in spray, liquid, cream, or powder form. If a fabric needs dry cleaning, have it done as soon as possible.

Repairs. Set aside time once a week for small repair jobs. This is a smart

part of your care system for three reasons: (1) you have to get out your sewing equipment only once to do several jobs, (2) you take care of minor repairs before they become major, and (3) you keep all your clothes wearable. The drawings on page 354 show you how.

Storage. Good storage is part of your clothes-care system too. Drawer or shelf storage space should be clean, smooth, and easy to reach. You can use it for knits, underwear, and accessories. Store similar items together. Putting all your belts together, for example, makes them easy to find. For clothes that hang, choose the right hanger for the type of garment. Use a plastic or padded hanger for delicate clothes. Use multiple hangers to save space.

CLEANING

Clothes collect dirt in normal wear. Some fibers attract dirt more easily than others. Garments are soiled by visible dirt, like mud or grease, and by perspiration and body oils. All clothes need to be cleaned regularly.

Care Labeling. Clothes today are made of many types of fabrics. Each requires a certain kind of care. Have you ever washed a woolen sweater and found that the clean sweater was three sizes too small? Using the wrong method of cleaning can ruin a garment. Before you clean a garment or fabric, check its *permanent-care label*. By law, this label must provide care instructions to help you maintain the garment. See page 354 for examples.

Washing and Drying. There are several ways to wash and dry clothes. Many people have a washer and a dryer at home. Some people machine wash their clothes at home and hang them outside on a line to dry. Others use coin-operated laundry equipment. No matter which way you launder your clothes, the basic steps are the same:

• Sort clothes into piles. Separate white clothes from colored ones. Separate clothes that need hot water from those that need warm or cold water.

• Check for stains and heavy soil. These need pretreating or presoaking.

• Choose the right water temperature for each load. Hot water works well on white and light-colored cottons. Dark or bright-colored fabrics wash well in warm water. Delicate and synthetic fabrics also wash well in warm water.

• Load the washer, being careful not to overload it. Add the correct amount of detergent.

• Choose the right temperature for the dryer. Untreated cotton can take hot temperatures; synthetic fabrics need low drying temperatures.

• Take clothes out of the dryer as soon as they are dry. This is especially

A Clothes-Care Clinic
Have everyone in your class bring in garments that need clothing care. These might be items that are stained or need repair. Look at each garment separately. As a group, talk about the particular problem and how it can be solved. Remember to read the care labels and review care procedures. Be original and creative in repairing rips and tears. After the group has decided on the best repair or cleaning procedure, return the garment to its owner. Set aside a class period for the cleaning, stain removal, or mending of the garments. After the clothes have been cared for, look at them again to evaluate the results.

Take clothes out of the dryer as soon as they are dry. Then take the time to fold them right away. If you stuff everything into the laundry bag, you may have to do unnecessary ironing later.

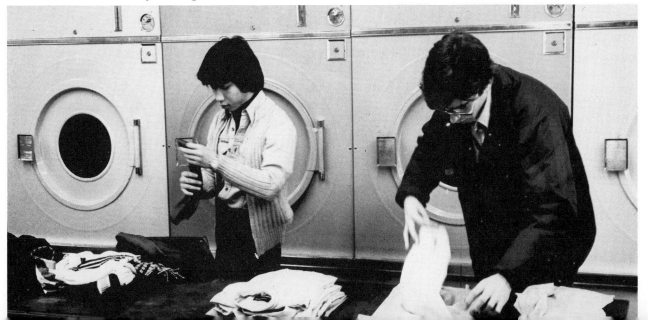

STAIN REMOVAL FOR WASHABLE FABRICS

Blood

While stain is fresh, soak in cold water. Work in detergent paste. Launder in warm water. If stain persists, soak again with bleach. Then relaunder.

Chewing Gum

Harden gum by rubbing it with ice. Scrape off excess with dull knife. If stain remains, sponge with a dry-cleaning fluid, rinse, and then launder.

Chocolate and Cocoa

Soak in cold water. If colored stain remains, pretreat with detergent paste and launder in water as hot as is safe for the fabric.

Cosmetics

Pretreat with detergent paste. Launder in hot water.

Grass and Foliage

Rub detergent paste into stain. If necessary, use a mild bleach. Launder in hot water.

Grease and Oil

Scrape off as much grease as possible. Rub detergent paste into stain. Launder in hot water with plenty of detergent.

Ink (ball point)

Rub white petroleum jelly into stain. Pretreat with detergent paste and launder. If fabric permits, add bleach.

Perspiration

Pretreat stain with detergent paste. If stain persists, apply ammonia to fresh stain and white vinegar to old stain. Rinse with water and then launder.

Soft Drinks

Sponge immediately with cool water. Launder.

Care Labels

Collect as many care labels from fabric and ready-made garments as you can find. Using those labels and the ones on page 354, discuss with your class what the labels mean. Were the labels interpreted differently? How could you improve the labels?

important for no-iron synthetic fabrics. They will wrinkle if left to sit.

Minimum-Care Fabrics. Many of today's clothes need only a little care and attention. These include knits, synthetics or blends, and fabrics with special finishes. They are often called *minimum-care fabrics.* You can put them through the automatic washer and dryer and then wear them with little or no ironing. These fabrics do need some special handling, however. Use small loads for both washing and drying to prevent wrinkles. Set your machine on a gentle *agitation* (movement or motion) cycle. Never use hot water. Set the dryer on a low temperature. Often minimum-care fabrics do not need machine drying. They can be put on a hanger to air dry. Some people prefer to wash delicate items by hand. Hand laundering can become part of your daily care system.

Dry Cleaning. Some fabrics require dry cleaning. When buying a garment, remember to consider the added expense dry cleaning will add to the original cost. Dry cleaning can be done by a professional cleaner. Or you can do the job yourself in a coin-operated machine.

In dry cleaning, clothes are cleaned in a large machine with liquid *solvent,* chemicals that remove grease and dirt. No water is used in this cleaning process. After the dirt has been removed, the solvent is forced out of the clothes and they are tumbled dry. They are then hung on hangers and covered with plastic bags.

If you use the coin-operated method, you can usually save money

Be sure the ironing board is a comfortable height for you to work on. If you have to bend over, the board is too low.

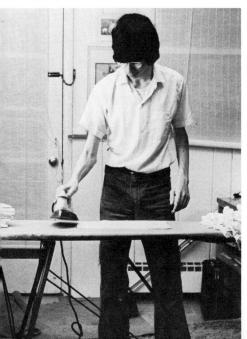

and still get good results. Before cleaning, brush the garment and *pretreat* any stains. Follow the operating directions on the machine. Be careful not to overload it. When the cycle is complete, place the garments on hangers. To remove the solvent odor, allow the clothes to air or put them through the dryer on a no-heat setting.

IRONING AND PRESSING

Ironing and pressing are the finishing stages of clothing care. *Ironing* is a back-and-forth motion. It is used on most woven fabrics. *Pressing* uses a lifting and lowering movement. It is used on knits and woolens to prevent stretching. Use steam to press. Here are some ironing and pressing tips:

• Read the care label for ironing instructions. Test the temperature of your iron first.

• Keep your iron clean. Use only the type of water recommended by the manufacturer.

• Use a clean, well-padded surface for ironing. A heat-resistant cover is a good safety measure. There are special pieces of pressing equipment, like sleeveboards and tailor's hams, to help you do a professional job. You can read more about them in Chapter 44.

• Use a lint-free pressing cloth, or turn the garment inside out to prevent shine.

Smart Energy Use

In home clothes care, you use energy for heating water, washing, drying, and ironing. Here are some tips for using this energy wisely:

• Wash only when you have a full load, but do not overload the washing machine.

• Use warm- and cold-water settings whenever possible.

• Use a cold-water rinse for any wash.

• Use a shorter wash cycle for lightly soiled clothes.

• Follow detergent instructions carefully so that you do not make too many suds.

• Keep the washer and dryer lint filters clean.

• Remove clothes from the dryer as soon as they are dry.

• Iron on the lowest temperature that will do the job.

• Unplug and turn off the iron when you are not using it.

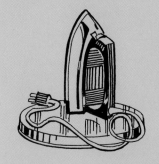

353

Care Labels

A permanent-care label gives you important information about the basic care needs of the fabric. The label often includes both what to do and what not to do. Here are some sample care labels:

DRY CLEAN
TOUCH-UP
WITH
WARM IRON

HAND WASH
DO NOT WRING
OR TWIST
DRY FLAT
STEAM IRON AT
WARM SETTING

DO NOT
DRY CLEAN
HAND WASH ONLY
DRIP DRY
IRON ON REVERSE SIDE
WITH COOL IRON

MACHINE WASH
AT COLD SETTING
—GENTLE CYCLE
DRIP DRY
IRON ON REVERSE
SIDE WITH COOL IRON

DO NOT BLEACH
MACHINE WASH
AND DRY AT
WARM SETTINGS
STEAM IRON AT
WARM SETTING

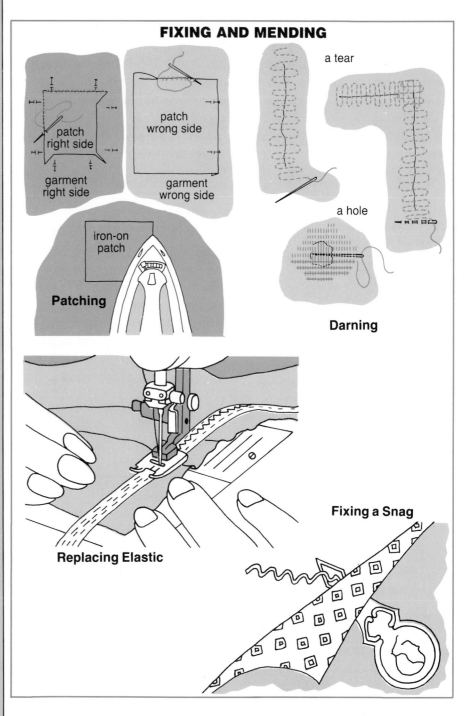

FIXING AND MENDING

patch right side

garment right side

patch wrong side

garment wrong side

a tear

a hole

iron-on patch

Patching

Darning

Replacing Elastic

Fixing a Snag

• When you are finished ironing, unplug the iron carefully. Allow it to cool standing on its heel.

• Remove any water, then store the iron in a safe place.

SEASONAL CARE

You probably have some clothes that you wear all year long. You may have others that are right for only part of the year. This is especially true if you live in a part of the country where the weather changes from season to season. Seasonal wardrobe changes need a special care routine. If you plan to store clothes for a few months, put them away in the best possible condition. At the same time, prepare your other clothes for the season ahead. The following are some tips for proper storage.

Remove any spots or stains before you store clothes. A stain left on a garment for several months may be impossible to remove. After removing any stains, wash and dry or dry-clean the garment. Do not iron clothes to be stored, since heat can cause discoloration. Do not starch these clothes, either, since starch-eating pests like silverfish can ruin a garment. Wrap clothes in tissue paper or plastic. Store them neatly hung or folded. There are many kinds of storage products available. Garment bags and see-through plastic boxes are examples. Cold-weather clothes like woolens need moth protection. This protection is available in spray, crystal, or cake forms.

A good clothes-care system is worth the time and effort. It helps you to practice good management and organization. You look and feel well put together. And you are ready for any occasion.

a quick review

1. Explain how you can take care of your clothes as you wear them.
2. What does routine mean? List the steps in routine clothing care.
3. What are permanent care labels? How do they help you take care of your clothes?
4. What are the steps in getting ready to machine wash clothes?
5. How are minimum-care fabrics handled differently from traditional natural-fiber fabrics?
6. What is the difference between ironing and pressing? Explain how each is done.

CHAPTER 48
Recycling

Turning something that is no longer usable into something you can use is called *recycling*. All through our history people have recycled things, usually because supplies and raw materials were hard to get. For example, old worn clothes were cut up and made into patchwork quilts or braided rugs. Animal fat was turned into candles and soap. Today resources are again becoming hard to find because they are being *depleted,* or used up. So paper is being recycled. In some areas garbage is being recycled as fuel. Glass bottles and tin and aluminum cans are also being recycled. This chapter is about recycling clothes.

MAKING CLOTHES OVER

One way to recycle your clothes is to make them over. This kind of recycling is especially good for clothes that are out of date but still fit. Updating clothes may mean shortening or lengthening them. It may mean adding a trim that is new and in style, such as an appliqué. It may also mean wearing a garment in a different way. For example, you might wear a pair of out-of-style pants tucked into high boots, or an old, loose sweater belted at the waist. Look through current magazines to spot styles you like. Then think about the out-of-date clothes you have. Can some of them be updated to look new?

Save pieces from your old shirts or worn jeans to use for small sewing projects.

Another *strategy,* or plan of action, is to change the whole look of a garment. Use your imagination and creativity. For example, turn a pair of pants into a pair of shorts. Cut the legs short and hem them. Make an old dress into a blouse or skirt. Change the look of a skirt or pair of pants by adding pockets made of contrasting material. Then make a vest of the contrasting fabric to wear with the skirt or pants. Sew ribbon or braid trim to the edges of a jacket or vest for a quick change. Even little touches, such as changing the buttons on a shirt or blouse to contrast instead of match, can alter the whole look of a garment.

Another way to recycle clothing is to change the color. You can use fabric dyes as directed on the package or bottle. Or, with a brush, paint the dye onto the garment in your own design, or tie-dye the garment. You can also buy special fabric paints that you can use straight from the tube to create any kind of look or design you choose.

Talk to your friends about how to change some of your clothing to get more wear out of it. Look in stores and magazines for ideas. Even if your first try does not work, keep trying. It is worth your time and can save you a lot of money. Of course, talk to your parents first before you recycle any clothing.

TRADING CLOTHES

Another way to recycle clothes is to trade them. If you have things that no longer fit or that you have stopped wearing, you might be able to arrange a swap. Some of your friends or relatives may also have things to swap. Have your parents approve the clothes you want to trade. They may know of someone who could use them. Before you make any trades, think of what clothes will be most

Patchwork Pillow

Materials:
- *old garments for patches and back of pillow*
- *35.5 cm-square (14 in-square) pillow form or polyester fiberfill*

1. Make a 10 cm-square (4 in-square) pattern from medium-weight cardboard.
2. Use this pattern to cut 16 squares of fabric.
3. Cut one large square 36.8 × 36.8 cm (14½ × 14½ in) for the back of the pillow.
4. Arrange the patches any way you like, in four rows of four.
5. With right sides together, sew the patches together in four strips.
6. Press seams open.
7. With right sides together, sew the four strips together. This makes the pillow front. Press seams open.
8. With right sides together, pin the patchwork pillow front to the pillow back.
9. Stitch a 1.3-cm (½-in) seam around all four sides, leaving about 25.5 cm (10 in) open along one side.
10. Turn the pillow right side out. Insert the pillow form or stuffing.
11. Slipstitch the opening closed.

357

PATCHES AND PATIENCE: QUILTS

What can you do with a stack of old fabric scraps? Make a quilt!

A *quilt* is a three-layer fabric held together with needlework. The inside layer, sometimes called the interlining, is usually made from cotton batting or down.

In ancient times the Chinese quilted jackets, the Romans quilted coverlets, and the Aztecs quilted tunics. During the Middle Ages, knights wore quilted clothing under their armor as extra protection from sword stabs. During a very cold spell in seventeenth- and eighteenth-century Europe, quilted clothing became very popular. People wore quilted coats, caps, and underwear.

In colonial America, new fabric was scarce. Many quilts were therefore made from tiny pieces—some-

useful to you. That way your trades will be good ones. Also, trade for clothes of equal value. For example, trade a jacket for a jacket, or perhaps two shirts for a good sweater.

RECYCLING FABRIC

If a garment is worn or out of date and no one wants it or can wear it, do not throw it away. Cut it apart and use the fabric for other things. First, take off all the buttons and trims. Put them with your sewing things. You may want to reuse them on another

garment someday. If the zipper is still good, save that too for something else.

Shirts, blouses, and dresses are all good sources of fabric for patchwork projects. Placemats, potholders, pillows, even another garment can be made from patchwork. Fabric from wool or wool-blend skirts, pants, and suits can be used to make braided items such as chair mats and rugs. Finally, clothes that are too worn out to be used for anything else can be saved for use as cleaning rags. Cotton

times from as many as four thousand scraps. Scraps of all sizes and shapes were made into "crazy quilts" by pioneers. At bees, or quilting parties, women would sit at quilting frames sewing and chatting.

There are two basic methods of design for quilts. The first is the *pieced,* or *patched, quilt.* There are at least three thousand recorded patching patterns. The second is the *appliqué* technique. This technique involves cutting out cloth into patterns and embroidering or sewing these patterns onto the original coverlet. This method became popular in about 1750 and was frequently used during the nineteenth century. Today several areas of the country are known for their special quilting designs. Some of these areas are the Amish country in Pennsylvania, the Appalachian area of Kentucky, and Hawaii.

There are also many methods of stuffing quilts. *Wadded* quilting is thickly stuffed all over. *Flat* quilting leaves out the thick middle layer. *Trapunto* is a combination of flat quilting and raised or stuffed quilting. *Corded* quilting has raised cords enclosed in lines of stitching.

Some Quilting Tips:
• Keep the lines of stitching far enough apart so the quilt will look flat.
• Use matching thread.
• Use the running stitch or a backstitch for the basic quilting. It is sturdier than embroidery stitching.
• Use the same or similar fabric for a patchwork quilt. For example, use all cotton or all silk.

Amazing Fact:
The largest known blanket was made by the readers of a woman's magazine. It was made from 20,160 knitted squares and measured 612 square meters (6800 square feet).

fabric makes the best cleaning rags. Rags come in very handy to wipe up oil or paint, to clean brushes, or to take up household dust.

a quick review

1. What is recycling?
2. Why is it a good idea to recycle clothes?
3. How can recycling clothes improve your wardrobe?
4. Name at least three ways to recycle clothes.
5. If a garment is too worn out to recycle, what can be done with it?

Drawstring Jeans Bag

Materials:
• *old pair of jeans or other pants*
• *0.95 m (1 yd) cord or rope*

1. From the upper part of one pants leg, cut off at least 35.5 cm (14 in).
2. Turn the cut piece inside out.
3. Close the narrow end by machine sewing a 1.3-cm (½-in) seam across it. Reinforce the seam by sewing it twice.
4. Measure down 3.8 cm (1½ in) from the open end on one of the pants side seams. Cut the seam open for 2 cm (¾ in).
5. Zigzag or overcast around the raw edges where you cut into the seam.
6. Turn the edge of the open end under 1.3 cm (½ in). Press.
7. Turn the new edge down 2.5 cm (1 in) and pin in place.
8. Stitch along the turned-under edge 0.6 cm (¼ in) from the fold line to form a tunnel, or casing.
9. Attach a large safety pin to one end of the cord or rope. Insert the cord into the casing and use the pin to work it around. Knot the ends together.

CHAPTER 49

Careers in Clothing and Textiles

There are probably more kinds of jobs in the clothing industry than in any other business. Artists design new garments. Scientists invent new products. Engineers look for faster or better ways of doing things. People with fashion flair, a very special skill, are important throughout the business. At every stage, marketing and salespeople are needed. And of course, stitchers and cutters and others who do the actual work of making a garment are the backbone of the industry. In this chapter you will learn about some of the jobs in the clothing industry and the ways some people started in clothing careers.

RESEARCH AND DEVELOPMENT

No business succeeds without looking for better and newer ways of doing things. This is especially true of the garment industry. New ideas are a big part of the job. *Research* is studying or looking for new products and better ways of working. For example, researchers are always seeking new synthetic fabrics and new fabric finishes. *Development* involves putting the research to work. That means finding a practical way to use it. For instance, a researcher may discover that a new kind of fabric requires a new sewing machine attachment. Then it is up to the people who work in development to invent the new attachment.

People in research and development are mostly scientists and engineers. A *textile chemist* may work in a laboratory on one fiber or fabric. Or this same chemist might supervise a team of people working on one or more special problems. There are different types of *research chemists*. Some work to develop new products. Others try to make old products better. And others test new products and ideas to make sure they are ready to be used. The people who test are called *textile testers*. A textile tester might run tests to see whether or not the colors will *bleed,* or run, when a fabric is washed or to find what is the best way to clean a garment.

Because time is so important in the garment industry, many special workers devote their days to finding faster and smoother ways of doing things. For example, *industrial engineers* may work on finding a faster machine to cut out a pattern or a quicker way to sew a garment.

The work that is done in research and development helps everyone who works in design and manufacturing.

DESIGN AND MANUFACTURING

Design and manufacturing are the branches of the industry where the idea for a specific garment is created and carried through to the final product. This final product is a finished piece of clothing. It is an exciting and

A designer may travel to where his clothes are being manufactured to check quality and be sure all changes have been made. A design may be changed several times from the time it is sketched to the final garment.

A Tailor

Jack Stahl is a tailor. He talks about his work:

"Even as a child, I loved to sew things. And I loved fabric. I took courses in school, and then after high school I was apprenticed to a tailor. That is how I learned most of what I know. After seven years as an apprentice, I went to work for another tailor. I wanted to see how someone else worked. I am saving my money so that I can open my own business some day. And I take courses in night school to learn about business."

A Chemist

Wilma Warren is a textile chemist. She talks about her career:

"I studied chemistry in college. I didn't plan to work in textiles. I started out working for a plastics company, trying to invent furniture that could use molded plastic. Then I took a job with a clothes manufacturer. First I worked on making a new fabric wrinkle-free. Now I spend my time inventing new finishes for fabrics. In a couple of years I will be promoted to manager of my department. Then I will spend less time in the lab and more time supervising other people."

361

A Patternmaker

Bob Burch talks about his job as a patternmaker:

"This is about the last job I ever imagined I would have. After high school I went to computer school at night and worked in the computer department of a bank during the day. I always loved to draw and used to dream about becoming a clothes designer. One day I saw an ad for a computer specialist with a clothes manufacturer. I applied for it. I learned that I could use my computer skills to work out patterns for clothes. I really like the work. I'm not a clothes designer, but I do get to use my drawing skills. I think of my work as creative."

Some History

The clothing business is often called the *garment industry* or *rag trade.* Here is some of its history.

The ancient Greeks made most of their cloth at home, but there were also fabric shops for the wealthy.

The Romans had a flourishing textile business. They imported fabrics from all over the world and built some of the first textile factories.

During the Middle Ages, cloth was once again mostly made at home. Professional clothmakers

(continued)

362

fast-paced area in which to work. Many skills from many types of workers are needed. The *fashion designer* is the person who comes up with an idea or look for a new garment. The designer draws a picture of the garment and often attaches a sample fabric. If the garment is approved, the design goes to the *product manager.* This person sees the design through from an idea to a finished garment. The drawing goes to a *patternmaker,* who figures out how to make a pattern for the garment. The decisions of the patternmaker are very important. They help determine how much time and fabric will be needed to make the garment. Those two factors have a lot to do with how much you pay for the garment when you buy it in the store. Patternmakers use computers to help them work out pattern layouts.

While the patternmaker is working, the *fabric buyer* is choosing and ordering fabric from the mills, or fabric manufacturers. It is the fabric buyer's job to decide which fabric will work best with a particular garment and to make sure that enough fabric is available. The fabric buyer may also order special dyes or finishes for a fabric.

Eventually the pattern and the fabric end up with the *cutter.* A cutter uses the pattern to cut out the pieces of fabric. Large machines can cut up to fifty layers of fabric at a time. *Stitchers* are the people who actually

A fabric designer designs the fabrics from which garments are made. Color, lines, and shapes are basic design elements.

The person who sews the design into the garment is called a sample maker. Most designs are sewn up in sample form and then tried on by a model. The designer can then make necessary changes for fit and comfort.

sew the garment together. Their work is planned very carefully by the industrial engineers. This shortens the sewing time. A good stitcher can often make a complete shirt in about 12 minutes.

The product manager checks each stage of manufacture to be sure that schedules are met. When the garment is finished, a *quality control inspector* looks it over very carefully. If a garment is well made, it is sent out to be sold. If it is flawed, the inspector decides whether or not it can be fixed without increasing the cost too much. If not, it is sold as a *second,* or flawed garment.

MERCHANDISING

After a garment is inspected, the *merchandising* team takes over. The manufacturer's salespeople sell the garments to a department store *buyer.* Buyers make decisions about what they think people will be wearing. If these decisions are wrong, the stores can lose a lot of money. Buyers must always consider other people's tastes. They must also be able to think several seasons ahead. They are often buying winter clothes in the middle of summer.

Within a store, the *department head* handles the display and sale of the clothes. Each department head super-

were organized into groups called *craft guilds.*

In the 1400s King Louis XI of France had silkworms brought to his country. Beautiful silks soon became the textile rage. The British began importing printed and dyed cottons from India in the 1600s. These also became very popular.

In the United States, the first cloth mill was built in 1638 by John Pearson of Massachusetts. In 1764 the *spinning jenny* was introduced. This machine could weave more than one yarn at a time. New dyes also made clothes more colorful and new color combinations possible. Finally, in 1790, the first real textile mill was set up in Pawtucket, Rhode Island.

Ready-made clothes were first sewn in nineteenth-century New England for sailors who had only short stays in port. This was the real beginning of the clothing trade. The gold rush of the 1840s and the Civil War of the 1860s also increased the need for "on the spot" clothes buying. In the United States, factory production of women's clothing began in 1859, men's clothing in the 1880s.

A Buyer

Lucille Church is a sportswear buyer for a big department store. She has this to say about her work:

"I started working in sales when I was still in high school. I went to college part-time. It took me seven years to get my degree in marketing. I got promoted to better and better jobs until I became a buyer. Three times a year I travel to California and Europe on buying trips, and twice a year I go to the Far East to buy fabrics. I love my work, and I know it is exciting, but there is also a lot of pressure. If I make some bad decisions about what people want to wear, I can cost my company a lot of money.

"At some point I could be promoted again. The

(continued)

(*Above*) Many people are involved in getting the garment to the retail stores and finally to the consumer.

(*Below, left*) Buyers and sales people meet regularly at conventions to show and sell the designers' newest lines. There are special apparel markets in major cities that hold these conventions. Minneapolis, Atlanta, Chicago, Dallas, and Los Angeles are several of these cities.

(*Below, right*) A color stylist knows which colors are important for the fashion season. Fabric buyers will need to find out what colors are being shown in order to make wise buying decisions.

A person who is an expert at garment construction and fit may work for a large department store or a small specialty store.

vises a sales staff. *Display artists* work at showing off the clothes inside the store and in the windows. They create and build clothing displays.

SERVICES

There are also several service careers that are part of the clothing business. *Tailors* and *sewers* make clothes or alter them to fit perfectly. *Dry cleaners* and *launderers* help maintain clothes. *Shoe repairers* take care of shoes and often repair and maintain handbags, too.

COMMUNICATIONS AND THE FASHION INDUSTRY

Finally, there is a group of related careers that combine journalism and fashion knowledge. Specialists in fashion writing write advertising for clothing manufacturers. Some people have made very successful careers out of writing about clothes and fashion.

a quick review

1. What is research and development? Why is it important to most businesses? Why is it especially important to the clothing business?
2. Why is so much planning involved in the design and making of a garment?
3. At what stages are salespeople needed in the clothing business?
4. Describe the workers in the service end of the clothing business. Why are they so important to the consumer?

problem would be that I would no longer be traveling. I think I will always stay a buyer."

▶ **Words to Know**
business: The production and sale of goods and services, or an organization engaged in such activities.
communication: The sending and receiving of information.
development: The act of bringing something into being; in industry, the creation of a new product or other item.
garment industry: The businesses that make and sell clothing.
industry: Production of goods on a large scale, or the businesses engaged in that production.
manager: A person who directs a business or part of a business.
marketing: The selling and advertising of goods.
product: An item made by a company for sale to consumers. In the garment industry, the product is an article of clothing.
research: Careful study of a subject.

Unit 6
FOODS

CHAPTER 50
Why People Eat

Food means many things in our lives. It keeps us alive. It also serves other needs. You may have heard the old saying "Some people eat to live, and other people live to eat." Think about what that means. Some people eat because their friends are eating or because it gives them something to do. Many people eat more than they need just because they enjoy food so much. Some people eat when they are bored, nervous, or unhappy. People who are both healthy and attractive have learned about eating. They know what to eat for growth, repair of body tissues, and energy. In this chapter you will read about people and food.

YOUR BODY NEEDS FOOD

Why do *you* eat? One important reason you eat is a physical reason. Your body, quite simply, needs the food. You are hungry.

Hunger is your body's sign that you need food. When you are hungry, your stomach may feel a little tighter, or it may even ache a little. Sometimes it may growl.

You also need food for *energy*. Energy is the strength you need to play or work. Without it, you would not be able to concentrate on your schoolwork. You would not be able to play sports. Even small jobs would seem like a heavy burden. Energy is what makes you feel fit and healthy.

Teens who participate in active sports often have larger appetites than those who are not as active.

YOUR MIND NEEDS FOOD

You also eat food for reasons that are not physical. These reasons related to your mental and emotional needs are called *psychological* reasons.

Food has a lot to do with emotions. *Emotions* are feelings. Have you ever decided to eat a candy bar because you were tired and bored and wanted something to do? Does nervousness make you eat? Perhaps it keeps you from eating.

Many people sometimes use food as an emotional crutch. These people are often overweight or underweight. They eat more or less than their bodies need for energy.

Another reason that people eat is because they are happy. Food is often the center of a celebration. People feel good when they eat birthday cake or

turkey and other traditional foods on holidays. These meals give people feelings of love and security.

Another psychological reason for eating is *conditioning*. Conditioning is the way in which behavior is shaped. A conditioned behavior is like a habit. Habits have much to do with when you eat. You may eat at about the same times every day. Even if your body does not give out hunger signals, you still may think you are hungry at these times. This is because you have been conditioned to think in this way.

You can also learn to like or dislike certain foods through conditioning. For example, if your best friend hates peas and refuses to eat them, you may decide you do not like them either. Peas might taste just as good

Changing Meal Patterns

How and when people in this country eat have changed a lot since your parents were your age. These factors are called meal patterns. Gone are three solid meals a day, with the noon dinner being the largest meal. Some families are able to eat only one meal a day together. That meal is usually dinner.

Many families rarely eat breakfast together.

Lunch for children in school and family members who work outside the home is often bought in diners, cafeterias, and coffee shops. Many people *brown bag* lunch; that is, they bring their own sandwiches to work or school.

Even dinner is not a guaranteed family effort since many family members plan activities for the evening hours. Some people work night shifts, which also means the family may not eat dinner together.

All this has led to an increase in snacking, which has become a way of life in the United States. Experts estimate that 25 percent of the food eaten by teenagers is junk food.

Eating Ethnic Foods

Each country or region of the world is known for some food specialties. Some of these specialties are listed below. Others are discussed in Chapter 71. How many of these foods have you eaten?

Eastern Asia is famous for *stir-fry cooking,* in which large amounts of vegetables and small amounts of meats or poultry are combined in a light sauce. The Japanese also eat *sushi,* raw fish wrapped in rice and seaweed.

Spain is famous for *paella,* a saffron-flavored dish that combines lobster, shrimp, other seafoods, and sometimes chicken, sausage, and other meats with rice.

The Middle East is known for its *pita bread.* This flat, thin bread has a pocket or slit in it. It is often filled with other foods and eaten like a sandwich. Pita bread is becoming popular in the United States. It can be bought in many supermarkets.

In India, *curry* is a common dish. It contains meat, fish, poultry, or vegetables in a sauce that is seasoned with curry powder, a blend of spices with a very strong flavor.

as any other food, but you have learned to associate them with something unpleasant. You have learned not to like them.

People are also conditioned to eat on certain occasions. For example, some people always expect to eat when they visit their grandparents. Others learn to want particular foods when they go to a baseball game or a party. People often expect to eat at a social gathering. This is not necessarily because they are hungry, but because they have been conditioned to eat on these occasions.

EATING FOR CULTURAL REASONS

You eat for cultural reasons also. For example, the kind of food you expect at a party may be very different from that expected by a friend. This is part of your cultural learning. Other cultural reasons for eating certain foods may be religious, ethnic, or regional. For example, some religions forbid the eating of pork.

Ethnic foods are those that are associated with particular places or countries. In many parts of the world, rice is an important food, and many people who have come to the United States from Latin American and Asian countries eat a lot of rice. Even if your family has no ethnic traditions, you may still eat ethnic foods. Does your family ever eat spaghetti? That is an Italian food. Do you ever eat tacos? They are a Mexican food. These ethnic foods are popular throughout the United States.

You also eat some foods because of the region of the country in which you live. Almost every region of the

Some foods are traditionally a part of family celebrations.

A family's background and origin will often determine the kinds of foods they serve on special occasions.

country is known for some special foods. For example, fresh salmon is popular along the northwest coast of the United States.

The foods people eat are also determined by *technology,* or the way that food is produced. For example, in the United States a large industry has grown up around the preparation and packaging of foods. Many Americans eat foods that are prepared, frozen, or canned. Until recently, few other countries had the technology to prepare quantities of food in this way.

It is important to think about what you eat and when you eat, since good eating habits are a key to physical and emotional health.

a quick review

1. List the two reasons that your body requires food.
2. How does your body tell you that you need food?
3. Describe three psychological reasons for eating.
4. What is conditioning? What does it have to do with eating habits?

▶ **Words to Know**

conditioning: A way that behavior is shaped or habits are created. It is one reason that you eat certain foods or eat at certain times.

cultural: Describing the beliefs and characteristics of a particular group of people.

hunger: The physical feeling that a body sends out to signal that it needs food.

junk food: Food that is high in calories but very low in nutrients.

technology: In the food industry, the way that food is produced, prepared, and packaged.

371

CHAPTER 51
Nutrients

Your body has a lot in common with a car. A car won't go without fuel. And your body won't run very long without food. Your car might run on the wrong fuel, but you get better mileage and go further with the right kind, in the right amounts. Likewise, your body has more energy and runs better when it has the kind and amount of food it needs, too. When you skip breakfast, do you ever feel tired by late morning? The reason is that you didn't get enough fuel. And how do you feel when you eat too many rich, gooey snacks right before dinner? They may be the wrong kind of fuel!

NUTRIENTS—BUILDING BLOCKS OF FOOD

Your body needs to be supplied with materials to make it work properly. These materials are called *nutrients* because they *nourish,* or support, the body. Over fifty different nutrients are grouped into six classes: protein, carbohydrate, fat, vitamins, minerals, and water.

Protein. Every cell in your body is made of protein, whether it is part of your skin, eyes, muscles, or hair. Protein is needed to repair tissues and to help you grow. Without it, your body couldn't grow properly or repair cuts, bruises, broken bones, or injured muscles. Did you know that 3 to 5 percent of your total body protein is replaced every day?

Protein is made from many different *amino acids,* which are sometimes called the building blocks of protein. When you eat protein, your body breaks it down into these smaller units. Then your body rearranges these units into new proteins, which your cells use. Most foods from animal sources have all of the eight "building blocks" needed to make new proteins. These foods are good sources of *complete,* or *high-quality,* protein. Many vegetable foods, on the other hand, contain only some of the essential building blocks. Such food supplies *incomplete,* or *low-quality,* protein.

Meat, poultry, fish, and eggs are excellent sources of high-quality protein. So are milk, cheese, and yogurt. Many people don't realize that peanut butter, baked beans, other nuts, and dry beans also contain high-quality proteins. Foods made from grain have low-quality protein.

Carbohydrate. Carbohydrates are your main energy source. Your body changes them into a special sugar called *glucose.* Glucose is used as fuel in your cells.

There are three kinds of carbohydrate: sugar, starch, and fiber. Sugar is the simplest carbohydrate. Starch is more complex. Many units of sugar link together to make starch. Fiber is also complex. Unlike starch, however, it cannot be broken down by the body. Fiber thus does not supply energy. Instead, it helps food and waste move through the body during digestion and elimination.

Sugar comes naturally from fruit, certain vegetables such as sweet potatoes and peas, and milk. Refined sugar is used to make soft drinks, candy, and pastry. Sugar with names you may not recognize—corn syrup, sucrose, and honey—is added to many foods. Good sources of starch are grain products such as rice, pasta, and bread, and vegetables such as potatoes and corn. Look for fiber in whole grain breads and cereals, vegetables, and fruits, especially the seeds and peels.

Fat. Gram for gram, fat gives more than twice as many calories as pure sugar. Fat also carries fat-soluble vitamins throughout your body. Too much fat, however, may not be good for you. Recent research indicates that damage to health from too much fat can begin early in life.

The makeup of fats determines their type. Fats can be saturated, unsaturated, or polyunsaturated. *Saturated fats* are solid at room temperature. *Polyunsaturated fats,* or oils, are liquid. *Cholesterol* is a fatlike substance in body cells. Many scientists think we should eat only moderate amounts of cholesterol for good health.

373

Food Labels

Food labels contain valuable information. Every label must state the name and form of the food. For example, pineapple is described as crushed, chopped, or sliced. The weight or volume of food must also be listed. Finally, every label must contain the name and address of the manufacturer, packer, or distributor.

Other information that is not required by law but which is showing up on many labels these days includes nutrition information.

When *nutrition information* is given, it states how many calories and how many grams of protein, carbohydrate, and fat are contained in each serving. The number of servings in the container is also noted. The percentages of the U.S. Recommended Daily Allowances of vitamins and minerals in the item are listed.

Ingredients are also listed on many containers. If they are not, it may be because the food is *standardized.* Standardized foods need not list their ingredients because all manufacturers have agreed that the same ingredients go into every container.

Fats come from two kinds of sources. The first are natural sources such as meat, poultry, fish, cheese, whole milk, nuts, seeds, and chocolate. The others are foods such as gravy, salad dressing, and fried foods. Fat has been added to these foods. Fat, like sugar, is hidden in many foods under different names, such as shortening, coconut oil, and lard. Sometimes it is laced through a juicy piece of meat. Cholesterol comes only from animal products.

Vitamins. Vitamins are regulators. Without them, your body could not function properly or use the nutrients in food. They do not provide energy. But B vitamins, for example, do help release the energy provided by carbohydrate and fat. Because vitamins form "partnerships" with other nutrients, the lack of a vitamin in a person's diet may affect the job of another nutrient.

The B vitamins (thiamin, riboflavin, and niacin) and vitamin C are *water-soluble.* This means that they dissolve in water, and thus in your body fluids. As a result, unneeded vitamins are discarded daily with body waste.

B vitamins, besides helping release the energy in nutrients, help keep your appetite and digestion normal, your nervous system healthy, and your skin smooth. Milk and milk products, whole grain and enriched grain products, and meat are good sources of B vitamins.

Vitamin C is found in citrus fruits, cabbage, tomatoes, and strawberries.

Fiber, one type of carbohydrate, is found in a variety of grain products.

Refer to the food composition tables on pages 511–516 to learn what other foods are good sources. People who don't get enough vitamin C over a long time bruise easily and have frequent colds and bleeding gums.

Vitamins A, D, E, and K dissolve in fat. As a result, your body can store extra amounts of these vitamins. You can get an overdose of them by taking large doses of vitamin pills, but probably not by simply eating vitamin-rich foods.

Vitamin A helps keep your skin healthy and helps your eyes adjust to darkness. Good sources of vitamin A are deep yellow and dark-green leafy vegetables and fruits.

Vitamin D is called the "sunshine" vitamin. Your own body makes it when your skin is exposed to sunlight. Vitamin D helps your body use calcium and phosphorus to build bones and teeth. Vitamin D is added to most milk. Vitamin E helps protect cell tissues. Your body makes vitamin K. It helps blood clot when you are injured. Both vitamin E and K are found in a variety of foods.

Minerals. You know minerals as rocks. But your body needs very small amounts of minerals as regulators. They work as vitamins do, helping other nutrients and body processes to function normally.

Calcium and *phosphorus* work as a team. Most of the calcium and phosphorus in your body is in your bones and teeth. Calcium also helps control your heartbeat and muscles. Your body needs more calcium than phosphorus. You can get similar amounts of both by eating dairy products. You also get phosphorus by drinking carbonated drinks. If you drink too many carbonated beverages and too little milk, you can have too little calcium and too much phosphorus for good health.

Iron, found in red blood cells, carries oxygen throughout your body. Without the iron-oxygen combination, you could not turn food into energy. Anemia is often caused by a lack of iron in the blood. When blood is lost, as from an injury or during a menstrual period, iron is lost too. Your body can recycle and store iron. But you still need to eat enough iron-rich foods. Iron is found in meat, eggs, leafy vegetables, and whole grain and enriched cereals.

Iodine helps the thyroid gland make the hormone that controls growth. *Goiter,* a disease caused by a lack of iodine, was common in the past. Most people now get enough iodine by eating iodized salt.

Sodium, potassium, and *chloride* are the minerals that control water balance. Table salt is sodium chloride. Today many snack foods such as pretzels, potato chips, and fries are heavily salted. Processed foods such as cured meats, condiments—including

Hidden Fat
- More than 90 percent fat:
  - salad oil
  - lard
- More than 80 percent fat:
  - butter
  - margarine
- More than 70 percent fat:
  - mayonnaise
  - pecans
- More than 50 percent fat:
  - walnuts
  - bacon
  - baking chocolate
  - dry unsweetened coconut
- More than 30 percent fat:
  - spare ribs
  - broiled loin steak
  - cheddar cheese
  - potato chips
  - french dressing
  - chocolate candy
- More than 20 percent fat:
  - pot roast
  - frankfurters
  - lean ground beef
  - most cookies
- More than 10 percent fat:
  - most broiled fish
  - most broiled chicken
  - cottage cheese
  - beef liver
  - creamed soups

Adapted from: Ronald M. Deutsch, *Realities of Nutrition,* Bull Publishing Company.

Why Is Milk Important?

Milk and milk products are the best sources of calcium. To get the same amount of calcium as there is in 250 mL (1 c) of milk, you would need to eat any one of the following:

- 16 slices of enriched bread
- 36 apples
- 18 medium potatoes
- 3.6 kg (8 lb) of beef
- 1875 mL (7½ c) of cooked carrots
- 1000 mL (4 c) of cooked brown rice
- 250 mL (1 c) of cooked collard greens
- 500 mL (2 c) of cooked broccoli

catsup, steak sauces, and barbecue sauces—and cheese contain sodium, too. Sometimes people eat more sodium than they really need. High blood pressure among adults may relate to eating too much salt.

Trace elements are other minerals that you need in tiny amounts.

Water. Water is essential to life. You can survive for only three to four days without it. But you could live for several weeks without a bite of food.

Water is part of every cell. It makes up about two-thirds of your body. Ninety percent of blood is water. The water in blood carries nutrients to cells and removes waste. Water also helps keep body temperature just right. Perspiration, which is water evaporating from your skin, keeps you cool.

You lose water in perspiration, in urine, and by breathing. So you need six to eight glasses of liquid daily. Water is in everything you eat. Beverages are mainly water. Fruits and vegetables are good sources, too. Even meat is 80 percent water.

NUTRIENTS . . . HOW MUCH?

Good nutrition is more than eating a little of each nutrient. Your body needs enough nutrients to work properly. A little calcium along with vitamin D, for example, may protect you from a disease called rickets. But you need a larger amount to help your bones grow normally.

The Recommended Dietary Allowances (RDA) are guidelines for nutrient and calorie intake for healthy people. Some people may need more, and

People need water to survive. Fresh water is inexpensive, and unlike carbonated beverages, it does not increase the amount of sugar in the diet.

Hamburger is one of the most popular protein foods.

others may need less. RDA charts are divided by age and sex because nutrient and calorie needs change throughout life. Teenagers need the most because of growth and active living. Pregnant or nursing women also need more nutrients.

GUIDELINES FOR THE 1980s

Most of us eat more fat, sugar, and sodium and less starch and fiber than people ate 75 years ago. Many scientists think that this new eating pattern is causing a widespread increase in diseases such as heart attacks, high blood pressure, and diabetes. The Dietary Guidelines for Americans (see page 382) were created to encourage moderation and variety in food choices. Moderation in eating and a varied diet can help promote and even improve health.

a quick review

1. How does food relate to health?
2. What does the term *high-quality protein* mean? Give some examples.
3. What function do carbohydrate and fat share?
4. How could you moderate fat in your diet? Sugar? Sodium?

▶ **Words to Know**

calories: The energy stored in food.

cell: The basic structural unit of the body.

cholesterol: A fatlike substance found in foods from animal sources.

enrich: To add to a food the nutrients that were lost in processing.

fat-soluble vitamins: Vitamins that dissolve in fat.

fiber: A complex carbohydrate that cannot be fully digested.

glucose: Sugar in the blood that powers body cells.

high-quality protein: Protein that contains all the essential amino acids. Also called complete protein.

low-quality protein: Protein that does not contain all the essential amino acids. Also called incomplete protein.

perspiration: Sweat.

polyunsaturated fat: Fat that is liquid at room temperature; oil.

saturated fat: Fat that is solid at room temperature.

starch: A complex carbohydrate made of linked units of sugar.

trace elements: Minerals needed in very small amounts by the body.

water-soluble vitamins: Vitamins that dissolve in water.

377

CHAPTER 52
Guidelines for Nutrition

Keeping track of the nutrients in everything you eat and drink each day is a big job. The Daily Food Guide can help. It was developed to make planning nutritious meals and snacks easy. It divides foods into five groups according to the nutrients each contains. All you need to do is eat the amount listed from each group every day. Then you will get the nutrients your body needs for good health.

Balanced daily menus have enough servings from four of the food groups. These are the vegetable and fruit group, the bread and cereal group, the milk and cheese group, and the meat, poultry, fish, and beans group. The fats and sweets group just adds extra calories and flavor.

Serving size is important to know. For example, a four-ounce glass of milk does not count as a serving. Instead, it is a half-serving from the milk and cheese group.

A balanced meal has food from at least three of the four food groups. The meat, poultry, fish and beans group is the exception, since you need only two servings from it daily. When you eat balanced meals, you get a variety of nutrients. Your body needs this variety to do its work. You also should eat a variety of foods from within each food group. Then you are more likely to get enough of each of the nutrients.

DAILY FOOD GUIDE

Food Group	Daily Servings
Vegetable and Fruit	**4** (one rich in vitamin C each day and one rich in vitamin A three to four times a week)
Bread and Cereal	**4**
Milk and Cheese	**2 to 3** for children under 9 **3** for children aged 9 to 12 **4** **2** for adults (1 extra during pregnancy) (1 extra when breastfeeding)
Meat, Poultry, Fish, and Beans	**2**
Fats and Sweets	none recommended

Can Snacks be Healthy?

Snacking has become a way of life for many people in the United States. After-school snacks and coffee breaks on the job are taken for granted. When friends visit, do you offer them food?

Snack foods are often high in sugar and calories but low in nutrients. However, with some planning you can substitute smart snacks for the more common potato chips and soft drinks. Try these nutritious snacks:

- raw vegetables such as carrots, cauliflower, cucumbers, green peppers, and turnips
- raw vegetables and fruits dipped in yogurt
- fresh fruits that are in season
- two round slices of a cored apple with peanut butter or cream cheese in the middle
- dried fruit filled with cream cheese
- celery filled with cream cheese
- hard-cooked eggs
- cubes of cheese
- heated cider with a stick of cinnamon

How many of these fruits and vegetables can you name? Which ones are especially high in vitamin C? Which ones are a good source of vitamin A?

VEGETABLE AND FRUIT GROUP

Raw, cooked, dried, and liquid forms of fruits and vegetables are grouped together. Legumes and lentils such as dry peas and kidney beans are grouped with meat, poultry, fish, and beans.

Citrus fruit, strawberries, cantaloupe, cabbage, papaya, tomatoes, and green peppers are some of the foods that are high in vitamin C. Dark green and deep yellow vegetables and fruit such as broccoli, carrots, greens, sweet potatoes, and apricots are rich in vitamin A. Peels and seeds are especially high in fiber.

Everyone needs at least four daily servings from the vegetable and fruit group. You should eat one item that is rich in vitamin C every day. And at least three times every week, you should eat one item that is rich in vitamin A.

One serving can be any of the following:

- 1 medium fruit
- a bowl of tossed salad
- a lettuce wedge
- 1 medium potato
- 125 milliliters (½ cup) of sliced fruit or vegetable
- 125 milliliters (½ cup) of juice
- ½ medium grapefruit

Grain products such as breakfast cereals, crackers, breads, rice, oatmeal, and pasta in many shapes make up the bread and cereal group.

BREAD AND CEREAL GROUP

Foods made of whole grain or enriched flour or meal are grouped together. These foods include breads of all kinds, biscuits, muffins, waffles, breakfast cereals, pasta, rice, barley, and bulgur.

Grain products are excellent sources of carbohydrate, iron, and B vitamins. Whole grains also provide fiber.

Everyone needs four servings a day. One serving can be any of the following:

- 1 slice of enriched or whole grain bread

- 125 milliliters (½ cup) of cooked cereal, rice, pasta, or grits
- 250 milliliters (1 cup) of ready-to-eat cereal
- 1 enriched or whole grain muffin, biscuit, or roll

MILK AND CHEESE GROUP

Many foods made from milk, such as yogurt, cottage cheese, cheddar cheese, and ice cream, make up this group. Pudding and creamed soups count too, since milk is one of their major ingredients.

Milk and milk products are the best sources of calcium, phosphorus,

381

Top: Foods in the milk and cheese group are good sources of calcium and protein. But some of these foods are richer in calcium per serving than others.

Bottom: Foods in the meat, poultry, fish, and beans group supply protein, iron, thiamin, and niacin. What other foods in this group can you name?

and riboflavin. They are also good sources of high-quality protein. Milk is often fortified with vitamin D, too.

The number of servings people need daily depends on their ages. People between nine and twelve years old need three servings. Teenagers need at least four.

One serving of milk or yogurt is 250 milliliters (1 cup).

The following portions of other foods in this group have the same amount of calcium as there is in one serving of milk:

- 45 grams (1½ slices) of cheddar cheese
- 500 milliliters (2 cups) of cottage cheese
- 250 milliliters (1 cup) of pudding
- 375 milliliters (1½ cups) of ice cream

MEAT, POULTRY, FISH, AND BEANS GROUP

Beef, pork, lamb, fish, poultry, organ meats, and eggs are included in this group. Nuts and legumes like chick peas, soybeans, kidney beans, and peanuts are good meat substitutes. That is, they are good sources of high-quality protein.

In addition to high-quality protein, this group supplies iron, thiamin, and niacin.

Children, teenagers, and adults need two servings daily.

One serving of cooked lean meat, poultry, or fish without bones is 60 milliliters (2 ounces).

The following portions of other foods in this group have the same amount of protein as there is in one of the above servings:

- 2 eggs
- 60 milliliters (¼ cup) of peanut butter
- 125 milliliters (½ cup) of nuts
- 250 milliliters (1 cup) of cooked dry legumes

FATS AND SWEETS

This group includes two kinds of food: sweets such as candy, jam, soft drinks, and syrup; and fats such as butter, margarine, and salad dressing. Breads and pastries made with refined but unenriched flour belong here, too.

These foods are good sources of fat, carbohydrate, and sometimes water. They are called empty-calorie foods because they supply calories but few nutrients. Use small amounts of these foods to add variety and flavor. But make balanced meals and nutritious snacks come first.

For a balanced diet, eat adequate servings from the first four food groups in the Daily Food Guide. Add variety and extra calories with small servings from the last group.

- Eat less candy, soft drinks, ice cream, cakes, and cookies.
- Eat fresh fruits, or canned fruits without sugar or with light syrup. Avoid heavy syrups.
6. *Avoid too much sodium.*
   - Learn to like unsalted foods.
   - Cook with only small amounts of added salt.
   - Go light on the salt shaker.
   - Limit the salty foods you eat, such as potato chips, salted nuts, popcorn, bacon, ham, and pickles.

▶ **Words to Know**

balanced meal: A meal that has one serving each from the vegetable and fruit group, the bread and cereal group, the milk and cheese group, and the meat, poultry, fish, and beans group.

Daily Food Guide: A simple guideline for planning nutritious meals and snacks and for judging food choices.

empty-calorie foods: Foods that have calories but few nutrients other than carbohydrate and fat.

meat substitute: A food that can be eaten in place of meat because the nutrient content is similar.

serving: A single portion of food with a size specified under food group guidelines.

a quick review

1. What is a balanced diet?
2. How could you use the Daily Food Guide to plan a meal?
3. Why is there no recommended number of daily servings from the fats and sweets group?
4. Why is variety important in your diet?

CHAPTER 53
Weight Control

Why are so many people always dieting? Even slim people want to be slimmer. Some people are never happy with their weight. Magazines and television advertisements tell us that thin is "in." What they should be doing is encouraging us to be our own best weight.

WHAT IS YOUR BEST WEIGHT?

Body weight is hard to judge. Because you and your friends probably have different heights and body builds, you each have a different weight that is best for you. A doctor is the best judge of proper weight. The following guidelines can also be used to determine your normal body weight.

A mirror can give an honest opinion. Look at yourself in a bathing suit. Stand tall. Do you look fat? A bulge here and a roll there may be signs that you are overweight. Perhaps you need exercise to firm up. Extra muscle may also help if you are too thin.

There is a layer of fat below the skin. That fat keeps you warm and protects you from injury. The thickness of this layer can also be used to find out if you are underweight, overweight, or at your ideal body weight. Doctors use a special tool to take an exact measurement. A pinch test gives a rough estimate. Simply pinch

Making smart food choices every day is the key to easy weight control. Look at the foods shown here. Which ones do you think are highest in calories? Which ones are lowest? Check your answers with a calorie chart.

your skin on the upper arm or midriff up to the muscle. The normal size of the layer of fat is 1.3 to 2.5 centimeters (½ to 1 inch). If you have less fat, you *may* be underweight. If you have more fat, you *may* be overweight.

Most height-weight charts are meant for adults, not children or teenagers. Unless you have a chart designed for your age group, do not use one. Charts are simply averages for a large group of people. Your best weight may be quite different from the figure on the chart.

CALORIES

You have probably heard the word *calorie* many times. Do you know what a calorie is? You cannot touch it or see it. It is not a nutrient. Rather, it is the energy in food. Your body burns energy, or calories, to keep you going and to power activities like running or swimming.

The number of calories you need depends on your age, sex, size, weight, and amount of activity. First, you need calories for *basal metabolism.* That is the rate at which your body burns calories for processes such as

Facts About Fat

• *Obesity,* or being overweight, is a major health problem in the United States. Experts think that fifty million people in this country are too heavy.

• There are many ideas about why people become overweight. Some weight problems are caused by gland imbalances, but these are very rare.

Another explanation is the "fat cell" theory. This says that because a person is overfed, she or he develops more and larger fat cells than normal-weighted people.

(continued on page 386)

Facts About Fat
(continued from page 385)

Heredity is a third reason given for obesity. However, many doctors believe that family eating habits are much more important than inherited traits.

- Eighty-five percent of obese children grow up to be obese adults.
- Heavy children have more accidents and more high blood pressure than other children.
- In general, the obese have a 150 percent higher death rate than the normal-weighted. Obesity is also linked to heart disease, diabetes, kidney problems, and some cancers.
- Studies with rats show that obese rats live longer than rats who suffer from "yo-yo syndrome"—constantly gaining and losing weight.
- A National Institute of Health study says that the very underweight have death rates almost as high as the obese.
- If you eat 1 percent more food than usual each day for a year, you will gain between 2 and 5 kilograms (5 to 10 pounds).
- If you are overweight, why not exercise, eat less sugar, remove skin from your meat, avoid butter, stop frying your food, and eat fruit instead of cake for dessert?

your heartbeat, breathing, blood circulation, elimination of waste, and production of new cells.

Exercise uses calories, too. The calories burned in physical activity depend on three things: the kind of activity, how long you do it, and how strenuously you exercise.

To control weight, you must eat as many calories as you burn. You gain weight when you eat more. You lose weight when you eat less.

Calorie charts tell you how many calories each food contains. Check the serving size and how the food was prepared. Both affect calorie value.

SENSIBLE TIPS FOR WEIGHT LOSS

Maintaining normal weight is good for your health. Some diseases, such as heart disease and diabetes, are more common among people who are considerably overweight. Keeping yourself at your best weight will also make you feel better about yourself. If you stay slim while you are young, you will have a better chance of being slim as an adult. Why not make normal weight a lifetime goal?

The best weight-loss program includes eating fewer calories and burning up more calories.

- Choose foods from the first four food groups. Cut down on foods from the fats and sweets group.
- Eat smaller portions.
- Eat slowly.
- Don't skip meals. You will probably eat even more calories by snacking later.

Burn extra calories through exercise, the other half of a weight-loss program.

- Begin a regular program of physical activity.
- Look for ways to get more exercise every day. Use stairs instead of elevators.

EATING TO GAIN WEIGHT

Extreme underweight can be bad for your health. Without enough food, you will not get the nutrients you need. You may get tired easily.

Check Your Calorie Needs

No two people need the same number of calories. The numbers below in parentheses indicate a range. Within that range, the calories you need depend on how active you are and on your basal metabolic rate.

Age	Females	Calories Males
7–10	2400 (1650–3300)	2400 (1650–3300)
11–14	2200 (1500–3000)	2700 (2000–3700)
15–18	2100 (1200–3000)	2800 (2100–3900)

Physical exercise is an important factor in weight control. The number of calories burned depends on the type of activity, how strenuously you exercise, and the length of time you exercise.

Calories in Common Foods	
apple pie, ⅛ of a 23-cm (9-in) pie	403
chocolate shake, 375 mL (12 oz)	391
cheese pizza, ¼ of 36-cm (14-in) pie	354
hamburger on bun, 85–g (3-oz) patty	305
fruit yogurt, 250 mL (1 c)	225
peanuts, 125 mL (¼ c)	211
fried chicken, 84 g (3 oz)	201
fried, breaded perch, 84 g (3 oz)	193
peanut butter, 30 mL (2 Tbsp)	186
bagel, 1	165
whole milk, 250 mL (1 c)	150
milk chocolate bar, 28 g (1 oz)	147
vanilla ice cream, 125 mL (½ c)	138
raisins, 68 mL (4½ Tbsp)	123
cottage cheese, 125 mL (½ c)	120
potato chips, 10	114
cheddar cheese, 28 g (1 oz)	113
rice, 125 mL (½ c)	112
noodles, 125 mL (½ c)	100
soft drink, 250 mL (8 oz)	96
baked potato, medium size	90
hard-cooked egg, 1	82

Your body may not be able to fight illness. Also, you may not think as clearly.

To gain weight, you need to eat more calories than your body burns.

• Eat more foods from the first four food groups.

• Eat larger portions of food, or eat more often if your appetite is small.

MAKING WEIGHT FOR SPORTS

Body weight is important to many sports. Wrestlers compete in weight classes. In football, extra weight is often an advantage, especially for the defense. Gymnasts and skaters have to keep their weight down.

Achieve proper weight for competition in a sensible way. The tips suggested earlier are useful for most athletes, too. Athletes who starve themselves and refuse to drink liquids before a weigh-in may become *dehydrated*. Their bodies do not have enough water. Also, crash dieting prior to an event does not provide nourishment for top performance.

Overeating before a game is not healthy either. Muscle, not fat, gives a

387

The first step in controlling your weight is to control or even eliminate snacks. Heavy after-school snacks such as pizza and soda contain many calories, and it takes a good deal of exercise to burn these calories away.

gain the weight back. This is because eating habits are not changed. Sometimes these methods, when misused, even result in serious illness or death.

Diet pills are usually not effective. And they can be dangerous. Many reduce the appetite. Diet pills may also cause nervousness or drowsiness. Many are *addictive,* or habit-forming. *Diuretics,* which cause water loss, are harmful, too. Because they move food through the digestive tract quickly, they may cause excessive water loss. In that case, fewer nutrients are absorbed. Furthermore, drugs do not help a person to lose body fat.

Diet candies swell to fill the stomach. Hunger pangs go away for a short time. However, candy before mealtime does not teach new food patterns. Hence, the weight lost often goes right back on.

Crash, or fad, diets do not work for many reasons. They are often boring. Many are not nutritious. Some are expensive. Others are not realistic for the way people live and eat. Most crash diets do not teach people new ways to eat. In Chapter 54, common fad diets for weight loss are discussed.

competitive edge. The best way to build muscle mass is to eat extra calories and to exercise regularly.

DANGERS OF REDUCING DRUGS AND CRASH DIETS

There are many ways to lose weight. Some of them are bad for you. Diet pills, diet candies, and crash diets are examples. People usually

a quick review

1. What are the advantages of maintaining your best weight? *feelgood*
2. Describe two ways to judge proper body weight. *pinch + cook*
3. How does your body use calories? *metabolism*
4. Describe a healthful diet for losing weight and one for gaining weight.

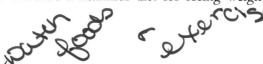

Many claims are made about food. Have you ever heard, for example, that eating carrots makes your hair curly? Or that an apple a day keeps the doctor away? Or that potatoes are fattening? None of these is true. The foods you eat do affect how you look and feel. But people have many wrong ideas about foods. You won't curl your hair by eating carrots. But vitamin A, made from the carotene found in carrots, does help to keep your hair shiny. Other sources of vitamin A, such as sweet potatoes or liver, will do the same.

FOOD MYTHS—FACT OR FICTION?

Are good looks and physical energy important to you? For most people, they are. Food *quacks,* people who promote misinformation about foods, often take advantage of consumers who want good health. Quacks know that people like easy answers—a quick, magic way to get slim, to have stronger muscles, or maybe to cure an illness. So they appeal to your emotions with statements like "Melt away 10 ugly pounds in ten easy days with this quick weight-loss program," or "Drink protein-fortified Lion's Milk for strong muscles."

A food myth, or quackery, is false or only partly true information about food. Some food myths may be very

CHAPTER 54
Food Fads

fiction: Chemical fertilizers poison the soil.

fact: Chemical fertilizers are needed to grow enough food for all the people in the world.

fiction: An apple a day keeps the doctor away.

fact: Apples have no special health-giving qualities. A balanced diet with a variety of foods can help keep the doctor away.

fiction: Toast has fewer calories than untoasted bread.

fact: Both have about 65 calories per slice.

fiction: Drinking milk and eating fish in the same meal will make you sick.

fact: Any foods that can be eaten separately can be eaten together.

fiction: Brown eggs have more nutrients than white eggs.

fact: Both have the same nutritional value. The color of the shell depends on the breed of hen.

fiction: Athletes need extra protein to build muscles.

fact: Most athletes and nonathletes need about the same amount of protein.

fiction: The food we buy is so low in vitamins that everyone needs vitamin pills.

(continued)

popular for a short time. When another quick, easy diet appears, people follow it. Diets like these are called *fad diets.*

Have You Heard About These? Books, magazines, and talk shows promote many different food myths, especially fad diets for weight loss.

The Air Force Diet, the Scarsdale Diet, and the Atkins Diet are all high-protein/low-carbohydrate diets. Different variations of these diets appear again and again under new names. Meat, poultry, and fish are allowed, but milk, grain products, and many vegetables and fruits are often discouraged. For a short time people lose weight. However, they do not get enough of many nutrients. These diets, if followed over long periods, can even cause damage to the kidney and liver.

Another kind of diet is the single-food diet. These diets stress eating one food, such as bananas or grapefruit, over and over. The dieter therefore does not get a variety of nutrients. Also, eating one food often gets boring quickly. Most people do not stay on these diets for long.

Fasting is not eating at all. Some diets promote fasting for a short time. The stomach is supposed to shrink. That is not true, however. The weight that is lost is mainly water. When the faster eats again, the pounds go back on.

Doctors sometimes use liquid protein diets to help very heavy people lose weight. The patients are watched carefully. People should not use such a diet on their own. Liquid protein can be dangerous when it is the only food source. Several deaths have been linked to these diets.

Sorting fact from fiction isn't easy. And sometimes misleading statements can do much harm. By following a food myth, you may delay getting the medical help you may need. Some food fads are costly, too. Remember that many quacks are out to make money. Fad weight-loss diets are also often less effective than traditional ways to lose weight.

WHAT ARE HEALTH FOODS?

Some different types of foods are called *health foods.* They can be the low-salt and low-sugar foods that supermarkets often carry for people on special diets. Or they can be the many foods that health food stores sell for their so-called health-giving properties. This term is misleading, however. Foods carefully chosen from grocery stores are just as healthful.

Organically grown foods are foods grown without the use of chemical fertilizers or pesticides. Organic fertilizers such as manure and compost are used to make the soil fertile. Animals raised organically are not given hormones to speed their growth.

Foods grown organically are not more nutritious than others. Plants can not tell the difference between organic and chemical fertilizers. Both kinds put the same nutrients into the soil. And pesticides are important to keep crops from being destroyed. There are laws to keep the amount of pesticides at safe levels.

Organically grown foods are usually more expensive. They cost more to produce. They may spoil faster, too. Sometimes foods that are sold as organic aren't really organic. So consumers do not always get what they think they are buying. In addition, organic fertilizers may spread bacteria and illness.

What does the term *natural foods* mean to you? If you asked five people, you might get five different answers. Advertisers use the term all the time. But no law regulates the meaning. The term is often used to mean that no preservatives were added or that the product was not heavily processed.

Eating fewer processed foods has some advantages. Nutrients are lost when some foods, such as white flour, are processed. When manufacturers *enrich* these foods, they put back some nutrients, but not all. Often, however, the nutrient loss is very small. For example, frozen orange juice is as nutritious as fresh.

How long could you stay on a diet that consisted of nothing but grapefruit and grapefruit juice? What are the disadvantages of this kind of diet?

fact: Many nutritious foods are available in the stores. A varied and balanced diet provides all the vitamins and other nutrients you need daily.

fiction: Potatoes are fattening.

fact: Any food is fattening if you eat too much. A medium-sized potato has only about 80 calories. The butter, sour cream, or gravy you put on it add extra calories.

fiction: White bread does not have any nutrients.

fact: White bread is made from flour that has had the bran and the germ removed from the grain. Nutrients are lost then, too. But some nutrients—thiamin, riboflavin, niacin, and iron—are added back. Most white bread is made from enriched flour.

fiction: Honey is better for you than refined sugar.

fact: Honey and table sugar both break down into the same two simple sugars when digested. Both have the same number of calories per gram. Honey is stickier and more harmful to your teeth.

fiction: Grapefruit breaks down body fat.

fact: No food can break down body fat. Weight is lost by eating fewer calories than you use.

Words to Know

additives: Substances added during food processing for specific reasons.

enrich: Put nutrients back into food after processing.

fad diet: A popular diet that promises extraordinary results in a short period.

fasting: Not eating for a period of time.

fertilizers: Substances that put nourishment in the soil.

food myth: Wrong information about food.

natural foods: A term with many meanings; foods with no preservatives or processing.

organically grown foods: Foods grown without chemical fertilizers.

pesticides: Chemicals used to control insects.

preservatives: Additives to keep food safe to eat for a longer time.

processing: Any change made in a food before eating.

quack: Someone who promotes misinformation about food or health.

Gardens need fertilizer to produce the best results. One type of organic fertilizer is compost. Compost is decayed organic matter such as decayed food. Chemical fertilizers and pesticides are used in nonorganic gardens.

Natural foods are not necessarily better. "Natural" granola is high in sugar. Read labels carefully so you know what you are buying.

It is true that some food-processing methods destroy nutrients. And we do not know the long-term effects of using many additives, though additive use is carefully watched. However, we do not know about the dangers of some substances in natural foods, either. Also, modern methods of growing and preserving foods must be used if we are to grow enough food and market it safely.

Use good sense in making food decisions. Eat more fresh fruits and vegetables and fewer processed convenience foods. Learn to enjoy whole grain breads and cereals.

a quick review

1. How can food myths be harmful?
2. Why is the term *health food* misleading?
3. What are the differences between organically grown foods and those grown with chemical fertilizers?
4. Would you consider granola, which is made with honey, no preservatives, but other additives, a natural food? Why or why not?

W hat would you do if tomorrow night's family dinner were up to you? Where would you eat? What would you eat? What kind of thinking and planning would you have to do before you started to cook?

WHO WILL EAT?

Before you decide on what food to serve and how much of it to prepare, you need to know who will be eating. Will your whole family be together, or will someone be away? Will there be a guest? If so, you will want to know if there are any foods your guest cannot eat. Religion or custom may also affect what foods you will serve.

WHEN WILL YOU EAT?

Consider the schedules of all your family's members. Think about when you will eat, where you will eat, and how you will serve the meal. If there are small children in the family, the meals should be served on a regular schedule. Older children and adults can be more flexible. In a family with teenagers, it is often difficult to find a time when everyone will be available for a meal. This is often because of the activity schedules of the teens, but it also can be a result of increased activities for the adults. For these times, it is essential to plan meals that can be reheated and eaten later.

CHAPTER 55
Planning Meals

HOW MUCH TIME DO YOU HAVE?

When planning any meal, consider how much time you have to prepare it. Consider also if anyone will be there to help you. Before you decide to use a certain recipe, read it thoroughly. Does the recipe call for a great deal of chopping, mixing, or waiting? How long must the food cook or chill? Do you have that much time? You might choose a recipe that needs last-minute preparation—for example, stir-fried vegetables. If so, select a dish to go with it that can be prepared in advance, like baked chicken. Good planning can help you avoid a lot of last-minute preparation.

Another way to save time in the kitchen is to use the available equipment. If you have a slow cooker or microwave oven, learn to use it.

WHAT FOODS DO YOU HAVE?

Plan meals around food already in the kitchen. Learn to use leftovers. Before shopping, check your kitchen to see what food supplies you already have. If you planned to serve broccoli but find fresh spinach in the refrigerator, you could substitute one for the other without losing food value.

HOW MUCH SHOULD YOU SPEND?

Menu planning is one key to keeping within a food budget. There are also many other ways to stretch food dollars and still eat well.

Before you go shopping, make a list of what you are going to buy. Otherwise, when you get to the store, you may give in to impulse buying. *Impulse buying* is buying something

Good planning can make a family meal a relaxed and pleasant occasion.

just because it looks or smells good. Impulse works especially well on a hungry stomach, so eat before you shop. If you can't eat before you shop, make a real effort to stick to your list and avoid impulse buying.

As you shop, look for *unit pricing.* Unit pricing tells you the price of an item per pint, pound, gram, or liter. This makes it easier for you to compare prices when items are packaged in different sizes. Also, be flexible. If you wanted chicken for a casserole but see that turkey is less expensive, make the substitution.

Be sure that you have storage space at home for the groceries you buy. Store the groceries properly as soon as you get home.

PLANNING FOR NUTRITION

Plan for good health as you plan your menu. The best way to ensure good nutrition is to follow the Daily Food Guide, which appears in Chapter 52. Use this guide to help you select foods that contain a variety of nutrients. By following the guide daily, you will have the nutrients that your body needs for growth and health.

MEALS WITH APPEAL

As you plan, picture how the meal will look on the plate.

Color. Foods come in so many colors that it is hard to imagine a meal all one color. But consider a dinner plate with roast chicken, mashed potatoes, creamed cauliflower, applesauce, and biscuits. How much color variety would there be? Now imagine broccoli spears substituted for the cauliflower. The dark green color of the broccoli adds appeal to this meal.

Texture. Variations in *texture,* the way a food feels in the mouth, also add interest to meals. For example, carrot sticks are crisp and crunchy. Their texture is very different from that of, say, soft mashed potatoes. In the above menu, the substitution of broccoli for cauliflower also helps to vary the texture.

Shape. Serving foods with different shapes is another way to make a meal more attractive. In the above menu, the food shapes were mostly round. The substitution of broccoli spears helps to vary the shapes. Cut broccoli would not be a help because it looks too much like the cauliflower. Carrots, which can be cut in lengthwise strips or round slices, are an easy way to vary shape in a meal. Another example of contrasting shapes is raw spinach served with onion rings.

Flavor. The way a food tastes is its *flavor.* When making up a menu, you should combine foods that taste good together. A strongly flavored, spicy food, such as tomato sauce, tastes

Meals are more interesting when the shapes of the foods vary. The shapes of most of the foods in the meal on the left are round. In the meal on the right, the shapes have been changed but the foods are nearly the same.

good balanced with a mild or bland food, such as spaghetti.

SETTING PRIORITIES

Deciding what is most or least important to you is called *setting priorities.* Your priorities will probably change many times as you grow older. Right now your chief consider-ation in meal planning may be taste. Later, when you have your own home or apartment, you may be more interested in how foods look or what it costs. If you have a very busy schedule, you will probably often choose foods that need little preparation. People are different and will set different priorities.

a quick review

1. Why is it helpful to know who will be eating before you plan a meal?
2. Name two timesaving pieces of kitchen equipment. Explain how they help you to save time.
3. What may happen to a hungry food shopper? What may happen to a food shopper without a list?
4. How can you provide variety and contrast in a meal?

How many different ways have you seen food served? Do you enjoy eating the same way every day, or do you like a change of pace? In this chapter you will read about some ways that food can be served.

FAMILY SERVICE

Most families have their own way of eating. Many of them prefer "family style" meals. In these meals all the food is passed around the table on platters and in bowls. Then people help themselves. In some families the mother or father carves the meat or serves the casserole at the table and then passes the plates to the other family members or to guests. Salads and beverages may also be served at the table. In many families, serving at the table is reserved for holidays and for special occasions. Serving at the table does not work as well for a very large group of people because the food will get cold before everyone is served.

Another kind of family service is filling all the plates with food in the kitchen and then serving the plates to the people at the table. If someone wants a second portion, the plate is carried to the kitchen for refilling. This method works well when table space is limited. It also means fewer dishes to wash.

CHAPTER 56
Serving Food

History's Menus

Can you imagine what you might have served if you had lived in ancient Egypt, or what you might have eaten had you dined in early Greece?

Below are some imaginary menus from the past, the present, and the future.

Prehistoric People:

Cave Bear   Wild Boar
Bone Marrow
Wild Berries

Ancient Egyptians:

Roasted Antelope and
Stork
Beans   Quince
Wheat Bread
Melon

Ancient Hebrews:

Pottage (Thick Lentil Soup)
Bean Flour Bread
Honey
Goat Milk

Ancient Greeks:
One of the following:

Barley Porridge
Fish
Figs
Grapes
(continued)

Food is often served very informally.

BUFFET SERVICE

Benjamin Franklin invented buffet service about 200 years ago. He needed an inexpensive way to serve a large number of people. So he offered food to his guests on a long table and let them walk about the room informally with their refreshments.

Buffet style is still a popular form of entertaining, especially for large groups of people. It allows the guests to select the foods of their choice. It also frees the host from serving. With some advance planning, you can prepare many buffet foods ahead of time.

When planning a buffet menu, choose foods that vary in color, texture, and taste. Also, choose foods that are easy to eat. Foods that can be eaten with the fingers or that can be cut easily with a fork are a good choice. Foods that contain a lot of liquid are not a good idea because they are easily spilled.

Keep the menu simple, so that each guest needs only one plate. Many casseroles are easy to make and serve. Be sure to keep hot foods hot to avoid food poisoning. You can do this by putting your serving dishes either on warming trays or inside shallow pans filled with hot water.

The buffet table is often set up in the center of a room to allow guests to walk around it easily as they serve themselves. If the serving table is placed near the kitchen, it makes it easier to remove empty dishes and refill empty serving platters.

For the convenience of the diners, food and eating utensils should be arranged on the table as people will use them. Sometimes the eating utensils are placed on a separate table. Sometimes tables are set with the eating utensils. When they are included on the buffet table, the clean plates should be placed first, appetizers next, then salads, main course, vegetables, and bread. Desserts and beverages should be placed at the end of the table. Arrange flatware and napkins near the plates or at the end of the table. Place sauces, dressings, and garnishes near the foods with which they are to be eaten. Don't forget the centerpiece. It can be anything attractive, but flowers are always a good idea.

Since it is often hard to eat while walking or standing, think about seating arrangements. Try to have enough chairs or cushions for everyone. Whenever possible, set up small tables around the room so guests can sit and eat more comfortably. Lap trays also make buffet eating easier.

FORMAL SERVICE

Formal service is used most often at luxury restaurants or at special affairs such as weddings. With this type of service, one person brings food from the kitchen and serves everyone at the table. Before each new course is served, the dishes from the previous course are taken away.

When a buffet table is arranged like this one, the eating utensils are set at individual places or on a separate table. This arrangement is used when the buffet table is small, when place settings can be put elsewhere, or when an additional table is available.

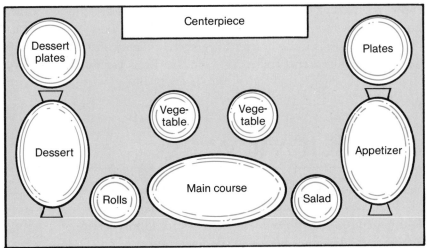

Ancient Romans:
One of the following:

Oysters
Fish
Eggs
Wheat Bread
Plums
Dates
Pastry

Europeans of the Middle Ages:

Chicken
Eggs
Cabbage   Turnips
Black Bread

Native Americans:

Wild Turkey
Sweet Potatoes   Corn
Pumpkin
Nuts

Present-Day Americans:

Hamburger
French Fries   Cole Slaw
Milkshake

Future Menu:

Algae Casserole
Marama Beans
Fish Crackers
Carob-Coated Locusts
Soy Milk

399

Lunch Box Ideas

People often take their lunch to school or work. This is known as *brown bagging* because the lunches are often carried in brown bags. Here are some tips for adding interest and variety to these lunches:

• Freeze small cans of fruit juice and pack one in a lunch box to keep your lunch cool.

• Include hard-cooked eggs, leaving the shells.

• Use wide-mouth vacuum bottles for carrying soups, salads, or stews.

• When packing cut fresh fruit, dip the edge in lemon or orange juice. This keeps the fruit from browning.

• In place of a sandwich, pack cubes of chicken, ham, or cheese.

• If you are packing someone else's lunch, add a card or a funny drawing.

▶ **Words to Know**

buffet service: Food is placed on a large table in serving dishes. Guests serve themselves.

family service: Food is passed around the table in serving dishes, and people serve themselves.

formal service: A waiter or waitress serves guests the filled plates.

tea or reception service: Similar to buffet service but less food is served.

You may want to try using formal service for a special occasion at home. Just remember that all the food is served and removed from the left side. However, beverages are served and removed from the right. To clear the table, remove all serving platters and bowls first. Then remove all the dirty dishes from in front of each person in turn. Never scrape or stack dishes in front of the guests.

TEA OR RECEPTION SERVICE

Teas or receptions are other ways to entertain large groups of people. A *tea* is an informal gathering at which light refreshments are served. A *reception* is somewhat more formal than a tea. It usually includes a receiving line, in which the host formally greets all the guests as they arrive.

Teas are very similar to buffets. The food is placed on a table, and the guests serve themselves. However, the menu for a tea is quite different. It generally includes tea, coffee, or punch served along with small sandwiches, cakes, fancy cookies, nuts, and candies.

Teas and receptions can be used for friendly get-togethers, club parties, or almost any time you want to bring a large group together. Such gatherings are generally come-and-go parties. Guests are expected to arrive between the times given on the invitation, stay awhile, enjoy the food, and then leave to make room for others. Guests may stay the whole time, but they are not expected to do so.

There are many types of people and many different reasons for people to get together. Therefore, there should be many different ways to serve guests. For smaller groups, choose family or formal service. Buffets, teas, or receptions work best for large gatherings. It is up to you to decide how formal you want the occasion to be. You can be as creative as you want when deciding on a theme for your party. Be sure to give each gathering plenty of thought and planning, and it is certain to be a success.

a quick review

1. What are two different ways to serve food to your family?
2. For what types of occasions would you use buffet service?
3. How should food be served and cleared for informal service?
4. What is the difference between a tea and a reception?

Have you even gone to a dinner and not known which salad or napkin was yours? Have you noticed that restaurants vary in their table settings? Usually, the more expensive the restaurant, the more formal the table setting and the service. Would you feel comfortable in a formal situation? If you learn a few simple rules, you will feel comfortable in any eating situation. You can also make your friends feel important as well as comfortable when you entertain by setting a beautiful, appetizing table.

SETTING THE TABLE

An orderly arrangement of knives, forks, and spoons is easier to handle than a confused one. By following a few patterns, you can turn table setting into a natural skill.

A table may be set for formal occasions, such as dinner parties, or informal occasions, such as buffets, barbecues, or after-the-game get-togethers. Formal service means that one person will bring the food from the kitchen and serve everyone at the table. Informal service allows people to serve themselves. In any case, the traditional table-setting rules remain the same. Some of these rules are as follow:

• A tablecloth should fit the table properly. The cloth should not be so

CHAPTER 57
Table Setting

Knives, Forks, and Spoons

Knives and spoons have been used for thousands of years. The fork, however, is a fairly new invention.

The earliest knife was probably made of stone. The steel knife finally appeared in the 1300s. Until the 1500s, people in Europe carried their knives in their belts. They used them for hunting or whittling wood as well as for cutting food.

Spoons and ladles were used by early cavemen. Later, the Egyptians had ivory, slate, and flint spoons. The Greeks and Romans used bronze, silver, or brass spoons. Many of these had spiked handles. The Chinese had spoons made of porcelain. In Europe in the 1500s, silver spoons became popular among the upper classes.

The first fork used for eating at the table dates back to the eleventh century in Italy. A dainty woman, the daughter of a nobleman, claimed that she was too weak to pick up heavy meats with her fingers. A tiny two-pronged fork was made for her out of gold. It was shaped like the larger meat forks used for serving and carving. Forks soon became popular eating utensils throughout Italy.

(continued)

short that you can see the table underneath. Nor should it be so long that it gets in the way when you sit. Place mats should be set near the edge of the table and an equal distance apart from each other.

• The napkin should be folded and placed with the open edge near the left side of the fork. The napkin should be about 2.5 centimeters (1 inch) from the edge of the table.

• Flatware is arranged in the order of use, from the outside in. It too should be placed about 2.5 centimeters (1 inch) from the edge of the table.

• Dinnerware is placed so it is within easy reach of the diner's hand.

• Glasses are arranged above the dinnerware and knife and spoons.

• A centerpiece may be placed in the middle of the table or anywhere else on it, as long as the table looks attractive and people can see each other.

TABLE MANNERS

Your table manners are a reflection of you. Be considerate of others and show pride in yourself by following standard table manners.

Your Appearance. Be sure your hands and face are clean when you go to the table. If you have been doing a dirty job, such as working on the car or cleaning out the garage, change your clothes before going to the table.

Conversation. Enter into the table conversation. Avoid arguments or unpleasant topics. Also, be a good listener. Meals are even more enjoyable with lively conversation.

Can you find three errors in this table setting? Look at the diagram on page 404 for assistance.

Glassware comes in many different styles. Handles make the glassware easier to hold and pour from.

Use of Napkins. Keep the napkin on your lap throughout the meal, unless you wish to lightly blot your lips. When the meal is over, place the napkin beside your plate.

Use of Flatware. The knife is used to cut pieces of food on the plate and, if there is no butter knife, to spread butter, cheese, or jelly on bread or rolls. Forks are used to hold solid foods and to cut soft foods, such as vegetables or cake. Forks and knives are used together to cut one or two bite-sized pieces of food at a time. When you are finished cutting, place the knife across the top of the plate.

The spoon is used for eating soft or liquid foods, for stirring liquids, and for tasting beverages. Between bites or after all the food has been eaten, place the spoon on the saucer or plate that is under the bowl or cup.

Passing Food. When passing food at the table, pass it all in the same direction so that no one is handed food from two sides at once.

The English at first considered the fork to be jewelry. The first king to use one to eat was James I, in the 1500s. But the three-pronged fork was not used by the English upper classes until at least a hundred years later. Governor John Winthrop of Massachusetts was the first to bring the fork to America.

Imagine taking your own knife, fork, and spoon with you whenever you go out to a restaurant. Yet this practice of taking personal utensils along on every journey did not come to an end until the 1700s.

Superstitions About Knives, Forks, and Spoons:
• If you drop a knife, the direction in which it leans if it sticks into the ground is important. This is the direction from which company or good news will arrive.
• If you drop a knife and it does not stick into the ground, be prepared for disappointment or for some bad luck.
• Do not cross a knife and a fork, or misfortune will be at your doorstep.

Table Coverings

Table coverings are tablecloths or place mats. They look attractive and help to protect the table. You can select a paper, plastic, or fabric covering. Paper and plastic cloths have the advantage of easy cleanup. Fabric cloths give a more formal look. They are available with easy-care finishes so that stains can be washed away and little or no ironing is necessary. Fabric cloths come in many colors. Place mats can also be quite attractive. They can be made of paper, plastic, straw, or fabric. Your choice will depend on your needs and the look you wish to create. For a "different" look, you may wish to try layering. *Layering* is using several layers of tablecloths, along with place mats or *runners,* which are lengths of fabric that go down the middle of the table and hang over the edge.

Napkins

Napkins are used to protect your lap from spilled food. They also can be used to keep your hands and face clean while eating. Either paper or cloth napkins can be used.

BASIC STEPS IN TABLE SETTING

Set a table to fit the menu you are serving. Napkins can be placed either at the left of the forks or in the center of the dinner plates.

Location of knife and spoons

Location of napkin and forks

Location of bread-and-butter plate

Location of salad plate

Location of salad plate with bread-and-butter plate

Location of drinking glasses

Location of cup and saucer

Colorful placemats and napkins that are coordinated with the dishes and glassware can make the table setting interesting, especially when the items are arranged neatly and correctly.

a quick review

1. Where should you place the knife, fork, soup spoon, and teaspoon when setting a table?
2. How can a knowledge of table setting help you feel comfortable in social situations?
3. Why are napkins used?
4. What are two common table coverings? What is layering? Why might it be used?
5. Describe good table manners in terms of appearance, conversation, passing food, and use of flatware and napkins.

CHAPTER 58
Eating Outdoors

Many people think that food tastes better outside, especially when it is cooked outside. But whether you are thinking of an outdoor picnic or a barbecue, you will enjoy it more if you plan ahead. You will have to decide what food and equipment you need and how you are going to carry everything. The menu should be carefully planned. Some foods are more suited to outdoor eating than others.

PICNICS

A picnic is an event in which you carry prepared food to an outdoor spot and eat it there.

Follow the same guidelines for meal planning as those in Chapter 55. Since you will be carrying the food, keep in mind that some foods pack better than others. Some are also easier to eat in an outdoor setting. For example, sandwiches and other foods that you can eat with your fingers are convenient at a picnic. They are also easy to pack. Soup, on the other hand, is difficult to *transport* (carry) without spilling. Also, it is difficult to eat if there is no table.

Food spoils quickly in warm weather. A good rule to remember is to keep hot foods hot, above 60°C (140°F), and cold foods cold, below 5°C (40°F). Ice chests, vacuum containers, and insulated bags will help keep food at the proper temperature.

Simple outdoor meals are the most enjoyable ones.

Picnic Food Tips
- Wash hands before handling food.
- Wash hands after handling raw meat, fish, or poultry.
- Thaw all meats and poultry in the refrigerator before cooking them. This will reduce the chance of food poisoning.
- Keep mayonnaise in a separate container. Mix it with other ingredients just before serving.
- Keep foods covered. Flies and other insects carry disease.
- Do not fill the cooler too full. This prevents the foods from staying as cool as they should. Leave space for ice between the foods.
- Keep hot and cold foods in separate thermal containers until ready to serve. Immediately after serving, return leftovers to the thermal containers. Leaving foods at room temperature for more than an hour increases the chance of food poisoning.

Hot foods such as casseroles can be kept in their original containers. Wrap them in layers of newspaper, and pack them in insulated bags. Cold foods should have plenty of ice surrounding them at all times.

Check in advance to see if the picnic grounds have tables, cooking facilities, or food stands. You may need to take a canteen of water if you are not sure that the area has safe drinking water. Be careful not to drink from streams or lakes. If there are tables, bring a paper or plastic tablecloth to ensure a clean eating area. Otherwise, use a clean blanket or cloth placed on the ground. Disposable paper or plastic plates, cups, napkins, and utensils make cleanup easy. Keep all food covered while you eat, to avoid attracting insects.

Leave the picnic area clean. Dispose of all trash properly. If there are no barrels, carry the trash until you can dispose of it properly.

BARBECUES

A barbecue is a picnic at which the food is cooked over an open fire or on a grill. The word *barbecue,* which comes from the French, means "whiskers to tail," which is how game animals are placed on a spit for roasting.

Food for Hiking

A hiking or backpacking trip means special food planning. You need foods that are light in weight. You also want foods that do not have to be kept cool. Finally, you want foods that do not need much cooking or equipment. Here are some suggestions.

Stores that sell camping supplies often carry foods especially prepared for the outdoors. Many are *dehydrated* or *freeze-dried*. This means that the water has been taken out. Simply add water and heat.

Dried soups, instant potatoes, and powdered juice mixes are good for hiking. All you have to do is repackage them in small amounts. Plastic bags work well for this.

Also, think about foods you can eat just as they are. Dried fruit, nuts, breads, and cheeses are good ideas.

▶ Words to Know

barbecue: A picnic at which food is cooked over an open grill.

insulated bag: A food-storage bag lined with material that keeps the contents either hot or cold.

picnic: An event in which you carry prepared food to a spot and eat it there.

transport: Carry an item from one place to another.

Barbecuing has come a long way since the days of the cave dwellers. Besides charcoal grills, we now also have gas and electric barbecues. However, charcoal grills are less expensive and more portable. The type of grill really does not matter. A large, fancy, covered grill cooks just as well as a simple, small model.

Besides the grill, you need fuel and starter, long matches, *insulated* (heat-proof) gloves, and cooking utensils with long handles. Charcoal briquettes give the most uniform and long-lasting fire. Stack the briquettes in a pyramid in the center of the base of the grill. A charcoal starter will speed up the fire. Never use gasoline or kerosene to start a fire. Never douse lit charcoal with starter fluid. In about thirty minutes, the briquettes will become covered with a gray ash. This means that the fire has reached the perfect temperature for cooking.

The cooking times for food, especially meats, vary according to the cut, thickness, shape, temperature when placed on the grill, weather conditions, and degree of cooking desired. Foods that take longer to cook should be placed about 15 centimeters (6 inches) away from the coals to avoid charring the outside of the food before the inside is cooked. All foods should be turned every five to eight minutes to prevent burning and loss of juices. Long-handled tongs or spatulas are best for turning. Basting sauces, marinades, or barbecue sauces add extra flavor to the food.

Charcoal grills should never be used inside a house or camper. The fumes given off by the burning charcoal are extremely dangerous and need a well-ventilated area to escape. Never leave the grill unattended. A container of water should be kept near the grill at all times in case the fire should flare up. When you have finished cooking, put out the fire by sprinkling it with water. Do not leave the site until the charcoal has become completely cool.

a quick review

1. How does a picnic differ from a barbecue?
2. Name five foods that are suitable for taking on a picnic.
3. What safety rule should be remembered when carrying food from your house to the picnic grounds?
4. What safety precautions should be taken when barbecuing?

Shopping for food is an interesting and challenging task once you know how to do it. Many people enjoy selecting the foods they will later eat.

KINDS OF STORES

There are many different kinds of stores in which to shop for food. They vary in the kinds of foods offered, services provided, and prices.

Supermarkets. The most popular food stores are *supermarkets.* They offer the widest variety of foods. In some parts of the country, supermarkets are open twenty-four hours a day. They sell many kinds and brands of canned and prepackaged foods. They also have fresh produce, meat, and dairy and bakery products. The cost of food in a supermarket varies from one store to another. Some are known for very high quality food at equally high prices. Other supermarkets sell food at very low prices. Their service may not be quite as good as in a more expensive market.

A discount supermarket is a newer kind of food store. At such a store, you can buy fewer kinds and brands of food. The emphasis is on keeping the prices down. There are usually few services. Customers are sometimes expected to bring their own boxes or bags for the food. Prices may

CHAPTER 59
Shopping for Food

Farmers' markets are found in cities as well as rural areas. Farmers bring their fresh produce to these markets to sell directly to the consumer.

be marked on signs rather than on each food item. Some discount supermarkets specialize in selling food in large quantities. Other supermarkets sometimes give discounts for quantity, too.

Specialty Food Stores. Stores that sell only one kind of food or special foods are known as *specialty food stores.* Those that sell only one kind of food include coffee and tea shops, spice shops, and ethnic food stores such as Italian or Chinese shops. Gourmet food stores sell many kinds of unusual or prepared foods. Delicatessens, or delis, sell cold cuts and prepared foods such as cole slaw and potato salad. The prices at such stores are often high. Prepared foods usually cost more, and some of these stores sell only expensive brands.

Farmers' Markets and Produce Stands.

Farmers' markets and produce stands are good places to buy fruits and vegetables. They are fairly inexpensive, and you can buy large or small amounts. A farmers' market is like a food fair. The food growers bring their products and sell them to customers who walk from stand to stand. Produce stands can be found on both city streets and country roads. The service is often warm and personal, and prices are kept down unless the produce is unusual or of extremely high quality.

Co-ops.

Co-ops are nonprofit organizations that sell food to their members. Usually the food must be bought in large quantities. Co-ops work well for families or groups who are willing to divide up what they buy. Customers often serve themselves and drive to a central place where the food is delivered on a set schedule.

Neighborhood Stores.

Neighborhood stores are smaller than supermarkets. They carry fewer kinds of foods and fewer brands. Often the food

costs more, particularly if the store is open around the clock.

THE ART OF SHOPPING

Most people like a store that is open when they want to shop and located near their home. There are, however, other things to consider when choosing a food store:

• Is the cold food refrigerated well? Is the meat fresh? Are the canned and dry foods sections well organized?
• Are prices reasonable and clearly marked?
• Are the employees friendly and helpful?
• Is the store clean? Does the food smell fresh and unspoiled?
• Are the fruits and vegetables fresh?

Stores usually stock up on supplies during the day on Friday because many people shop on weekends. The busiest hours are usually later afternoon and early evening. Early to middle afternoon on a Friday is a good time to shop since the stores are well stocked at that time. On other days the stock may be low, and the produce may not be fresh.

Good shoppers are organized shoppers. Begin by making a list of everything you need. In most places, local newspapers advertise food sales in the newspapers. Using these advertise-

SHOPPING LIST

2 gal. skim milk
1 lb margarine
(house brand)

3 packages frozen
green beans (house brand)
4 packages frozen
spinach (use coupon)
1 head romaine lettuce
1 bag carrots
2 cucumbers
3 lb bag onions
5 lb potatoes
(use coupon)

chuck roast (special)
3 lb ground beef
2 roasting chickens
(special)

salt
2 lb box rice

The Shopping List

A shopping list offers many clues to how economy-minded a shopper is. How many money-saving clues can you spot in the list above?

First, notice that the list is arranged by food groups—dairy products, frozen foods, fresh foods, meats, and staples are each listed together. That saves time when you are shopping in the store.

Buying store brands cuts costs. Using coupons and watching for specials and other sales also cut costs.

(continued on page 412)

Shopping List

(continued from page 411)

The cuts of meat are all economical. Combined with reduced prices on two of them, they may be the best money-savers on the list.

The choice of romaine lettuce shows that this is probably a winter or early spring shopping list. Romaine is least expensive during these months. In other months, various greens are a better buy. The other fresh vegetables on the list are less expensive this time of year and throughout the summer months.

Finally, buying large packages of onions and rice is a good way to save money, provided you will use them.

▶ Words to Know

co-op: A nonprofit organization that sells food to members at prices lower than in stores.

farmers' market: A central area where food growers may sell produce directly to customers.

neighborhood store: A small food store with fewer kinds of food and brands than a full-service supermarket carries.

produce stand: A stand that sells fruits and vegetables only.

specialty food store: A special store where only one kind of food or

(continued)

Using coupons wisely can save you money.

ments to plan a shopping list can save a lot of money. Here are some other money-saving tips:

• Before you shop, check your refrigerator for any foods on hand that will soon spoil. Use them in place of foods on your shopping list. Also check your shelves for any items on your list. If you find any, take them off the list.

• Use coupons whenever possible. Present the coupon when the food is paid for.

• Shop on "double-off" coupon days whenever possible. Coupons are worth twice as much on those days.

• Buy vegetables and fruits in season, when they are cheaper.

• Buy store brands of canned and prepackaged foods when possible.

• Buy fresh foods you can prepare rather than prepackaged, processed foods. You usually pay extra for the packaging of food items.

• Buy whole chickens and unboned meat. They are cheaper than cut-up chickens and boned meat.

• Buy large sizes when you can use

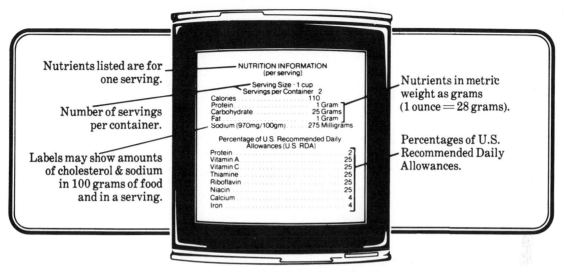

Nutrients listed are for one serving.

Number of servings per container.

Labels may show amounts of cholesterol & sodium in 100 grams of food and in a serving.

NUTRITION INFORMATION
(per serving)

Serving Size - 1 cup
Servings per Container 2

Calories	110
Protein	1 Gram
Carbohydrate	25 Grams
Fat	1 Gram
Sodium (970mg/100gm)	275 Milligrams

Percentage of U.S. Recommended Daily
Allowances (U.S. RDA)

Protein	2
Vitamin A	25
Vitamin C	25
Thiamine	25
Riboflavin	25
Niacin	25
Calcium	4
Iron	4

Nutrients in metric weight as grams (1 ounce = 28 grams).

Percentages of U.S. Recommended Daily Allowances.

Nutrition labeling on packages may differ. Some labels give more information than others. But the format is always the same: per-serving information on top and percentages of U.S. Recommended Daily Allowances below.

them. Always check the price against the *unit price,* though, to be sure the large size is the cheapest size. The unit price tells you the cost of an item per ounce, pound, or some other unit of measure.

• Learn how to read labels. They contain valuable information on nutrition and money-saving consumer information.

Good shopping is a skill that anyone can learn. It is an important part of being an efficient cook.

certain, usually expensive, brands of food are sold.

supermarket: A large, full-service food store.

unit pricing: A method of noting food price by ounce or pound so that shoppers can compare the prices of different-sized packages of an item.

a quick review

1. What are some differences between a regular supermarket and a discount supermarket?
2. Describe some of the reasons that you might choose to shop in a specialty food store.
3. How are neighborhood stores different from supermarkets? What are the advantages of each kind of store? What are the disadvantages?
4. What should you keep in mind when choosing a food store?
5. How can a shopping list help a food shopper?

CHAPTER 60
Eating Out

People in the United States eat more meals outside their homes than anyone else in the world. How often you eat out and where you eat depend on several things. Some of these are your family's likes and dislikes, the amount of money you have for eating out, and the activities of the family members.

There are many reasons that people choose to eat out. Sometimes they eat out to celebrate a special event. It may be a birthday or a new job. Sometimes they eat out just because it provides a nice break in their daily routine. Whoever does the cooking in the family gets a break from that task. Usually, however, eating out is more expensive than preparing a meal at home.

THE ORIGIN OF RESTAURANTS

Restaurants are places where you can buy and eat food. Restaurants as we know them today first developed in France during the late 1700s. In the 200 years since then, restaurants have become a major business in many countries. In the United States today, many restaurants rely on machines to do most of the work. Fast-food chains are an example. You also find restaurants that rely on the skills of a chef. Elegant restaurants, where every dish is especially prepared, are examples.

Fast-food chains offer a limited menu and usually reasonable prices along with fast service.

KINDS OF RESTAURANTS

There are many different kinds of restaurants. They vary in the type of food served, the service, and the price.

Fast-Food Chains. Fast-food restaurants serve a few types of food quickly. Fast-food chains are made up of many identical fast-food restaurants in different locations. They became popular during the early 1960s. They are very convenient for busy working people who have little time to prepare meals. In some fast-food chains, only one or two kinds of food are served. For example, one fast-food chain may feature fried chicken. Another chain may feature hamburgers and french fries, or tacos. Fast-food chains do not have kitchens. Instead, they have food preparation areas. The food is brought in partially prepared. Then it is fried or cooked in some other way. Food is generally cooked in large batches. Then it is kept warm until someone orders it.

In a fast-food restaurant, people serve themselves. They usually walk up to a central serving area and give their order. The food quickly arrives on a tray, and the customer carries the food to a nearby table. After eating, the customer is often expected to throw out the paper cartons the food was served in and clean up the table.

Fast-food restaurants offer food at inexpensive prices. A family of four can often eat for about one-half of what they would pay in another kind of restaurant. Certainly, fast food is far cheaper than food served in a fancy, full-service restaurant. However, much of the food from fast-food restaurants is very high in calories, fat, and sodium.

Family Restaurants. Family restaurants offer a larger variety of food than fast-food chains. They also serve the food to the customer at a table. They make up the single largest group of restaurants.

One type of family restaurant is the *diner,* which is small in size and usually has a counter and some tables. Diners are patterned after the Pullman dining cars that were first attached to trains in the late 1860s. However, the original Pullman diners served very elegant food. Diners today usually serve a larger variety of basic or plain foods.

Steak houses are another popular kind of family restaurant. They developed in the late 1880s after Chicago began supplying beef to cities throughout the United States. Steak houses specialize in serving a variety

of steaks, usually with a baked potato and a salad. The price can range from inexpensive to quite expensive. This depends on the quality of the steaks and the extent of the service.

Cafeterias first began in the late 1800s in New York City. The very first customers helped themselves to their food and ate it standing up. Today, cafeterias are everywhere. They provide tables and pleasant, comfortable surroundings. They still display the food and customers make their selections as they pass by. As the customers choose their food, they place it on a tray and pay the cashier at the end of the line.

A family restaurant may specialize in one kind of food, as steak houses do, or it may serve a variety of foods. Usually some foods, such as pies and breads, are prepared outside the restaurant. Much of the food preparation and actual cooking is done in the restaurant's kitchen.

Family restaurants range from very cheap to fairly expensive.

Luxury Restaurants. Luxury restaurants serve food that is prepared to individual order in the restaurant's kitchen. Few prepared or frozen foods are used. Luxury restaurants often have a large menu. Some luxury restaurants prepare only a few dishes. Then they change their menu every day. Others are known for preparing just a few dishes very well.

Children accustomed to fast-food restaurants often need to learn to wait for service in a family restaurant. Although serving takes time, it gives the family a chance to talk. Children also enjoy choosing food from a menu.

The service in a luxury restaurant, like the food, is very special. Because of all the work involved and the special foods that are offered, these restaurants are usually expensive.

Ethnic Restaurants. Americans are fortunate that so many different kinds of people settled here. This means that the foods of many different countries are available in restaurants throughout the country. Restaurants that specialize in serving the food of a particular country are called *ethnic res-* *taurants.* Chinese restaurants are a popular type of ethnic restaurant. Italian restaurants are another. Ethnic restaurants may serve elaborate and expensive meals, or they may specialize in only a few foods at relatively inexpensive prices. The type of service also varies.

GOOD MANNERS AND TIPPING

Good manners belong everywhere. They are just as important at an at-home family dinner as they are in an

Healthy Eating in Fast-Food Restaurants

· Select a fast-food restaurant that has a salad bar.

· Limit the amount of fried foods you order.

· Ask for cheese, lettuce, and tomato on your sandwich.

· Order milk or juice instead of a soft drink.

· Avoid milkshakes if you are watching your weight.

· Bring fresh fruit from home so you won't eat sweets on the menu.

· Stop at a frozen yogurt stand for a nutritious dessert.

417

► **Words to Know**

cafeteria: A family restaurant in which food is chosen by customers who then put it on a tray, pay for it, and carry it to a table to eat.

ethnic restaurants: Restaurants that serve the food of a particular country.

family restaurant: A restaurant that features sit-down service at moderate prices, with a menu slightly larger than that of a fast-food chain.

fast-food restaurant: A restaurant that features fast, inexpensive food and service, usually with a limited number of foods.

luxury restaurant: A restaurant that features individually prepared meals and excellent service, often at high prices. Menus vary from small to quite large.

restaurant: A place where people go to buy and eat meals.

service: The way the table is set and how the food is served.

steak house: A restaurant that features steaks, usually served with a baked potato and salad.

tip: To leave extra money for the waiter or waitress. This is in addition to the cost of the meal.

Some restaurants specialize in a particular type of food. Here, various types of seafood are featured.

elegant restaurant. Mostly, good manners are nothing more than showing consideration for others. This means not talking with your mouth full of food and not waving flatware around. It also means saying "please" and "thank you." Refer to Chapter 57 for more information about good table manners.

Americans *tip,* or leave extra money, for the people who wait on them in restaurants that have sit-down service. The usual tip is 15 to 20 percent of the total bill. Of course, the better the service, the larger the tip. A tip is a way to thank the people who have made a restaurant meal especially pleasant for you.

a quick review

1. What are some of the reasons that people choose to eat out?
2. Describe each of the three general groups of restaurants. Tell how the foods are prepared and what kinds of foods are served.
3. What is an ethnic restaurant? Why does the United States have so many ethnic restaurants?
4. What is the purpose of tipping? How large a tip should you leave in most restaurants?

Preparing food can be a lot of fun. And it can have good-looking, good-tasting results. What does your kitchen look like during and after the preparation of a snack or a meal? If it looks neat, you were probably well organized. How long did it take you to prepare the snack or meal? If it didn't take more time than you had, you were probably organized.

Being organized in the kitchen means knowing what you are doing. It means finding the food and equipment you need before you start, and cleaning up as you go along. Have you ever started to cook and halfway through the recipe discovered that you were missing one of the ingredients? What did you do?

Some people would borrow from a neighbor. Others would just throw the dish out. If you had known that you were missing something, you might have chosen another recipe. Or someone in your family might have been able to pick the item up at the store.

WORKING IN THE FOODS LAB

Preparing food at school requires even more organization than cooking at home. This is mainly because your class period is only so long. And when class is over, the lab must be cleaned up and left ready for the next group. Some schools have double-

CHAPTER 61
Working in the Kitchen

Cooperation in the Foods Lab

Working in the foods lab requires a lot of cooperation. You, your teacher, your lab partners, and your other classmates must all be able to work together.

Cooperation also means following directions. Before entering the lab kitchen, listen closely to your teacher's directions. Then:

• Take off any outside clothes. Outside clothes may be soiled. Bulky sweaters can get in your way. Long, loose sleeves can knock things over, drag through food, or even catch fire from the stove.
• Put on an apron.
• Tie back your hair if it is long. This will keep it out of the food.

Here are some tips for helping the lab go smoothly:

• Use the exact amount of food for your recipe. Leave the leftovers for the next class.
• If you don't understand a step, ask your teacher.
• Offer help when a lab partner needs it.
• Help with the cleanup whenever you can and at the end of the lab.
• Stay in your own lab kitchen.
• Talk quietly while working in the lab.

period labs that last up to an hour and a half. Most schools have lab periods that are much shorter. Some are as short as 30 minutes. Even in a short lab, however, you can finish many projects. You can do so if you have a good work plan that divides the jobs among all the students in your lab group.

Planning for the Lab. Good planning is necessary for an effective food lab. The first step is to select a recipe. In many schools the recipe is chosen by the teacher. The recipe should be one that can be finished in a short time or started one day and finished the next. Recipes that require chilling are easy to continue the next day. Your teacher can help you to find other recipes than can be completed over a two-day period.

After the recipe is selected, list the ingredients needed and their amounts. Give this list to your teacher. This list is your market order. If the entire class is making the same dish, this step is not necessary. But if many different items are being prepared, your teacher will want to combine the different market orders before ordering whatever supplies are not on hand.

Your work in the foods lab will be most effective if everyone in your group knows exactly what her or his responsibilities are. First, make a list of all the equipment you will need for this particular lab. If it is a two-day

lab, list the equipment needed for each of the two days.

Next, list all the jobs or tasks that need to be done. Begin with

• get out equipment
• pick up food supplies
• set up dish water

To these, add whatever special tasks your recipe calls for.

Now decide who is going to do what. Try to divide the tasks evenly. Some tasks can be done at the same time as others.

When the tasks have been divided, start setting up a time schedule for your recipe. The class period can be divided many ways. You can save time by dovetailing. *Dovetailing* means doing different jobs at the same time. For example, while one student picks up the food ingredients, another can be setting out the utensils. Or, while one student blends the dry ingredients, another can grease the pans, and another can measure and blend the liquid ingredients. For your plan to work, you need to estimate how long each task will take. This will become easier with experience.

During the Lab. When you are working in the foods lab, it is important to follow your plan. That may mean that you will work little on some days and more on others. To prepare your dish or meal in the time you have, you must perform your

Read the recipe completely before you begin to cook. Then follow the directions step by step through the preparation.

Cleanup is an important part of working in the kitchen. Good cleaning keeps the kitchen sanitary. Cleaning up as you work makes the final job that much easier.

Here are some cleanup tips:

• Remove any food from utensils before washing them or placing them in the dishwasher.

• Soak greasy pots and pans in hot water before washing.

• Soak starchy pans in cold water before washing.

• Fill the dishpan or one side of the sink with hot, soapy water. The hot water along with the dish detergent will kill any bacteria on the utensils. It will also remove any greasy or sticky foods.

• Use hot water for rinsing.

• Use clean dishcloths, sponges, and towels. Soiled dishcloths and towels can spread harmful bacteria.

• Whenever a piece of equipment is used or dropped on the floor, it should be washed in hot, soapy water.

• After the dishes are washed, rinse out the dishpan, the sink, and the dishcloth. Hang the dishcloth and towel up to dry or place them in the lab laundry.

tasks when needed. You must also understand these tasks before attempting them. You must also cooperate with your lab partners. Sometimes you will need to help them. You can help your group keep on schedule by cleaning up whatever is no longer needed. The final cleanup will then be much easier.

After the Lab. In each lab class you will learn more about working with food. As time goes on, you will be able to follow more complicated recipes in the same amount of time. The reason is that you will all be better able to plan and work together. One way to find out how you are progressing is to evaluate each lab. To do this,

421

Spiced Apple Muffins
(makes 6)

160 mL (⅔ c) flour
45 mL (3 Tbsp) sugar
7.5 mL (1½ tsp) baking
 powder
0.6 mL (⅛ tsp) salt
0.6 mL (⅛ tsp) cinnamon
80 mL (⅓ c) milk
15 mL (1 Tbsp) beaten egg
7.5 mL (1½ tsp) butter or
 margarine, melted
80 mL (⅓ c) raw apples,
 finely chopped

1. Grease 6 muffin pans.
2. Mix together flour,
 sugar, baking powder,
 salt, and cinnamon.
3. In a separate bowl,
 combine the milk, egg,
 and melted butter or
 margarine.
4. Add the dry ingredients
 to the liquid ingredients
 and mix (batter will be
 lumpy).
5. Fold in apples.
6. Fill muffin pans two-
 thirds full.

Topping:

10 mL (2 tsp) sugar
0.6 mL (⅛ tsp) cinnamon

1. Preheat oven to 218°C
 (425°F).
2. Combine sugar and
 cinnamon.
3. Sprinkle mixture over
 top of unbaked muffins.
4. Bake 20 minutes or until
 toothpick inserted in
 middle comes out clean.
5. Remove from pan and
 cool on a cooling rack.

LAB PLAN FOR SPICED APPLE MUFFINS
(Class meets from 10:03 to 10:43.)

Student	Task	Time
No. 1	Pick up ingredients	10:05
	Measure dry ingredients	10:10
	Combine dry ingredients	10:12
	Add dry ingredients to liquid ingredients and mix	10:14
	Fold in apples	10:15
	Bake	10:20–10:40
	Put away equipment	
No. 2	Get out equipment	
	Grease pans	10:05
	Measure liquids	10:08
	Combine liquids	10:10
	Fill muffin pans	10:12
	Place on cooling rack	10:17
	Dry equipment	10:40
No. 3	Set up dishwashing	
	Pare, chop, and measure apples	10:05
	Prepare topping	10:07
	Place topping on batter	10:12
	Wash equipment	10:25

In this group, each person has specific jobs to do. These job assignments were planned ahead of time.

Timesaving Tips

• Read your recipe all the way through before beginning.

• Check to be sure you have all the necessary ingredients before beginning.

• Be sure you have all necessary equipment before beginning.

• Assemble all the ingredients before starting work. That way, you should have to make only one trip to the refrigerator and can avoid wasting time.

• Use as few utensils and appliances as possible.

• Pare and peel fruits and vegetables over a paper towel. The towel can be thrown away later, making cleanup easier.

• Line the broiler pan with foil to make cleanup easier.

• Clean up as you work.

• Dovetail when possible. For example, while the water heats, peel the vegetables.

• What went well in this lab?
• What did not go well?
• How could we improve?

To really make progress, you and your lab partners must follow your suggestions for improvement.

WORKING IN YOUR KITCHEN AT HOME

Often when preparing food at home, you are working alone. This means organizing your work slightly differently. You should still become familiar with the recipe and make certain you have all the ingredients and equipment. Time, though, is usually not as big a problem at home as it is in school. At home you can usually spend more than 40 minutes in the kitchen. Sometimes the cleanup at home is a bigger problem. At school you generally have lab partners to help you. At home, the job is yours. Sometimes students forget this. If you want your parents to encourage your "kitchen experiments," you have to be responsible for the cleanup. Of course, it is always easier if you clean up as you go along.

a quick review

1. What are three steps that help you to be organized in the kitchen?
2. How is working in the school foods lab different from working in your home kitchen?
3. What should you consider when selecting a recipe to use in school?
4. How can your lab group make the best use of time in the foods lab?

Market Order for Spiced Apple Muffins

flour: 160 mL (⅔ c)
sugar: 55 mL (3 Tbsp + 2 tsp)
baking powder: 7.5 mL (1½ tsp)
cinnamon: 0.6 mL (⅛ tsp)
salt: 0.6 mL (⅛ tsp)
apples: 80 mL (⅓ c), chopped
milk: 80 mL (⅓ c)
egg: 15 mL (1 Tbsp)
butter or margarine: 7.5 mL (1½ tsp)

Your teacher may tell you to use margarine or to share an egg with another kitchen group.

▶ **Words to Know**

dovetail: To do more than one task at a time.
effective: Productive or competent.
evaluate: To determine the value of something.
foods lab: A classroom equipped with kitchens for student use.
ingredient: A food used in a recipe.
pare: To cut off the outer layer, such as in paring an apple.
peel: To take off the outer layer, such as in peeling an orange or a banana.
responsibilities: Tasks for which you are accountable.
simultaneously: At the same time.
task: A job, duty, or assignment.

CHAPTER 62
Kitchen Equipment

Kitchen equipment comes in many different styles and brands. This equipment is often interesting and fun to work with. Because there is so much to choose from, it is important to know which items are *essential* (necessary) and which ones would just be nice to have. Many tasks or jobs can be done by more than one piece of equipment. Sometimes an inexpensive item can do the job just as well as an expensive one. For example, you can chop onions with a knife or with a food processor. Yet many people buy food processors, and for many different reasons. You need to know your cooking needs before buying any kitchen equipment.

Working in a foods lab will give you the chance to use different pieces of equipment. Then you can decide for yourself which ones you think are really necessary and which ones are luxuries. The time and money you have to spend on cooking are also factors. Your needs may change at different times in your life.

This chapter will focus on small appliances and kitchen utensils.

KITCHEN APPLIANCES

Most small kitchen appliances are fun to use as well as functional. When you buy one, be sure to care for it properly. Read the instruction book carefully and follow it exactly. The following are some common small kitchen appliances. Remember, you do not have to have all of them to be an efficient, quality cook.

Electric Mixer. There are two types of electric mixers: portable hand mixers and stand mixers. You must hold the portable mixer in your hand when you use it. Portable mixers are ideal for basic mixing jobs that do not require a powerful motor. A stand mixer is a heavy-duty mixer that sits on the countertop. It usually comes with its own bowl. It can do everything a hand mixer can do and more, such as kneading bread dough and mixing heavy batters. It also leaves your hands free for other tasks.

Electric Frypan. These come in a variety of shapes (round, square, rectangular). All have an adjustable thermostat and temperature dial. Electric frypans can be used to fry, roast, pan-broil, bake, or simmer foods. The frypan will automatically maintain whatever temperature you set until you change it or turn it off. Electric frypans offer more uniform heat control than cooking on top of the range.

Before you use any electrical appliance, be sure you understand the correct and safe way to use it.

Portable Hand Mixer

Stand Mixer

Electric Frypan

Toaster Oven

Liquid Measuring Cup

Dry Measuring Cups

Measuring Spoons

Timer

Thermometers

Electric Coffee Makers. There are two types of electric coffee makers: percolators and drip. Both brew good coffee and will keep it hot for hours after brewing. A drip coffee maker can also be used to heat water for instant coffee, tea, or cocoa.

Toaster. Most electric toasters have two or four slots on the top for bread or special toaster products. Toasters will evenly brown both sides of bread at once, to the shade you choose. Some will automatically adjust to any type of bread, thick or thin, and toast each to the shade desired without any resetting of the controls.

Toaster Oven. This versatile, energy-saving appliance offers all the advantages of a toaster plus those of a small oven. Small items can be baked in the toaster oven. Some units can also broil foods. Since a toaster oven is smaller than a conventional oven, it uses less energy.

Blender. Blenders have high-speed motors and whirling blades. They are used to blend, mix, grate, chop, shred, puree, or liquify foods. Blenders can do some of the same jobs as mixers, but since they do not mix in air with the food as they work, they cannot completely take the place of a mixer. For example, a cake prepared in a blender would not rise as high as one prepared with a mixer.

Food Processor. A food processor has a very powerful motor and a round, plastic work bowl. It can do everything a blender can do and more, such as slicing, shredding, and grating. It, too, cannot completely take the place of a mixer. It works so fast that it does not mix in as much air while working. Thus it is not suitable for all recipes.

Microwave Oven. A microwave oven can cook food up to 75 percent faster than a conventional range. This saves both time and energy. A microwave oven can be a countertop unit or part of a large oven. Microwave ovens cook by agitating the molecules in food, thus producing heat. The heat does not come from outside the food, as in a conventional oven, but from within. Microwave cooking requires some special techniques and some special cookware. The main difference in cookware for a microwave oven is that you cannot use metal. But you can use many plastics.

Convection Oven. Convection ovens also save time and energy, but not as much as microwave ovens. Convection ovens too can be part of a larger oven or a separate portable countertop unit. In convection cooking, a high-speed fan circulates the hot air within the oven. This produces uniform heat throughout the oven and speeds up the cooking.

KITCHEN UTENSILS

Stores today offer a large selection of gadgets to make life in the kitchen easier. Not many kitchens have room enough for all of the utensils that are available. And few people want to spend the money to "have one of everything." Again, it is important to know what the different utensils can do and which kitchen tasks you do often. Most utensils are simple, well-designed tools that have been around for years. The following items belong in every well-equipped kitchen.

Measuring Utensils. Measuring cups and measuring spoons are important for following recipes accurately. Measuring cups are of two types. Some are dry measuring cups, used for measuring items such as flour, sugar, and shortening. Others are for measuring liquids. Dry measuring cups are generally sold in sets. They are made so that you can fill them to the brim, then level off the contents with a straight-edged utensil. Liquid measuring cups are made of glass or plastic so that you can see

An electric blender can puree vegetables for soup in a few seconds.

Mixing Bowls

Rubber Spatula

Hand Beater

Pastry Blender

Colander

427

Strainer

Pastry Brush

Tongs

Kitchen Shears

Funnel

through them. They may have more than one scale of measure printed on the side.

Timer. A timer lets you do other tasks while baking a casserole or simmering a stew. A timer should have clear markings from 1 to 60 minutes and a loud bell.

Thermometers. There are several types of thermometers for use in cooking. A meat thermometer will show how hot it is inside the meat or poultry you are roasting. With it you can determine when the roast is rare, medium, or well done. The temperature range of a meat thermometer is 54 to 90°C (130 to 195°F). A candy thermometer is a great help when making candy or jelly. Its temperature range is 15 to 221°C (60 to 430°F). A deep-fat frying thermometer will help you to maintain oil at a constant temperature. Its range is also 15 to 221°C (60 to 430°F). An oven thermometer will let you know if your oven is heating to the temperature you set. It measures temperatures from 93 to 260°C (200 to 500°F).

Mixing Equipment. A great variety of mixing equipment is available.

• *Mixing bowls.* Mixing bowls can be made of glass, metal, plastic, or ceramic materials. They come in a wide variety of sizes. They are used for holding the different ingredients during food preparation.

• *Mixing spoons.* These are long-handled spoons used for combining ingredients. They can be made of metal, plastic, or wood.

• *Rubber spatula.* A rubber spatula is used to scrape out bowls or bottles and for folding in ingredients such as egg whites. It has a plastic or wooden handle and a flexible plastic or rubber blade.

• *Hand beater.* A hand beater can be used for mixing thin batters such as puddings and cake mixes.

• *Pastry blender.* A pastry blender is used to cut in or blend shortening into flour when making piecrust or biscuits.

Preparation Equipment. Many items are used to prepare ingredients for cooking.

• *Colanders and strainers.* Both colanders and strainers are used for draining foods. Colanders can stand by themselves and have larger holes and either one or two handles. They are used for draining noodles, fruits, or vegetables. Strainers have small holes and one long handle. They are used to separate solids from liquids. For example, you use a strainer to separate the pulp from the liquid in orange juice.

• *Pastry brush.* A pastry brush is a small brush used to brush liquids or glazes onto pastries, breads, or pies.

• *Vegetable brush.* A vegetable brush is a larger brush used for cleaning vegetables.

• *Kitchen shears.* Kitchen shears are great for cutting meat, poultry, vegetables, pastry, and dried fruit. They may look much like regular shears, but they are heavier and do not rust when wet.

• *Tongs.* Tongs are perfect for turning meats, handling barbecued and fried foods, removing eggs or baked potatoes, or for handling ice cubes. Tongs have long metal arms with gripping sections on the ends.

• *Rolling pin.* A rolling pin is used for rolling out pastry, biscuit, and cookie dough. It can be made of plastic or wood.

• *Pastry cloth.* A pastry cloth is used for rolling out dough so that it will not stick to the counter. It is made of heavy fabric, such as canvas.

• *Food mill.* A food mill is used to puree foods. The food is placed in the bowl section, and when you turn the handle, the food is crushed and pushed through the holes in the bottom of the bowl.

• *Fruit juicer.* A fruit juicer is used for squeezing the juice from fresh citrus fruits.

• *Cutting boards.* Cutting boards come in all shapes and sizes. They may be made of wood or plastic. They protect your countertop from knife marks.

• *Parers.* These have floating blades

A microwave oven can bake four potatoes in 16 minutes. A conventional oven would take more than 1 hour.

Double Boiler

Loaf Pan

Pie Pan

Muffin Pan

Narrow Spatula

429

Your Family Kitchen: A Place to Save Energy

Here are some tips from the U.S. Department of Energy to help your family save energy in the kitchen.

• If you have a gas stove, be sure the pilot light burns properly with a blue flame. A low flame means the stove is not working properly.

• Boil water in a covered pan. It will boil faster and use less energy.

• When using the oven, make the most of the heat by cooking as many foods as you can at one time. In hot weather, bake in the cool hours of the day.

• Use smaller cooking appliances like toaster ovens, electric frypans, microwave ovens, pressure cookers, and slow cooking pots instead of a large oven whenever you can. They use less energy.

• Range-top cooking also uses less energy than the oven.

• Do not keep your refrigerator too cold. An energy-saving temperature is 3° to 4°C (38° to 40°F) for the fresh food compartment and −15°C (5°F) for the freezer section. For a separate freezer appliance, −20°C (0°F) is cold enough.

• Defrost the refrigerator often (unless it is a frostfree model).

that move along the edge of fruits or vegetables to trim off the skin.

• *Graters.* Graters have several different-sized cutting edges to produce coarse or finely shredded foods. They are used for grating fruits, vegetables, and cheeses or for slicing foods such as tomatoes.

• *Funnel.* A funnel is the only gadget in your kitchen that will allow you to pour liquids from a large container into a smaller one without spilling a drop. They can be made of metal or plastic and come in several sizes.

• *Can opener.* A hand-held or wall-mounted can opener is used to cut a can lid out completely and smoothly.

• *Knives.* Knives come in a variety of shapes and sizes to fit many different household needs. For example, a paring knife has a short blade and is used for paring and cutting fruits and vegetables. A bread knife has a long, narrow blade and is used for slicing bread.

• *Narrow spatula.* A narrow spatula has a flexible blade and is used for leveling off ingredients.

• *Pancake turner.* A pancake turner is used for turning foods such as pancakes or hamburgers or for removing cookies from a baking sheet.

Cookware. Pots and pans used for cooking on top of the range come in a variety of shapes and sizes designed for different tasks.

• *Saucepan.* A saucepan has a single long handle. It can be very small or large. It is probably the most versatile piece of cookware in the kitchen.

• *Frying pan.* A frying pan, sometimes called a skillet, is a shallow pan with a long handle. It is used for frying, sauteeing, and panbroiling.

• *Double boiler.* A double boiler has two sections, both of which look like saucepans. The bottom pan holds water. The second pan fits snugly over the bottom pan and holds the food. When the water in the bottom sec-

Compare the energy costs of different models of an appliance to determine which will cost the least to operate. Refrigerators, room air-conditioners, freezers, washers, and dishwashers all carry Energy Guide labels.

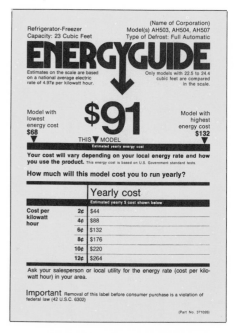

tion boils, the food in the top section is heated. A double boiler is used for heating delicate foods such as egg sauces or chocolate.

Baking Equipment. Bakeware can be made of metal, glass, or ceramic materials. Metal bakeware has finishes that vary from a nonstick coating for easy food removal to a dark surface that helps to brown the food. The following are the pieces used most often. The sizes are standard.

• *Cake pans.* Round or square cake pans are used for baking layer cakes. The round pans are 20 or 22 centimeters (8 or 9 inches) in diameter. The square pans are 20 or 22 centimeters (8 or 9 inches) square.

• *Loaf pans.* Loaf pans are used for meat loaves or breads. The most common size is 22 × 12 × 7 centimeters (9 × 5 × 3 inches).

• *Baking sheets.* Baking sheets, cookie sheets, or jelly roll pans are rectangular, shallow pans. They are used for baking jelly rolls, thin sheet cakes, and cookies.

• *Tube pans.* Tube pans are round and deep with a hollow tube in the center. They are used for baking angel food, chiffon, or bundt cakes. The most common size is 2.9-liter (12-cup), or 25 × 10 centimeters (10 × 4 inches).

• *Pie pans.* Pie pans are round and usually 20, 22, or 25 centimeters (8, 9, or 10 inches) in diameter. They have sloping sides.

• *Muffin pans.* Muffin pans have individual cups to hold muffins or cupcakes. They come in 6- or 12-cup pans with varying-sized cups.

• *Cake racks.* Cake racks are made of metal wire. The racks are used to hold cake pans or cookies while they are cooling. The racks allow air to circulate around the cake or cookies.

• *Casseroles.* Casseroles come in a wide variety of shapes and sizes. They are used for baking and serving foods from the same utensil.

• *Custard cups.* Custard cups are generally made of heatproof glass. They are used for baking custards and popovers.

Guidelines For Buying Equipment

Prices vary greatly for all kinds of kitchen equipment. Although the price is usually related to quality, the best is not always the most expensive.

In order to be truly satisfied with the appliance you choose, you must first decide if you really need it. The following guidelines will help.

• Do you really want the appliance?
• Do you need all the functions of the appliance?
• Will you use it frequently?
• Do you have space to store it?
• Is the appliance worth its cost to you?

▶ **Words to Know**
essential: Something that is necessary or basic.
molecule: A very small part of a substance.
task: Job or assignment.
thermostat: A device that regulates temperature.

a quick review

1. What is the difference between an electric frypan and a frying pan?
2. What is the difference between a toaster and a toaster oven?
3. What are the two types of measuring cups? How do they differ?
4. Name three types of thermometers used in the kitchen. How do they differ?

CHAPTER 63
Using Recipes

Have you ever tried to prepare a food or dish without using a recipe? Sometimes it works. Sometimes it does not. Or have you ever been given a recipe and found that it didn't contain enough directions?

RECIPES

To be useful, a recipe must have two parts. The first part lists the ingredients needed and the exact amount of each. For example, a recipe may call for 30 milliliters (2 tablespoons) of honey. Normally, too, the units of measure are *abbreviated,* or shortened, so that the example just given would look like this: 30 mL (2 Tbsp) honey. The second part of the recipe gives directions. It may direct you to "cream honey with butter." A good recipe will tell you what you need, how much of it you need, and what to do with it. It will also tell you how many people it will serve.

Formats. Several formats are used for recipes. The four most common ones are the standard form, the action form, the narrative form, and the descriptive form.

The format most commonly used in cookbooks is the *standard form.* It first lists each ingredient in the recipe. In front of each one is the exact amount needed. Next come the directions. These may be given in one paragraph or as numbered steps.

The *action form* first tells you what to do. Then it gives the amount and name of the ingredient. Here is an example:

Cook together in boiling salted water:
- 4 medium-size carrots, pared and quartered
- 3 medium-size potatoes, pared and quartered

The *narrative form* leaves out the list. It gives ingredients, amounts, and directions in one paragraph.

The *descriptive form* is a three-column arrangement. The first column lists the ingredients. The second states the amount. The third gives directions. Each column is spaced so that an ingredient, its amount, and directions for its use are in line.

Abbreviations. Abbreviations, shortened forms of words, are used for units of measure. They appear in the singular form, even if the item is plural. For example, 120 mL is the abbreviation for 120 milliliters. Abbreviations in the metric system include:

$$L = \text{liter}$$
$$g = \text{gram}$$
$$°C = \text{degrees Celsius}$$

EQUIVALENT MEASURES

Customary Measure	Equivalent Customary Measure	Approximate Metric Equivalent
1 gallon	4 quarts	3.8 liters
1 quart	4 cups	470 milliliters
1 pint	2 cups	240 milliliters
1 cup	½ pint, 16 tablespoons	250 milliliters
¾ cup	12 tablespoons	180 milliliters
⅔ cup	10 tablespoons plus 2 teaspoons	160 milliliters
½ cup	8 tablespoons	120 milliliters
⅓ cup	5 tablespoons plus 1 teaspoon	80 milliliters
¼ cup	4 tablespoons	60 milliliters
⅛ cup	2 tablespoons	30 milliliters
1 tablespoon	3 teaspoons	15 milliliters
1 teaspoon		5 milliliters
½ teaspoon		2.5 milliliters
¼ teaspoon		1.25 milliliters
⅛ teaspoon		0.5 milliliters
1 pound	16 ounces	450 grams
½ pound	8 ounces	225 grams
1 ounce		28 grams

Recipe Terms

bake: Cook by dry heat in the oven.

blend: Mix two or more ingredients until smooth.

boil: Cook in liquid at boiling temperature.

broil: Cook over or under direct heat.

chill: Refrigerate until completely cold.

chop: Cut into small pieces.

cool: Lower the temperature, usually to room temperature.

fry: Cook in hot fat.

grease: Rub butter, margarine, shortening, or other fat over a food or container.

knead: Work dough with the hands until it is springy, using a folding and pressing motion.

pare: Remove the skin of a fruit or vegetable by using a knife or parer.

preheat: Bring an oven to the recommended temperature before cooking food.

roast: Cook meat or poultry in the oven by dry heat.

sift: Shake flour in a sieve or special sifter; also, to shake dry ingredients together in the same way.

simmer: Cook in liquid just below the boiling point.

toss: Mix gently.

whip: Beat with a handbeater or an electric mixer until fluffy or stiff.

433

To follow a recipe accurately, you must use standardized measuring cups and measuring spoons.

Stir-frying

An interesting way to cook vegetables and meat is to stir-fry them. Vegetables are fried quickly in a little bit of oil with high heat. They must be stirred constantly so that they will not burn or stick to the pan. Then a lid is put on the pan, and the vegetables are steamed with a little water for a short period of time.

Stir-frying has long been popular in the Far East as a way of cooking vegetables. Many people use a special cone-shaped, round-bottomed pan called a *wok* for stir-frying, but a heavy skillet with a snug lid works just as well.

Abbreviations for the measurements used in the English customary system include:

$$
\begin{array}{rcl}
c & = & cup \\
pt & = & pint \\
qt & = & quart \\
gal & = & gallon \\
tsp & = & teaspoon \\
Tbsp\ or\ T & = & tablespoon \\
oz & = & ounce \\
lb & = & pound \\
°F & = & degrees\ Fahrenheit
\end{array}
$$

Abbreviations for units of time are:

$$
\begin{array}{rcl}
hr. & = & hour \\
min. & = & minute \\
sec. & = & second
\end{array}
$$

Measuring Accurately and Following Directions. If you want a recipe to turn out successfully, you must do two things. First, you must measure ingredients accurately. Second, you must follow directions exactly.

The first step in measuring accurately is to know your equipment. Measuring equipment consists of dry and liquid measuring cups along with measuring spoons.

Dry measuring cups are easy to use with dry ingredients such as flour or sugar. They come in sets of different sizes. The most common sets include cups that measure ¼ cup, ⅓ cup, ½ cup, and 1 cup. To measure a dry ingredient, fill up the cup that is the size you need. Then, using the straight edge of a knife or spatula, level off the ingredient along the top of the cup. The exact amount that you want is now in the cup.

Liquid measuring cups have marks on the side to show specific amounts. Some have metric measures on one side and English customary measures on the other side. Liquid measuring cups also have space at the top to allow for a full measure without spilling. These cups are made of clear plastic or glass. Because you can see through them, you can see the liquid as it fills up the cup. Then you can stop pouring when you have enough. To be sure you are measuring liquids accurately, put the measuring cup on a flat surface. That way you will know

FORMS OF A RECIPE

Peach Melba (Standard Form)

1 450-g (1-lb) can of cling peach slices
1 280-g (10-oz) pkg. of frozen raspberries
60 mL (¼ c) sugar
15 mL (1 Tbsp) cornstarch
15 mL (1 Tbsp) lemon juice

Drain peaches, reserve 60 mL (¼ c) juice. Drain thawed raspberries, reserve all juice. Combine sugar, cornstarch, and lemon juice in a saucepan with raspberry and peach juice. Stir and heat until thick. Add peaches and raspberries. Serve warm over vanilla ice cream.

Peach Melba (Action Form)

Thaw:
1 280-g (10-oz) pkg. of frozen raspberries

Drain:
1 450-g (1-lb) can of cling peach slices, reserving 60 mL (¼ c) juice

Raspberries, reserving all juice

Combine, heat, and stir until thick:
60 mL (¼ c) sugar
15 mL (1 Tbsp) cornstarch
15 mL (1 Tbsp) lemon juice

Add:
Raspberries and peaches

Serve warm over vanilla ice cream.

Peach Melba (Narrative Form)

Drain a 280-g (10-oz) package of frozen raspberries. Reserve all of the juice. Drain a 450-g (1-lb) can of cling peach slices. Reserve 60 mL (¼ c) juice. Combine in a saucepan: raspberry and peach juice, 60 mL (¼ c) sugar, 15 mL (1 Tbsp) cornstarch, 15 mL (1 Tbsp) lemon juice. Heat in a saucepan and stir until thick. Add peaches and raspberries. Serve warm over ice cream.

Peach Melba (Descriptive Form)

Frozen raspberries	280-g (10-oz) pkg.	Drain and reserve juice
Canned peach slices	450-g (1 ib)	Drain and reserve 60 mL (¼ c) juice.
Sugar	60 mL (¼ c)	Combine sugar and cornstarch in
Cornstarch	15 mL (1 Tbsp)	saucepan.
Lemon juice	15 mL (1 Tbsp)	Add lemon juice and other juices to saucepan.
		Heat, stirring until thick. Add peaches and raspberries. Serve warm over ice cream.

Which Recipe Should I Use?

Before you select a recipe, ask yourself these questions:

• Do I understand the directions? Can I do the steps the recipe calls for?

• Do I have the ingredients on hand? Or will I need to go shopping?

• What equipment will I need? Do I have it? If not, can I borrow it?

• Is this recipe expensive? Does it fit into the budget?

• How long will it take to prepare this recipe? Do I have that amount of time? Do I have some extra time in case it is needed?

• How many servings will the recipe make? Do I need to increase or decrease the amount?

▶ **Words to Know**

abbreviation: A short form of a word.

action form: A recipe format in which the ingredients needed are listed under the relevant step in the directions.

descriptive form: A recipe format in which the ingredients, amounts, and directions are written in three columns.

dry measuring cups: Cups used to measure dry ingredients such as flour.

English system: A customary measuring
(continued)

To measure the correct amount of liquid, set the measuring cup on a flat surface. Make sure it is at eye level as you read the amount.

that the cup is level. Then bend down and get eye level with the cup so that you see the measuring marks clearly. Liquid measuring cups have pouring lips to make pouring easy.

Do not confuse measuring spoons with flatware. *Measuring spoons* are used to measure tablespoons, teaspoons, and parts of teaspoons when following a recipe. Flatware, by contrast, varies in size. It is not an accurate measure. Measuring spoons, like dry measuring cups, come in sets of different sizes. The most common

sets include spoons that measure 1 tablespoon, 1 teaspoon, $\frac{1}{2}$ teaspoon, and $\frac{1}{4}$ teaspoon. Notice that the fractions are not the same as for dry measuring cups. To use a measuring spoon, simply dip it into the ingredient, then level it off with a straight edge.

The second step in measuring accurately is to know how to measure different ingredients. Different ones require different ways of measuring.

Liquids such as milk, juice, water, vinegar, oil, and melted fats are measured easily and accurately in liquid measuring cups. If liquid measuring cups are not available, you can use dry measuring cups, but take care to fill the cup all the way without spilling it. If you use a measuring spoon, do not measure the liquid over your bowl of ingredients. One spill can change the outcome of your recipe.

Shortening, butter, and margarine are solid fats. They are usually measured with dry measuring cups. As you fill the cup with the fat, press firmly until it is full. Then level the cup off with a straight edge.

Eggs come in different sizes. It is best to use medium or large eggs in recipes, unless another size is called for.

Flour is best measured in dry measuring cups. If the recipe calls for sifted flour, sift it before measuring. Then spoon the flour into the cup until the measure overflows. Level the cup with a straight edge. Do not pack the flour or shake or tap the cup. If the recipe does not specify sifted flour, simply spoon the unsifted flour into the measuring cup and level it.

Whole grain flour is not sifted, but you should stir it with a spoon or fork before measuring it.

Sugar is measured just like unsifted flour. Brown sugar, however, is different. It must be firmly packed into the dry measuring cup. When it is turned out of the cup, it will hold the shape of the cup.

THE METRIC SYSTEM

The United States is in the process of changing from the customary English system of measurement to the metric system. The metric system is used worldwide. It is easier to work with than the English system. All calculations are made in units of ten. Parts and multiples are noted by prefixes. Weight is measured in grams. Volume is measured in liters. Heat is measured in degrees Celsius.

As you do more cooking, you may find recipes with metric measurements. It is possible to *convert*, or change from one measuring system to the other. But you will have better results if you use metric utensils and follow the recipe as written.

system that measures weight in pounds and ounces and volume in cups, pints, quarts, and gallons.

format: The style in which a recipe is written.

ingredients: The foods used in a recipe.

liquid measuring cups: Cups used to measure liquid ingredients such as water and milk.

measure: Obtain the exact amount of a specific ingredient.

measuring spoons: Spoons used to measure small amounts, such as tablespoons and teaspoons.

metric system: A measuring system that measures weight in grams and volume in liters.

narrative form: A recipe format in which all the information is written in paragraph form.

recipe: The ingredients, amounts, and directions needed for making a particular dish.

standard form: A recipe format in which all the ingredients and amounts are listed first, then the directions are given either in steps or paragraphs.

a quick review

1. Which recipe form is most often found in cookbooks?
2. How do dry measuring cups differ from liquid measuring cups?
3. Name the two base units of the metric system used in cooking.
4. Why must you get eye level with the cup when measuring liquids?

CHAPTER 64
Safety in the Kitchen

A student was once heard to say, "My grandmother always makes a big deal about washing hands before cooking. Why, she even made me wash the cutting board twice while we prepared a picnic lunch. Then I spilled some oil on the floor, and you would have thought I poured the entire bottle out on purpose. She made me wipe it up and clean the floor before I could finish the sandwiches. Why the fuss?"

The answer is simple. Even the smallest things can become health and safety problems in the kitchen. If a cutting board is not washed properly, it may transmit harmful bacteria and cause food poisoning. If spills are not cleaned up immediately, you or someone else may fall and get hurt. Imagine what might happen if you fell with a knife in your hand. Safety in the kitchen is very important.

HANDLING FOOD PROPERLY

If you have ever been up half the night with an upset stomach and aching head and body, then you may have had a mild case of *food poisoning*. The symptoms of food poisoning can be similar to those of the "flu." People usually don't die from food poisoning, but it can be very uncomfortable.

Food poisoning may be caused by *bacteria,* which are very tiny organisms in food. Bacteria are actually present everywhere, even in the air we breathe. But not all bacteria in food are harmful. Our bodies can even handle a small amount of harmful bacteria. It is only when the bacteria count is very high that we become ill.

SAFE PREPARATION OF FOODS

The most important thing to remember about keeping food free of dangerous bacteria is to keep all food either hot or cold and to keep ourselves and the utensils we use clean.

Keep Hot Foods Hot. After cooking, food should be kept hot, above 60°C (140°F), or chilled. Never leave food at room temperature for more than two hours. At room temperature, bacteria grow rapidly. Heat leftovers thoroughly. High temperatures will destroy many harmful bacteria.

Keep Cold Foods Cold. Foods such as meat, poultry, eggs, and cheese must be stored in the refrigerator at temperatures below 5°C (40°F). These food items should be purchased last in the supermarket and refrigerated or frozen as soon as you get home. Custards, meringues, and cream pies should be stored in the refrigerator as soon as they have cooled slightly. When taking food outdoors, keep perishables in an ice chest or cooler. Lunch boxes keep food cooler than paper bags. Vacuum containers are great for keeping soups or stews hot, salads or liquids cold.

Keeping Clean. Keeping clean is important to prevent food from being *contaminated,* or infected with harmful bacteria. When handling food, be sure your hands are clean. Wash often, especially after coughing or sneezing, playing with pets, or handling raw food. Remember, your hands may carry harmful bacteria to the food and cause food poisoning. Utensils such as forks, knives, and spoons should also be kept clean. Cutting boards should be cleaned after each use. If you have an open cut or sore, do not handle food unless you wear household gloves. Bacteria from the wound can cause food poisoning.

KITCHEN SAFETY

Carelessness is the cause of most accidents that take place in the kitchen. Touching a hot pot can cause a nasty burn. Climbing on the counter to reach something on the top shelf can result in a fall and a broken ankle. Placing knives in a sink filled with soapy water can cause a painful cut. All of these accidents can be prevented.

Safety with Appliances. Before you use any electrical appliance, be sure you understand the right way to use

Guidelines for Kitchen Safety

- Turn cookware handles toward the back of the range. Tighten loose handles with a screwdriver.
- Dispose of any broken utensils.
- Wipe any spills or food from the floor immediately.
- When reaching for something from the top shelf, stand on a sturdy step stool or ladder.
- Knives should be washed separately and stored in special compartments. When cutting food, always cut away from yourself. When handing a knife to another person, do so with the blade pointed away from the recipient. Keep knives sharp. Dull knives can cause injuries, since you need to press harder when cutting and the knife may slip.
- Keep all cabinet doors and drawers closed.
- Never buy or use any can that is bulging or leaking or appears damaged in any way.
- Do not use an appliance for other than its intended use. Be sure to read the instruction booklet before using the appliance.
- If an appliance seems to be working incorrectly, stop using it immediately. Then have it checked by a parent, teacher, or appliance repairer.

TEMPERATURE OF FOOD FOR CONTROL OF BACTERIA

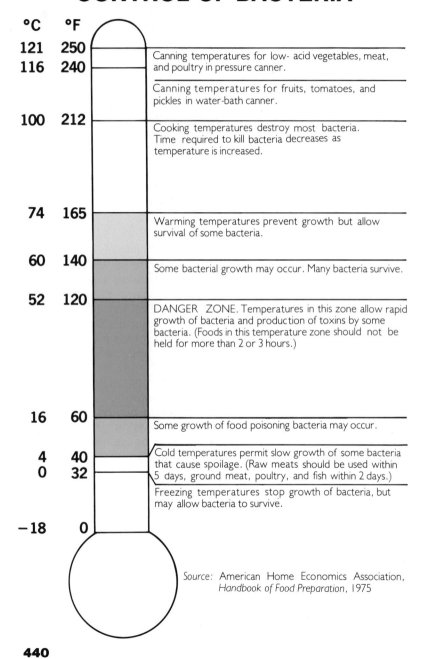

°C	°F	
121	250	Canning temperatures for low- acid vegetables, meat, and poultry in pressure canner.
116	240	
		Canning temperatures for fruits, tomatoes, and pickles in water-bath canner.
100	212	Cooking temperatures destroy most bacteria. Time required to kill bacteria decreases as temperature is increased.
74	165	Warming temperatures prevent growth but allow survival of some bacteria.
60	140	Some bacterial growth may occur. Many bacteria survive.
52	120	DANGER ZONE. Temperatures in this zone allow rapid growth of bacteria and production of toxins by some bacteria. (Foods in this temperature zone should not be held for more than 2 or 3 hours.)
16	60	Some growth of food poisoning bacteria may occur.
4	40	Cold temperatures permit slow growth of some bacteria that cause spoilage. (Raw meats should be used within 5 days, ground meat, poultry, and fish within 2 days.)
0	32	Freezing temperatures stop growth of bacteria, but may allow bacteria to survive.
−18	0	

Source: American Home Economics Association, *Handbook of Food Preparation,* 1975

it. In school, your teacher may demonstrate this. Or a group of students may read the instruction book, then demonstrate the use and care of an appliance for the class. Here are some other guidelines for using appliances:

• Be sure your hands are dry when using electrical appliances. Wet hands could cause electrical shock.

• If an appliance has a separate cord, plug the appliance end of the cord in first, then the outlet end. To unplug the appliance, hold onto the plug and pull it gently from the outlet. Never yank on the cord to remove the plug from the outlet.

• With an electric mixer, always insert the beaters before plugging in the mixer. Use a rubber scraper to scrape the sides of the bowl. Never use wooden spoons or narrow spatulas. They can get caught in the beaters and hit your hand.

• Keep the cord out of the way when using an appliance. Do not let it hang over the countertop. The appliance could get pulled over. Accidents like this cause many burns.

• Only plug one kitchen appliance into an outlet at a time. Plugging two or more appliances into the same outlet at once can overload the circuits. This could blow a fuse, throw a breaker switch, or even cause a fire.

Safety When Cooking. Many kitchen accidents occur while people are actually cooking. The following

When tasting food while cooking, use a clean spoon. Using the mixing spoon to taste introduces harmful bacteria into your food.

safety precautions are important to remember. Keep them in mind whenever you are cooking.

• When you cook in deep fat, be sure the food is dry. Water on the food will cause the fat to splatter. This can cause burns.

• Use dry, heavily padded pot holders to handle hot pans or oven racks. Wet ones form steam, and steam can burn your hands.

• Keep books and papers away from the range top.

• If fat catches on fire, do not throw water on it. This will spread the flames. First, turn off the burner or the appliance. Then carefully cover the utensil or put baking soda on the base of the flames.

The kitchen can be a fun place to work. You can make it a safe place, too. Remember to keep your hands clean when working with food, and avoid coughing and sneezing around food. Keep hot food hot and cold food cold to prevent food poisoning.

Types of Food Poisoning

• *Staph* is caused by bacteria found in foods containing milk, meat, or mayonnaise. These foods must be refrigerated when they are stored.

• *Salmonella* is caused by bacteria found in raw eggs and raw meat.

• *Botulism* is also caused by bacteria. These bacteria are found in improperly canned low-acid foods. Examples of low-acid foods are meat, poultry, and all vegetables except tomatoes. Never use food from bulging, leaking, or damaged cans.

• *Trichinosis* is caused by a very small worm found in raw fresh pork. This worm is destroyed by cooking. Never eat fresh pork that is pink.

• *Hepatitis* is caused by eating food that has come in contact with sewage or contaminated water.

▶ **Words to Know**

bacteria: Microscopic plants.

contaminated: Infected with harmful bacteria.

food poisoning: Illness caused by harmful bacteria in food, improper handling of food, or poor sanitation habits around food.

a quick review

1. Name three types of food poisoning caused by bacteria.
2. How can trichinosis be avoided?
3. Name five safety practices that can help prevent accidents in the kitchen.
4. How can you keep food cold when you are on a picnic or in school?

CHAPTER 65
Meat, Fish, Poultry, Eggs, and Beans

The different kinds of foods in this group have something in common. They can all provide the protein that your body needs to grow. Some of these foods are better sources of protein than others. Some of them cost more. Some of them take longer to prepare. This chapter will help you learn about selecting and preparing these protein-rich foods.

MEAT

Beef, which is the flesh of year-old cattle, is the most popular meat in the United States. Veal, lamb, and pork are also popular. *Veal* is the meat of a young calf, and *lamb* is the meat of a young sheep. *Pork* is the meat of a mature hog. *Variety meats* are the internal organs of animals, such as the liver, heart, kidneys, brains, and tongue. Sweetbreads, which are a gland of young animals, tripe, which is the stomach wall of cattle, and chitterlings, which are the intestines of hogs, are also variety meats.

Meat is a good source of high-quality, or complete, protein. It also contains iron, phosphorus, and the B vitamins. Meat contains muscle, connective tissue, and fat. The toughness or tenderness of meat depends on the amount and strength of the muscle tissue. Breeding, age, exercise, and feeding of the animal all affect its tenderness. Meat from young animals, such as veal and lamb, is more likely

"Steak" comes in many different cuts. Starting at the left and moving clockwise, here are a porterhouse, a filet mignon, a sirloin, and a club steak, which is the large side of the porterhouse.

to be tender than meat from older animals. Injecting the animal with enzymes or aging the meat in the packing plant helps tenderize the meat.

The part of the animal that the meat comes from also determines the tenderness. Those parts that were exercised the most are the least tender. This means that meat cut from the leg, shoulder, or neck is tougher than meat cut from the rib. These less-tender cuts are generally less expensive. The tender cuts of meat usually cost more. However, all cuts are equally nutritious. Cooking less-tender cuts of meat properly can make them more tender.

Processed Meats. Processed meats are those that have been changed in some way (other than cutting) before they get to the store. In this country most meat processing is done by industry.

Sausage is one of the oldest processed meats. Sausage was made in the Mediterranean countries as long ago as 1000 B.C.

Sausage is sold in links, rings, rolls, patties, and loaves and in bulk form. It contains one or more kinds of chopped meat. The mixture of the chopped meat, other ingredients, and spices is then usually stuffed into a casing to hold it together.

Wholesomeness of Beef

U.S.
INSPECTED AND PASSED BY DEPARTMENT OF AGRICULTURE
EST. 38

This round stamp, normally colored purple, is placed on a piece of meat to show that that piece has passed inspection by the U.S. Department of Agriculture. Such meat is safe to eat. The purple dye of the stamp is harmless. All meat that is processed in one state and sold in another must have this mark on it.

Freezing Meats
Whatever is used to wrap meat for storage should provide a moistureproof, airtight compartment for the food.

Mark each package with the name of the food it contains and the date on which it was put into the freezer. Keep an inventory of the foods stored in the freezer.

This shield-shaped grade mark is a guide to the tenderness, juiciness, and flavor of meat. The U.S. Department of Agriculture grades the meat of packers who want it done. There are three commonly used grades of meat: prime, choice, and good. Prime meat is the most tender. It is also the grade most often served in better restaurants. Choice meat is generally the grade sold in supermarkets. It is popular because it is tender and can be cooked in many ways. Good meat is less tender because it doesn't have as much *marbling*—evenly distributed mixtures of fat and lean—as the better grades.

Standard and commercial are two other grades of meat. They are of lesser quality and are not often found in supermarkets. They are tough.

Many different sausages, hot dogs, and cold cuts are available. The differences among them in taste and texture depend on several things. These include what kind of meat is used, what ingredients are added, and how thoroughly the meat is chopped. Read the label carefully to see what is in the product.

Dried beef is cured, smoked, dried meat from the beef carcass. Bacon and ham are cured pork products. Curing and smoking are methods once used to preserve meat, before refrigeration was available. Now curing and smoking are done to add flavor. It is important to cook these products thoroughly if they are not precooked.

Buying Meat. Most food stores prepackage fresh meat in see-through containers. Meat is also sold frozen. Convenience foods, such as hamburger patties and prepared meals, are commonly sold this way.

Some meats, such as corned beef, and deviled ham, are available canned. Since you cannot see the products, reading labels is important.

Most meat is sold by the pound or by the kilogram. As a guideline, plan on 12 g (¼ lb) of boneless meat per serving. Of course, there are some people who will eat more than one serving at a meal.

Storing Meat. Fresh meat should be refrigerated and used within two or three days after it is bought. If it must be kept longer, wrap it tightly in freezer paper or aluminum foil or seal it tightly in plastic bags. Then

Processed meats include many varieties of sausage, luncheon meats, bacon, and hot dogs.

Antipasto, a common Italian appetizer, consists of a variety of foods arranged attractively on a platter. The one shown here has many different foods—eggs, peppers, cherry tomatoes, celery, shrimp, mushrooms, asparagus, scallions, radishes, salami, ham, pickles, onions, and beans.

you can store it in the freezer for three to four months. Meat that is stored in the freezer should be sealed so that no air reaches it. The cold air of the freezer will dry the meat. This is called freezer burn. Freezer burn does not make the meat unsafe to eat, but it does change the taste by drying the meat and causing it to lose some of its tenderness.

Meat that has been frozen should be thawed in the refrigerator or in a microwave oven. It should not be thawed at room temperature. The reason for this is that the outside of the meat can reach room temperature before the inside is thawed. At room temperature, bacteria grow quickly. This increases the possibility of food poisoning.

It is best to thaw meat in the wrapper to keep it from drying out. A large roast may take a day or two to thaw. Small cuts of meat will take less than a day.

Thawed meats should not be refrozen. There are two reasons for this. First, freezing does not kill bacteria. So the increased number of bacteria will grow even more the second time

1. Center food on the sheet.

2. Bring opposite sides of sheet together.

3. Double fold.

4. Double fold ends.

5. Tightly press wrapping around food.

6. Snugly press ends to package. Secure with freezer tape as necessary.

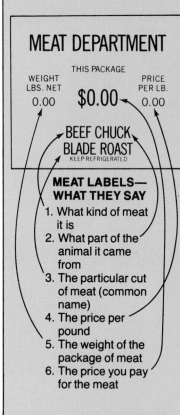

MEAT DEPARTMENT

THIS PACKAGE

| WEIGHT LBS. NET | | PRICE PER LB. |
| 0.00 | $0.00 | 0.00 |

BEEF CHUCK BLADE ROAST
KEEP REFRIGERATED

MEAT LABELS— WHAT THEY SAY
1. What kind of meat it is
2. What part of the animal it came from
3. The particular cut of meat (common name)
4. The price per pound
5. The weight of the package of meat
6. The price you pay for the meat

Ways to Tenderize Meats

marinate: Soak the meat in oil, seasonings, and vinegar or lemon juice.

braise: Brown the meat in hot fat, add a small amount of liquid, and cook slowly until done.

stew: Cover the meat with liquid and simmer for two hours or more.

cube: Cut the meat into small pieces to break the tough fibers.

pound: Break the fibers with a small mallet.

chop or *grind:* Use a meat grinder to break the meat into very small pieces.

the meat thaws. This greatly increases the chance of food poisoning. Second, as meat thaws, moisture is removed. If it were to thaw a second time, the meat would become very dry.

Cooking Meats. Most people like meat that is tender, flavorful, and juicy. The two methods of cooking meat are moist-heat cooking and dry-heat cooking. Braising—cooking in a covered container with a small amount of liquid—and stewing—cooking in a large amount of liquid—are moist-heat methods. Cooking in moisture over low heat helps to tenderize meat because it breaks down the connective tissue. The liquid used for cooking can be water, juices, or sauces such as tomato sauce. The liquid can also be used to flavor other foods being cooked at the same time, such as vegetables.

Dry-heat cooking, such as broiling, roasting, or frying, does not use liquid. This type of cooking is used for tender cuts of meat. It does not make the meat more tender. If dry-heat cooking is not done properly, it may make the meat tough.

Broiling is cooking meat directly over heat, such as on a charcoal grill, or directly under an electric or gas-heating unit. Broiling browns the surface of the meat rapidly and seals in the juices. Since the heat is so high, care must be taken to avoid burning and toughening the meat.

Roasting is cooking meat uncovered in an oven. Roasting pans are often used with a rack. The cooking temperature is kept medium to low, 175 to 150°C (350 to 300°F). The amount of time it takes to cook a roast depends on the weight of the meat and the temperature of the oven. Many cookbooks are available to help you estimate how long to cook a roast. A meat thermometer inserted into the thickest part of the roast will enable you to cook a roast to the exact degree of doneness you wish. It is important, however, that the thermometer not touch a bone. If it does, it will not indicate the right degree of doneness.

Frying is cooking meat with a small amount of fat in an uncovered pan on top of the stove. Deep-fat frying is cooking in a large amount of fat.

Extenders. Other ingredients, usually called *extenders,* can be mixed with meat to increase the number of servings. Extenders spread the flavor through the entire dish, causing the protein to be extended, or to go further.

Textured vegetable protein can be used with hamburger to get more servings from the same amount of meat. Vegetable protein is made from soybeans, which are high in protein. Other foods can also be used to stretch meat servings. Rice added to

Try a sauce on fish. Or try rolled fish fillets wrapped in bacon, skewered with vegetables, and cooked over charcoal.

chopped meat will give more stuffing for green peppers. Bread crumbs added to ground meat help give more servings of meat loaf. Spaghetti and noodles are also served with meat dishes so that the dish will feed more. Casseroles, stews, and ground-meat dishes often include extenders.

Meat extenders add to the flavor of the dish. However, some people do not like the taste of extenders.

When deciding whether to save money by stretching a meat dish, consider the nutrition and taste preferences of the people who will be eating it.

FISH

Fish are generally divided into two groups, fin fish and shellfish. Both are good sources of protein. There are many different types of fish. Some of the more popular fin fish include cod, tuna, trout, flounder, catfish, and salmon. Some fish come from freshwater lakes and rivers, others from the salt water of the ocean.

Fish are sold in several ways. *Whole fish* are those that are sold just as they come from the water. *Dressed fish* are scaled fish with their heads, tails, fins, and insides removed. *Filleted fish* have all the bones removed. Fish are also sold in sticks, which can be frozen, or fish cakes, which are breaded.

Shellfish have a hard outer covering. Popular types of shellfish include clams, crabs, lobsters, oysters, scallops, and shrimp.

Fish are as good a source of protein

The Great American Hamburger and Other Meats

The hamburger had its origin in Russia. There people called the Tatars, or Tartars, shaped it and ate it raw. German sailors traveling there brought the idea back to Hamburg, Germany, where the people of Hamburg, called Hamburgers, were the first to cook the ground meat.

In 1904, at a large fair in St. Louis, hamburgers were first served on buns.

Today 30 percent of all the meat served and bought in the United States is hamburger.

Meat makes up 30 to 40 percent of the diets of people in the United States and Europe. In India and Africa, that figure is 20 percent.

Tired of beef as your main protein source? In 1931 the first commercial packaging of rattlesnake meat was begun in Florida. You can still buy it if you have a taste for it.

Amazing Fact: If you eat meat, you will probably eat 12 sheep, 23 hogs, 14 cattle, 35 turkeys, 880 chickens, 2 calves, and 770 fish in your lifetime.

Amazing Fact: The largest hamburger on record was made in Texas in 1978. It weighed 33.3 kilograms (74 pounds).

447

This shield, printed on an egg carton, indicates the quality of the eggs inside. There are three grades of eggs: U.S. Grades AA, A, and B. U.S. Grade AA represents the highest quality.

Eggs are labeled and sold according to the weight of a dozen.

U.S.D.A. Sizes	Weight in Ounces
Jumbo	30
Extra Large	27
Large	24
Medium	21
Small	18
Peewee	15

The size of eggs has nothing to do with their quality.

The interior quality of the egg is determined by *candling*. This is done by holding an egg in front of a light so that the inside can be checked.

The colors of the shell and the yolk are determined by the hen's diet. Color is no indication of quality.

These chicken crepes make an attractive main dish. The crepes, which are like thin pancakes, are filled with chicken salad and topped with a cheese sauce and almonds.

as meats and usually contain little fat. They also contain important minerals. Examples are iodine, calcium, and phosphorus.

Fresh fish are packed in ice to keep them fresh for a short time. If fish are sent long distances from where they were caught, they are processed and frozen. Fish can also be preserved by smoking, salting, or canning.

Since fresh fish do not keep well for long periods of time, freshness is important. Fresh fish should be cooked within a day of being bought. Fish that are beyond their peak of freshness may have a slime on the skin and a stale odor.

Keep fresh fish as cold as possible without freezing when storing. Wrap them tightly in plastic wrap. This will keep their odors from mixing with the odors of other foods.

Frozen fish are very popular and convenient. Fish that are fast-frozen after being caught can then be safely shipped to all parts of the country. Breaded shrimp and fish sticks are popular ways of buying frozen fish.

Canned fish is generally an inexpensive and convenient way to buy and store fish. Tuna fish is a popular canned fish that may be used in a casserole, salad, or sandwich. Labels on the cans tell the type of fish and whether it is packed in oil or water.

Cooking Fish. Fish may be cooked whole or in pieces. Because of the high percentage of protein in fish, a low-to-medium cooking temperature is best. Fish are usually considered done when the flesh flakes or separates easily with a fork. Overcooking will make the fish dry and tough.

POULTRY

Poultry includes various birds, especially ducks, chickens, turkeys, geese, and Cornish hens. Poultry contains the same high-quality protein as meat. It is also a good source of iron and B vitamins. In general, it contains fewer calories than meat.

Poultry is sold in many different stages of processing. Fresh whole poultry usually has the head, feet, internal organs, and feathers removed. It is commonly sold in halves and quarters. Poultry parts can be bought separately as well. Poultry is also sold in pressed, deboned, and rolled forms.

If poultry is bought fresh, it should be refrigerated and used within two or three days.

Frozen poultry should be kept frozen until it is to be cooked. It should be thawed in the refrigerator. Thawing poultry on a countertop greatly increases the chances of food poisoning. Thawed poultry should be cooked as soon as possible. Bacteria can breed in uncooked poultry. Because of this, clean cutting boards and knives are important.

Canned poultry is also available. It is convenient, and there is usually no waste. Canned poultry may be used much the same way as canned fish.

Cooking Poultry. Cooking poultry at a medium-to-low temperature keeps it juicy and tender. Poultry can be prepared in a variety of ways: fried, roasted, stewed, or broiled. Cooked poultry can be used in soups, pot pies, salads, and casseroles. Roasted poultry is often stuffed just before it is put into the oven. Storing stuffed uncooked chicken or turkey is not safe. The chicken acts as an insulator for the stuffing. It does not allow the stuffing to cool fast enough to avoid the growth of bacteria.

Hard-cooked eggs should not be boiled. Boiling them causes the white to become tough and the shells to crack. Boiling them for a long time causes a green ring to form around the yolk.

Omelets

Making an omelet can be an exercise in creativity and skill. Making an omelet is easier with an *omelet pan,* a frying pan with sloped sides. Omelets may be plain and taste much like scrambled eggs, or they may be an adventure in eating. They may contain diced cheese, ham, cooked vegetables, mushrooms, seafood, or tomatoes or any combination of these and other foods.

Plain Omelet

• Beat with a fork until blended:

  4 eggs

• Beat in:

  62 mL (¼ cup) milk or cream
  ¼ teaspoon salt
  ⅛ teaspoon paprika

• Melt in a skillet:

  1 tablespoon butter

When the butter is fairly hot, add the egg mixture. Cook it over low heat. Lift the edges with a spatula and tilt the skillet to permit the uncooked custard to run to the bottom of the pan. When it is all an even consistency, fold the omelet over and serve it immediately.

449

Beans, Peas, and Lentils

Dry beans, peas, and lentils are often food bargains. They provide a wealth of energy for a nominal cost.

Buying Tips: Usually only the highest grade of beans, peas, and lentils are sold on the supermarket shelves. Try to buy them in "see-through" packaging. Then look for bright color, uniform size, and absence of damage, such as cracked seeds or foreign matter in the package.

Store beans, peas, and lentils in tightly covered containers in a dry, cool place.

Some Common Names of Beans:

kidney or pinto	*Use:* chili con carne
lima, "cowpeas" (black-eyed peas)	*Use:* main-dish vegetable or succotash

Some Common Names of Peas:

green and yellow dry	*Use:* boiled with butter
dry split	*Use:* split-pea soup
lentils	*Use:* paired with fruits and meats

Chili, made from chopped beef, tomatoes, and beans, is a popular dish in the southwest. Because chili is tasty, economical, and a good source of protein, it is becoming popular in other parts of the country.

EGGS

Eggs are a low-cost, convenient source of protein and of vitamins A and D, riboflavin, and iron.

Eggs can be used in many ways. Sometimes they are the main dish in a meal, such as an omelet. They are also used with other foods—to thicken them (custard), to coat them before frying (fried chicken), or to bind several ingredients together (meat loaf). Eggs also are used to help make some foods rise, such as popovers. Sometimes when they are used this way, the whites are beaten separately until stiff. Eggs are also used to flavor and color certain foods.

Occasionally, eggs are prepared un-cooked, as in eggnogs. However, eggs are usually cooked. They can be fried, scrambled, poached, baked, or cooked in the shell. Eggs are cooked at low to medium heat.

Eggs cooked in the shell are called *hard cooked* or *soft cooked*. Boiling eggs makes them tough and rubbery. When cooking eggs in the shell, place them in cold water. Bring the water to the boiling point. Then turn the heat down, cover the pan, and turn off the heat. Let the pan stand for three minutes for soft-cooked eggs. Let it stand for twenty minutes for hard-cooked eggs. Pour off the hot water and quickly cool the eggs with cold water. This makes them easier to peel and prevents overcooking. Overcooking can result in a greenish ring around the yolk and a tough white.

Eggs are most often bought fresh. Fresh eggs should always be kept in the refrigerator. Eggs are sold in cartons of a dozen. Some eggshells are brown and some are white. The color of the eggshell makes no difference either in the food quality of the egg or in the way it tastes.

Dried eggs keep for a long time. There are several mixes on the market that contain dry eggs along with other ingredients. Cake mixes and pancake mixes are examples of products that use dried eggs. Backpackers find dry eggs a light, convenient form of high-protein food.

Egg substitutes are also sold. They contain similar vitamins and protein, but little of the fat or cholesterol contained in real eggs. They can be used to replace eggs in many recipes.

BEANS AND NUTS

Dry beans, peas, and nuts are sometimes used in main dish recipes. All are good sources of low-quality, or incomplete, protein and food energy. They contain B vitamins and minerals, too.

There are many different kinds of beans, including soy, navy, pinto, and lima beans. Some require soaking before cooking. This may take a long time. Cooked, canned beans are time-savers.

Beans are often used in combination with other foods. Combining them with meats helps provide complete protein. Chili con carne is an example of a bean-and-meat combination dish.

Beans can be used in casseroles, soups, salads, and sauces. Baked beans, three-bean salad, and refried beans are favorite dishes in different parts of the United States. Beans can provide a tasty, inexpensive, high-quality food in the diet.

a quick review

1. What determines the tenderness of a cut of meat?
2. Why is a moist-heat method of cooking good for preparing less-tender cuts of meat?
3. List three ways to extend the flavor of meat and to lower the cost.
4. List five ways eggs can be used in cooking.
5. Why is temperature important in the preparation of foods high in protein?

▶ **Words to Know**

broil: Cook meat directly over heat, with fat dripping away.

curing: A method of preserving meat or fish, such as salting or smoking.

extenders: Substances such as rice, bread, and noodles that, when added to meat, increase the number of servings.

filleted fish: Fish with the bones removed.

freezer burn: Brownish discoloration of the surface of meat that has been exposed to air while frozen.

fry: Cook in a small amount of fat, usually in an uncovered pan.

lamb: Meat from a young sheep.

roast: Cook meat uncovered, with dry heat.

sausage: A mixture of chopped meat, spices, and other ingredients stuffed into a casing.

simmer: Cook in a liquid just below boiling temperature.

stew: Simmer meat in liquid that covers the food. Can be done with or without vegetables.

variety meats: Internal organs of animals, such as the liver, heart, kidneys, and tongue.

veal: Meat from a young calf.

451

CHAPTER 66

Milk and Cheese

Ancient people first began to raise animals such as cows, oxen, goats, and sheep in about 9000 B.C. They raised the animals mostly for the hide or meat or some other part that could be used for food. The milk these animals gave was probably discovered by accident. However, milk and milk products quickly became an important part of many people's diets.

People in the United States drink more milk than any other beverage except water. One important reason is that milk is a leading source of many nutrients. Milk is also used as a basic ingredient in many other common foods and recipes.

MILK PRODUCTS

Milk is an important source of nutrients. It is a major source of calcium, which is needed for bone growth and maintenance. It is also a source of high-quality, or complete, protein. Milk and milk products contain phosphorus, as well as riboflavin and thiamin, two important B-complex vitamins. Milk is also a source of vitamin A, and often vitamin D is added.

Because teenagers grow rapidly, they especially need to include milk in their daily diet. As a rule of thumb, if you drink a glass of milk with every meal, you will get the amount of milk

Drinking milk as a snack, as well as with meals, helps you meet your daily calcium and protein requirements.

you need each day. A liter (1.06 quarts) of milk provides about half the daily requirement of protein.

Milks. Milks include whole milk, skim milk, low-fat milk, flavored milk, and yogurt. Whole milk, skim milk, and low-fat milk contain varying amounts of fat. Of the three, whole milk has the most fat, skim milk has less fat, and low-fat milk has the least fat. *Cultured buttermilk* is low-fat or skim milk that has been commercially soured. *Yogurt* is another commercially soured milk product that is far thicker than milk. *Flavored milks* are those to which chocolate, cocoa, or other sweeteners have been added. Flavored milks contain more calories than unflavored milk.

Concentrated Milk Products. Concentrated milk products are made by removing some of the water from whole milk. *Evaporated milk,* which comes in cans and costs less than whole milk, becomes whole milk again when water is added. *Dried whole milk* is milk with most of the water removed. *Nonfat dried milk* is milk from which the water and fat have been removed. It is a powder. *Sweetened condensed milk* is milk with some water removed and a sweetener added. All of these products are cheaper than whole milk. And they can be stored for a long time on a shelf.

Creams. *Cream* is a liquid composed almost entirely of milk fat. Whipping cream, or heavy cream, has

453

• Powdered milk has been around for a long time. Genghis Khan's soldiers dried mares' milk in the sun. To mix it, they would add water, put the mixture in a pouch, and attach it to a horse. After a day of riding, the milk would be mixed.

• Each member of one Kenya tribe drinks 9 to 13 liters (9 to 14 quarts) of milk each day, yet the entire tribe has low cholesterol levels.

• If you drink skim milk, you may not get enough calcium. You should drink skim milk with meals that include some fat.

• Nonfat milk provides incomplete protein because of the heating process it undergoes.

• Raw milk, that is, milk that is not pasteurized, has the most protein of all milks.

• In the Middle East, people drink goat's milk; in India, buffalo's milk; in Lapland, reindeer's milk.

Amazing Fact: In 1937, Andy Faust of Oklahoma broke the hand milking record. He got 456 liters (120 gallons) in twelve hours of milking.

the greatest amount of fat. Light cream, sometimes called coffee cream, has the next highest amount of fat. Half-and-half is a mixture of equal parts of milk and cream. It has a lower fat content than any other cream. Sour cream is cream that has been commercially soured. It has about the same amount of fat as light cream.

Frozen Dairy Desserts. Frozen desserts made with milk include ice cream, sherbet, frozen custard, and ice milk. Ice cream is made from cream, sugar, and flavoring. Sherbet is made from milk and sweetened fruit juice.

Frozen custard is like ice cream except that eggs are used in the base mixture. Ice milk is made with ingredients like those in ice cream, but milk is used instead of cream.

COOKING WITH MILK

Custards, soufflés, puddings, cream soups, and some casseroles are dishes that may have milk as a major ingredient. Milk is also an ingredient in breads, cakes, and pasta dishes. Milk is a primary ingredient in white sauce, which is used in many dishes.

Milk burns easily. Because of this,

Putting fruit and milk on cereal increases the food value of the cereal and makes it more appealing.

The diagram below gives the names of these cheeses.

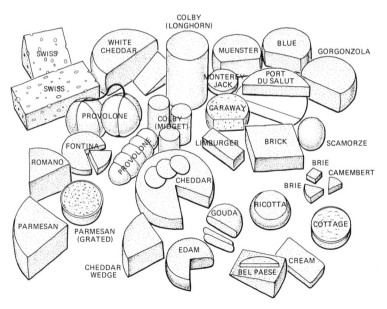

SWISS
SWISS
WHITE CHEDDAR
COLBY (LONGHORN)
MUENSTER
BLUE
GORGONZOLA
MONTEREY JACK
PORT DU SALUT
PROVOLONE
COLBY (MIDGET)
GARAWAY
FONTINA
PROVOLONE
LIMBURGER
BRICK
SCAMORZE
ROMANO
CHEDDAR
BRIE
CAMEMBERT
BRIE
GOUDA
RICOTTA
PARMESAN
PARMESAN (GRATED)
COTTAGE
EDAM
CREAM
CHEDDAR WEDGE
BEL PAESE

Surprising Facts About Cheese

• Over the last forty years, cheese consumption in the United States has increased. On the average, each person in this country eats about 5 kilograms (11 pounds) of cheese per year. Over the average lifetime, this may add up to 450 kilograms (½ ton) of cheese.

• There are more microbes (tiny organisms) in just over 1 kilogram (2½ pounds) of cheese than there are people on Earth.

• There are over 350 different kinds of cheeses. Many countries are known for their special cheeses. Some of these famous national cheeses include:

Belgium: Limberger
Denmark: Havarti
France: Roquefort
Germany: Tilsit
England: Cheshire
Greece: Feta
Italy: Parmesan
Netherlands: Edam
Norway: Jarlsberg
Switzerland: Gruyere
United States: Colby

Amazing Fact: The heaviest cheese of all time was a Wisconsin cheddar. Made in 1964, it weighed in at 15,566 kilograms (34,591 pounds).

455

Cheese Ideas

Cheese is a *versatile* food. This means it can be used many ways. Have you ever tried a grilled cheese sandwich made with Swiss cheese? What about a sandwich with grilled cheese, tuna fish salad, and sliced tomato? There are many variations of the grilled cheese sandwich. Can you think of others?

Another popular way of using cheese is to serve it grated. Some uses of grated cheese are:

- adding it to a salad
- sprinkling it on top of hot soup
- adding it to tacos
- mixing it with a meatloaf mixture before cooking
- adding it to bread dough
- mixing it with yogurt for a dip
- blending it into scrambled eggs
- sprinkling it on baked potatoes
- using it as a topping on cooked vegetables
- using it as a topping on warm apple pie

Cubes of cheese make great snacks. Try serving different kinds of cheese cut into cubes.

Cheese fondue is a mixture of cheeses, milk, and seasonings. It is heated and served with cubes of French bread for dipping.

Grilled cheese sandwiches can be turned into special treats by adding fish salad. Sole has been used here, but tuna or salmon also work well.

you should take special care when cooking anything with milk in it. Baked dishes with milk are usually cooked at a moderate temperature, usually about 150 to 175°C (300 to 350° F). Custards are often baked in a pan that has been set in another pan filled with water. When cooking milk on top of the stove, use a double boiler whenever possible.

THE WORLD OF CHEESE

Almost every part of the world except for Asia and Africa, where there are few milk products of any kind, is known for some variety of cheese. The countries of Western Europe and the Middle East make many different kinds of cheeses.

How Cheese Is Made. Cheese is a by-product of milk. Legend says it was discovered by a traveler who carried a pouch made from a cow's stomach. The pouch contained milk. Many hours into his trip, the traveler discovered that the milk had soured. It had separated into a liquid substance and a solid substance. He tasted the solid substance. He found he liked its taste. The solid substance came to be called cheese.

Cheese making, despite the arrival of technology, has changed very little over the years. It begins with warm milk. The warm temperature creates an acid, which sours the milk. Rennet, the substance that came from the cow's intestine in the first cheese, is added to make the liquids and solids separate. The liquids are called *whey*. The solids are called *curds*. The liquids are removed. The curd, or cheese, is then aged. Usually, it is pressed into a single solid shape. Sometimes herbs or spices or even mold, which makes the world-famous blue cheese, is added.

Cheese is made from many different kinds of milk. The milk can come from cows, reindeer, goats, or sheep. Cheese is a highly variable product. This means that humidity, temperature, and even various kinds of bacteria in the air all influence the taste of cheese. A cheese made in one area will not taste the same if it is made in another area, even if it is made in exactly the same way. This is part of what makes cheese so special. There are hundreds of kinds of cheeses, but all fall into one of three groups.

The first group of cheeses includes natural, unripened cheeses. Among these are Brie, Camembert, and other "soft" cheeses. The second group includes semihard cheeses such as brick and Muenster. The third group includes hard cheeses such as Edam, Gouda, Parmesan, and cheddar.

There are also processed cheeses, which account for over one-half of the cheese sales in the United States. These cheeses are a combination of bits and pieces of other cheeses, along

Eating ice cream is a fun way to meet part of your daily milk and cheese requirement.

by-product: An extra material that is left over when something else is made. For example, when you make butter, the by-product is the buttermilk that is left over.

cheese: A by-product of milk made by separating and removing liquids. The remaining solid ripens to become cheese.

concentrated milk product: A form of milk in which some of the water content has been removed. All water content may be removed to produce dried milk or only some, to produce condensed milk.

cream: Milk fat that rises to the top when milk is allowed to settle. It can be converted to butter by whipping.

curds: The solids that separate out of milk during the making of cheese.

double boiler: A two-part pan in which the bottom part holds boiling water and the top part holds the food.

frozen dairy dessert: A dessert made from frozen milk products.

whey: The liquid that separates out of milk during the making of cheese.

with seasonings and preservatives. They are cheaper than other cheeses. They are also bland, which makes them an important food source for people on some special diets. They keep for a long time, and they melt easily when cooked.

COOKING AND STORING CHEESE

Like milk, cheese does not take well to long cooking or high temperatures. It becomes stringy and tough. One way to avoid this is to grate or shred the cheese before adding it to the other ingredients to be cooked. It is also helpful to bring the cheese to room temperature before cooking with it. When cheese is cooked in the oven, the cooking is done at a low temperature. When cheese is cooked on top of the stove, the cooking should be done in a double boiler or over very low heat.

Cheese is used in pastries, fondues, soufflés, soups, as a filling for pasta, and in Welsh rarebit, which consists of melted cheese sauce over toast.

Cheese will keep if it is wrapped very well before storing and placed in the refrigerator. Some cheeses have a tendency to form mold as they age. This is not harmful. In some cheeses, blue cheese for example, the mold is considered the best part.

Dairy products are delicious and interesting foods. No other food comes in so many shapes and forms, is used in preparing so many dishes, and is so consistently a part of the diet of so many peoples throughout the world.

a quick review

1. Why is milk important nutritionally?
2. Describe the different kinds of milks.
3. What should you keep in mind when cooking with milk?
4. What should you keep in mind when cooking with cheese?

right color, lively taste, and good nutrition are what make fruits and vegetables so important to our appetites and diet. Even the names of these foods have interesting origins. The word *vegetable* comes from the Latin word *vegetus,* meaning "lively." The word *fruit* comes from another Latin word, *fructus,* meaning "enjoyment." No one has recorded when or how fruits and vegetables were first eaten. However, these foods have been enjoyed throughout the ages. Fruits and vegetables are rich in vitamin A, the B-complex vitamins, and vitamin C, as well as important minerals. Fruits and vegetables are also a good source of fiber and the acids that help your body regularly eliminate waste.

FROM APPLES TO ZUCCHINI

Modern food-processing techniques have made out-of-season fruits and vegetables available all year round. The best and most nutritious time to eat fruits and vegetables is when they are fresh, that is, right after they are picked. But that is not always possible, especially if you do not live in a farming area.

Fruits and vegetables are at their best right from the garden. Exposure to heat and air may cause them to lose some of their nutrients. Fresh fruits and vegetables that have been

CHAPTER 67
Fruits and Vegetables

The Surprising Potato

The first potatoes, which were grown in South America, were the size of peanuts. The Indians dried them. Then they walked on them to rub off the potatoes' skins. In 1539 the Spanish brought potatoes back to Europe. Like tomatoes, potatoes were only used as a decoration until the Germans began cooking and eating them. Today, potatoes are the world's second most important crop.

stored a long time or shipped great distances often lose food value as well as flavor. Companies that process foods often build their plants right next to farming areas to save time and to allow the fruits and vegetables to reach the peak of ripeness. They are then picked at the right moment and prepared, canned, or frozen. Foods processed this way are often more nutritious than they would be if they had been sold as fresh produce. This is because fruits and vegetables lose some of their nutrients if left exposed to the air for more than a couple of minutes.

Because they are not cooked as long, frozen vegetables keep their flavor and color better than canned vegetables. However, canned fruits and vegetables can be stored for longer periods of time and are often easier to use.

Dried fruits and vegetables have many uses. Dried fruits such as apricots, apples, and prunes are good eaten alone or combined with nuts as snacks. Dried vegetables are often used in mixtures such as dried soups, sauces, and casseroles. Instant potatoes, which are actually dried potatoes, are widely used.

WHAT IS A FRUIT, WHAT IS A VEGETABLE?

A vegetable is a plant that is grown because parts of it can be eaten. The term is also used for the parts that are eaten. Plants have several parts, all of which provide us with familiar foods. These parts are the seed, root, stem, leaf, flower, and fruit.

Seeds. Examples of vegetables that are seeds of plants include beans, peas, corn, and nuts. These seeds can be planted to produce additional vegetables.

Roots. These vegetables grow underground. Common examples are carrots, beets, potatoes, and onions. All these foods have a green leafy top

Fruits and vegetables are often used together in salads to add variety in color, shape, and flavor.

A summer fruit salad served in a watermelon shell is an appealing addition to any meal. It can even be used as a centerpiece.

that grows above the ground. Many people do not like the taste of that part of the plant because it is bitter. However, it is an excellent source of nutrients such as vitamins A and C.

Stems. Asparagus, broccoli, celery, and rhubarb are vegetables that are the stems of plants. Stem vegetables are a good source of fiber. They are best cooked when they are fresh. As they mature, they become tough and stringy.

Leaves. Spinach, turnip greens, mustard greens, kale, and cabbage are leafy vegetables. Many leafy vegetables—lettuce, parsley, watercress, romaine, and escarole—are popular leafy salad greens. Any leaf of a plant that you cook and eat is classified as a leafy vegetable. Many of them are good raw or cooked, but some are eaten only in their raw form. Spinach, for example, tastes delicious cooked or served raw in salads. But lettuce is usually eaten raw.

Leafy vegetables are excellent sources of vitamins A and C. The darker the green of the leaf, the more vitamin A the vegetable contains.

Flowers. The buds or flowers of some plants are eaten as vegetables. Examples include broccoli and cauliflower. Both can be cooked or eaten raw in salads or as appetizers.

The Mighty Mushroom

There are over 38,000 different varieties of mushrooms in the world.

Mushrooms come in many different shapes. Some look like ears, some like birds' nests, some like lumps of jelly. And they can be very large or very small. One mushroom found in Australia weighed over 7.6 kilograms (17 pounds) and measured over 1.5 meters (5 feet) around. Mushrooms also have many smells. They can smell like soap, cod liver oil, sweet flowers, fish, or garbage.

Today mushrooms that are used for food are often grown in mushroom houses where the environment is kept cool and moist. Kennett Square, Pennsylvania, is called the "Mushroom Capital of the World" because there are so many mushroom houses in that area.

There have been many myths and strange beliefs about mushrooms through the centuries. Egyptian pharoahs believed that mushrooms were magical. Romans considered them food for the emperors, though they were sometimes also given to soldiers for strength. Mushrooms were sacred in Mexico and Central and South America, and one Latin American tribe is

(continued)

Fruit. Cucumbers, peppers, and squash, usually thought of as vegetables, are really fruits. The fruit of a plant appears after the flower or blossom. You are familiar with common fruits such as apples, oranges, and pears. Other fruits include pumpkins, tomatoes, watermelons, and cantaloupes. In all these foods, the seeds are protected by the fleshy part of the food, which we eat.

BUYING FRUITS AND VEGETABLES

Shopping for fruits and vegetables can be a pleasant experience. There is a large variety of colors, shapes, and tastes to select from. It is fun to sample new foods and to explore the different ways of preparing them.

Fresh Fruits and Vegetables. Fresh fruits and vegetables can be selected from a garden, purchased from a farm market, or bought in a supermarket. In the supermarket, they will be found in the *produce* department. Wherever you buy them, make sure they look fresh and crisp. Brown leaves and limp stems mean that the vegetables are not fresh. Very soft fruits are overripe. Do not buy them unless you can use them right away. For example, overripe bananas can be used in banana bread.

Canned Fruits and Vegetables. Fruits and vegetables are canned in many different forms. They may be whole, halved, sliced, or in pieces. The form you buy depends on how you plan to use the product. Canned foods may be stored indefinitely at room temperature. Since they are cooked during the canning process, they require no further cooking. But many people prefer to heat them.

Frozen Fruits and Vegetables. Be sure frozen foods are frozen solid at the time you buy them. Then take them home and store them in the freezer as soon as possible. Letting frozen foods thaw and then refreezing them increases the growth of bacteria in the food. This increases the chances of food poisoning.

COOKING FRUITS AND VEGETABLES

It is easy for fruits and vegetables to lose some of their vitamins. They also change flavor, texture, color, and shape as they mature and when they are cooked. When cooking fruits and vegetables, how do you retain the nutrients? How do you maintain the flavor or improve it? How can you keep the colors bright?

Keeping the Nutrients. Fruits and vegetables that are dark green or deep yellow are good sources of vitamin A. The darker the green or the deeper the yellow, the more vitamin A the food contains. For example, carrots and spinach are very good sources of vitamin A. White potatoes and onions contain very little.

Even though white root vegetables such as potatoes, parsnips, and turnips contain little vitamin A, they are a good source of vitamin C. If cooked correctly, a serving of these vegetables can provide up to one-fourth of your daily requirement of vitamin C. Many of the seed vegetables are rich in vitamin B.

Fruits and vegetables can be cooked many different ways. The most common methods are boiling, baking, and frying. The following facts are important to remember when cooking fruits and vegetables:

• The B vitamins, vitamin C, and minerals dissolve easily in water. Therefore, the less water used when cooking vegetables, the more vitamins and minerals saved.

• The B vitamins and vitamin C are easily destroyed by exposure to heat and air. By cooking vegetables containing these vitamins in a closed container for a short period of time, you keep more of the vitamins.

• Vitamins B and C are destroyed by exposure to oxygen. Boil the cooking water a few minutes before adding the raw vegetables. This will allow excess oxygen to escape from the cooking water and prevent some vitamin loss during cooking.

• Vitamins A, D, and E dissolve in

Fresh vegetables are often packaged before being placed on sale in supermarkets.

fats. They are drawn out into the cooking liquid when fats such as bacon drippings or butter are added to vegetables during cooking.

• The more inner surface of the fruit or vegetable exposed to water and air, the greater will be the nutrient loss in cooking. Cook vegetables whole or in large pieces.

• Many of the nutrients are near the surface of the vegetable. If the skin must be removed, cut as little of the vegetable as possible when paring

known to have worshipped the plant. Long ago in Ireland it was believed that fairies joined hands and danced in rings each night. The circles of mushrooms—or "fairy rings"—that sprang up overnight were thought to be their tracks.

You should never eat mushrooms unless you know they are safe. Some are poisonous. Some are not.

Meatless Eaters: Vegetarians

A *vegetarian* is a person who eats no animal flesh. Many vegetarians do eat eggs and milk products in addition to vegetables, fruits, nuts, grains, and seeds. These are called *lacto-ovo-vegetarians*. But some eat only food from plants. These are called *vegans*.

The idea of a meatless diet is not new. In the sixth century B.C., the Greek philosopher Pythagoras tried to convince his countrymen not to eat meat. But modern vegetarianism did not begin until 1847, when the Vegetarian Society of Manchester, England, first used the word.

There are many reasons why people choose to become vegetarians. These include:

• *religious beliefs:* Hindus, Buddhists, and others have strict religious laws restricting meat eating.
• *moral beliefs:* Many people think it is wrong to kill animals.
• *health reasons:* Today animals are treated with chemicals. Also, meat is colored and preserved with additives that some say may cause harm to humans. Meat is also high in fats and cholesterol and is difficult to digest.

(continued)

Vegetables can be prepared many different ways. They combine easily with other vegetables as well as with other kinds of foods. Their colors add appeal to meals.

it. Paring vegetables after cooking saves the most nutrients.

• Many vegetables, such as cabbage and spinach, contain acid that will destroy the color during the cooking process. To prevent this color loss, cook these vegetables as rapidly as possible. Leave the pan uncovered so that the acid may pass off in the steam.

• Baking soda will destroy some vitamins. It should not be added to vegetables, even though it will shorten the necessary cooking time.

• To preserve food value and flavor, cook vegetables only until tender.

• Do not overcook such vegetables as cabbage and onions. Overcooking causes their flavor to become strong and unpleasant.

These facts are the basis for the following guidelines for cooking vegetables and fruits. Follow these guidelines to get the best flavor and nutrition from your cooked vegetables and fruits.

• Leave vegetables and fruits whole when cooking them, or cut them into large pieces only.
• Do not soak vegetables and fruits, especially after they have been peeled.
• Cook vegetables and fruits in a small amount of water. Watch them to prevent burning.
• Cover the pan as vegetables or fruits cook, except when cooking strong-flavored vegetables or fruits.
• Start vegetables and fruits in rapidly boiling water. Cook them as quickly and briefly as possible.

• Serve the cooking liquid with the vegetable or fruit, or save it to use in sauces or soups.

Some fruits, such as pared apples and peeled bananas, turn brown if left out in the air. To prevent this, dip them into an acid liquid such as lemon juice or pineapple juice. There are commercial products on the market that are a mixture of ascorbic acid (vitamin C) powder and sugar. This mixture can be sprinkled directly onto the sliced fruit. You can also mix it with water and add it to the fruit to keep the fruit from browning.

Adding sugar to the cooking water helps preserve the shape of a fruit. If you are cooking fruit to use in a salad or as a garnish, add the sugar early in the cooking process. If you are making applesauce, add the sugar after the fruit has cooked to a softened state.

a quick review

1. How are vegetables classified? Can you name some from each category?
2. What are the basic things to look for when you are buying fruits and vegetables?
3. What are five facts to remember when cooking fruits and vegetables?
4. How can you keep sliced fruit from browning?

• *financial reasons:* Compared to other protein sources, meat is very expensive.
• *world hunger:* Many people think that meat production is inefficient because it takes so much grain to raise meat-producing animals. For every 4.5 kilograms (10 pounds) of grain that beef cattle eat, they produce only 450 grams (1 pound) of meat.

Vegans must be sure to get enough protein. This can be done by eating a great variety of grains, nuts, legumes and other vegetables, and fruits.

Vegans must also be certain to get enough vitamin B12, which comes mostly from animal products, as well as calcium and iron. This can be done by taking vitamin and mineral supplements.

▶ **Words to Know**
fruit: That part of a plant that appears after the flower.
vegetable: A plant grown because parts of it can be eaten.
versatile: Having many uses.

CHAPTER 68
Breads and Cereals

Since the earliest times, people have grown cereals and harvested their seeds for food. In early times, cereal grains were pounded or ground, mixed with liquid, and cooked into little cakes or crackers. Modern breads such as tortillas from Mexico are still made in this manner.

At first, whole grains were used in bread making, just as they sometimes are today. Whole grain flour makes delicious, nutritious bread. However, there are two problems involved in using whole grain flour. First, the bread is somewhat dark and coarse in texture. Second, whole grain cereal products are apt to spoil quickly. This is because the *germ,* or life-giving portion of the seed, is relatively high in fat.

Over time, ways were found to remove the *bran,* which is the hard outer coating of cereal grains. Milling techniques were also developed to remove the germ. These milling techniques leave the soft, whitish grain center, which can be ground into very fine particles. The finely ground product is then called *white flour,* or *refined flour.* Refined flour, with the germ removed, makes breads that keep better than those made with whole grain flours. These breads also have a much finer texture.

A problem with refined flour is that it is the bran and the germ in grain that contain most of the B vitamins, iron, and roughage. Most of this food value is removed when the grain is refined. The nutrients must be put back in the flour if it is to be nourishing. Flour to which the iron and vitamins of the bran and germ have been restored is called *enriched flour.* The federal government has set standards for enrichment. Manufacturers who use the word *enriched* must follow these standards. The highly nutritious wheat germ is packaged and sold separately. People buy it to sprinkle on cereals or fruits or to add to homebaked products.

TYPES OF CEREAL PRODUCTS

We often think of cereal as breakfast food only, but it is hard to plan a meal that does not include at least one kind of cereal product. Rice, macaroni products, and all breads are cereal products. Sauces and gravies are often thickened with cereal.

Bread. Bread is the most frequently eaten cereal product. Modern breads come ready prepared, partially prepared, or in mix form. These breads save time, have uniform quality, and add variety to meals. Homemade bread is easy to make if you understand the basic principles involved and have the necessary time available. Cookbooks separate breads into *yeast breads* and *quick breads.* Yeast breads

Many quick breads contain fruits and nuts. This adds both nutrients and calories. Banana bread and date nut bread are examples.

contain yeast and take time to *rise,* or become light and larger. Quick breads do not contain yeast. They rise because of baking powder or baking soda. They do not take as long to rise, which is why they are called "quick."

Amazing Bread Fact:
The longest loaf of bread ever baked was 205.3 meters (684 feet 6 inches) long. It was baked in Australia in 1978.

467

Breakfast in a Bowl: Cereal

Grains were cultivated in Central Asia as early as 5000 B.C. These were eaten both moist and dry, just as cereal is today.

The word *cereal* comes from the Roman goddess of grain, called Ceres. Each year from April 12 to 19, the Romans honored Ceres with a festival called the *Cerealia*. The aim was to win Ceres' favor so that she would protect farmers from drought and provide good harvests.

Cereal provides more food energy for less work than any other crop. Cereal products made from wheat, oats, rice, and corn fill more than 20 billion breakfast bowls in the United States each year.

The average person in the United States eats about 3.6 kilograms (8 pounds) of corn flakes every year. Corn flakes were invented by Dr. John Kellogg and his brother, Will. They wanted an easily digestible food for patients in a hospital. They had no idea that their invention would become such a hit.

Many nutrients are destroyed when the cereals are processed, although since 1941 manufacturers have been restoring iron and some of the B vitamins. Today many cereals are sprayed with additional synthetic vitamins.

Breakfast Cereals.   Many people in the United States are used to eating cereal for breakfast. Cereal is a good energy food to start the day, but that is not the only time you can eat it.

Some of the breakfast cereals on the market are already cooked. These are called *ready-to-eat cereals*. When you buy ready-to-eat cereals, you pay extra for the precooking and for the convenience of not having to prepare them yourself. These cereals provide a quick breakfast or snack.

Oatmeal and cream of wheat are common hot breakfast cereals. These cereals are cooked in water or other liquids. Many of them have been processed to cook in a very few minutes. When buying such cereals, notice whether the package is labeled regular, quick-cooking, or instant. If it is labeled quick-cooking, you will need to cook it only a short time. If it is labeled instant, all you need to do is add boiling water.

Other Cereal Products.   Macaroni, spaghetti, noodles, and rice are also cereal products. Rice and other cereal grains such as buckwheat are often used in casseroles.

PREPARING CEREALS

The main purpose of cooking cereal is to soften the starch in it for easier digestion. If you follow the cooking guidelines on the package, your cereal dishes will have the texture and appearance that you want.

Cereals.   When you cook a cereal, you need to take certain steps so that it will not be lumpy. Before you begin, read the package directions. Follow them carefully.

In most cases, you pour the cereal into boiling water. The important step is to pour slowly and stir constantly. If you pour the cereal in all at once, it will probably stick together in lumps. Also, if you do not keep stirring, the starch in the cereal will again probably stick together in lumps. It is also important to measure accurately and to time the cooking carefully.

When you have finished cooking the cereal, fill the pan with cold water and let it soak for a few minutes. This will make the pan easier to clean later by keeping the cereal from drying and sticking to the sides of the pan.

BUYING CEREALS

Hot cereal usually costs less than cold cereal. However, the amount of nutrients in different cereals varies considerably. Read the label to see what nutrients are found in each product. If a nutritional claim is made in the advertising, the label must state how many grams of protein, fat, and carbohydrate there are per serving, and the size of the serving. The label must also state the amount of vitamins and minerals per serving. This is shown as a percentage of the recommended daily allowance for that particular nutrient.

A cereal product must also carry an ingredient list showing all the ingredients that it contains. The ingredient that is present in the largest amount is listed first. The others follow in descending order. This list is especially helpful for finding out how much sugar is contained in a cereal product. In many cereals, sugar is the leading ingredient. Too much sugar in the diet of people in this country is considered to be one of the major causes of tooth decay.

When buying cereal, be sure to compare the prices of different-sized packages and of different brands. Try

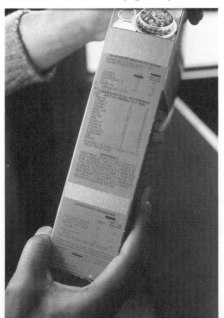

Nutrition labeling is usually printed on cereal boxes. The nutrients in different cereals vary greatly.

different brands to see if you can tell the difference. If not, you should buy the less expensive one. If you can tell the difference, you have to decide which is more important to you, price or quality.

PREPARING BREAD

Bread is made from flour, liquid, shortening, sugar, eggs, and leavening. In yeast bread, the *leavening agent* is yeast. The leavening agent causes the bread to *rise,* or to increase in volume. This increase takes time. Some yeast breads take up to 4 hours to make. Others can be prepared a day ahead and left in the refrigerator up to 48 hours before baking. There are many varieties of yeast bread, including homemade white bread, commercial white bread, raisin bread, whole wheat bread, and French bread.

Quick breads get their name from the fact that they take less time to prepare than yeast breads. Usually the leavening agent is baking powder. But sometimes baking soda or air is the leavener. Examples of quick breads include muffins, biscuits, coffee cakes, nut breads, popovers, pancakes, and waffles.

BUYING BREAD

Whether buying commercially prepared bread, a bread mix, or ingredients to make bread, it is helpful to do some comparison shopping. Compari-

Other Kinds of Noodle Products

Spaghetti, macaroni, and noodles have many interesting relatives.

• *Spinach noodles* are green noodles that have spinach as an ingredient. There is a light hint of spinach in the taste.

• *Whole wheat noodles* are brown noodles made from whole wheat flour. The texture is just a bit grainier than that of white-flour noodles.

• *Egg noodles* are noodles that contain more eggs than other noodles. They have a rich flavor and are more yellow in appearance.

• *Manicotti noodles* are large, fat, hollow noodles that are often filled with a vegetable or cheese mixture after cooking.

• *Ravioli* are flat, square noodles with a slit. In that slit is put meat, cheese, or vegetable filling.

• *Lasagna noodles* are long, wide, thick noodles that are layered together after cooking with meat, cheese, and tomato sauce to create a very popular and delicious main dish called lasagna.

Amazing Bread Fact:

In ancient Egypt, if a baker ruined his bread, he could be killed.

1. Mix together the dry ingredients.

2. In a separate bowl, mix the liquid ingredients.

4. Fill the greased muffin tins ⅔ full. Bake until a wooden toothpick inserted in the middle of a muffin comes out clean.

3. Add the liquid ingredients to the dry ingredients and stir only until all ingredients are combined. The mixture will be lumpy.

5. The finished product looks like this. The top is only slightly rounded. If the top is pointed, it is due to overmixing.

6. There should be no large holes inside the muffin.

STEPS IN PREPARING BISCUITS

1. Measure dry ingredients and cut in shortening.

2. Add milk.

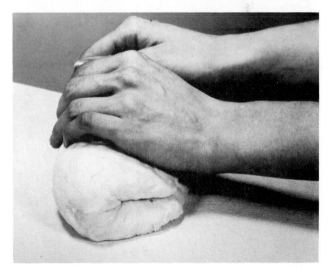

3. Stir until all ingredients are blended.

4. Knead.

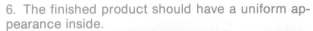

5. Roll out dough on a floured cloth and cut into desired shapes. Place on a greased baking sheet and bake until lightly browned.

6. The finished product should have a uniform appearance inside.

Comparing Ingredient Labels for Ready-to-eat Cereals and Cooked Cereals

One of the most important things you can do when shopping for cereals is read the ingredient labels.

Food manufacturers are required by law to list the ingredients in their products in the order of how much is used. In other words, if a lot of one ingredient is used, it will be at or near the top of the list. Look at the ingredients of a cereal you know is sweet tasting. Sugar is probably one of the top two ingredients. Now look at the ingredients of a cereal that looks as if it may have very little sugar. Sugar is still fairly high on the list!

Several of the heavily sweetened cereals also contain many chemicals and additives, which tend to make the price of these cereals fairly high. Some of these additives are there to keep the cereal fresh over a long time. Others make the cereal more nutritious.

Now look at the list of ingredients of a cereal that needs to be cooked. You probably won't see sugar or a lot of chemicals listed. Cooked cereals do not need additives to keep them crisp.

This balanced breakfast is made up of orange juice, cereal with fruit and milk, toast, butter or margarine, and hot chocolate.

son shopping involves taking the following steps before buying:

• comparing prices of the same product in different stores
• comparing prices of different brands in the same store
• comparing the flavor, appearance, and nutritive content of different products and different brands

After making these comparisons, decide which product is the best buy for you. It may be the least costly, the best tasting, the best looking, or some combination of these.

PREPARING OTHER CEREAL PRODUCTS

Spaghetti, macaroni, and noodles are all cooked in the same way. Fill a large pan with water and bring it to a *rapid boil*. Water is at a rapid boil when it bubbles vigorously in the middle. You should have 6 to 7 liters (6 to 7 quarts) of water for each 450 grams (1 pound) of noodle product you are cooking. Add to the water 15 milliliters (1 tablespoon) of salt and 15 milliliters (1 tablespoon) of vegetable oil. The oil helps keep the noodles from sticking together. Add the noodles, spaghetti, or macaroni to the boiling water slowly, taking care to keep the water boiling. To keep the water boiling, add the noodles or spaghetti strands a few at a time. Do not add them all at once. Time the cooking very carefully according to your recipe or the directions on the package. When the noodles are tender but still firm, they are done. Drain off the water carefully or pour it and the noodles into a colander. The spaghetti, macaroni, or noodles are now ready to serve or combine with sauces or other foods. *Hint:* If you are cooking macaroni or noodles for a casserole that will be baked, take a few minutes off the cooking time. That way you will not overcook the noodles during the baking stage.

There are several types of rice available in most areas. These include brown rice, long grain, and raw white

Noodle products come in a variety of shapes and sizes.

rice. Several types of processed rice are also available. To cook these, follow package directions.

Rice expands during cooking, so 0.25 liter (1 cup) of raw white rice will yield 0.75 liter (3 cups) of cooked rice. Processed rices do not expand so much, as they have already been partially cooked.

For each cup of raw white rice you want to cook, put 0.5 liter (2 cups) of water into a pan. For each cup of brown rice, use 0.6 liter (2½ cups) of water. Add about 4 milliliters (¾ teaspoon) of salt and, if you like, 15 milliliters (1 tablespoon) of butter. Bring the water to a boil. Then, stirring the

Storing Bread and Restoring Freshness to It

Many people keep bread in a special container called a bread box. The purpose of a bread box is to keep bread cool and dry, which helps it stay fresh. If you do not have a bread box, you can keep bread easily in tightly sealed plastic bags. Bread can also be stored in the freezer for several months. Stale bread can be freshened very easily. Wrap it in foil and seal tightly. Then heat it in a warm, about 71 to 93°C (150 to 200°F) oven for 20 to 25 minutes.

473

Rice is often used in combination with other foods.

BUYING OTHER CEREAL PRODUCTS

There are about 200 different varieties of noodles, spaghetti, and macaroni. The best way to become familiar with these is to experiment with the different sizes and shapes and determine which ones you prefer. Then compare prices among different brands and in different stores.

Different types of rice vary in their nutritive value, cooking time, and price.

Regular white rice is lower in nutritive value. For this reason, many manufacturers add vitamins and minerals to make the rice *enriched.*

Precooked or instant rice is rice that has been cooked, then dried and packaged. It takes only a short time to cook but is usually more expensive than regular rice. Rice can also be purchased in flavored mixes.

Brown rice is very nutritious and has a nutty flavor. It takes longer to cook than regular rice.

Wild rice is usually the most expensive.

▶ Words to Know
cereal products: A group of foods made from grain. They include breakfast cereals, rice, and noodles.
enriched flour: Refined flour with iron and vitamins added.
leavening agent: An ingredient that makes baked products rise.
quick bread: A bread that does not use yeast as the leavening agent.
refined flour: Flour with the bran and germ removed. Also called *white flour.*
rise: In baking, to become larger and lighter.

boiling water, add the rice slowly so the boiling does not stop. Cover the pan and turn the heat down low. Stir the rice occasionally. White rice will cook in 25 to 30 minutes. Brown rice will take 40 to 50 minutes, or until all the water is absorbed.

a quick review

1. What is the difference between refined flour and enriched flour?
2. What is the difference between yeast breads and quick breads? Give two examples of each.
3. When is a cereal manufacturer required to put nutritional labeling on a package?
4. What is comparison shopping?

474

In 1979 people in the United States ate an average of 41 kilograms (91 pounds) of refined sugar per person. There is growing concern about the effect all this sugar has on our health. Fats, too, are eaten in great amounts by people in this country. While some fat is needed in our diets, too much fat has been shown to cause serious problems for the heart and the circulatory system.

SUGAR

Sugar is available in solid and liquid forms. Most of the sugars in use have been refined and processed from sugar beets and sugarcane plants.

Granulated sugar is the most familiar form of sugar. It is what most people in the United States put into their sugar bowls. It comes from sugar beets or sugarcane. It has many uses. When a recipe calls for "sugar," it means granulated sugar.

Brown sugar is granulated sugar with molasses added to it. The more molasses it contains, the darker the color and the stronger the flavor. Brown sugar is used in many baked goods to add color and flavor.

Confectioner's sugar, or powdered sugar, is very finely processed sugar that looks like fine white flour. Confectioner's sugar can be made at home by putting granulated sugar in a blender jar and blending at high speed for a few seconds. Confection-

Facts About Sugar

• Sugar was known in India as early as 3000 B.C. In ancient China, sugarcane juice was dried and called stone honey. During the Middle Ages, honey was a popular food since it was the by-product of the beeswax needed for candles. In Italy in the 1500s, sugar sculptures were sometimes used as centerpieces.

• Each person in the United States eats an average of 41 kilograms (91 pounds) of refined sugar per year. This compares with about 4.5 kilograms (10 pounds) per person in some developing countries.

• All green plants make sugar, but most of the sugar you eat comes from sugarcane or sugar beets. *Fructose* is fruit sugar. *Maltose* is malt sugar. *Lactose* is milk sugar. *Glucose,* found in fruits and vegetables, is also called blood sugar. In the body, other sugars are broken down into glucose.

• When you eat a lot of sugar, your pancreas sends insulin into your bloodstream to work on it. After a time, this process greatly lowers your blood sugar. When this happens, you may feel tired, nervous, or depressed. Some doctors think that many emotional and mental problems are really the
(continued)

476

Many fruits are made into jams and jellies. Most of these products are very high in sugar.

er's sugar is used mostly for frostings and candies.

Honey, made by bees, is sold in two forms: extracted as a liquid and on the honeycomb. It has a greater sweetening ability than sugar, but it gives a chewy texture to baked goods. It has about as many uses as granulated sugar. If it *crystallizes* (becomes solid) in the jar, you can put the jar in warm water and melt the honey back down to liquid form.

Molasses is the juice that is made from boiling sugarcane. It is not as sweet as sugar. Table molasses is light in color. Blackstrap molasses is dark in color.

Syrups are liquid sugars made from maple, cane, and corn. They have many different uses. Maple syrup is made from the sap of maple trees. It is used to make candy or maple sugar, or as a topping for pancakes. Cane syrup is made from the sap of sugarcane. It is a substitute for molasses. It is also used as a sweetener in many processed foods. Corn syrup is made from corn. It can be purchased as light corn syrup or dark corn syrup. It is used in jellies and processed foods.

Many experts feel that people in this country eat too much sugar for good health. You can easily cut down on the amount of sugar you consume by eating apples, bananas, or other fruit instead of cake or cookies. Drink fruit juice instead of carbonated beverages, and try to stay away from candy.

Sugar is an ingredient in many recipes, especially for baked goods. Always use the type of sugar that your recipe calls for. Since different sugars have different textures and sweetening abilities, the kind you use has a great effect on the flavor, texture, and appearance of the final product.

FATS

Fats add flavor to foods, tenderize foods, and give baked items their appetizing brown color. There are several different forms of fat used in cooking. Liquid fats are called *oils*. *Vegetable oils* are extracted from different seeds (sunflower, soybean, corn), fruits (coconut, olive), and nuts (peanut, hickory, walnut). Processing makes these oils very much alike in taste. However, many oils cannot take the high heats of some types of cooking. They begin smoking or burning before high heat is reached. They are therefore said to have "low smoking points."

Solid fats include butter, margarine, and shortening. *Butter* is made from cream. It gives a rich, sweet taste to baked goods. *Margarine* is a butter substitute. It is usually made from milk and vegetable oils. When used in cooking, it produces only a slightly different taste from that of butter. It is usually less expensive than butter. *Shortening* is a solid form of fat. It is made from different types of oils, including corn, peanut, and soybean. Shortening is ideal for baking because it produces a soft, delicate texture. It can be used as a substitute for butter in baking. It is less expensive than butter or margarine.

Many people in the United States eat too much fat. Extra fat is hard for the body to handle. Eventually it can endanger your health. A very easy way to cut down on the fat in your diet is to stop eating a lot of fried foods. Snack items such as potato chips have a high fat content. Cut down on pastries and other sweet baked items because in addition to fat, they also contain a lot of sugar. When cooking meat, trim away the extra fat. Some meats, such as bacon, sausages, and hamburgers, can be put on paper towels before they are served to "blot" away extra fat.

Many different types of recipes call for fats. Salad dressings, for example, use fats as a basic ingredient because their oily quality helps the dressing coat the salad. Vegetable oil or olive oil is generally used for salads.

Many foods, including meats, vegetables, and pastries, can be *deep fat fried,* or fried in a large amount of fat.

result of the body's inability to handle too much sugar. In addition to depression and nervousness, a craving for sweets, certain allergies, an inability to concentrate, and low blood pressure may also be results of eating too much sugar.

• Eating too much sugar can do great physical damage, too. In Natal, South Africa, the local Indian population eats nine times as much sugar as the Indians of India. The South African Indians have the highest diabetes rate in the world.

• Eating large amounts of sugar has also been linked to heart disease, hardening of the arteries, and, of course, tooth decay. Sugar, including honey, slows down the stomach's juices and lessens the stomach's ability to move. As a result, digesting other foods becomes more difficult. Digesting sugar also robs the body of B vitamins.

• Sugar is a very concentrated food. Eating 140 grams (5 ounces) of sugar a day is like eating 1125 grams (2½ pounds) of sugar beets a day.

Deep fat frying gives foods a special flavor and a generally tender texture. Shortening and most vegetable oils can be used for deep fat frying.

Pan frying is another method of cooking with fat. In pan frying, foods are fried in a small amount of fat, usually vegetable oil or shortening.

CAKES

Cakes contain many of the same ingredients as breads, but in different amounts. More eggs and sugar are used in cakes.

Cakes can be divided into those with shortening and those without. Most cakes with shortening have baking powder or baking soda as leaveners. Most cakes without shortening have air as a leavener.

Many people like to use commercial cake mixes. These mixes are easy to use and save time and energy. You can also buy many different kinds of frozen cakes.

COOKIES

Cookies can be served as dessert or snacks or used as gifts. Many people enjoy baking fancy cookies for special holidays.

Cookies are made from many of the same ingredients as breads or cakes. Usually, however, more short-

Deep-fat fried foods contain more fat and calories than the same foods cooked other ways. To avoid accidents, be alert when deep fat frying.

ening and sugar are added than are put into other baked goods. You can mix up your own cookie dough, or you can buy frozen cookie dough that is ready to bake. Packaged cookie mixes are also available for many different types of cookies.

PIES

Pies, unlike cakes and cookies, are not usually divided into groups. There are two-crust pies and one-crust pies. Two-crust pies are often filled with fruits such as apples and blueberries. One-crust pies are sometimes baked with the filling. Pumpkin pie is an example. Other pies use a baked pie shell. That is, the crust is baked by itself. Then the filling is added. Lemon meringue pie is an example.

Piecrusts are very important to good pies. They are usually made with flour, salt, shortening, and water. The shortening makes the crust tender and flaky. And it gives a golden brown color.

Making your own piecrust is not difficult if you follow the recipe exactly. Piecrust mixes are available in different forms. Usually you just need to add the liquid and shape the crust. Also available are frozen piecrusts, ready to be baked and filled.

Piecrusts can also be made from crushed graham crackers or cookies. These crumb crusts are most often used with cream, custard, or pudding pies. Making piecrusts becomes easier with experience. Follow these tips:

• Roll the pie dough on a lightly floured pastry board.

• Roll the dough from the center out, lifting the rolling pin at the edge.

• Use metal pie pans with a dull finish for even browning. Glass pie pans also work very well.

a quick review

1. What are four different forms of sugar?
2. How do cakes, cookies, and bread differ?
3. Why is fat used in cooking?
4. Why should you reduce the amount of sugar and fat in your diet? List several ways to do so.

▶ **Words to Know**

brown sugar: Granulated sugar with molasses.
butter: Fat made by beating cream.
cholesterol: A fatty substance found in foods from animal sources.
confectioner's sugar: A very fine sugar, also called powdered sugar.
corn syrup: A liquid sugar made from corn.
deep fat frying: Cooking in enough fat to completely cover the food.
fructose: Natural sugar found in fruit.
glucose: A sugar found naturally in many foods.
granulated sugar: Table sugar.
honey: A sweet substance made from the nectar of flowers by bees.
margarine: A solid fat often used in place of butter.
molasses: A thick, brown syrup separated from raw sugar in the manufacture of sugar.
oil: A liquid fat.
processed foods: Foods that have been treated in some way before reaching the consumer.
refined sugar: Sugar that has all of the molasses removed so that it is white.
shortening: A soft solid fat.
syrup: Liquid sugar.

CHAPTER 70

Regional Foods of the United States

Imagine a huge countrywide fair that featured all the foods people eat everywhere in the United States. It would be a wonderful display. No other country anywhere has drawn its people from so many different parts of the world. English settlers began arriving here in the early 1600s. Other early settlers were the Dutch, Spanish, Italians, and French. Various African peoples have also long been in this country. All of these peoples brought special ideas about food. Each group brought a love for certain ingredients and spices and herbs, along with unique food dishes. Later, groups of immigrants came from Eastern Europe. Chinese immigrants settled in New York and San Francisco, creating two major Chinese communities where their styles of cooking were offered. Eventually other groups came to America, too.

Who settles in a *region,* or area, what kind of climate it has, and what crops can be grown there all have a strong influence on local foods. Today each major region of the United States is known for its food *specialties,* which are foods popular in that particular area. Most major cities are also known for their variety of ethnic foods.

King crab is more plentiful in its native Alaska than in the other forty-nine states. Other foods in this buffet are fiddlehead ferns, hollandaise sauce, Russian rye bread and mushrooms, cranberry catsup, red cabbage, and wild blueberry cake.

THE NORTHEAST AND MIDDLE ATLANTIC STATES

Long, cold winters in the Northeast led to much salting and drying of foods. The summer growing season is long enough for many vegetables to be grown. Maple trees give syrup to use on top of plentiful berries that grow throughout the area. The berries were also used to make jams and jellies. Clam chowder is a popular dish. Another popular meal is the *New England boiled dinner.* It consists of boiled corned beef and vegetables. Dried corn is used in many dishes, such as johnnycakes, puddings, and mush.

Parts of the Northeast coastline and the Middle Atlantic States are known for their seafood—clams, scallops, lobsters, and many kinds of fish. The Middle Atlantic States are also the home of the Pennsylvania Dutch. Among their favorite foods are apple

Foods the First Settlers Found

The first permanent white settlers in the United States encountered many plants and animals that were unlike anything they had ever seen before. When they did encounter a familiar food, such as salmon or strawberries, they were amazed at its size.

The coastal waters of the New World contained lobsters and clams, along with trout, cod, mackerel, and bass. There was plenty of game, too, including raccoon, bear, deer, and rabbit.

To go with these foods, the people found blackberries and raspberries, among other things. There were also wild mushrooms. The settlers soon learned to grow such vegetables as sweet corn, squash, and beans.

Despite these findings, the first settlers barely made it through the first year, for they did not know which foods could be eaten safely.

Gradually, the settlers learned enough from the Native Americans and from their own experiments to survive on their own.

Creole Cookery

Creole cooking, which is native to New Orleans and the surrounding area, is one of the best known of regional United States cooking styles. It combines French, African, Native American, and Spanish food. From the French, it takes cooking methods and the names of most of its recipes. For example, fish is often cooked *en papillote,* or in a sauce and wrapped in a paper bag. *Bouillabaisse,* an elaborate fish stew, is another creole specialty.

The African influence is shown in the long hours of simmering stews in a large pot and in the use of okra, a green African vegetable that also functions as a thickener in gumbo, a stew or hearty soup.

The Choctaws, a Native American people from Alabama and Mississippi, discovered the use of filé, which is ground sassafras leaves. Filé works as a thickener in gumbos much the same way that okra does.

The Spanish contributed tomatoes, peppers, and the idea of combining meat, poultry, and rice in one dish.

Other specialties in creole cooking include crawfish, soft-shell crab, and a combination of rice, beans, and vegetables.

butter, bread-and-butter pickles, watermelon-rind pickles, green-tomato relish, pickled eggs or hard-boiled eggs in beet juice, and an array of desserts and baked goods.

THE SOUTH

Southerners take great pride in their Southern-style cooking. Among the foods that Southern cooks work with are chicken, pork, rice, and such vegetables as okra, corn, beans, and sweet potatoes. Traditional Southern dishes include fried chicken; sugar-cured, smoked ham; spare ribs; pigs' feet prepared with greens; spoonbread; and hoppin' john, which is a combination of black-eyed peas, rice, and beans. Pecan pie is another Southern specialty. Southern cooking also includes soul and creole food.

THE MIDWEST

The Midwest is frequently called the "breadbasket of the nation" because much of the U.S. food supply comes from its fields. Beef, pork, and lamb are plentiful. There are also many dairy farms. Farmers need a heavy breakfast before they take on a day's work, so eggs, bacon, cereal, and toast are a common breakfast. A typical Midwestern dinner consists of steak, fresh corn on the cob, fresh sliced tomatoes, baking-powder biscuits, and strawberry shortcake. It should come as no surprise that Midwestern cooks "put away," or can, the

food that is not eaten right away. Throughout the winter, people eat corn relish, pickles, tomatoes, and green beans that were canned or frozen in the summer.

THE SOUTHWEST

Texas is known for its chili, which is thought to have been invented in San Antonio sometime after the Civil War. Many Texans like their chili extraordinarily hot, and they would never put beans in it. Texans also eat kid, or young goat, which they barbecue. Much of the Southwest is known for Tex-Mex food, a special blend of American and Mexican food that developed along the border between the two countries. Tex-Mex food, like chili, is highly spiced. Favorite dishes are made with tortillas and chilies. Other Tex-Mex foods include little desserts served with honey, called *sopapillas.* These are fried dough. The Southwest has a hot, dry climate, which, as in so many other cultures, may account for the love of hot food. Spicy foods make people sweat, and people in hot climates need that.

THE WEST AND NORTHWEST

The West and Northwest of the United States were settled last and by more different peoples than any other region in the country. However, these regions have fewer food specialties

In New England, clambakes are popular along the coast.

Barbecues

Although barbecuing is common in several other countries, such as Greece and Turkey, it is a style of cooking that most people think of as belonging especially to the United States. Whether or not this is so, it is a favorite pastime in this country and has been almost since the first settler set foot on North American soil.

Barbecuing is a method of cooking meat and other foods over an open fire. The Native Americans were barbecuing long before the first European settlers arrived, and they taught the settlers how to use this cooking method with the wild game that was so plentiful in North America at that time.

Texans are the people who have the greatest reputation for barbecuing. A typical menu at a Texas barbecue might include potato salad, cole slaw, corn on the cob, sourdough biscuits, and two very special barbecue sauces for the meat. One sauce is doused on the meat before and during cooking. The other sauce goes on the meat after it is cooked, right before it is eaten.

than any other. Perhaps by the time people moved west, they had forgotten about their ethnic foods. Instead, people in the West and Northwest eat all the wonderful food that lies right at their fingertips. They are great suppliers of fruits and vegetables to other parts of the United States. They also eat such local favorites as avocado, papaya, Chinese cabbage, and artichoke. Shrimp and salmon are caught in local waters and often served simply baked or grilled.

San Francisco has several special dishes of its own. One is *cioppino,* an excellent seafood stew with Spanish overtones. There is also tasty sourdough bread. San Francisco, like New York, has outstanding Chinese food, thanks to the large Chinese population.

In the past few years, buffalo (bison) has again become a popular meat in the West, mainly because it is raised locally. It remains to be seen whether or not the popularity of this meat will spread to other parts of the United States.

Alaska is known for several foods, including king crab, snow crab, and salmon. The arctic region of Alaska is not suitable for farming, but the climate in the southern region is surprisingly mild. The climate, combined with the extremely long summer days, produces huge vegetables—20-kilogram (50-pound) cabbages, rhubarb 120 centimeters (4 feet) tall, and huge tomatoes and strawberries.

THE HAWAIIAN ISLANDS

The climate in Hawaii is mild enough for farming, but the land is not well suited to it. Even so, Hawaii is the country's chief exporter of pineapple. Other popular Hawaiian foods include mangoes, papayas, coconuts, and *poi,* which is a paste made from the taro plant. There are many wonderful kinds of seafood in the waters around the islands, including mahi mahi, trout, black bass, and other fish that have been imported to Hawaiian waters. The Kona crab is considered a delicacy, and Kona coffee is known all over the world. Hawaiian dishes often combine meat and fish. Coconut is often found in climates where milk-giving animals are rare. Its milk is a cooking substitute for cow's milk, and coconut fat resembles butter.

Luaus are popular in Hawaii. They are elaborate feasts at which a stuffed pig is cooked outdoors and served with a wide variety of Hawaiian foods.

Although eating habits in the different parts of the United States have become increasingly uniform, each region does have its special foods and dishes. And the best way to sample these is to travel throughout the country, seeking out local foods wherever possible.

a quick review

1. What are some of the groups of people that have settled in the United States? What effect have they had on the foods you eat today?
2. How does climate affect the foods that are eaten in a particular region of the country?
3. Why is the Midwest called the "breadbasket of the nation"?
4. How did the climate in the Northeast affect the way its food customs developed?
5. What is Tex-Mex food? How did it get its name?

World foods vary from hot and spicy foods to very bland. Bland foods have very little taste. Many foods that you enjoy are also popular in other countries, where they may be prepared and served quite differently. Each country has special ways of combining available ingredients and special cooking processes. These methods of combining the available ingredients with particular methods of cooking make up the *cuisine,* or cooking style, of a particular region. You may have heard people speak of "French cuisine." The cuisine of a country is determined by the climate, the culture, and the geography of the country. Geography refers to physical characteristics such as mountains or flat plains. It can be fun to explore these different foods. This chapter will describe and show you some of the foods typical of various regions of the world. The way people live in these different regions is sometimes called their *culture.* A culture is the combination of the beliefs, lifestyles, and social characteristics of a group of people. A culture is usually associated with a particular geographic area.

CHAPTER 71
Foods of Other Cultures

African dishes are made mainly of fish and seafood, along with vegetables.

Chinese dishes include sweet and sour pork. Rice is served with most dishes.

AFRICA

There are many countries in Africa. Food customs vary considerably. In the barren wastelands, the natives eat wild berries along with any meat they can get by hunting. Near the seacoasts, fish and shellfish are plentiful.

Much African cooking relies on combinations of foods. For example, spices such as paprika, red pepper, ginger root, cinnamon, and nutmeg may be mixed with vegetables and lamb. This stew is usually served with rice.

Popular side dishes may include mangoes, grated cucumbers, mashed apricots, chopped carrots, dates, onions, or nuts. A flat wheat bread called pita bread is commonly served in Africa.

CHINA

Rice is the basic food of the Chinese diet. Vegetables are more important to a meal than meat. They are usually stir-fried, cooked over high heat for a short time. Vegetables help make the meal more economical. The Chinese eat very little beef. They do, however, eat pork. Sweet and sour pork is a common dish. Fish and other seafood are very popular along the coast.

Eggs are important in Chinese cooking. They are sometimes used in soup, such as *egg drop soup,* which is a chicken broth made with beaten eggs. The most common beverage is tea.

486

ENGLAND

English food is hearty and filling. Familiar fried eggs, bacon, sausage, and not-so-familiar fried bread make up a hearty breakfast.

Dinner, the main meal of the day, is often served at noon. It usually includes meat, potatoes, vegetables, and gravy. One of the more popular English dinners is roast beef with Yorkshire pudding. *Yorkshire pudding* is a quick bread similar to a popover, baked in the drippings of a roast. *Fish and chips,* fried fish served with potatoes similar to french fries and wrapped in newspaper, is another popular meal in England.

In the late afternoon, many English people enjoy tea with pastries.

FRANCE

The French are known for their cooking. They use a great many sauces. This often results in a high calorie content.

People often shop for fresh produce and bread every day. The main meal of the day is usually served at noon. A salad of crisp, fresh greens is often served at the beginning of a French dinner, usually as a separate course. One of the famous French specialties is *bouillabaisse,* a fish stew.

Pastries are very popular desserts in France. *Napoleons*—many-layered, cream-filled pastries—and *eclairs*—long pastries filled with cream—are two examples.

487

A common English meal is roast beef with Yorkshire pudding (shown at right and top).

France is known for fresh-food stands. Here fish and produce are displayed.

This German family is eating wiener schnitzel and knockwurst.

Curried dishes are popular in India. They are usually served in combination with rice.

GERMANY

The Germans' main meal of the day is at noon, but unlike the French, they rely on meat and potatoes as the basics. Their traditional wiener schnitzel—veal—and sauerbraten—a variation of pot roast—are very common, along with potato pancakes, red cabbage, and apple strudel. Other German basics include sausage and bread. The Germans are known for their sausages and cold cuts, which are usually part of the evening meal.

In Germany you can travel throughout the countryside ordering the same items and yet find very different tastes.

INDIA

Indian dishes use very spicy, hot sauces containing peppers and *curry,* a blend of different spices. Curry dishes are often served with minced meats, rice, nuts, and dried fruits. Many people in India do not eat meat of any kind. They are vegetarians and rely on foods such as lentils and yogurt for protein. Those who are not vegetarians rely on lamb as their main source of meat. Beef is not eaten because cattle are considered holy. Desserts often use yogurt and other milk products as a base.

Indians traditionally use their fingers to dip the meat and rice from sauce to sauce. It is customary for people to sit at large, low tables covered with many small dishes.

488

ITALY

There are great regional differences in Italian food. Southern Italy is known for its extensive use of tomato sauces. This is because farming conditions make meat expensive. So sauces are used to stretch the meat. Some of the popular foods are lasagna and spaghetti.

Northern Italy is a more fertile and industrialized area. Food is less expensive. White sauces are often used in place of tomato sauces, and meats are used more often.

Italians generally eat a small breakfast. The noon meal is the largest, and the evening meal is usually light.

JAPAN

Japan is an island with little room for grazing animals, so much of the food comes from the sea. Raw or steamed fish, as well as octopus, squid, and seaweed, are basics.

Rice is most important to the Japanese diet. It is steamed and served plain along with other foods. Many vegetables are produced in Japan, and they are often mixed together.

The Japanese, like the Chinese, cook most of their food in bite-sized pieces. Foods are steamed, broiled, or stir-fried. Many foods are prepared at the table.

Japanese food is traditionally served at low tables. Chopsticks are used. Soup is drunk from the cup rather than eaten with a spoon.

489

An assortment of Italian foods is shown here. Included are Italian bread, stuffed artichokes, roast turkey, spaghetti, and cheese-filled pastries.

In Japan, all foods except soups and finger foods are eaten with chopsticks.

Mexican dishes include tacos and gazpacho, a delicious tomato-based soup that is served cold.

Middle Eastern foods include shish kebab, baklava, and *chelo*, which is a special dish made with rice.

MEXICO

Peppers and corn are an important part of Mexican cooking. So are *tacos* and *enchiladas,* in which corn meal wrappers surround ground beef, hot tomato sauce, beans, and cheese.

Beans are another common food. *Refried beans* are beans that are cooked until soft, then mashed and fried. Often they are served with grated cheese.

The avocado, a bland-tasting fruit, is often used with other foods. *Guacamole* is a dip made from tomato, onion, and mashed avocado. It may be served with tortilla chips. Other common fruits are bananas, papayas, and pineapples.

MIDDLE EAST

The Middle East covers a large area including Iran, Iraq, Saudi Arabia, Lebanon, Turkey, and Egypt. These countries are hot and dry. Sheep and goats, which live easily in this climate, are the staple meat sources.

The basic ingredients in Middle Eastern cooking are eggplant, tomato, garlic, and green pepper. *Shish kebabs* are pieces of lamb broiled on a skewer with vegetables. *Dolmas* are ground lamb and spices wrapped in grape leaves. Rice is popular in the Middle East. Although many spices are used in cooking, the foods are not hot and spicy. Fruits such as figs, melons, and pomegranates are common desserts.

490

The United States Department of Agriculture (USDA) has set up several programs that are related to food. These programs include school and day-care feeding programs; the Women, Infants, and Children Program; the food stamp program; and programs for the elderly.

Public Law 94-105. Public Law (PL) 94–105 was passed by Congress in 1975. It has four parts: school lunches, school breakfasts, child-care food programs, and summer food programs. Under this law, the USDA is required to give funds to any qualifying school that requests them. Many schools are a part of this program. When a PL 94–105 program is adopted by a school, all children are eligible to participate.

When the first school lunch program was begun in 1946, it had two goals. The first was to meet the nutritional needs of school-age children. The second was to use up agricultural *surpluses*. Surpluses are excess farm crops or products that are not sold in the market. These goods are purchased by the government.

A school breakfast program was first established as the result of a 1966 congressional study. The study showed that millions of children in the United States were coming to school hungry. It also showed that children who did not eat breakfast

CHAPTER 72
Government Food Programs

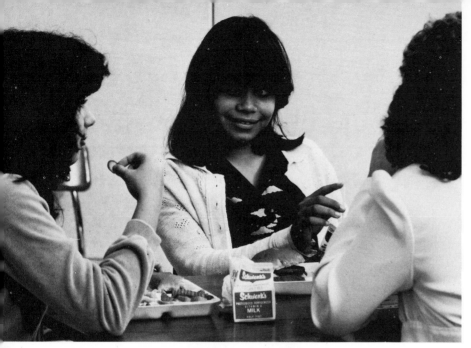

School lunch programs that receive federal funds must meet nutritional requirements. One of the requirements is that milk be served.

Food and the Aged
Many older people in this country are malnourished.

Some Solutions: Some elderly people have joined food cooperatives. A *food cooperative* is a group of people who join together to buy food wholesale. The members pay low prices for all items and receive an additional discount if they work.

Another solution is cooperative gardening. More and more older people are growing their own food on donated or rented farm plots. Seeds and plants are given by local businesses.

one school district. The program worked so well that it was expanded.

The USDA recognizes the need for a balanced meal. Therefore, it sends schools not only funds to buy food, but also lists of requirements of what must be served. These lists are updated from time to time. The chart on this page lists the current requirements for USDA school breakfast and lunch programs.

To help children not enrolled in the public school system, the law was expanded to include the Child-care Food Program. This program is for children who are attending a day-care center, a Head Start program, a recreation center, or a family day-care center. A Summer Food Program was also set up to meet children's nutritional needs when school is not in session. This program may be run by school districts, recreation centers, summer camps, churches, and other

were more restless, irritable, and less able to concentrate or learn than other children. Based on this information, a first program was started in

Requirements for School Breakfast and Lunch Programs

FOOD ITEM	BREAKFAST	LUNCH	
		Elementary	Secondary
Fluid milk	240 mL (1 c)	240 mL	240 mL
Fruit/juice Vegetable/juice	120 mL (½ c)	180 mL (¾ c)	240–360 mL (1–1½ c)
Bread	1 slice	1 slice	1–3 slices
Meat or alternate*	as often as possible	57 g (2 oz)	85 g (3 oz)

*egg, poultry, fish, cheese, peanut butter

community agencies. For an area to qualify to receive summer food, at least one-third of the children living there must be in the reduced-rate or free-meal category during the school year. The Child-care Food Program and the Summer Food Program may offer a combination of breakfast, lunch, dinner, and snacks. Sponsors are required to serve balanced meals similar to those outlined in the school breakfast and lunch programs.

WIC. WIC stands for the Women, Infants, and Children Program. Its aim is to supplement the diets of pregnant, breast-feeding, and *postpartum* women (women who have recently given birth), as well as those of infants and small children to the age of five. Aid is given to low-income women and children who are found to be not getting sufficient amounts of nutrients.

Food Stamps. This program was begun in 1961 to help low-income families get enough food for good nutrition. Local offices distribute coupons ("stamps") to qualifying families. Coupons are then exchanged at grocery stores for food.

Programs for the Elderly. The Older Americans Act of 1965 provides older people with funds to buy food. To qualify, a person must have a limited income and be over age 60.

Many communities offer food programs to the elderly. These programs offer nutritious food and companionship to older people.

a quick review

1. What four programs exist under Public Law 94–105?
2. What did a 1966 congressional study discover about schoolchildren and breakfast?
3. Which program helps newborn babies and their mothers?

CHAPTER 73
Careers in Foods and Nutrition

You already know that food is important to people's health and enjoyment. Because food is such a big part of our lives, the food industry is a very large one. People interested in working with food find many careers open to them. They also find many different ways to prepare for and enter those careers.

How do you know when a food career interests you? How do you know if you will be good at working with food? If you enjoy eating, that is a good sign. It means you like food, and it probably also means that you have a good sense of taste and smell. If you have tried cooking or other kinds of food preparation and found that you really liked the experience, that is another clue that a career in the food industry might be right for you.

This chapter contains brief descriptions of the general job areas in which a person may work with food. This chapter also describes many different kinds of careers in each area. In addition to what you learn here, more information may be found in the library. There you may read more about any food-related career that interests you.

Another good way to learn about careers in the food industry that interest you is to find a job working with food. You may even want to work in several areas with food before you de-

This commercial baker is preparing dinner rolls for a large hotel.

cide on the particular area that interests you and suits your skills.

Food careers generally fall into three groups. The first group is the *food service industry.* This group includes restaurants, cafés, cafeterias, food stands in parks and at baseball stadiums—anyplace where food is prepared and served to people. In a sense, grocery stores and other food stores are also part of the food service industry because they prepare and serve food to people. Grocery stores are also considered part of the food-processing industry, because they are the last stop in the food-processing chain that begins with the farmer.

The *food-processing industry* is the part of the food industry that deals with everything that happens to food from the time it is grown or raised until it reaches a place—either a res-

taurant or a grocery store—where it can be served or sold to the consumer.

The third major area of the food industry is *home economics.* People who work as home economists handle a variety of jobs, ranging from dietetics and nutritional planning to communications to education. Let us take a closer look at the jobs available in each category.

FOOD SERVICE INDUSTRY

Persons who work in the food service industry are often involved with food preparation. Some of these people, such as chefs or assistant chefs, have had special training. Other people with less training or no training at all may work at various stations, or departments, within the professional kitchen. For example, they may pre-

Career Ladder—Dietitian
Judy Van Train, Dietitian:
"When I started junior college, I had no idea what I wanted to do. I signed up for some home economics courses because I had enjoyed them and done well in them in high school. The first course I took was one in nutrition. It was very hard, but I liked it. More important, I discovered that I loved learning about food. I decided to major in foods and nutrition.

"After graduation, I worked for a large company testing recipes. I learned much there, but after a couple of years, I knew that I was more interested in working with people. So I decided to complete my internship in dietetics. That meant I had to work in a hospital, then join the American Dietetics Association and pass a national test. Boy, did I ever study for that test!

"I then took a job as a dietitian in another hospital. When patients are put on special diets for diseases, I plan menus for them.

"I have started to take some courses toward my master's degree. If I want to become a nutritionist at this hospital, I will need a master's degree. And with a master's, I could teach classes about nutrition either at the hospital or at the local college."

495

The equipment in this milk processing plant requires careful checking by technicians and engineers.

A Food Service Center Career Ladder
Kitchen helper (entry level)
Assistant cook (assistant level)
Cook (supervisory level)
Food service supervisor (managerial level)

What education and experience would a person need to begin at each of these levels and to move from one level to another?

pare soups and salads or set up dessert plates. Such persons earn little money in the beginning unless they have specialized or vocational training. However, with experience often comes more responsibility in the kitchen and better pay.

Other people who work in food service include waiters and waitresses, busboys, stewards, and table captains. Except for stewards and captains, these people need no special training. Entry-level jobs are easy to get, but more money is paid to experienced workers. There is little room for advancement. However, persons who work in this area of food service often move on to better restaurants, where the pay is also better.

Because cleanliness is so important wherever food is prepared, several kinds of workers are needed for sanitation occupations. These workers include dishwashers, pot scrubbers, and maintenance people, who completely clean the kitchen and food service area. These jobs do not pay well, but they also do not require any special training. There is not much advancement, and most persons who want more money find a new place to work.

Food service managers include restaurant owners, managers, executive chefs, other specially trained chefs, and dietitians. All these persons have special training, which may vary from vocational training and apprenticeship for chefs to a master's degree in business or home economics for the others. Advancement opportunities and pay are usually good. The hours are sometimes very long, and the work may involve much physical labor.

FOOD-PROCESSING INDUSTRY

Food processing begins with the farmer, who decides which food crops to plant and livestock to raise. The farmer is in charge of the food until it is sold to a distributor, if it is to be sold fresh, or to a food processor, if it is to be used in manufacturing a food item. Farming was once a major occupation in the United States, but now the number of farmers is shrinking every year. Most farms today are large, and much special equipment and heavy machinery is necessary to operate them. Until about a generation ago, most farmers passed their farms on to their children, who learned how to farm by helping with the farming chores. Today, however, many persons who manage large farms and ranches have college degrees in agriculture in addition to farming experience.

Many other careers are also available in food processing. Much work must be done in factories to make prepackaged, canned, or frozen foods. Large numbers of workers are needed to fill jobs in the factories. Home economists are needed for various duties, as are persons with business backgrounds, who serve as managers. Factory work requires little education after high school. With time and experience, you may handle jobs of greater responsibility right up to the position of plant manager.

Another area in which workers are needed is food transportation and distribution. Truck drivers are needed to transport food throughout the United States. Engineers and business managers are needed to plan the distribution of the food.

Wholesale and retail food stores are the final step in the food-process-

```
Patricia Vakos
322 McKinley
Anderson, Indiana 46016

Job Objectives:
Junior position working in res-
taurant management.

Job History:
Summer, 1980, worked as waitress in
delicatessen.  Did some food prep-
aration.  Summer, 1979, worked as
waitress at Lookout Resort.  Served
two meals daily and worked buffet
table on Saturdays.

Education:
High School junior specializing in
home economics.  Plan to go on to
college and study restaurant man-
agement.

References on Request.
```

```
                    322 McKinley
                    Anderson, Indiana 46016
                    May 12, 1982

Ms. Eileen Simcox
Manager
So Good Restaurant
12th and Jackson Streets
Anderson, Indiana 46016

Dear Ms. Simcox,

   I am writing to ask about the
possibility of obtaining a summer
job in your restaurant.
   I have just completed a course
in restaurant management, and I
am now interested in obtaining
some firsthand restaurant experi-
ence.
   I am available for interviews
any weekday after 4 p.m. and on
Saturday.  I hope we can meet to
discuss this matter further.
   I have enclosed a copy of my
resume, which will tell you more
about my experience.
                    Sincerely,
                    Patricia Vakos
                    Patricia Vakos
```

Résumé

A résumé is a sheet of paper that describes your work experience and education and the job you hope to get. A résumé should be neatly typed. A beginning résumé should run no longer than one page. On the left is a sample résumé.

Cover Letter

When you send a résumé to a possible employer, you should also send a cover letter. This is a very short letter stating that your résumé is enclosed and that you hope to be able to meet with the person to whom you are writing for further discussion about the job. On the left is a sample cover letter that might go with your résumé.

This nutritionist is teaching children about nutrients in foods. A parent of one of the students is assisting her for the day.

ing industry. They supply food to the consumer. Some specialized workers, such as butchers, work in grocery stores. Other workers generally have high school educations and little special training. The pay is low, but experience often brings increased pay and responsibility. It is not unusual for a checkout clerk to rise to the position of assistant manager in a grocery store.

HOME ECONOMICS

The last group of food-related careers is in home economics. Workers in this field have home economics degrees. Some have graduate degrees in home economics or in business, communications, or a related field.

Many home economists teach. Home economics courses are offered in college, high school, junior high school, and elementary school. Other home economists educate people through their work in communications or consumer affairs rather than through teaching in school. They write about food products and food uses for the consumer. Some of these people work on newspapers, writing feature articles about food, and others work for magazines that either specialize in food features or are entirely devoted to food. Home economists who work in communications may also work in private industry, writing promotional materials for food products or for industry organizations such as the Egg Council or the Meat Board. Many home economists work for large companies, where they may manage a food product or handle some other aspect of the food-processing industry. Sometimes they work in test kitchens developing recipes for products.

Another large group of home economists works in nutrition, dietetics, and food research. Most of these persons have degrees in foods and nutrition. To become a dietitian, you must have a college degree, serve an internship, and pass an examination. Nutritionists in hospitals are dietitians with advanced degrees who work in nutrition education. Researchers create new food products or new uses for foods and study new ways in which our bodies use food. These people usually have advanced degrees and a strong background in chemistry. Dietitians, nutritionists, and researchers work for hospitals, private businesses, medical schools, and community and public health organizations, as well as in diet therapy supervision, planning and managing special diets for others.

Many home economists also work for the Extension Service of the U.S. Department of Agriculture. They plan and teach classes on nutrition, home economics, consumer education, safety and health, and food management. Some extension home economists write educational materials published by the government. Extension home economists must have at least a bachelor's degree. Sometimes a master's degree is required.

As you can see, there are many directions and several ways to begin a food-related career. Many students work in some of the fields that are easy to enter before they make a final decision to study food in college.

a quick review

1. What are the three major areas of the food industry?
2. How can a worker gain more responsibility and money?
3. What kind of experience and education is needed to be a farmer? How has this changed over the last few years?
4. Where can you find out more about a specific career in which you are interested?

RESOURCES

- Recipes
- Recommended Daily Dietary Allowances
- Food Composition Tables
- Index

Meat, Fish, Poultry, Eggs, and Beans

The Hamburger Master Mix
Serves 4

Nutrition Information per Serving (approximate):
calories 360
protein 27 g
fat 16 g
carbohydrate 27 g
sodium 1540 mg

5 Meals
15 mL (1 tablespoon) butter or margarine
2.25 kg (5 pounds) ground beef
600 mL (2½ cups) chopped onion
240 mL (1 cup) chopped green pepper

1120 mL (5 cups) chopped celery
5 cans tomato soup, undiluted
2.1 kg (5 15-ounce cans) tomato sauce
25 mL (5 teaspoons) salt
2.5 mL (½ teaspoon) black pepper

1 Meal
5 mL (1 teaspoon) butter or margarine
454 g (1 pound) ground beef
120 mL (½ cup) chopped onion
45 mL (3 tablespoons) chopped green pepper
240 mL (1 cup) chopped celery
1 can tomato soup, undiluted
425 g (1 15-ounce can) tomato sauce
5 mL (1 teaspoon) salt
dash of black pepper

1. Melt butter or margarine over low heat in 8-quart skillet or pot.
2. Crumble beef into skillet, increase heat, and cook until red color disappears.
3. Add onion, green pepper, and celery. Cook until beef is brown and vegetables are tender.
4. Add soup, tomato sauce, salt, and pepper.
5. Cover and simmer for 30 to 45 minutes, stirring occasionally.
6. Cool and divide equally into one-meal portions. Freeze. May be thawed and used for a variety of family dinner meals.

Egg Foo Yung (Chinese)
Serves 5

Nutrition Information per 240 mL (1 cup) (approximate):
calories 150
protein 8 g
fat 12 g
carbohydrate 2 g
sodium 325 mg

30 mL (2 tablespoons) salad oil
3 eggs
240 mL (1 cup) bean sprouts, drained
120 mL (½ cup) chopped cooked pork (almost any other cooked meat or tuna may be substituted)
30 mL (2 tablespoons) chopped onion
15 mL (1 tablespoon) soy sauce
Sauce (recipe below)

1. Heat oil in large skillet or electric frying pan.
   2. In separate bowl, beat eggs until thick and lemon-colored.
3. Stir in bean sprouts, pork, onion, and soy sauce.
4. Pour 60 mL (¼ cup) of mixture at a time into hot skillet. With broad spatula, push cooked egg up over meat to form a patty. When patties are set, turn to brown other side.
   5. Serve hot with sauce.

Sauce

5 mL (1 teaspoon) cornstarch
5 mL (1 teaspoon) sugar
5 mL (1 teaspoon) vinegar
120 mL (½ cup) water

1. Combine all ingredients in small saucepan.
2. Cook, stirring constantly, until mixture thickens and boils. Boil and stir for one minute.

HOW TO USE THE HAMBURGER MASTER MIX

Product	Mix	Other ingredients	Directions
Beefaroni	1 freezer container	225 g (1 8-ounce) package elbow macaroni	Heat meat mix. Cook macaroni. Mix meat and macaroni and serve hot.
Chili	1 freezer container	480 mL (2 cups) drained canned kidney beans 5 mL (1 teaspoon) chili powder	Heat meat mix. Add beans and chili powder. Cover and simmer for 10 minutes.
Pizza	1 freezer container	Biscuit or yeast dough (canned biscuits may be used) 5 mL (1 teaspoon) Italian seasoning Olives, frankfurters, pepperoni, or sliced Italian cheese Parmesan cheese, grated	Add Italian seasoning to meat mix. Simmer meat sauce until it thickens. Line pizza pan with thinly rolled dough. Spread meat sauce over dough and garnish as desired. Sprinkle with Parmesan cheese. Bake in moderate oven (375°F or 190°C) for 15 to 20 minutes. Cut and serve at once.
Spaghetti	1 freezer container	225 g (1 8-ounce) package spaghetti 5 mL (1 teaspoon) Italian seasoning Parmesan cheese, grated	Heat meat sauce. Add Italian seasoning and simmer for 15 minutes. Cook spaghetti according to directions on package and drain. Mix meat and spaghetti and sprinkle with Parmesan cheese.
Spanish Rice	1 freezer container	720 mL (3 cups) cooked rice	Heat meat sauce. Add cooked rice. Cover and simmer 5 to 10 minutes.
Sloppy Joe	1 freezer container	1 package of 8 hamburger buns	Simmer meat sauce for about 1 hour or until thick. Toast buns. Serve meat sauce on hot toasted buns.

WHITE SAUCE 240 mL (1 cup)

Type	Butter or margarine	Flour	Salt	Pepper	Milk
thin	15 mL (1 tablespoon)	15 mL (1 tablespoon)	2.5 mL (½ teaspoon)	dash	240 mL (1 cup)
medium	30 mL (2 tablespoons)	30 mL (2 tablespoons)	2.5 mL (½ teaspoon)	dash	240 mL (1 cup)
thick	45 mL (3 tablespoons)	45 mL (3 tablespoons)	2.5 mL (½ teaspoon)	dash	240 mL (1 cup)
very thick	60 mL (4 tablespoons)	60 mL (4 tablespoons)	2.5 mL (½ teaspoon)	dash	240 mL (1 cup)

Nutrition Information per 240 mL (1 cup) medium sauce (approximate):
calories 420
protein 10 g
fat 32 g
carbohydrate 23 g
sodium 1465 mg

1. Melt butter or margarine in top of double boiler over boiling water in bottom of double boiler.
2. Add flour, salt, and pepper, and stir until smooth.
3. Add milk slowly, stirring constantly.
4. Cook slowly, stirring constantly, until smooth and thickened.

Note: White sauce may also be made in a saucepan over direct heat. Use low heat and stir constantly.

CHEESE SAUCE

Nutrition Information per 240 mL (1 cup) (approximate):
calories 740
protein 37 g
fat 57 g
carbohydrate 20 g
sodium 2115 mg

Make 240 mL (1 cup) thin white sauce. Add 240 mL (1 cup) grated American cheese, and stir until melted.

MUSHROOM SAUCE

Nutrition Information per 240 mL (1 cup) (approximate):
calories 665
protein 15 g
fat 49 g
carbohydrate 41 g
sodium 1990 mg

Make 240 mL (1 cup) medium white sauce. Heat 22.5 mL (1½ tablespoons) butter or margarine in skillet, and add 180 mL (¾ cup) drained canned mushrooms and 5 mL (1 teaspoon) chopped onion. Cook until onion is golden brown, stirring 2 or 3 times, and add to white sauce.

EGG SAUCE

Nutrition Information per 240 mL (1 cup) (approximate):
calories 570
protein 22 g
fat 42 g
carbohydrate 26 g
sodium 1570 mg

Make 240 mL (1 cup) medium white sauce. Add 2 hard-cooked eggs, coarsely chopped, and 10 mL (2 teaspoons) chopped pimiento, and stir.

Baked Cheese Fondue
Serves 4

Nutrition Information per Serving (approximate):
calories 260
protein 14 g
fat 18 g
carbohydrates 12 g
sodium 625 mg

240 mL (1 cup) soft bread crumbs
240 mL (1 cup) grated American cheese
2.5 mL (½ teaspoon) salt
few grains pepper
15 mL (1 tablespoon) butter or margarine, melted
3 eggs, separated
240 mL (1 cup) milk

1. Place bread crumbs, cheese, salt, pepper, and melted butter or margarine in mixing bowl, and mix well.
2. Beat egg yolks until thick and lemon-colored, and add milk.
3. Add to bread-crumb-cheese mixture, and stir.
4. Beat egg whites until stiff, and fold into mixture.
5. Pour into greased baking dish.
6. Set in pan containing hot water up to about two-thirds depth of baking dish.
7. Bake in moderate oven (177°C or 350°F) for 30 to 40 minutes, or until firm.
8. Insert tip of knife in center of fondue, and if knife comes out clean, fondue is done.
9. Serve immediately in dish in which it was baked.

Breads and Cereals

All-Purpose Master Mix
Makes 3120 mL (13 cups)

Note: To measure the Master Mix, pile it lightly into cup and level off with spatula.

Nutrition Information per 240 mL (1 cup):
calories 670
protein 12 g
fat 35 g
carbohydrates 76 g
sodium 690 mg

2160 mL (9 cups) sifted all-purpose flour
80 mL (1/3 cup) baking powder
15 mL (1 tablespoon) salt
10 mL (2 teaspoons) cream of tartar
60 mL (1/4 cup) sugar
240 mL (1 cup) nonfat dry milk
480 mL (2 cups) shortening

1. Sift together the flour, baking powder, salt, cream of tartar, sugar, and dry milk.
2. Cut in shortening with pastry blender or two knives until mixture looks like coarse cornmeal.
3. Store in covered containers at room temperature.

German Dessert Pancake
Serves 4

Note: Strawberries may be served over the pancake instead of the lemon.

Nutrition Information per Serving (approximate):
calories 145
protein 5 g
fat 9 g
carbohydrates 11 g
sodium 130 mg

80 mL (1/3 cup) sifted all-purpose flour
1.25 mL (1/4 teaspoon) baking powder
80 mL (1/3 cup) milk
2 eggs, slightly beaten
30 mL (2 tablespoons) butter or margarine
15 mL (1 tablespoon) confectioners' sugar
4 lemon wedges

1. Preheat oven to 218°C (425°F).
2. In small bowl, combine flour and baking powder.
3. Beat in milk and eggs, leaving batter a bit lumpy.
4. In a 25-cm (10-inch) skillet with heatproof handle, melt butter or margarine. When butter is very hot, pour batter in all at once.
5. Bake 15 to 18 minutes until pancake is golden.
6. Sprinkle with sugar. Serve hot with lemon wedges to squeeze over pancake.

HOW TO USE THE ALL-PURPOSE MASTER MIX

Product amount	Mix	Sugar	Water	Eggs	Other ingredients	Amount of mixing	Temperature/time
Biscuits (15–20)	720 mL (3 cups)		240 mL (1 cup)			Until blended. Knead 10 times.	205°C (400°F) 10 minutes
Muffins (12)	720 mL (3 cups)	30 mL (2 tablespoons)	240 mL (1 cup)	1		Until ingredients are just moistened.	205°C (400°F) 20 minutes
Coffee cake	720 mL (3 cups)	120 mL (½ cup)	160 mL (⅔ cup)	1	For topping: 120 mL (½ cup) brown sugar, 45 mL (3 tablespoons) butter, 2.5 mL (¼ teaspoon) cinnamon	Until blended.	205°C (400°F) 25 minutes
Griddlecakes (18) or Waffles (6)	720 mL (3 cups)		360 mL (1½ cups)	1		Until blended.	
Oatmeal Cookies (4 dozen)	720 mL (3 cups)	240 mL (1 cup)	80 mL (⅓ cup)	1	5 mL (1 teaspoon) cinnamon; 240 mL (1 cup) quick rolled oats	Until blended.	177°C (350°F) 10–12 minutes
Drop Cookies (4 dozen)	720 mL (3 cups)	240 mL (1 cup)	80 mL (⅓ cup)	1	5 mL (1 teaspoon) vanilla; 120 mL (½ cup) nuts or chocolate bits	Until blended.	177°C (350°F) 10–12 minutes
Yellow Cake	720 mL (3 cups)	300 mL (1¼ cups)	240 mL (1 cup)	2	5 mL (1 teaspoon) vanilla	Add two-thirds liquid, and beat 2 minutes. Add rest of liquid, and beat 2 minutes.	177°C (350°F) 25 minutes

Fruits and Vegetables

Tortilla Chip Salad
Serves 8

Nutrition Information per Serving (approximate):
calories 440
protein 23 g
fat 26 g
carbohydrates 31 g
sodium 700 mg

1	head lettuce
225 g (8 ounces)	fresh spinach
454 g (1 pound)	ground beef
3.75 mL (¾ teaspoon)	seasoned salt
2.5 mL (½ teaspoon)	*each* onion powder, garlic powder, chili powder
0.6 mL (⅛ teaspoon)	cayenne red pepper
4 drops	red pepper sauce
160 mL (⅔ cup)	water
392 g 1 can (14 ounces)	kidney beans, drained
4	tomatoes, cut in eighths
170 g 1 package (6 ounces)	tortilla chips
114 g (1 cup) (about 4 ounces)	Cheddar cheese, grated
240 mL (1 cup)	chopped onion
120 mL (½ cup)	mayonnaise or salad dressing
15 mL (1 tablespoon)	pickle relish
30 mL (2 tablespoons)	chili sauce

1. Wash lettuce and spinach; tear into bite-sized pieces. Chill.
2. Cook and stir ground beef in large skillet until brown; drain. Stir in seasonings, water, and kidney beans; heat to boiling. Reduce heat; simmer uncovered 15 minutes, stirring occasionally. Cool 10 minutes.
3. Combine greens, tortilla chips, cheese, and onion in large salad bowl.
4. Mix mayonnaise, chili sauce, and pickle relish; toss gently with salad mixture.
5. Pour warm ground beef mixture over salad; toss gently. Serve immediately.

Gelatin Mold
Serves 5

1 85-g (3-ounce) package fruit-flavored gelatin (lemon, orange, cherry, raspberry, etc.)
240 mL (1 cup) hot water
240 mL (1 cup) cold water or fruit juice

1. Place gelatin in mixing bowl, add hot water, and stir until gelatin dissolves.
2. Add cold water.
3. Pour into mold, and chill until gelatin sets.
4. Unmold, and serve as a salad or dessert.

Variations

Fruit: Substitute 180 mL (¾ cup) fruit juice for 240 mL (1 cup) cold water. Add 240 mL (1 cup) grape halves, drained, canned, crushed pineapple, sliced bananas, or combinations of fruits, and 60 mL (¼ cup) chopped nuts, if desired. Add fruits when gelatin has partially thickened, and return to refrigerator until gelatin sets.
Vegetable: Use lemon-flavored gelatin, and add 240 mL (1 cup) chopped cabbage, chopped celery, grated carrots, or a combination of vegetables. Add vegetables when gelatin has partially thickened, and return to refrigerator until gelatin sets.

RECOMMENDED DAILY DIETARY ALLOWANCES, REVISED 1980

The Recommended Dietary Allowances (RDA) are designed for the maintenance of good nutrition for practically all healthy people in the United States. They list the maximum amount of selected nutrients that most healthy people need daily under usual environmental stress. The RDA are based on scientific research, and they are used to plan and evaluate the diets of *groups* of individuals. The diet itself should include a variety of common foods, which will also provide other nutrients for which human needs have not yet been determined.

	Age (years)	Weight (kg)	Weight (lb)	Height (cm)	Height (in)	Protein (g)	Fat-Soluble Vitamins Vitamin A (μg R.E.)[a]	Fat-Soluble Vitamins Vitamin D (μg)[b]	Fat-Soluble Vitamins Vitamin E (mg αT.E.)[c]	Water-Soluble Vitamins Vitamin C (mg)	Water-Soluble Vitamins Thiamine (mg)	Water-Soluble Vitamins Riboflavin (mg)
Infants	0.0–0.5	6	13	60	24	kg×2.2	420	10	3	35	0.3	0.4
	0.5–1.0	9	20	71	28	kg×2.0	400	10	4	35	0.5	0.6
Children	1–3	13	29	90	35	23	400	10	5	45	0.7	0.8
	4–6	20	44	112	44	30	500	10	6	45	0.9	1.0
	7–10	28	62	132	52	34	700	10	7	45	1.2	1.4
Males	11–14	45	99	157	62	45	1000	10	8	50	1.4	1.6
	15–18	66	145	176	69	56	1000	10	10	60	1.4	1.7
	19–22	70	154	177	70	56	1000	7.5	10	60	1.5	1.7
	23–50	70	154	178	70	56	1000	5	10	60	1.4	1.6
	51+	70	154	178	70	56	1000	5	10	60	1.2	1.4
Females	11–14	46	101	157	62	46	800	10	8	50	1.1	1.3
	15–18	55	120	163	64	46	800	10	8	60	1.1	1.3
	19–22	55	120	163	64	44	800	7.5	8	60	1.1	1.3
	23–50	55	120	163	64	44	800	5	8	60	1.0	1.2
	51+	55	120	163	64	44	800	5	8	60	1.0	1.2
Pregnant						+30	+200	+5	+2	+20	+0.4	+0.3
Lactating						+20	+400	+5	+3	+40	+0.5	+0.5

	Water-Soluble Vitamins (Cont.)				Minerals					
	Niacin (mg N.E.)[d]	Vitamin B₆ (mg)	Folacin (μg)	Vitamin B12 (μg)	Calcium (mg)	Phosphorus (mg)	Magnesium (mg)	Iron (mg)	Zinc (mg)	Iodine (μg)
Infants	6	0.3	30	0.5	360	240	50	10	3	40
	8	0.6	45	1.5	540	360	70	15	5	50
Children	9	0.9	100	2.0	800	800	150	15	10	70
	11	1.3	200	2.5	800	800	200	10	10	90
	16	1.6	300	3.0	800	800	250	10	10	120
Males	18	1.8	400	3.0	1200	1200	350	18	15	150
	18	2.0	400	3.0	1200	1200	400	18	15	150
	19	2.2	400	3.0	800	800	350	10	15	150
	18	2.2	400	3.0	800	800	350	10	15	150
	16	2.2	400	3.0	800	800	350	10	15	150
Females	15	1.8	400	3.0	1200	1200	300	18	15	150
	14	2.0	400	3.0	1200	1200	300	18	15	150
	14	2.0	400	3.0	800	800	300	18	15	150
	13	2.0	400	3.0	800	800	300	18	15	150
	13	2.0	400	3.0	800	800	300	10	15	150
Pregnant	+2	+0.6	+400	+1.0	+400	+400	+150	e	+5	+25
Lactating	+5	+0.5	+100	+1.0	+400	+400	+150	e	+10	+50

a   Retinol equivalents. 1 retinol equivalent = 10 international units (I.U.) vitamin A or 1 μg retinol or 6 μg βcarotene.

b   As cholecalciferol. 10 μg cholecalciferol = 400 international units (I.U.) vitamin D.

c   α-tocopherol equivalents. 1 mg d-α-tocopherol = 1α T.E.

d   Niacin equivalents. 1 niacin equivalent = 1 mg niacin or 60 mg of dietary tryptophan.

e   The increased requirement during pregnancy cannot be met by the iron content of habitual American diets nor by the existing iron stores of many women; therefore, the use of 30 to 60 mg of supplemental iron is recommended. Iron needs during lactation are not substantially different from those of nonpregnant women, but continued supplementation of the mother for 2 to 3 months after giving birth is advisable to replenish stores depleted by pregnancy.

Adapted from: Recommended Dietary Allowances, Ninth Edition (1980), with the permission of the National Academy of Sciences, Washington, D.C.

NUTRITIVE VALUES OF EDIBLE PARTS OF FOODS

Note: dashes indicate that amounts are unmeasurable or that no figures are available.

Food and Approximate Measure	Amt.	Food Energy Cal.	Protein g	Fat g	Carbohydrate g	Calcium mg	Iron mg	Vit. A I.U.	Thiamine mg	Riboflavin mg	Niacin mg	Ascorbic Acid mg	Sodium mg
MEAT, FISH, POULTRY, AND EGGS													
Egg, fried in butter	1	85	5	6	1	26	.9	290	.03	.13	trace	0	135
Egg, hard-cooked	1	80	6	6	1	28	1.0	260	.04	.14	trace	0	54
Egg, scrambled in butter, milk added (omelet)	1	95	6	7	1	47	.9	310	.04	.16	trace	0	144
Fish stick, breaded	1 oz	50	5	3	2	3	.1	0	.01	.02	.5	—	—
Haddock, breaded and fried	3 oz	140	17	5	5	34	1.0	—	.03	.06	2.7	2	150
Salmon, canned	3 oz	120	17	5	0	167	.7	60	.03	.16	6.8	—	444
Shrimp, canned	3 oz	100	21	1	1	98	2.6	50	.01	.03	1.5	—	—
Shrimp, french fried	3 oz	190	17	9	9	61	1.7	—	.03	.07	2.3	—	159
Tuna, canned in oil	3 oz	170	24	7	0	7	1.6	70	.04	.10	10.1	—	—
Tuna salad	1 c	350	30	22	7	41	2.7	590	.08	.23	10.3	2	—
Bacon, broiled or fried crisp	2 slices	85	4	8	trace	2	.5	0	.08	.05	.8	—	153
Beef, pot roast (lean and fat)	3 oz	245	23	16	0	10	2.9	30	.04	.18	3.6	—	—
Beef, pot roast (lean only)	3 oz	140	22	5	0	10	2.7	10	.04	.17	3.3	—	—
Beef, hamburger	3 oz	235	20	17	0	9	2.6	30	.07	.17	4.4	—	—
Beef roast (lean and fat)	3 oz	375	17	33	0	8	2.2	70	.05	.13	3.1	—	—
Beef, sirloin steak (lean and fat)	3 oz	330	20	27	0	9	2.5	50	.05	.15	4.0	—	48
Beef, sirloin steak (lean only)	2 oz	115	18	4	0	7	2.2	10	.05	.14	3.6	—	—
Beef, dried, chipped	2.5 oz	145	24	4	0	14	3.6	—	.05	.23	2.7	0	3047
Bologna	1 slice	85	3	8	trace	2	.5	—	.05	.06	.7	—	369

NUTRITIVE VALUES OF EDIBLE PARTS OF FOODS

Note: dashes indicate that amounts are unmeasurable or that no figures are available.

Food and Approximate Measure	Amt.	Food Energy Cal.	Protein g	Fat g	Carbohydrate g	Calcium mg	Iron mg	Vit. A I.U.	Thiamine mg	Riboflavin mg	Niacin mg	Ascorbic Acid mg	Sodium mg
MEAT, FISH, POULTRY, AND EGGS (cont.)													
Lamb chop, broiled (lean and fat)	3 oz	360	18	32	0	8	1.0	—	.11	.19	4.1	—	—
Lamb chop, broiled (lean only)	2 oz	120	16	6	0	6	1.1	—	.09	.15	3.4	—	—
Liver, beef, fried	3 oz	195	22	9	5	9	7.5	45,390	22	3.56	14.0	23	—
Sausage, brown and serve	1 link	70	3	6	trace	—	—	—	—	—	—	—	—
Frankfurter	1	170	7	15	1	3	.8	—	.08	.11	1.4	—	—
Veal cutlet	3 oz	185	23	9	0	9	2.7	—	.06	.21	4.6	—	41
Chicken, ½ breast, fried	3 oz	160	26	5	1	9	1.3	70	.04	.17	11.6	—	—
Chicken, leg, fried	1.3 oz	90	12	4	trace	6	.9	50	.03	.15	2.7	—	—
Chicken, half, broiled	6 oz	240	42	7	0	16	3.0	160	.09	.34	15.5	—	—
Chicken a la king	1 c	470	27	34	12	127	2.5	1130	.10	.42	5.4	12	760
MILK AND CHEESE													
Cheddar cheese	1 cu in	70	4	6	trace	124	.1	180	trace	.06	trace	0	120
Cottage cheese, small curd	1 c	220	26	9	6	126	.3	340	.04	.34	.3	trace	481
Cream cheese	1 oz	100	2	10	1	23	.3	400	trace	.06	trace	0	67
Mozzarella cheese, whole milk	1 oz	90	6	7	1	163	.1	260	trace	.08	trace	0	—
Mozzarella cheese, part skim milk	1 oz	80	8	5	1	207	.1	180	.01	.10	trace	0	—
Swiss cheese	1 oz	105	8	8	1	272	trace	240	.01	.10	trace	0	201
American cheese	1 oz	105	6	9	trace	174	.1	340	.01	.10	trace	0	318
Cream, half-and-half	1 Tbsp	20	trace	2	1	16	trace	20	.01	.02	trace	trace	7
Cream, heavy (whipping)	1 Tbsp	80	trace	6	trace	10	trace	220	trace	.02	trace	trace	5
Cream, whipped topping (pressurized)	1 Tbsp	10	trace	1	trace	3	trace	30	trace	trace	trace	0	—
Milk, whole	1 c	150	8	8	11	291	.1	310	.09	.40	.2	2	122

		Cal.	g	g	g	mg	mg	I.U.	mg	mg	mg	mg	mg	mg
Milk, lowfat (2%)	1 c	120	8	5	12	297	.1	500	.10	.40	.2	2	2	150
Milk, lowfat (1%)	1 c	100	8	3	12	300	.1	500	.10	.41	.2	2	2	—
Milk, skim	1 c	85	8	trace	12	302	.1	500	.09	.37	.2	2	2	127
Milk, buttermilk	1 c	100	8	2	12	285	.1	80	.08	.38	.1	2	2	—
Mil, evaporated	1 c	340	17	19	25	657	.5	610	.12	.80	.5	5	5	297
Ice cream, hardened	1 c	270	5	14	32	176	.1	540	.05	.33	.1	1	1	84
Ice cream, soft serve (frozen custard)	1 c	375	7	23	38	236	.4	790	.08	.45	.2	1	1	109
Sherbet	1 c	270	2	4	59	103	.3	190	.03	.09	.1	4	4	19
Custard, baked	1 c	305	14	15	29	297	1.1	930	.11	.50	.3	1	1	209
Yogurt (whole milk)	8 oz	140	8	7	11	274	.1	280	.07	.32	.2	1	1	115
FRUITS AND VEGETABLES		Cal.	g	g	g	mg	mg	I.U.	mg	mg	mg	mg	mg	mg
Apple, raw	1	80	trace	1	20	10	.4	120	.04	.03	.1	6	1	
Apple juice	1 c	120	trace	trace	30	15	1.5	—	.02	.05	.2	2	2	
Apple sauce, sweetened	1 c	230	1	trace	61	10	1.3	100	.05	.03	.1	3	5	
Apricots, dried	1 c	340	7	1	86	87	7.2	14,170	.01	.21	4.3	16	34	
Banana	1	100	1	trace	26	10	.8	230	.06	.07	.8	12	1	
Blueberries, raw	1 c	90	1	1	22	22	1.5	150	.04	.09	.7	20	1	
Cherries, raw	10	45	1	trace	12	15	.3	70	.03	.04	.3	7	—	
Fruit cocktail, canned, in heavy syrup	1 c	195	1	trace	50	23	1.0	360	.05	.03	1.0	5	13	
Grapefruit, raw, white	½	45	1	trace	12	19	.5	10	.05	.02	.2	44	1	
Grapefruit juice, canned, unsweetened	1 c	100	1	trace	24	20	1.0	20	.07	.05	.5	84	—	
Grapefruit juice, canned, sweetened	1 c	135	1	trace	32	20	1.0	30	.08	.05	.5	78	3	
Grape juice, canned	1 c	165	1	trace	42	28	.8	—	.10	.05	.5	trace	5	
Grape drink, canned	1 c	135	trace	trace	35	8	.3	—	.03	.03	.3	—	3	
Cantaloupe	½	80	2	trace	20	38	1.1	9240	.11	.08	1.6	90	33	
Orange	1	65	1	trace	16	54	.5	260	.13	.05	.5	66	2	
Orange juice, canned, unsweetened	1 c	120	2	trace	28	25	1.0	500	.17	.05	.7	100	2	
Pear, raw	1	100	1	1	25	13	.5	30	.03	.07	.2	7	3	

NUTRITIVE VALUES OF EDIBLE PARTS OF FOODS

Note: dashes indicate that amounts are unmeasurable or that no figures are available.

Food and Approximate Measure	Amt.	Food Energy (Cal.)	Protein (g)	Fat (g)	Carbohydrate (g)	Calcium (mg)	Iron (mg)	Vit. A (I.U.)	Thiamine (mg)	Riboflavin (mg)	Niacin (mg)	Ascorbic Acid (mg)	Sodium (mg)
FRUITS AND VEGETABLES (cont.)													
Pineapple, canned, crushed, chunks, tidbits	1 c	190	1	trace	49	28	.8	130	.20	.05	.5	18	3
Pineapple juice, canned, unsweetened	1 c	140	1	trace	34	38	.8	130	.13	.05	.5	80	3
Raisins	1 c	420	4	trace	112	90	5.1	30	.16	.12	.7	1	1106
Strawberries, raw	1 c	55	1	1	13	31	1.5	90	.04	.10	.9	88	1
Asparagus, cooked	4 spears	15	2	trace	2	13	.7	470	.10	.08	.7	16	1
Lima beans, cooked	1 c	210	13	trace	40	63	4.7	400	.16	.09	2.2	22	2
Green beans, frozen, cooked	1 c	35	2	trace	8	54	.9	780	.09	.12	.5	7	5
Beets, canned, sliced	1 c	65	2	trace	15	32	1.2	30	.02	.05	.2	5	401
Broccoli, frozen, chopped, cooked	1 c	50	5	1	9	100	1.3	4810	.11	.22	.9	105	28
Brussels sprouts, frozen, cooked	1 c	50	5	trace	10	33	1.2	880	.12	.16	.9	126	22
Cabbage, raw, shredded	1 c	15	1	trace	4	34	.3	90	.04	.04	.02	33	18
Carrot	1	30	1	trace	7	27	.5	7930	.04	.04	.4	6	34
Carrots, canned, sliced	1 c	45	1	trace	10	47	1.1	23,250	.03	.05	.6	3	366
Cauliflower, raw	1 c	31	3	trace	6	29	1.3	70	.13	.12	.8	90	—
Celery	1 stalk	5	trace	trace	2	16	.1	110	.01	.01	.1	4	50
Corn, canned, cream-style	1 c	210	5	2	51	8	1.5	840	.08	.13	2.6	13	604
Corn, canned, whole kernel	1 c	140	4	1	33	8	.8	580	.05	.08	1.5	7	389
Lettuce	¼ head	20	1	trace	4	27	.7	450	.08	.08	.4	8	15
Peas, canned	1 c	150	8	1	29	44	3.2	1170	.15	.10	1.4	14	401
Potato, baked	1	145	4	trace	33	14	1.1	trace	.15	.07	2.7	31	6
Potato, french fried	10 strips	135	2	7	18	8	.7	trace	.07	.04	1.6	11	3

	Measure	Cal.	g	g	g	mg	mg	I.U.	mg	mg	mg	mg	mg
Potato chips	10	115	1	8	10	8	.4	trace	.04	.01	1.0	3	—
Potato salad	1 c	250	7	7	41	80	1.5	350	.20	.18	2.8	28	1320
Sauerkraut	1 c	40	2	trace	9	85	1.2	120	.07	.09	.5	33	1755
Spinach, raw, chopped	1 c	15	2	trace	2	51	1.7	4460	.06	.11	.3	28	39
Spinach, cooked	1 c	40	5	1	6	167	4.0	14,580	.13	.25	.9	50	90
Sweet potatoes, candied, 2¾ × 1 in.	1 piece	175	1	3	36	39	.9	6620	.06	.04	.4	11	44
Tomato, raw	1	25	1	trace	6	16	.6	1110	.07	.05	.9	28	4
Tomato catsup	1 Tbsp	15	trace	trace	4	3	.1	210	.01	.01	.2	2	156
Tomato juice, canned	1 c	45	2	trace	10	17	2.2	1940	.12	.07	1.9	39	486
BREADS AND CEREALS		**Cal.**	**g**	**g**	**g**	**mg**	**mg**	**I.U.**	**mg**	**mg**	**mg**	**mg**	**mg**
Biscuit	1	105	2	5	13	34	.4	trace	.08	.08	.7	trace	175
Bread, raisin	1 slice	65	2	1	13	18	.6	trace	.09	.06	.6	trace	91
Bread, rye	1 slice	60	2	trace	13	19	.5	0	.07	.05	.7	0	139
Bread, white	1 slice	70	2	1	13	21	.6	trace	.10	.06	.8	trace	142
Bread, whole wheat	1 slice	65	3	1	14	24	.8	trace	.09	.03	.8	trace	132
Oatmeal, cooked	1 c	130	5	2	23	22	1.4	0	.19	.05	.2	0	523
Bran flakes with raisins	1 c	145	4	1	40	28	16.9	0	.58	.71	5.8	18	212
Corn flakes, sugar-coated	1 c	155	2	trace	37	1	1.0	2350	.46	.56	4.6	14	267
Shredded wheat, spoon-size	½ c	90	2	1	20	11	.9	1880	.06	.03	1.1	0	1
Cracker, graham, 2½ in. square	2	55	1	1	10	6	.5	0	.02	.08	.5	0	95
Cracker, saltine	4 sqs	50	1	1	8	2	.5	0	.05	.05	.4	0	123
Doughnut, yeast, glazed	1	205	3	11	22	16	.6	25	.10	.10	.8	0	99
Noodles	1 c	200	7	2	37	16	1.4	110	.22	.13	1.9	0	3
Pancake	1	60	2	2	9	27	.4	30	.06	.07	.5	trace	152
Rice, instant	1 c	180	4	trace	40	5	1.3	0	.21	—	1.7	0	450
Roll, frankfurter and hamburger	1	120	3	2	21	30	.8	trace	.16	.10	1.3	trace	202
Roll, hard	1	155	5	2	30	24	1.2	trace	.20	.12	1.7	trace	313
Spaghetti	1 c	190	7	1	39	14	1.4	0	.23	.13	1.8	0	1

NUTRITIVE VALUES OF EDIBLE PARTS OF FOODS

Note: dashes indicate that amounts are unmeasurable or that no figures are available.

Food and Approximate Measure	Amt.	Food Energy Cal.	Protein g	Fat g	Carbohydrate g	Calcium mg	Iron mg	Vit. A I.U.	Thiamine mg	Riboflavin mg	Niacin mg	Ascorbic Acid mg	Sodium mg
BREADS AND CEREALS (cont.)													
Spaghetti in tomato sauce with cheese	1 c	260	9	9	37	80	2.3	1080	.25	.18	2.3	13	955
MISCELLANEOUS													
Carbonated beverage (cola)	12 oz	145	0	0	37	—	—	0	0	0	0	0	—
Soup, beef noodle	1 c	65	4	3	7	7	1.0	50	.05	.07	1.0	trace	936
Soup, tomato	1 c	90	2	3	16	15	.7	1000	.05	.05	1.2	12	990
Popcorn	1 c	25	1	trace	5	1	.2	—	—	.01	.1	0	trace
Pizza, plain	1 slice	145	6	4	22	86	1.1	230	.16	.18	1.6	4	456
Pie, apple, 1/7 of pie	1 slice	345	3	15	51	11	.9	40	.15	.11	1.3	2	405
Pie, lemon meringue, 1/7 of pie	1 slice	305	4	12	45	17	1.0	200	.09	.12	.7	4	337
Pie, pumpkin, 1/7 of pie	1 slice	275	5	15	32	66	1.0	3210	.11	.18	1.0	trace	278
Cake, angelfood, 1/12 of cake	1 slice	135	3	trace	32	63	.2	0	.03	.08	.3	0	143
Cake, chocolate with chocolate icing, 1/16 of cake	1 slice	235	3	8	40	41	1.0	100	.07	.10	.6	trace	150
Brownies with nuts	1	95	1	6	10	8	.4	40	.04	.03	.2	trace	50
Cookies, chocolate chip, 2 in. diameter	4	205	2	12	14	40	.8	40	.06	.06	.5	trace	200
Cookies, oatmeal with raisins, 2½ in. diameter	4	235	3	8	38	11	1.4	30	.15	.10	1.0	trace	84
Peanut butter	1 Tbsp	95	4	8	3	9	.3	—	.02	.02	2.4	0	97
Sugar	1 Tbsp	45	0	0	12	0	trace	0	0	0	.0	0	trace
Butter	1 Tbsp	100	trace	12	trace	3	trace	430	trace	trace	trace	0	140
Margarine	1 Tbsp	100	trace	12	trace	3	trace	470	trace	trace	trace	0	140
Salad dressing, French	1 Tbsp	65	trace	6	3	2	.1	—	—	—	—	—	219
Salad dressing, French, low-calorie	1 Tbsp	15	trace	1	2	2	.1	—	—	—	—	—	126
Mayonnaise	1 Tbsp	100	trace	11	trace	3	.1	40	trace	.01	trace	—	84

INDEX

(Figures in boldface indicate the page where a term is defined.)

PICTURE CREDITS

394—Robert Capece/McGraw-Hill; 396—Green Giant Company; 397—Elihu Blotnick/Woodfin Camp; 398—Gabe Palmer/Image Bank;
401—Beryl Goldberg/Woodfin Camp; 402—E. Silva/Alpha; 403—Sunkist Growers; 405—Zimmerman/Alpha; 406—National Broiler Council;
407—Rothwell/Freelance Photographers Guild; 409—Gabe Palmer/Image Bank; 410—Richard Choy/Peter Arnold, Inc.;
412, 414—Robert Capece/McGraw-Hill; 415—Lester Sloan/Woodfin Camp; 417—Robert Capece/McGraw-Hill; 419—Kenneth Karp;
421—Mimi Forsyth/Monkmeyer; 422—Paul Conklin/Monkmeyer; 425—Beryl Goldberg/McGraw-Hill; 427—Oster; 429—Tupperware;
434—Pedro Noa/McGraw-Hill; 436—Robert Capece/McGraw-Hill; 441—Marvin Lyons/Image Bank; 442—Tupperware; 443—Jillson/Alpha;
444—Sigrid Owen/Freelance Photographers Guild; 445—Rudy Muller/Alpha; 447—North Atlantic Seafood Association; 448—American Soybean Association;
449—American Egg Board; 450—Michael Skott/Image Bank; 452—Robert Capece/McGraw-Hill; 453—Poinciana, Florida; 454—Alpha;
455—United Dairy Industry Association; 456—North Atlantic Seafood Association; 457—Larry Voigt/Photo Researchers; 459—Robert Capece/McGraw-Hill;
460—Best Foods/Hellman's Mayonnaise; 461—California Table Grape Commission; 463—Tupperware; 464—Margarin Studios/Alpha;
466—Whirlpool Corporation; 467—California Tree Fruit Agreement; 469—Robert Capece/McGraw-Hill;
470-471—Betty Crocker Food and Nutrition Center, General Mills, Inc.; 472—Bill Debold/Freelance Photographers Guild;
473—William Hubbell/Woodfin Camp; 474—The Rice Council; 475—Argo and Kingsford's Cornstarch/Best Foods; 476—Karo Corn Syrup;
478—Co-Ed Magazine; 480—Whirlpool Corporation; 481—Joe Rychetnik/Photo Researchers; 483—Fred J. Maroon/Photo Researchers; 485—Alpha;
486—(t) Brian Seed/Black Star, (b) Argo & Kingsford's Corn Starch/Best Foods; 487—(t) Robert Capece/McGraw-Hill, (b) Richard Kalvar/Magnum;
488—(t) Robert Capece/McGraw-Hill, (b) Freelance Photographers Guild; 489—(t) Bart J. Devito/Image Bank, (b) W.H. Hodge/Peter Arnold, Inc.;
490—(t) Spindel/Freelance Photographers Guild, (b) Mazola Corn Oil/Best Foods; 491—Kenneth Karp; 492—Sepp Seitz/Woodfin Camp; 493—Tupperware;
494—Shakespeare/Freelance Photographers Guild; 495—Restaurant Business Magazine; 496—Arthur d'Arazien/Image Bank;
498—American Dietetic Association/Doyle Pharmaceutical Company